Alma Sedonia Knobloch
Maidservant of the Divine Plan

In deep gratitude to all Bahá'í authors and publishers
whose high-quality literature has contributed my spiritual
development and intellectual life
and has made this book possible

Alma Sedonia Knobloch

Maidservant of the Divine Plan

Jennifer Redson Wiebers

GEORGE RONALD
OXFORD

George Ronald, Publisher
Oxford
www.grbooks.com

© Jennifer Redson Wiebers 2023
All Rights Reserved

A catalogue record for this book is available from the British Library

ISBN 978-0-85398-654-6

Cover design Steiner Graphics

CONTENTS

Preface and Acknowledgements   vii
Introduction   1

1	The Knobloch Family	4
2	Discovery of the Bahá'í Faith	10
3	Mírzá Abu'l-Faḍl	17
4	The Church	21
5	Bringing the Black Community into the Faith	27
6	A Missed Pilgrimage	30
7	Homefront Pioneering in New York State	34
8	Dr Edwin Fisher	50
9	Edwin Fisher Raises the Call in Germany	60
10	Alma's Call to Germany	63
11	Unusual Confirmations	68
12	Rapid Expansion in Stuttgart	78
13	Bahá'í Identity, Community Building and Consolidation	83
14	Alma and Edwin Fisher	91
15	Invitation to the Holy Land, and the Passing of Amalie Knobloch	95
16	Pilgrimage	101
17	Distractions	110
18	Germany 'As Long as Possible'	120
19	Beyond Stuttgart	135
20	The Stuttgart Board of Counsel	125
21	The Role of Women in the Community	135
22	Two Dreams, Two Meetings	139
23	Steadfastly Building Community	148
24	Tablets to the German Believers	155

25	The German Bahá'ís Meet 'Abdu'l-Bahá in London and Paris	163
26	Lady Blomfield and the Stuttgart Bahá'í Community	172
27	Leipzig at Last	186
28	Summer of 1912	190
29	Alma's Family in Leipzig	195
30	Petitions to the Master	198
31	'Abdu'l-Bahá in Germany	206
32	Fanny's Illness and Recovery with Alma and 'Abdu'l-Bahá	232
33	The Stuttgart Bahá'í Community 'Abdu'l-Bahá Created	235
34	The 'American Girl' Teaches Throughout Germany	238
35	The War to End All Wars	252
36	Crisis and Victory during the War	266
37	The Crucible of War and the Revelation of the Divine Plan	275
38	The Love of God that Bubbles Over	288
39	In America Again	299
40	The Ascension of 'Abdu'l-Bahá	303
41	The German Bahá'í Community after Alma	308
42	The Sad Story of Wilhelm Herrigel	311
43	Return to Germany?	317
44	Serving the Guardian in the United States	325
45	Cabin John, Maryland, and a Year of Reflection	348
46	In the South One Last Time	356
47	The Last Years	371

Bibliography — 381
Notes and References — 389
Index — 455
About the Author

PREFACE AND ACKNOWLEDGEMENTS

O my God! O my God! Thou seest me in my lowliness and weakness, occupied with the greatest undertaking, determined to raise Thy word among the masses and to spread Thy teachings among Thy peoples. How can I succeed unless Thou assist me with the breath of the Holy Spirit, help me to triumph by the hosts of Thy glorious kingdom, and shower upon me Thy confirmations, which alone can change a gnat into an eagle, a drop of water into rivers and seas, and an atom into lights and suns? O my Lord! Assist me with Thy triumphant and effective might, so that my tongue may utter Thy praises and attributes among all people and my soul overflow with the wine of Thy love and knowledge.

'Abdu'l-Bahá
Prayer for the Southern States
Tablets of the Divine Plan

In the early 1990s, travelling through the sweet-smelling fragrant forest of Great Falls National Park in Cabin John, Maryland and admiring its natural beauty while contemplating the deeper meaning of life, I stopped by the roaring waterfalls. I prayed the prayer for the southern states in the *Tablets of the Divine Plan* revealed by 'Abdu'l-Bahá, the Centre of the Covenant of the Bahá'í Faith. I cried out, '*A gnat into an eagle, a drop of water into rivers and seas* . . .' I was searching for purpose in my life.

Looking back, it seems that I was not alone. Later I learned that less than fifty years earlier in Cabin John, Alma Knobloch, a little-known hero of the Bahá'í Faith, slipped into the world of immortality on 23 December 1943. She was one of the three exemplary people referred to in the *Tablets of the Divine Plan*.

This magical spot in Cabin John captivated me and I started to bring groups of youth from the Washington Bahá'í Centre to the waterfalls to pray. I also brought my future husband Carsten Wiebers there and we laughed when I fell into the water and was soaked head to foot!

Since those days, I have been drawn step by step towards writing Alma's story. There were so many confirmations on the way. After Carsten and I married, he brought me to Germany in 1993. Later, in 1997 while visiting my father, he told me that he had a treasure, a lock of hair of the Master that had been given to him by my grandfather. He took me to see it in the safe deposit box. When I opened the case, I was surprised to learn that it had been a gift to my grandfather from Carl Hannen, Alma's nephew who had spent considerable time living with her in Germany. Later, while writing the book I learned that some of the first Bahá'ís to pioneer to Berlin from Leipzig in the 1920s lived in an apartment on Friedrichsruher Strasse about 100 metres from the apartment building my husband's grandmother lived in at that time, the home where my husband grew up and his family lived until 1980; the year and the place where he and his parents accepted the Bahá'í Faith together. All these events guided my life like a compass. This book is the result.

Alma was a humble servant, a drop of water who became as a river and sea. Her spiritual station is preserved through eternity in the many Tablets of 'Abdu'l-Bahá to her and her family.

Many of the Tablets in this book have been published in collections such as *Tablets of Abdul-Baha Abbas* or in *Star of the West*; however, the book also includes some Tablets from the archives of various early believers and are quoted here with the permission of the Bahá'í World Centre. These are the original English translations made at the time, and although they are of variable quality and may not always provide a suitable impression of the original Tablets, it has been decided to include them as they are the translations that Alma and the early believers received, copied and shared amongst themselves, and thus provide a historical context. They were used as a preliminary form of Baháʼí scripture at prayer gatherings and they guided the lives of the early Western Baháʼís. The provenance of each Tablet is given in the Notes and References at the back of this book.

There are many people whose support have made this book possible. First and foremost, I am indebted to my dear and loyal husband Carsten, whose encouragement, enthusiasm and support carried me through this long project. Many evenings when he returned home from work I greeted him with dramatic stories, and sometimes it took him a moment to realize that I was talking about things that had happened more than 100 years earlier! He also helped with the proofreading of the document and happily cared for our three children Clara-Lisa, Caio and Emily while I was travelling to visit different archives.

I deeply appreciate the assistance I received from the many archivists who supported my research for this book. They helped me to collect not only the relevant letters and documents but also many of the photographs which bring the story to life.

The archivists Lewis Walker, Edward Sevcik and Roger Dahl supported my research at the United States National Baháʼí Archives (USBNA). Lewis spent many hours working with me and was always cheerful and fun to work with. He drew my attention to the many letters written in the German language at the USBNA, and at times copied boxes of these letters which he shipped to me in Germany. None the less, due to the extensive amount of material in the archives, it became apparent that I needed to travel to the United States to visit the archives personally. My sister Juli Redson-Smith joined me on my trip to Wilmette and her dear friend Valerie Dana kindly hosted us at her apartment. We spent a week copying and scanning at the USBNA, which was at the time located in the basement level of the Baháʼí Temple. These days were full of memories; more than 40 years earlier my three sisters and I had all attended Minnie Hadley's Baháʼí childrens' classes in another room in the basement of the Temple. In 2013, Valerie was serving on the National Spiritual Assembly of the United States. I shall never forget the spiritual atmosphere of her home; we shared morning and evening prayers, it was very special.

My next stop was the Baháʼí Archives in Washington DC. In the early 1990s I had attended the famous firesides at the home of Nasir and Ziba Bashirelahi which had a great influence on my life. They are good friends of our family, and it was a joy to stay with them while I was working at the Washington Archives. Helia Ighani Hock, the archivist in Washington DC, was also a great support.

I am greatly indebted to Gisbert Schaal at the National Baháʼí Archives of Germany for his support throughout this project. Gisbert helped me to locate documents and photos at both the National Archives and the Baháʼí Archives in Stuttgart and Esslingen. He is a member of the family of Consul Schwarz and was quick to organize many interesting interviews with members of various older German Baháʼí families. We spent many days together in Stuttgart touring the places ʻAbdu'l-Bahá had visited and sharing stories. He has become a very good friend to me.

I would like to express my appreciation to Susanne Pfaff-Grossmann who kindly shared letters and files from the Grossmann Archive Collection. Her dear brother, former Member of the Universal House of Justice Hartmut Grossmann, also shared stories and provided much inspiration and encouragement to me over the years.

Lutz Unkrig and Gerda and Gunther Haug helped decipher the many letters which were written in the old German alphabet, for which I am thankful. In addition, I am grateful to my daughters Clara-Lisa and Emily and my good friend Kirsten Wetz who all helped with proofreading.

I am grateful for the insights I received from Judy Hannen Moe, a descendant of the Hannen/Knobloch family, whose book *Aflame with Devotion* covers additional details about Alma and her sisters. Judy generously shared many family photographs which have greatly contributed to the quality of this book. She answered questions and shared her recollections throughout the project. We have become good friends, as were our grandfathers. Judy's book on Fanny Knobloch (in progress) will be especially of great interest to the Bahá'ís in South Africa where Fanny pioneered for many years. Of the three Knobloch sisters, Fanny's handwriting was by far the most difficult to decipher!

When the road was long, Earl Redman encouraged me to keep moving forward, and as the book started to take shape he kindly offered his help to edit the text. Earl is a true friend to me, always willing to listen and help in any way. His contribution to Bahá'í history is an inspiration to all Bahá'í authors and his books will illumine hearts and minds for generations to come. Earl has uncovered countless stories of Bahá'í heroes all over the world, illuminating the path of service for all those who attempt to follow.

I was fortunate to have contact with Nell Golden shortly before publication, whose sharp memory provided insights into the early years of the first Bahá'í communities in Georgia and South Carolina. Nell's lively spirit is inspiring and her enthusiasm is contagious.

Finally, I especially want to thank the remarkable May Hofman, whose thorough editorial work, patience and loving guidance added invaluable quality to these pages. She always knew the right questions to ask, discovered any inconsistencies, and gently guided me through the delivery of this, my first book. Her stalwart dedication and deep knowledge of the Bahá'í Faith are a powerful asset to the entire Bahá'í community. I am also grateful to Erica Leith for typesetting and for her help in organizing the photographs for the book. It was a great privilege to publish this book with George Ronald. May Hofman, Erica Leith and Wendi Momen deserve much gratitude and great respect for their outstanding contribution to the literature of the Bahá'í Faith over the years.

INTRODUCTION

> *... how easily, where unity existeth in a given family, the affairs of that family are conducted; what progress the members of that family make, how they prosper in the world. Their concerns are in order, they enjoy comfort and tranquillity, they are secure, their position is assured, they come to be envied by all. Such a family but addeth to its stature and its lasting honour, as day succeedeth day.*
>
> 'Abdu'l-Bahá

Amalie Knobloch, her three daughters Fanny, Alma and Pauline and her son-in-law Joseph Hannen were united like the fingers of one hand animated by love and steadfast dedication to Bahá'u'lláh. Each one provided spiritual, material, emotional and mental support to the other, enabling them to expand their spiritual capacities and seize any opportunity to serve the Bahá'í Faith. The result was an example to the individual, the community and the world.

This book focuses on the services of Alma Knobloch, whom 'Abdu'l-Bahá called a 'Herald of the Kingdom' and who was one of the three people mentioned in the Tablets of the Divine Plan. Alma declared her Faith in 1903 and had the bounty of being trained by Mírzá Abu'l-Faḍl in Washington DC. In 1904, Alma became the first Bahá'í in the West to be expelled from a Christian Church because of her Faith. She raised up the first African-American community in the United States of America, and she taught the first coloured believer in Canada.

In 1907, 'Abdu'l-Bahá sent Alma to Germany to support the

teaching efforts of Dr Edwin Fisher. Through the financial support of her generous hard-working sister Fanny, Alma served in Germany for 13 years. Upon her arrival in Stuttgart there were four believers; through Alma's outstanding explanations of the Bible, almost an entire church congregation joined the Bahá'í Faith, raising the number of active believers to more than 50 in just six months and more than 100 throughout Germany in the following year. Alma taught different social groups including working single women and established upper-class families. It was a time of 'entry by troops', the consolidation of which involved many challenges for these groups of people to surrender their own cultural ideas, take on a new religious identity and turn to 'Abdu'l-Bahá.

Throughout the First World War Alma and the German Bahá'í community focused on peace. Soldiers who had attended Bahá'í devotionals entered the battlefields with Bahá'í prayers and quotations against their breasts. Alma spent much of the time during the war opening new communities in Germany and she spread the Faith amongst the aristocracy in Munich. At the end of the war, she emerged from the bomb shelters of Mannheim to receive great confirmations in large halls overflowing with hundreds of people who came to hear the message of Bahá'u'lláh throughout Germany.

In addition to her work in Germany, Alma taught the first believers in Austria and the Czech Republic, as well as future Hand of the Cause Hermann Grossmann, and the first European martyr, Adam Benke.

In December of 1920, Alma returned to the United States, where she once again focused on race unity in the Bahá'í communities of Washington DC, New York City, and Springfield, Massachusetts. After the passing of 'Abdu'l-Bahá, Alma dedicated the rest of her days to Shoghi Effendi. She worked with Louis Gregory, the National Teaching Committee, travel teachers and other homefront pioneers to spread the Faith and build up lasting communities and assemblies in Florida, Georgia, and South Carolina. In the deep South, Alma worked for race unity. Despite the dark days of the Jim Crow laws, Alma was a fearless

INTRODUCTION

white woman who crossed the racial and social barriers to build up coloured communities in the Southern States.

The Knobloch sisters left behind a detailed correspondence that records the names and contributions of many early Baháʼís in many locations. This book captures these details as follows: Chapters 2-6: Washington, DC; Chapter 7: New York State and Canada; Chapters 8-43 Germany and other European countries; Chapters 44-47: United States, primarily Eastern Southern States. May future Baháʼí historians find this book a useful reference for their precious work.

1
THE KNOBLOCH FAMILY

*'Be on the alert, especially after 1868,
for the coming of our Lord!'*

Deep in the heart of Europe, surrounded by the Kingdoms of Austria-Hungary, Prussia, Bavaria, and the remains of the Holy Roman Empire, was the Kingdom of Saxony, sometimes referred to as the 'cockpit of Europe'. Its tactical position made it a particularly turbulent place during the Napoleonic wars which ravaged Europe from 1805 to 1815. When choosing alliances, unlucky Saxony always chose the wrong side to support. After the loss of 22,000 soldiers while fighting Prussia at the Battle of Jena in 1806, Saxony switched sides to support Napoleon. Subsequently, Napoleon and Saxony were forced to capitulate at the Battle of the Nations in Leipzig in October 1813, leaving an estimated 80,000–110,000 casualties behind. Napoleon's troops retreated to France and approximately 60 per cent of northern Saxony was annexed by Prussia. Napoleon never returned but he left behind a civil system that secured religious and secular freedom, abolished tithes, banned guilds, and changed the legal system including laws regarding marriage, divorce, and property rights. Church land was sold to the people and there was a new level of social mobility.[1]

It was there, in the small agrarian village of Wittendorf in the Kingdom of Saxony on the Polish border, where Karl August Knobloch was born in 1832. Growing up in Saxony at this time, Karl Knobloch was a beneficiary of the Napoleonic reforms. He was well educated: his father Gottfried Knobloch

Alma Knobloch

Alma's father Karl August Knobloch

Alma's mother Amalie von Rössler Knobloch

Amalie Knobloch's parents Karl Gabriel and Johanna Christine Gehde von Rössler

Alma with her brother Paul and sister Pauline

Alma in her youth

Left to right: Alma's fiancé, Alma, Joseph Hannen, Pauline

Left to right: Unidentified, Alma's brother Paul, Fanny, Alma's fiancé, Alma, Pauline

Alma with her mother Amalie

Fanny and Alma

was a renowned teacher and was awarded the Medal of the Council (*Ratsmedaille*) for his work in a High School in Bautzen.[2] A new freedom of intellectual thought was sweeping across Europe, awakening and empowering the people. Thinkers of the time envisioned new concepts of individual rights and freedoms, including Karl Marx and Friedrich Engels who wrote the Communist Manifesto in nearby Berlin in 1848. Karl Knobloch and his brother Wilhelm received an excellent secular education and were surely inspired by the spirit of the age. Wilhelm later became a Professor at the University of Leipzig.

Beyond the secular education, the boys received an additional wind of inspiration from the religious side. Their minds were open to the possibility of spiritual renewal through their mother Johanna Christine Gehde, a Prussian Templer[3] and an avid student of the Bible. She raised Karl and his brother Wilhelm to 'be on the alert, especially after 1868, for the coming of our Lord!'[4] The Templers were a messianic society whose apocalyptic millennial beliefs led them to establish settlements in the Holy Land, including Haifa, at the base of Mount Carmel. Early Templer founders and supporters came from Württemberg and Prussia. Today their historic, red-roofed homes still line Ben Gurion Avenue, leading to the Bahá'í Terraces on Mount Carmel.

Karl Knobloch, a learned man with many creative ideas and high principles, found his true love in the virtuous Amalie von Rössler (1837–1908). She was born in Böblitz, near Bautzen. Her father Karl Gabriel von Rössler was from an aristocratic family, as indicated by his title 'von'. They married in St Peter's Church in Bautzen, on 11 May 1858. St Peter's was the first '*Simultankirche*' ('shared church') in Germany. Established at the end of the Thirty Years' War, whose horrors claimed the lives of up to 60 per cent of the population in some areas of Germany, St Peter's embodies the concept of peace and religious unity in worship of God; Protestant and Catholic congregations worship God simultaneously, sharing the Church up to today.[5] Four of the Knobloch children: Fanny (1859–1949),

Ida (1861–1869), Alma (1864–1943), and Martin (1866–1894) were christened in St Peter's Church.

The Kingdom of Saxony enjoyed peace as a member of the German Confederation from 1815 until 14 June 1866, when Saxony voted against Prussia in the German Assembly in Frankfurt, thereby forfeiting its position of neutrality. Thus began the Austro-Prussian war, in which Saxony once again sided with the losing side, Austria. Tired of war and the poverty it entails, the year 1867 was one of the peak years of German emigration to the United States,[6] with approximately four million Germans emigrating during this time.[7] The von Rössler family was made up largely of military officers. Perhaps that is why all of Amalie's brothers emigrated to the United States, with the exception of Bruno, who remained in Bautzen to care for their parents. In the United States, the German immigrants supported each other in small communities and made big contributions in many American cities, including the design and construction of the US Capitol building in Washington DC.

At age 35, Karl Knobloch had had enough of Saxony, and on 1 June 1867 he departed Hamburg for New York taking with him his seven-year-old daughter Fanny.[8] It was an auspicious time in the United States; the Civil War had ended two years earlier and a period of freedom and reconstruction had begun. On 21 March 1868, Amalie, four-year-old Alma and little Paul Martin arrived in New York on the steamer *Germania* from Hamburg to reunite the family.[9] Throughout Alma's life, the German and American families maintained close contact. Saxony continued to suffer from war and disease until 1871, when Bismarck unified Germany and Saxony became part of the German Empire.

The Knoblochs established themselves in Washington DC. Amalie never spoke English fluently, but her children quickly learned English at school. Education was always important to the family and the scholastic accomplishments of the Knobloch children are recorded in the *Evening Star* newspaper. Alma made the merit roll of the fifth grade.[10]

Karl and Amalie had two more children in the United

States. Sadly, their son Bruno born in 1872 passed away shortly after birth. Two years later, in 1874, Pauline was born. She was a cheerful child and brought much joy to the family. Often referred to as the 'angel' of the family, Pauline had an unusual spiritual awareness. This 'little angel' indeed years later became the 'spiritual mother' of her entire illustrious family.

The Knoblochs were trusted, dedicated and hard-working church members. Until 1905, Alma spent most of her free time working for the Lutheran Concordia Church, organizing social events, participating in and teaching adult Bible study classes and Sunday School to children. She supported the minister in many of his duties and like her mother and sisters she had a deep profound love for Jesus Christ and the Bible.

Karl supported the family by working in various creative positions as an architect, a wood carver and an inventor.[11] He was very interested in chemistry and the properties of natural substances. On 27 May 1879, Karl patented a new technique in wood distillation.[12] He further developed this technique, known as the 'Knobloch Process of Dry Distillation'.

The Knoblochs moved to Wilmington, North Carolina, where Karl, known as Professor Knobloch, founded the Carolina Chemical Company which used his patented distillation process to produce medicinal products. Karl developed a Pinole Extract, a Corina Chill Cure, and a Carolina Balsam,[13] all produced from bark and plant extractions from species grown in North Carolina.[14] Census records indicate that Alma and Amalie maintained a family residence in Washington DC at this time.

After the American Civil War, life in North Carolina was a mixture of opportunity and insecurity. 'Carpetbaggers' and 'Scalawaggers' from the North exploited cheap labour and land, as well as the broken political system in the war-torn region. North Carolina struggled to find its social and political identity during Reconstruction. Many did not trust the state's judicial institutions. Racism was a normal part of life in North Carolina at that time: of the 58 lynchings that were recorded in North Carolina from 1880 to 1900, 45 victims were Black and 13

White.¹⁵ This discrepancy made a strong impression on the Knobloch children. Years later, Pauline recounted: 'When I was a little girl in Wilmington North Carolina, teachings and environment had made me regard Black people with something like terror. I had known of the frightful retribution visited by whites upon Negros for offenses of which I assumed they must be guilty.'¹⁶

Many German immigrants settled in Wilmington, and by the mid-1850s they began to raise funds to build St Paul's Lutheran Church for the German congregation. In 1882, the church established a 'Young Peoples Society' which was quite popular. Paul Martin and Fanny were very active in theatre and music productions.¹⁷

Karl's sudden death on 7 July 1887 was a terrific shock to the family. At age 50 Amalie was left behind with the four children. Women had limited legal rights and could not trade or conduct business activities in the United States at that time. Thus, it was left to the only son Paul Martin to carry on the family business which Karl had begun. His attempt to take over the Carolina Chemical Company production facilities as the chief pharmaceutical chemist was unsuccessful.¹⁸ In Autumn 1889 he left for New York City, where he performed with his band.¹⁹ By 1890 Paul had returned to Washington DC.²⁰

Two years after her father's death, at age 29, Alma became the first family member to return to Germany. After 25 years in the USA, she arrived in Bremen on the Nord Deutsche Steamer *Dresden*, on 26 July 1893.²¹ She visited friends and relatives and there was someone in Germany with whom she fell in love. Alma returned to Washington DC on 18 October to attend Pauline's wedding on 8 November 1893.²² Pauline married Joseph Anthony Hannen (1872–1920).²³ Joseph and Pauline moved in with the rest of the Knobloch family.

One year later, at the young age of 27, Paul Martin passed away.²⁴ The details of his passing are not known, but Alma recalled that he had a very gentle and sensitive disposition but a certain weakness in life. Fanny, Alma, Pauline and Joseph were left to earn the family money and care for Amalie.

At the turn of the century, unmarried women enjoyed legal rights that married women did not have, due to the concept of coverture. In many states, married women were deprived of property rights, had limited inheritance rights, and their wages went to their husbands. Men were responsible for family financial matters, but the debt of a man could fall on his wife! Alma and Fanny were not married, they earned and managed their own money. Fanny also managed the sales work of the women who worked for her, which was quite revolutionary for the time. In 1902, Alma and Fanny invested in real estate, which they later used to support themselves and their religious teaching activities as they grew older.[25] Their pragmatic investments were a good choice and helped to provide the necessary independence and financial stability for their services later in life.

Pauline and Joseph were blessed with three children: Carl in 1896, Gladys in 1898 and Paul in 1900. Little Gladys died shortly after birth. After the birth of Paul, Pauline moved with her family to live with Joseph's mother. Joseph worked in various positions, including that of a stenographer and a railroad company manager. Later, he worked with Fanny as a sales manager for Viavi, an innovative pharmaceutical company from San Francisco that produced gynaecological health products. Due to the personal nature of their products, Viavi depended upon saleswomen for marketing and sales. At the time, it was very unusual for women to work in administrative corporate positions; however, Fanny was a manager at Viavi and lived in Cumberland, Maryland, from 1900 to 1901.[26] She was well respected by those who worked with and for her. Alma cared for Amalie and had a dressmaking business in Washington DC, where she also employed a few Black women who helped her with the sewing work. Alma and her family became good friends with these women; they overcame racial prejudice and built genuine friendships.

2
DISCOVERY OF THE BAHÁ'Í FAITH

Mrs Sarah Etta Sargent worked with Joseph and Fanny at Viavi. Fanny recalled how Sarah introduced them to the Bahá'í Faith:

> . . . in November of 1902, in my official capacity, I was seated one morning at my desk when Mrs. Sargent, uninvited, entered the office and interrupted my work. I looked up questioningly and, to my surprise, was told of a Mrs. Wilt, whose prayer had wonderful power. PRAYER! What a subject during business hours! However, hearing that this prayer was being offered before dawn, I interrupted her with the remark, 'Why, she isn't half awake then, in the dark.' I was informed that Mrs. Wilt let the cold water run over her hands and bathed her face before praying. It was bitter cold winter weather and one's fingers would curl up if held under the cold-water faucet. So, her statement arrested my attention. I said, 'Your friend must love the one she prays for dearly, to get up before dawn in this dreadfully cold weather to pray.' Mrs. Sargent increased my amazement by adding, 'Yes, she is doing this for nineteen mornings, and she does not even know the young wife and mother whose life she has despaired of but who is now, thanks to God, holding her own.'
>
> A few days later Mrs. Sarah Etta Sargent was called in for further questioning because, during those intervening mornings, strange to say, I had awakened before dawn, pushed back the covers and, feeling the intense cold in the

room, had asked myself, 'Why, oh why, is this lady out in the northeast section of the city getting up now and praying on her knees for someone whom she does not know personally? What a remarkable woman she must be!'

Although not in the least inclined to have an interest in forms of religion, I found myself seeking an interview with this Mrs. Wilt, which was graciously granted. My sisters and brother-in-law, Mr. Joseph Hannen accompanied me to her home during a raging blizzard. My mental picture of so spiritual a person was that of a frail, fair-complexioned, spiritual looking woman, but, to my surprise, when the door opened, I was facing a dark, olive-complexioned lady possessing a sturdy figure. At the close of our visit, where we had been listeners, we were invited to come the following Sunday and meet her friends. When I was later asked by my brother-in-law Joseph, 'What did you get out of this talk?' my reply was, 'That lady's God is a living reality, not something ethereal or off at a great distance, but a <u>living reality</u>!'[1]

Sarah Etta Sargent moved away from Washington for the following two years,[2] but before she left, she introduced the Knobloch family to the small Washington Bahá'í community, who invited and included them in their activities.

Pauline was the first family member to become a member of the Bahá'í Faith. She recalled her remarkable experience as follows:

> In the year of 1902 this humble and unworthy servant was given the pearl of greatest price, the Glorious & Wonderful message of Baha'o'llah [sic] the returned Christ. Through Mrs. S. E. Sargent my sister Fanny Knobloch, my husband and myself were invited to call upon a Mrs. A. Jones who was and is well known for her gentleness and powerful prayers.
>
> This Saturday evening, it seemed to me, was a memorable one, it seemed to me it was an evening of symbols. We made our visit and were greatly attracted to these ladies

because of their joy and sincerity, and although no word concerning this Mighty Truth was spoken, I felt, rather than knew, that a great change in my life was soon to take place. So strong was this feeling that on our way home I spoke of it in this way. In the first place when we left home the moon and stars were shining brightly in the sky, during our visit, it thundered and lightened [sic], and the earth received a great down pour of rain. On leaving, the moon and stars were again shining brightly. Walking home I was very quiet and thoughtful. At last I spoke to my sister and husband saying it seems to me we are on the eve of great changes. They both smiled and asked why, then I said: We left home in clear beautiful weather, while visiting there was a terrible storm and now it is clear and calm again. This is the symbol to my mind, we are now contented in our old way of living and thinking, there will soon be a great upheaval and tempest of thought, perhaps, and then peace and contentment. They laughed and so did I at the picture, but this really was prophetic of my own condition.

 The next morning instead of going to my Church I went to Mrs. Jones prayer meeting she held every Sunday morning. Again, I was contented and happy, still no word concerning the truth of Baha'o'llah [sic]. At the close of the meeting Mrs. Sargent said to me, 'would you not like to visit a wonderful teacher from Persia? He is able to answer any questions you have concerning the Bible.'[3]

Pauline, slightly fearful of meeting an oriental man, asked her mother to accompany her to the meeting. The oriental man was none other than the illustrious Bahá'í teacher Mírzá Abu'l-Faḍl, who was assisted by his young translator Ali-Kuli Khan, later the Persian Chargé d'Affaires in Washington DC. The two men spoke in a direct and straightforward manner patiently and lovingly explaining the prophecies and proofs from the Bible as Pauline remained quietly captivated. There was a long silence. Pauline had no more questions. In her head she could only hear the words ringing in her ears, 'Christ has come again in the flesh.'⁴ Finally, Khan broke the silence and asked her if she was 'satisfied with the answers or if she needed more answers to be convinced?' Pauline 'suddenly beamed at them and said, "How could there be anything more wonderful than this great Faith? After you received this, what else in the world would you wish to possess?"'⁵ The encounter was a surprise for Ali-Kuli Khan, who later told Pauline, 'he felt he had wasted time and breath' as her 'face was a perfect blank, no sign of interest, denial, belief, opposition, surprise, nor the least sign of understanding'. Mírzá Abu'l-Faḍl, however had the deeper insight and told him, 'She was overcome with the spirit, she will be an active Believer and her saint of a mother also.'⁶

That night, 26 November 1902, after much pleading, Pauline took some family members to the home of Laura Barney where the Washington community was celebrating the Day of the Covenant for the first time at her home. Here they met people who were 'good and kind', learned more about the Faith and heard Mírzá Abu'l-Faḍl give a lecture for the first time.

Alma was engaged to be married, but her fiancé died before the wedding took place. The untimely death of her fiancé was a source of great suffering, she loved him very much. She travelled to Germany and Switzerland to recover with friends and family from 14 June 1901 until 9 February 1902,⁷ but she returned quite ill. The results of the trip were 'not what the family had hoped for'. Because she was sick, Alma was not included in the early visits to the Bahá'í gatherings. Her sisters had been praying for her at Mrs Jones's devotionals in Ledroit Park,⁸ where Mrs Jones assured them that Alma would become 'perfectly well'.

One afternoon in September 1903, Pauline came to Alma's room because she had something of great importance to tell her. 'While trembling all over' she told Alma that 'Christ had come again upon the earth and has left and His son 'Abdu'l-Bahá, who is in prison at Acca and is married, has children and is establishing the teachings.' Alma responded, 'We will inquire about all of this and see what it means.'⁹

The next day Pauline brought Alma a healing prayer to be said nine times before retiring. 'O my God! Thy name is my healing, Thy remembrance is my remedy . . .'[10] Alma wrote that she was touched by the way Pauline passed this little prayer to her and she was deeply impressed by the 'pleading and beautiful' look in Pauline's face. Still, Alma was proud to be a long-time Bible class teacher in the oldest Lutheran Church in Washington and was caught off-guard by Pauline.

Alma recalled, 'Imagine my surprise when using this prayer for the first time – such a strong spirit – unusual vibration passing through my entire body – by the time I had repeated it the ninth time I full realized that I here to for had not prayed at all – in fact, I had only repeated words, such was the effect of this healing prayer.'[11] Soon Alma joined her sisters attending the prayer meeting at the home of Mrs Jones. She wrote:

> The first visit to Mrs. Jones seemed strange: one hour of prayer between 11–12 AM. Those present that I can recall were Mrs. Jones, Mrs. Barnitz, Mrs. Phelps, and Grandma Phelps sitting in a semi-circle before an open hearth reading the Hidden Words and prayers then Mrs. Jones told me to read the 21st chapter of Revelations and said 'Abdu'l-Bahá was standing back of me showering myrtle [sic] over me. It was very strange.

Whenever Alma saw Mrs Jones, Mrs Jones always had something 'wonderful and strange' to tell concerning Alma's development. In 1903 Alma and every member of her family openly declared themselves as Bahá'ís.[12] They attended two or three times weekly the regular ten o'clock prayer meetings at the home of Mrs Jones where the holy Tablets and prayers were read and discussed. In the summer of 1903 Mírzá Abu'l-Faḍl left Washington to go to Green Acre Bahá'í School in New Hampshire. A French Bahá'í, Georgiana d'Astre, continued the meetings, always finding someone to teach the newly declared family as their faith grew stronger.[13] Mírzá Abu'l-Faḍl returned in the Fall to build up the Washington community and train a generation of Western Bahá'í teachers who would carry the Faith and build communities all over the Western world.

During this time, 'Abdu'l-Bahá suffered from the intrigues of His half-brother Mírzá Muḥammad-'Alí. Mírzá Abu'l-Faḍl organized nine believers in Washington including himself to pray for the Master's safety. Alma recalled:

> When kneeling and supplicating for Abdu'l-Bahá's safety, the power of the spirit was strong and powerful, and my entire body was greatly affected, feeling exhausted [I] finally laid down being wide-awake, I saw a most magnificent large sun its most glorious splendour casting its rays on the water, its waves gradually coming up closer and closer until they covered me . . .[14]

In November, Alma wrote to the Master. In those days, 'Abdu'l-Bahá was living under precarious circumstances, so all the letters written to Him from Western believers were posted to Ahmad Yazdi at Port Said, Egypt, and then forwarded safely to the Holy Land. Pauline encouraged Alma to write to 'Abdu'l-Bahá, and said, 'Make a wish and it will be granted.'[15] After sending her letter, Alma quietly wished to herself that it would be answered before Christmas. When she learned that Ahmad Yazdi often held letters in security at Port Said due to troubles in 'Akká, she felt quite sorry for having made such an impossible wish. But on Christmas Eve, to her great surprise, a Tablet from 'Abdu'l-Bahá addressed to her had arrived and was awaiting translation!

> O thou maid-servant of God!
> In these times thanksgiving for the Bounty of the Merciful One consists in the illumination of the heart and the feeling of the soul. This is the reality of thanksgiving. But, although offering thanks through speech or writings is approvable, yet, in comparison with that, it is but unreal, for the foundation is spiritual feelings and merciful sentiments. I hope that you may be favored therewith. But the lack of capacity and merit in the Day of Judgment does not prevent one from bounty and generosity, for it is the day

of grace and not justice, and to give every one his due is justice. Consequently, do not look upon thy capacity, nay, rather, look upon the Infinite Grace of the Bounty of Abha, whose grace is comprehending and whose bounty is perfect.

I beg of God through the confirmation and assistance of the True One thou mayest show the utmost eloquence, fluency, ability and skill in teaching the real significance of the Bible. Turn toward the Kingdom of Abha and seek the bounty of the Holy Spirit. Loosen the tongue and the confirmation of the Spirit shall reach thee.

As to that great Sun which thou sawest in a dream: that is His Holiness the Promised One and the lights thereof are His bounties. The surface of the water is transparent body – that is, pure hearts. Its waves are the moving of the hearts, the cheering of the souls – that is, spiritual feelings and merciful sentiments. Thank thou God for that thou hast had such a revelation in the world of dreams. As to the fact that man must entirely forget himself, by this is meant that he should arise in the mystery of sacrifice and that is the disappearance of mortal sentiments and extinction of blamable morals which constitute the temporal gloom, and not that the physical health should be changed into weakness and debility.

I humbly supplicate to the Threshold of Oneness that heavenly blessings and merciful forgiveness may overtake thy dear mother, sisters and loving relations, especially thy betrothed who suddenly departed from this world to the next one.[16]

3
MÍRZÁ ABU'L-FAḌL

Mírzá Abu'l-Faḍl was the foremost Bahá'í teacher of his time. He could clearly explain the Bahá'í teachings based on his large knowledge of the Christian and Muslim religions.

The first Bahá'í to bring the Faith to the United States was Anton Haddad, followed by Ibrahim Kheiralla, both arriving in 1892. Kheiralla was a successful teacher but he taught a mixture of Bahá'í teachings combined with his own personal religious ideas. When the first Western Bahá'ís met 'Abdu'l-Bahá on the famous Hearst pilgrimage in 1898, these differences became blatant, and confusion arose.

'Abdu'l-Bahá sent two early American believers, Lua Getsinger and Emogene Hoagg, to Egypt in 1899 and 1900 to study the Bahá'í teachings with Mírzá Abu'l-Faḍl. They returned to the United States and shared the things they had learned with the American believers. In addition, 'Abdu'l-Bahá sent some Persian teachers for additional support. The most loved and respected of these teachers was the unforgettable Mírzá Abu'l-Faḍl himself.

During his stay in the United States he taught summer courses at Green Acre and visited the friends in New York. It was the greatest bounty for the Washington DC Bahá'ís that he spent most of his four-year sojourn in America living in their community. His arrival aroused interest in the Washington DC press in 1902.[1] In 1904, the *Washington Times* dedicated the entire front page of its third section to him.[2]

Mirzá Abu'l-Faḍl and Ali-Kuli Khan were the key teachers who brought Pauline Hannen into the Faith. Pauline visited them repeatedly, listening so quietly to their explanations that

Ali-Kuli Khan wondered if she understood what they were talking about and if she was even interested! When Khan approached Pauline about this, she responded enthusiastically, 'How could there by anything more wonderful than this great faith?'³ After Pauline and Joseph accepted the Bahá'í Faith, they naturally began teaching their friends. In the Fall of 1903, Joseph had invited the Businessmen's Bible Class of the First Congregational Church to a talk by Mírzá Abu'l-Faḍl. The audience was quite large, more than a hundred listening to his talk about the Bible story of Christ feeding the multitude.⁴

In May of 1904, the 'Báb's celebration' was held in the home of Mrs Alice Barney, where Alma met Mírzá Abu'l-Faḍl and his young translator Ali-Kuli Khan for the first time. Mírzá Abu'l-Faḍl gave an impressive and unforgettable talk, which was later followed by a second lecture that was equally as popular.⁵ After his talk, Mírzá Abu'l-Faḍl gave Alma and Pauline stones with the special Bahá'í symbol of the Greatest Name of God (Alláh-u-Abhá) engraved on them and the sisters were invited to attend his weekly Bible class.⁶ These exciting meetings sometimes continued until the early hours of dawn. Mírzá Abu'l-Faḍl led a very serious and deep study of the Bahá'í Faith and the proofs in the Bible, while Ali-Kuli Khan and Ahmad Sohrab translated. Mírzá Abu'l-Faḍl told the participants that his course would be like a college course and that they should each bring a notebook and pencil with them. From the start he told his students that they 'were not to spread these teachings or give them out, for only Abdul Baha's interpretations were authentic'.⁷

Mírzá Abu'l-Faḍl organized these classes to train a generation of teachers who would be able to raise up new communities. He told the participants in this class that they 'would be scattered to teach the Faith throughout the world'.⁸ In fact, this is exactly what happened – Pauline and Fanny would be the first Bahá'ís to teach in Zimbabwe (then Rhodesia) while Fanny made three trips to teach in South Africa. Ahmad Sohrab served the Faith in many Western and Middle Eastern countries. Other class members included Charles Mason Remey who taught in Asia, the Middle East, Europe and America; Georgiana d'Astre and

Laura Clifford Barney who taught in Europe; Colonel Fitzgerald who brought the Bahá'í teachings to the western United States in 1906, where his teaching work received considerable publicity.⁹ Though Colonel Fitzgerald did not remain an active Bahá'í all his life, he is responsible for first mentioning the Faith to future Hand of the Cause and father of the Australian Bahá'í community, Hyde Dunn.¹⁰ Marjorie Morton, another classmate, also taught the Bahá'í Faith throughout the United States and served on national publishing and reviewing committees. On a pilgrimage to the Holy Land, she spent much time with the Greatest Holy Leaf, Bahíyyih Khánum, and wrote her obituary in *The Bahá'í World*.¹¹

From a modern perspective, Mírzá Abu'l-Faḍl's course was similar to the Ruhi Institute courses offered by the Bahá'í community today – a deep study of the Bahá'í writings combined with practical elements that translate words into deeds and build communities. He accompanied Alma as she brought her new religious knowledge into her classes at the Concordia Church. Alma's understanding of the Bible and religion became keen, and she became confident. In addition, Mírzá Abu'l-Faḍl encouraged his participants to identify and enter new fields of service. For her first Bahá'í service, Mason Remey invited Alma to support the Sunday afternoon meetings at the home of Mrs Powell in Baltimore in 1904.¹² Her second task was to write to 19 believers who no longer attended meetings. Alma received responses to 17 of her 19 letters and felt encouraged. After some time, the other two people also sent a cheerful response and Alma was empowered.¹³

These classes had a strong effect on the entire family. In the autumn of 1904, Alma and her sisters invited some friends, and Alma's brother in-law Joseph invited some of the elders of the Church, to their home to meet Mírzá Abu'l-Faḍl, Ali-Kuli Khan and Ahmad Sohrab.¹⁴ It was a courageous invitation. Although the letters do not mention any of their friends joining the Faith at this time, Annie Ripley, who later hosted the Master at her home in 1912 and carried out important early teaching activities in Florida, is mentioned in Alma's papers as serving on the

Concordia Church Board at that time. The Knobloch family was privileged to have Mírzá Abu'l-Faḍl teach in their home. Remembering these classes later, Alma wrote:

> We found Mírzá Abu'l-Faḍl most careful and precise in all his statements and when we had finished the course, which was rather difficult, Mírzá Kuli Khan [who had been our] translator – we were told not to give out our notes that we had been taken – we were not to spread his interpretations – that only Abdu'l-Bahá's interpretations are to be used and are authentic. I carefully put my notebook away and felt that another page of my life had been turned and [I] was starting a new, broad, and beautiful life.[15]

Alma later recalled that many years earlier, when her brother Paul had quit teaching Sunday classes at the Church he asked Alma how her conscience would permit her to teach the children. Alma replied, 'I shall go on until a better way is found and it will come someday, that is sure.'[16] Now she had finally found what she had been waiting for. In those early days, Pauline would often remark to Alma, 'How grand it would have been, had you known about the Bahá'í Teachings sooner, you could have told the Glad-Tidings to your friends across the sea.'[17]

Mírzá Abu'l-Faḍl's lessons were the foundation of Alma's Bahá'í identity, and what he taught her she shared with others throughout her life, wherever she went. To the great sorrow of the American believers, after four years of teaching Mírzá Abu'l-Faḍl left the United States on 29 November 1904. His classes and books had an immeasurable impact on the Western Bahá'í community.

In 1909, Joseph Hannen joined forces with other American believers and founded the Persian–American Educational Society which raised funds to sponsor Western teachers and Persian students to improve general education in Persia. In this way, the Western friends could give something back to the Persian friends in the East who had provided the basis for their spiritual education, in particular, Mírzá Abu'l-Faḍl!

4
THE CHURCH

In the early days of the American Baháʼí community the believers were drawn to the Faith from various perspectives. Some were attracted by a sense of romantic mysticism, others had esoteric interests, others were attracted to the principles which they felt promised secular reform, while still others were convinced through religious scripture, recognizing that Baháʼuʼlláh was the Promised One and the fulfilment of the biblical prophecies.[1]

The Knoblochs were devoted Christians and active members of the Concordia Church in Washington DC. Although the church could not answer all Alma's religious questions, she maintained a strong Christian identity and belief in the Bible and served the church with dedication. Concordia's active and united congregation was composed primarily of German immigrants and provided the social life of the Knobloch family. The Knoblochs did not give up their church membership when they joined the Baháʼí Faith; in common with many early Western Baháʼís, they maintained these memberships and it was natural for them to share the Baháʼí message with their church friends. In July 1904, Alma was elected treasurer for the Christian Endeavour group[2] and teacher at the Concordia Church.[3]

Mírzá Abu'l-Faḍl had taught a deeper understanding of the Bible and encouraged Alma to share the truths she had learned in her Bible class. On one occasion Pastor Menzel asked her to help with the Bible study class on the subject of Isaiah 9. He told the students that Alma and the teachers would explain this prophecy to them:

For unto us a child is born, unto us a son is given: and the government shall be upon his shoulder: and his name shall be called Wonderful, Counsellor, The mighty God, The everlasting Father, The Prince of Peace. Of the increase of His government and peace there shall be no end, upon the throne of David, and upon his kingdom, to order it, and to establish it with judgment and with justice from henceforth even forever. The zeal of the Lord of hosts will perform this.[4]

Alma was amazed – the verse had fascinated her since she was a small child. Mírzá Abu'l-Faḍl had helped her understand that this prophecy had now been fulfilled. Alma wondered, 'Could it be that the Pastor saw it with a new light?'

Later, Alma invited some of her Bible scholars to hear a talk by her Bahá'í friend Charles Mason Remey. She recalled, 'This added to the distress of Pastor Menzel who had been asked by the church Elders to turn over his Bible class to me, which was increasing in attendance as more became interested.'[5] Pastor Menzel looked sad when he visited the class; Alma wondered what he was thinking. Later he told Alma that Pauline had shared with him some Bahá'í literature, which he did not understand.

Becoming a Bahá'í had given Amalie Knobloch the desire to serve God. As with Alma, Pastor Menzel asked her if she would like to teach some children in the Sunday School class. She gladly accepted the offer and taught eight little girls. Everyone was quite happy, and the other teachers said she looked like an angel with the children.

While Pastor Menzel was attending the Christian Endeavor Congress in New York, he asked Alma to hold his two confirmation classes. Alma wrote, 'On Pastor Menzel's return he acted different and distant, I took this as a result of the Congress at NY, for they did not accept the Bahá'í Cause as a true religion, and it was not recognized as a spiritual Christian movement.' Later Alma found out that he returned after attending a Synod meeting in Baltimore where it was decided that Alma had become a 'danger to the church and that Pastor Menzel should see to it that she leaves'.[6]

The following Sunday Pastor Menzel discussed Luke 17 from the New Testament in his Sunday service. Alma referred to it as 'The End of the World', because it describes the Coming of the Kingdom of God and the Son of Man:

> ... so shall also the Son of man be in his day. But first must he suffer many things and be rejected of this generation. And as it was in the days of Noah, so shall it be also in the days of the Son of man. They did eat, they drank, they married wives, they were given in marriage, until the day that Noah entered into the ark, and the flood came, and destroyed them all. Likewise also as it was in the days of Lot; they did eat, they drank, they bought, they sold, they planted, they builded; But the same day that Lot went out of Sodom it rained fire and brimstone from heaven and destroyed them all. Even thus shall it be in the day when the Son of man is revealed.[7]

Afterwards, Pastor Menzel asked Alma to explain her beliefs to the Church Elders and Sunday School officers. Alma was glad to talk about it with anyone who was interested. Pastor Menzel told her there would not be too many people present and that they would meet an hour before the regular Sunday School meeting. When Alma arrived at 7 p.m. all were present. She felt tension in the room, everyone was quiet as Pastor Menzel nervously paced back and forth. He shut the door to the hall and pulled down all the shades on the windows. It seemed strange. Then he opened with a prayer and turned to Alma. She recalled,

> then [he] asked me to tell what my Faith was, what was my belief! – I asked him for his Bible – he did not move – asked him again please to hand me his Bible – no reply – Then I depicted his sermon of the previous Sunday and closed by saying 'And They will bring you before the elders, as you have done tonight'. Pastor Menzel was red in the face, stammered that he had been unusually busy that week and could not prepare his sermon. He asked if my mother believed as I did.[8]

In another account of the same event, Alma wrote that Pastor Menzel accused her of mentioning 'the name of Christ with Mohammed' and making 'some other remarks . . . Nervous and flushed he flouted several questions about believing in Mohammed and asked what I had to say to that all of which I quietly answered.'[9]

The President of the Concordia Church brought Alma home that evening. He told her, 'So sure as there is God in heaven, be assured that He will bless you for all you have done – we all love you.'[10] With tears in his eyes he said goodnight and Alma was comforted by his sincerity.[11]

At the end of the following Sunday sermon Alma and Amalie asked the Pastor if he would prefer that they no longer attend the Sunday School. He said after all that happened it would be better if they did not come. The Church Elders discussed the situation at their next meeting and informed Pastor Menzel that he should see to it that Alma and Amalie return or his resignation would be accepted. The students of Alma's Bible class threatened to quit if she did not return and sent two delegates to the Knobloch home to beg Alma and Amalie to come back. They recognized that Alma and Amalie's new beliefs did not cause them to lose their faith, but rather increased their services![12] For Amalie it had been only half a year since she had taken charge of the class of eight little girls, after she had accepted the Cause.

Alma concludes the story:

> Did we return? No. For my part I felt free like a bird – could go out and teach the Bahá'í Cause without restriction. All the friends had been kind and loving all these many years . . . A new life ahead . . . seemed clear that we could not 'put new wine into old bottles'. Only those who have gone through a similar experience can realize its meaning.[13]

Later some of the Elders visited the Knoblochs and told them they were missed. Alma and Amalie 'begged that they would not make any change on our account, the pastor was only doing his duty on behalf of the Synod and he has a large family of small children.'¹⁴

Alma wrote to Mírzá Abu'l-Faḍl:

> The Bible class had been invited to the social reunion at the home of one of my scholars . . . Two days before the date it was suddenly called off stating that under no consideration would they permit Bahais to come to her home & insisted that I recall the invitations. The task was not an easy one, [I] received unkindness but also many cheerful & encouraging words, the battle was a severe one, but I came out ahead this time. When the reunion did take place, I arranged a real Bahai evening under the name 'a trip to Klondike', gold being the topic. Sunday last was honoured at the German Orphan Asylum being asked to take entire charge of the instructions & will endeavour to instill [sic] the truth. Your humble scholar prays that the good seeds you sowed with us so much patient [sic] may bring forth fruits.¹⁵

Amalie Knobloch wrote to 'Abdu'l-Bahá regarding these eventful times and received the following reply dated 25 July 1906:

> O thou venerable maid servant of God
>
> Thy letter was duly received. Its contents signified true spirituality and steadfastness.
>
> O thou maid servant of God! Consider not merit and aptitude! Thou shouldst rather consider the favors and benefits of the Blessed Perfection.
>
> When we think of self, we find that merit and aptitude (ability) are lost. When we regard Truth, we discover that the Favors of God are infinite and not conditional upon merit and aptitude.
>
> Observe how the small seed grows and thrives by means of vernal showers, the heat of the heavenly sun and the zephyrs until it grows to a fruitful tree. Now see where the former state of the seed is, and the present state of stem, leaves, blossoms and the wonderful fruits, consequently the

Divine gifts make a sea out of one drop of water! And make out of one seed a heavenly tree.

I implore God to promote thee day after day in the stages of Eternal Glory and to make thee the instrument to spread the Word of God! Summon thou, the souls to the Law (Cause) of God, and bring them to the Divine Kingdom!

. . . I hope that thou mayest be chosen and not of the pretenders. Be thou gifted with speech and not silent! Be thou active and not passive! Be thou full of joyful tidings and not hopeless! Be thou existing and not lost, so that the eyes may see and darkness may be changed into illuminations! Strew thou pure seeds over purified land (souls) that thou mayest witness the Divine Bounty!

It would be in vain, if for a thousand years, thou plant seeds into salsuginous [salty] ground. In this case days simply pass and no result can be gained. Then spread the seeds over blessed ground and plant them until thou, in a very short time, viewest a very large harvest and the heavenly blessings will be inferred!

Express my best compliments to the maid servant of God Alma, and say unto her, 'Be thou not sad at the antipathy of others, and let not the accusations and rebukes of the clergy grieve thee! But be joyful, certainly thou shalt experience the hatred of enemies and rebuke of opponents! And shall be the target of the arrows of oppression, just as thou didst hear concerning the adversaries of the Beloved Ones in the Cycle of Christ and how they preferred the rebukes and the antipathies of others.[16]

So it was that Alma and Amalie Knobloch, who were bold enough to bring the Bahá'í teachings into their Christian Church, were the first to be rejected by a Christian Pastor and asked to leave that Church on the basis of their belief in Bahá'u'lláh. Their courage and the significance of this event attracted great confirmations to them both.

5

BRINGING THE BLACK COMMUNITY INTO THE FAITH

When one door closes, another opens. Alma found a new community to teach. Pauline recalled how the Knoblochs began building the Black Bahá'í community in Washington:

> The work among the Colored people was really started by my sainted mother and sister Alma, though I was the one who first gave the Message to Pocahontas Pope and Mrs Turner. My Mother and sister went to their home in this way meeting others giving the message to quite a number and started meetings. Then my sister left for Germany where she now teaches, and I took up the work.[1]

In 1903, at least three African-American women worked for the Knobloch family: Laura Burk, Carrie York and Pocahontas Pope, all of whom came to accept the Faith after they learned of it from the Knoblochs.

Laura Burk helped Alma, Fanny and Amalie with their household. One day she asked Amalie about the Knobloch's new faith. As Amalie was not very fluent in English, she asked Alma to talk to Laura. Alma took Laura to her room and explained the Bahá'í Faith to her. Later Amalie went upstairs and 'found Laura kneeling at the end of Alma's bed praying for the great blessings she had received'.[2] Laura's husband held a Bible class at his church and a government position, making him part of the African-American 'government official set', a core of Washington's stable middle class.³ Later, Alma shared the teachings with him as well.

Pauline explained the Bahá'í teachings to her washing woman Carrie York,⁴ and she accepted it. Alma employed Pocahontas Pope, who may have been of mixed native and African-American heritage,⁵ to help her as a seamstress in her dressmaking business.⁶ Alma's friendship with Pocahontas Pope confirmed her interest in the Faith. She became a believer and opened her home to share the teachings with interested friends and neighbours. This was the second of the 'Washington Houses of Faith'.⁷

Pocahontas and Laura asked Alma to give talks at their respective homes. These meetings were well-attended and a great success. Fortnightly, Alma gave classes to this interested group, and the receptivity was great. Many people gathered at the Pope home where they heard about the teachings of Bahá'u'lláh and the proofs of the Bible. Pocahontas's husband was a pastor who told her that she was following the Anti-Christ, but then he used the Bahá'í ideas she taught him in his sermons!

Pocahontas wrote to 'Abdu'l-Bahá in the Holy Land, and He replied with a Tablet to her in February 1907:

> Render thanks to the Lord that among that race thou art the first believer, that thou hast engaged in speaking sweet-scented breezes, and has arisen to guide others. It is my hope that through the bounties and favors of the Abhá Beauty [Bahá'u'lláh] thy countenance may be illumined, thy disposition pleasing, and thy fragrance diffused, that thine eyes may be seeing, thine ears attentive, thy tongue eloquent, thy heart filled with supreme glad-tidings, and thy soul refreshed by divine fragrances, so that thou mayest arise among that race and occupy thyself with the edification of the people, and become filled with light.⁸

'Abdu'l-Bahá also wrote to Alma concerning this, conveying his greetings to Pocahontas and commenting on how happy He was to receive the news that the Cause was being spread among the 'Colored race'.⁹ He also sent a message to Alma in a Tablet revealed to Charles Mason Remey on 12 December 1906:

> To Miss Alma Knobloch – Send to her my love and greetings and say: Blessed art thou that to you the white and the black are one. Whiteness is by the light of the heart, not the skin; and blackness is the blackness of the heart not the face. The reflection of a person is seen in the black pupil of the eye. How many there are who have black faces, but their characters are white and illumined. I am most happy on account of this work which you have been doing; it is the cause of the whiteness and illumination of your spirit.¹⁰

Alma's study classes with these friends replaced the classes she had once participated in at Concordia Church. Alma and Amalie walked past the church to study the Bahá'í teachings with the receptive African-American community. Alma did not feel any remorse, rather she felt elated to have found such a wonderful new group of friends! At the time, such relationships between members of the Black and the White races were extraordinary.

6

A MISSED PILGRIMAGE

In late 1904, Alma considered joining Mírzá Abu'l-Faḍl, Ahmad Sohrab, Howard MacNutt, Percy Woodcock, Georgiana d'Astre, Miss Hitchcock, Nathan Fitzgerald, and others to make her first pilgrimage to meet 'Abdu'l-Bahá in 'Akká. There was a bit of confusion regarding the logistics of this trip and the group of pilgrims.[1] The dates were not clear and then they were only fixed short term. Alma did not have permission from the Master to come to the Holy Land, so she consulted with Mírzá Abu'l-Faḍl, who replied on 22 November 1904:

> . . . although it is my utmost pleasure and joy and [I] pray to God for this great privilege that you may go and visit the Master, yet, in the way of friendship, I must tell you that if you could have permission from here, it is far better for you. For I have experienced during 30 years of my teaching this truth, that those people who had permission, and started from their own country to Accá could draw a greater benefit for their spiritual development and attained to the good pleasure of the Lord . . . Send a telegram to Ahmad Yazdi and ask [it] to be sent to the Master. Let the contents be the following: Mírzá Abu'l-Faḍl is going to travel with Mr. MacNutt, and a party to the Holy Land in the first of December. I pray that permission be given to this maidservant through Miss Barney. I hope that during these 8 days you will hear from the Master . . . But, know this, that going with permission and going without it, has opposite effects. I cannot explain more about this in a letter, except meeting with permission is beneficial to life.[2]

A MISSED PILGRIMAGE

At the time, the fastest way to communicate with 'Abdu'l-Bahá was to send a telegram to Ahmad Yazdi, a Bahá'í merchant who was also the Honorary Consul for Persia[3] in Cairo, who would then send it to the Master. A week later, Alma wrote to Mírzá Abu'l-Faḍl:

> In regard to my joining Mr. McNutt party, it seemed so hurried, the clerks at the telegraph office seemed doubtful and said it would take days to send the message, that we concluded that I had better wait and write to the Master for permission. Nothing could induce me to go if there were any doubts of my not receiving spiritual benefits, for it is the one and only wish that I may be worthy of the Cause and be permitted to work in this most glorious Truth, and humbly pray for strength to bear the tests bravely and grow stronger in the faith.[4]

The choice to remain home proved to be the best one. The MacNutt pilgrimage was encircled with difficulties which demonstrated the wisdom of 'Abdu'l-Bahá. During this time 'Abdu'l-Bahá borrowed a large sum of money from a Bahá'í in Paris to move the Bahá'ís of 'Akká to Egypt temporarily and His mail needed to be diverted.[5] The Covenant-breakers had aroused negative attention from the Turkish government against the Master in late 1904.[6] This pilgrimage occurred during the period when Mírzá Badí'u'lláh had repented of his unfaithful actions against 'Abdu'l-Bahá and was actively in contact with the Bahá'ís in 'Akká. He even met with the pilgrims in the MacNutt group.[7] Howard MacNutt himself was restricted to two visits to 'Akká for a total of five days, and for one of the visits he was smuggled into 'Akká in the back of a covered wagon.[8] The Master warned Howard, 'Your coming to 'Akká is not so dangerous to yourselves as it is to the Bahá'í friends who live here. They suffer the consequences of your coming to 'Akká after you have gone.'[9]

Typically, Alma turned her disappointment into a new opportunity by focusing on spiritual development and service.

Georgiana d'Ange d'Astre, a Bahá'í in Washington DC, was divorced and raising her daughter Odette, then an eighth grader,[10] alone. She embraced the Faith in the summer of 1903,[11] around the same time as Alma Knobloch. Georgiana was invited to join the group of pilgrims who travelled with Howard MacNutt to 'Akká in late 1904, but she could not leave Odette in Washington alone. Reluctant to ask Alma for help directly, Georgiana told Alma that Mírzá Abu'l-Faḍl had said that the Knoblochs should take custody of Odette while she, Georgiana, was away.

The Knoblochs agreed, but the decision was a difficult one. The relationship between Georgiana and the Knoblochs was burdened by nationalistic feelings between immigrants of French and German descent. Eventually, Alma and Fanny decided to ask Mírzá Abu'l-Faḍl directly.[12] He replied, 'It would be very good for Odette if the Knoblochs would . . .' take her.

Alma, Fanny and Amalie met with Georgiana, but the discussion did not go well. Old European prejudices continually tested their Bahá'í identities. Alma recalled that Georgiana was asking for a big favour from the Knoblochs, and yet she made many offensive remarks including, 'French women only consider men as real friends,' and 'French women hate the Germans,' to which Fanny replied, 'And you want to leave your daughter with the three of us ladies?' Amalie was so hurt that she left the room.

Later Amalie told Alma, 'You can decide, and I will accept your decision.' Alma decided to accept Odette as a test to prove her own faith. She felt that looking after Odette would be a contribution to the unity of mankind, which is a central teaching of Bahá'u'lláh. She realized that every Bahá'í must strive to overcome the old ideas which have led to so much war and hatred. As for herself, not having the permission to join the group of pilgrims and then being asked to look after a French child doubly tested her faith. Her decision to work for unity by taking Odette is a sign of her great character. It also shows religion as a true means of healing and uniting people.

Odette and Alma shared a room and became good friends.

Odette attended Alma's Sunday School and Bahá'í classes and accompanied Alma to the meetings at the home of Pocahontas Pope.[13]

After her pilgrimage, Georgiana remained in Europe and failed to return to Washington at the originally agreed time. Thus, Odette lived for two years with the Knobloch family. Joseph and Fanny finally contacted Odette's father to find out when Odette could return to her parents. Mr d'Astre told them that he had sent Georgiana a second ticket, and 'this time she is ready to come back'.[14] By 1907, Georgiana had returned to France with Odette and joined the Paris Bahá'í community. She married Joseph Roche, who adopted Odette.[15]

Alma had been a believer for only a short time but was already able to apply the teachings that would change the world. She had finished training with Mírzá Abu'l-Faḍl, started correspondence reaching out to estranged believers, started study circles with the Bahá'ís in Baltimore, taught the first African-American Bahá'ís in Washington, started Bahá'í meetings in their homes with their friends, and finally overcame strong nationalistic prejudices to accept responsibility for Odette d'Astre. What would come next?

7

HOMEFRONT PIONEERING IN NEW YORK STATE

In 1905, the Washington DC Community pitched tents and held the first solely Bahá'í Summer School in the United States at 'Camp Mineola' in Colonial Beach, Virginia, where Mrs Leone St. Clair Barnitz had spent her summer vacations teaching her friends since 1903.[1] Alma was camping with Pauline's son Carl, and Odette, and first met Margaret Mills Sprague from Buffalo, New York while struggling with her non-waterproof tent in the rain.[2] After a good laugh, a strong friendship evolved. Margaret and Alma were both 'on fire' with the spirit of the Bahá'í Faith.

Upon their return home, Alma and Mason Remey received invitations from Margaret to help establish the Bahá'í Cause in Buffalo. Since Remey could not go, he asked Alma if she could go instead. Alma replied, 'I sent my letter last night confirming that I would come!'[3] Alma spent three months teaching in Buffalo.

John Fell Mills, the first Bahá'í in Buffalo, had learned of the Faith through Howard and Mary MacNutt in New York.[4] Soon John's parents Henrietta and artist John Harrison Mills and his sister Margaret Sprague also joined the Faith. His parents held weekly meetings in their home trying to form an Assembly in Buffalo, for quite some time with little success.[5] Alma and Margaret worked as a united teaching team. They attended talks at the International Progressive Thought League of Buffalo, an organization founded by Grace Carew Sheldon and Elizabeth Marney-Conner. Grace, a prominent journalist and the daughter of Chief Justice James Sheldon, was acquainted with Margaret and supported her efforts. After a talk on the topic of fear, the audience was invited to share their thoughts. Grace was moved when Alma explained the concept of fear from a Bahá'í perspective. She invited Alma and Margaret for dinner at her home and a close friendship evolved. Alma wrote home that Grace accepted the Faith, but it seems she did not become an active believer. She did maintain a relationship with the Bahá'í Faith, however, and in 1912, she publicly invited 'Abdu'l-Bahá to visit Buffalo during His journeys in the United States.[6]

After three months, in November 1905, Fanny and Amalie asked Alma to return home.[7] As Alma planned to return to Washington, Margaret's sister-in-law Henrietta Mills wrote to the House of Spirituality in Chicago (the forerunner of the Chicago Local Spiritual Assembly), on 17 October 1905:

> Regret to say that outside of our own family I know of no one residing here who claims the name, though there are some who go to Green Acre and have heard of the teachings . . . we are newcomers just getting a foothold here . . . will be glad to meet anyone you may send to help us and will do all in our power to help all who are aiding the Cause, will invite any persons whose addresses you send together here and talk over the truth . . . 'These are the days of Faith and deeds, not the days of words – let us arise from the sleep of negligence . . .' Our family consists of Harrison Mills, John Fell Mills and yours faithfully Henrietta Fell Mills.[8]

The House of Spirituality responded on 6 November:

> We feel sure that Buffalo will present a field for a wonderful work and rejoice to hear of your intention to serve therein. It will indeed be of great benefit to establish such a gathering of which you speak, and we will do all in our power to assist in establishing the same. At the present writing,

we are unable to send you the names and addresses of any friends who may reside in Buffalo but hope to do so in the near future . . . The House of Spirituality C. Scheffler[9]

Less than a month after Alma returned home, she received a wonderful Tablet from 'Abdu'l-Bahá in which he told her to return to Buffalo.[10] In response, Alma moved to Buffalo and set up a seamstress shop in a commercial space owned by Henrietta Mills in Dunkirk. On 29 January 1906, Alma received loving encouragement from 'Abdu'l-Bahá:

> O thou seeker of the Kingdom!
> Thou hast forwarded thy photograph and it was considered. In thy face a brilliant light is apparent and that sparkling light is the love of God. All faces are dark except the face which is a mirror of the light of the love of divinity. This light is not accidental – it is eternal. It is not temporal but real. When the heart hath become clear and pure then the face will become illuminated, because the face is the mirror of the heart.
> I was indeed very happy to look at thy picture and pray God that thy face may become shining. Be happy and joyful and in this Age be it illuminated and full of light.[11]

Grace Sheldon's Progressive Thought League weekly meetings were well attended. Speakers of various religions, schemes and cults were invited to give lectures, which were then published in full in the largest Buffalo paper, *The Buffalo News*. Grace invited Alma to present the Bahá'í teachings at these meetings and her presentations were publicized. The response was tremendous: many letters were received, one even from as far away as Australia!

On 14 November 1906, in a Tablet sent to Mason Remey, the Master foreshadowed Alma's future role in Europe:

> Announce, on my behalf respectful greeting to the attracted maid-servant of God Miss [Alma Knobloch] and say: 'O

Alma with early Bahá'ís and friends in Washington DC, circa 1904

Náw-Rúz celebration at the Hannen home in Washington DC, 1906

Fanny in 1909
© USBNA

Karl Hannen and his Aunt Alma, Stuttgart, 1909
© USBNA

thou beloved maid-servant of God! Now is the time, now is the moment, in which, like unto Mary Magdelene (who loosened her tongue in the city of great Rome), thou mayest arise and become engaged in teaching the coming of the Kingdom of God and spread far and wide to the ears the glad-tidings of the Realm of Eternity!'

In brief! O thou servant of Baha! Strive ye that the souls be engaged, in all parts of Europe, with the utmost purity and sanctification, in the diffusion of the fragrances of God.

Undoubtedly teachers both from among the women as well as the men must go to Australia and New Zealand, whenever the means and opportunity are brought about. Now make ye an effort that perchance though correspondence some souls, in those parts, may become illumined with the Light of the Kingdom.[12]

Alma was receiving numerous invitations to present the Bahá'í teachings, opening new fields to spread the Cause. Soon she was invited to speak in two historic churches in St Catherines, Ontario, Canada.[13]

St Catherines, Ontario

In the antebellum era of American history, the interests of southern state slave owners increasingly clashed with the moral agenda of the abolitionists in the northern states. In 1850, pressure from the southern states pushed the US Congress to pass the Fugitive Slave Act, which gave legal rights to slave owners to retrieve fugitive slaves caught living in the northern states. Thus, the border to freedom was pushed further to the north to Canada West, now known as Ontario, where slavery had been abolished in 1834. Eventually, moral pressure from the northern states against the Fugitive Slave Act contributed to the outbreak of the US Civil War (1861–1865).

While Alma was teaching in Buffalo, she met the 83-year-old Amelia Cisco Shadd. Amelia was a distinguished member of the African-American community in Canada West who lived in St Catherines, Ontario, where her son ran a successful jewellery business. Through Alma, Amelia accepted and began to teach the Bahá'í Faith in 1906. 'Abdu'l-Bahá wrote to Alma:

> Convey my greetings to Mrs. [Williamson] and say: 'These seeds which are scattered here and there are spreading strong roots in the bosom of the earth and these will develop and grow until many harvests are gathered. Rest thou assured.'[14]

Alma is the first Bahá'í known to have taught the Faith in St Catherines.[15] Located 15 miles from the US border, the city served as a safe haven for fugitive slaves in the antebellum years and was the final destination of Harriet Tubman's famous Underground Railroad, which freed hundreds of people from the brutality of slavery. Many African-Americans permanently relocated to St Catherines, including much of Harriet Tubman's family and the renowned Reverend Anthony Burns, a fugitive slave who was captured by slave catchers in Boston and returned to his Southern owners in 1854. Widespread angry protests led the citizens of Boston to find, purchase and free him in 1855. After attending Oberlin College on scholarship, Anthony Burns served as a Minister at the Zion Baptist Church, located next to Harriet Tubman's Salem Chapel in St Catherines. He passed away in St Catherines on 17 July 1862 and a small monument has been erected to honour his memory.

In August 1906, Amelia Shadd Williamson arranged for Alma to speak in St Catherines to two large congregations of over 250 people at Anthony Burns's Zion Baptist Church and Harriet Tubman's Salem Chapel. In both churches, Alma proclaimed the 'Coming of the Kingdom', and shared the Glad Tidings of the coming of Bahá'u'lláh. She quoted the words of 'Abdu'l-Bahá: 'The Door of the Kingdom is opened, the Sun of Truth is shining upon the world.' Alma's presentation was very successful, many thanked her and a large number of people invited her to return.[16]

'Abdu'l-Bahá responded to Amelia's declaration of Faith in a Tablet addressed directly to her:

> O thou who art attracted to the Kingdom!
> Thy letter contained meanings full of sweetness. I therefore took it in my hand with the utmost love and became informed of thy desire.
> O thou maid-servant of God! Glad-tidings be unto thee! As thou art faithful and art going to remain firm, the favors of the Bounty of Abha will encircle thee; thou wilt become a cause of the illumination of the human world, and be assisted by the heavenly confirmation.[17]

This Tablet is quite remarkable. 'Abdu'l-Bahá wrote to Amelia that she would 'remain firm', and 'be the cause of the illumination of the human world'. These were incredibly strong words for a new believer to receive from the Master. But who was Amelia Shadd Williamson? Why does her name disappear from Bahá'í history after 1906?

A detailed investigation into the historical records of the time reveals the answer. Amelia's great-grandfather was a German soldier named Hans Schadd, who was injured while fighting for the British in the Revolutionary War. Hans was nursed back to health by a free Abyssinian woman named Elizabeth, whom he married in 1756. Hans and Elizabeth were industrious and well-respected business people who left their heirs with much valuable property in the state of Delaware. Education was of primary importance to the Shadd family, and they maintained a good standard of living down through the following generations, despite their mixed racial heritage.

Amelia's father was the well-known abolitionist Abraham Doras Shadd who served as a conductor on the Underground Railroad and later became the first Black man elected to a public office in Canada. Abraham and Harriet Shadd had 12 children, many of whom became famous role models for the African-American community.

Amelia Shadd Williamson was born in 1823. She married David Thomas Williamson, a self-emancipated former slave from West Virginia[18] and an exceptional watchmaker who passed the jewellery trade down to his sons. David Williamson passed away on 7 July 1889. Amelia's younger brother, Abram William Shadd, served in the 104th Regiment of Colored Troops in the US Civil War, as did Thornton Chase, who later became the first person in the United States to accept the Baháʼí Faith in 1894–5.[19] The 104th Regiment of Colored Troops consisted of 10 companies; Chase was Captain in Companies C and D until he resigned from the military on 14 November 1865. In addition, George Gregory, Hand of the Cause Louis Gregory's beloved stepfather, who paid Louis's law school tuition, served as First Sergeant in Company C.[20] The 104th Regiment, United States Colored Infantry mustered out 5 February 1866.

The Shadd family upheld principles that were far ahead of their time and that were in harmony with the teachings of Baháʼu'lláh: the abolishment of racial prejudice, the equality of men and women, and the emphasis on education as a means for releasing human potential. Abraham Shadd believed in the equality of men and women and worked hard to acquire the best possible education for his daughters as well as his sons, even moving the family to ensure the girls would be able to attend school. This paid off greatly; three of his daughters became famous abolitionists and set historical precedents for women: Mary Ann, Emeline and Amelia. Mary Ann Shadd Cary was a famous publisher, the first Black female enrolled in law school and the second to become a lawyer in the United States. Emeline Shadd Simpson was one of the first Black female professors. Amelia served as the associate editor for Mary Ann's famous newspaper *The Provincial Freeman* and became the first Black Canadian to accept the Baháʼí Faith.

Mary Ann Shadd founded *The Provincial Freeman* primarily to publicize her belief that the only way to uplift the African-American community out of its troubled position was to focus on morality and education as tools to achieve economic and political self-sufficiency.[21] In the early years, Mary Ann and Amelia used pseudonyms to hide their female identities, and published articles in *The Provincial Freeman* in which they discouraged any form of 'begging' for financial support for the Black communities in Canada West. This was a dangerous step, as it was in direct opposition to the practices of the African-American Churches in Canada West and, in particular, the powerful Refugee Home Society of the American Missionary Association which funded the Black schools. These organizations greatly exaggerated the needs of the Black communities in Canada so as to attract financial support which they distributed amongst the Black community. Mary Ann and Amelia rejected this as a form of humiliation, finding it counterproductive to the elevation of character. In addition, they maintained a 'universal concept of mankind', and rejected any form of 'racial identity'. They crossed the colour lines to work with anyone interested in the improvement of educational opportunities for all children including Blacks.

Mary Ann Cary and Amelia Shadd were very close to each other. Mary Ann married in Amelia's home and the two sisters lived near each other most of their lives. Mary Ann passed away in 1893, followed by her sister Emeline in 1894, before the Bahá'í Faith was taught in America. The illustrious contributions of the Shadd family towards the unity of mankind have left a mark in the history of the United States and Canada. It is easy to see how Amelia, coming from such a family, accepted the Bahá'í teachings.

Amelia passed away in St Catherines on 5 October 1906,[22] shortly after 'Abdu'l-Bahá revealed His remarkable Tablet in her honour. She was laid to rest in Victoria Lawn Cemetery. Amelia never met 'Abdu'l-Bahá. One may perhaps imagine that He thought of her as He passed through St Catherines on a train en route to Montreal in 1912. Shortly afterwards the town of St Catherines formed a Bahá'í community.[23]

In both the United States and Canada, Alma spread the Faith with complete disregard for skin colour. She connected souls to the Covenant whenever and wherever there was interest. She was not concerned with race, social position, or gender. For Alma, teaching was a matter of the heart.

The pace of service in Buffalo increases

By August 1906, the Mills family had established an 'Open Room' in their home for public teaching events, which were announced in the newspaper. Twelve people came to the first meeting and five came to the second, held three days later. Many invited Alma and Margaret to visit them with their friends to share the message. Alma made many calls and received many invitations organized by Margaret Sprague and Henrietta Mills.

Alma and Margaret visited Mrs Kaiser in Park Erie on the Canadian side. She wrote, 'Mrs. Kaiser accepted the Message simply out of the strength of Margaret's earnestness without proofs.' Alma and Margaret arranged meetings at Mrs Kaiser's home for people who had never heard of the Bahá'í Faith, and meetings for believers and familiar seekers were held at the Mills's home.[24] Pauline and Joseph gave a public talk during their visit.[25]

Far away in 'Akká, the Master was spiritually united with this small group of Bahá'ís. In September they received the translation of His confirmation:

> O ye spiritual assembly!
>
> As ye were gathered together in the meeting of hospitality with the utmost longing for the knowledge of God, that meeting was mentioned in the divine Kingdom and you became favored with special bounty. Such gatherings are very praiseworthy and acceptable, for all beget joy and fragrance, the hearts become illumined and the despondent souls become heavenly.
>
> Likewise, though I was remote in so far as the body is concerned, I was near to the friends in heart and spirit and close to the believers in that assembly.
>
> I entreat God that your assembly wax greater day by day and the meeting of the love of God become adorned with celestial attributes, so that the confirmations of the Kingdom of God descend continually.[26]

At this time, the term 'assembly' meant a 'group of Bahá'ís' and not yet an elected body.

The efforts Alma and Margaret made to share the message were physically and mentally exhausting. Their work for the Cause attracted Bahá'ís in other centres. Mary Agnew from Chicago praised their efforts and activities. Alma wrote home in August 1906:

> Mrs. Sprague is doing a most wonderful work here and needed help in every direction, she has been elected as superintendent of the Army and Navy NCJN to visit the sick, prisons and soon this gives us a chance to bring the truth to many and a very broad field to work in. There is no return for this work . . . Mrs. S. is still wearing the blue dress I made her and has no other, I have almost finished a blue cotton dress for her, and she is very glad to get something else to wear.[27]

Margaret became the Second Vice President at the International Progressive Thought League of Buffalo.[28] There were so many confirmations. Pauline wrote to Alma:

> Has Mama told you of her dream wherein you chose to make your bed a small room, and not here, the same night I dreamt that you received a Tablet from the Master, wherein He told you to work where you are, you would be greatly tested and that was a sign of God's favour. Don't you think that was strange, possibly that same night Mrs. Mills opened her home for your need and keep right on in the work that has opened up so wonderfully for you . . . how I would love to be at work with you, I have what you once wished for, children and a home, you have what I have always hoped for. So, it goes, now I pray most earnestly that you may reach many, many souls and that I may reach a few.[29]

Confusion arose due to different understandings of the Bahá'í teachings. In particular, the topic of reincarnation was not clearly understood and this became a sensitive issue.[30] Alma started considering other fields of service.

Mason Remey referred Alma to Ralph Osborne in Syracuse. He was a believer from Brooklyn who had served in 1900 on the 'Board of Counsel' of the Bahá'ís of New York City.[31] Since then, he had moved to upstate New York, where he lived with his parents and worked with his uncle. Mason and Ralph had been discussing the prospects of teaching in Syracuse, but no progress had been made.[32] Remey saw Ralph as 'a very staunch believer, and one who was anxious to serve the Cause', but he felt that the worldly influences that surrounded him held him back from teaching.[33]

Ralph invited Alma to help him in Syracuse.[34] Surely Remey had shared with him news of Alma's courageous efforts. Ralph wrote to Alma regarding teaching opportunities that he knew that 'we would have to get some woman to tell us how' and now he had 'gone and done it we will both see what you say'.[35] Perhaps he felt that Alma would have more social freedom than he did for such activities. His family members were all strong Catholics and he described himself as 'socially not very well acquainted'. Although he knew many people, he had not been able to 'mix in' and could not host any talks or lectures.[36]

Alma accepted his kind invitation, and he quickly organized a place for her to stay.[37] On 13 October 1906, she moved into the room he had arranged for her with friends of his acquaintances at 1005 Grape St.[38] The stress of these days was too much, though, for Margaret. That day a newspaper article reported that Margaret had been hospitalized for insanity.[39]

Ralph wrote Mason regarding the rental of a parlour where talks could be given, and Mason gladly offered 'to arrange with him for the deferral of this expense if it should be necessary to incur it'.[40] Mason wrote that he had 'several plans in preparation . . . but as yet these matters are not settled'.[41] Things in Syracuse did not materialize and by the beginning of November Alma had returned to her family in Washington.

Back in Washington, she was given a newly translated Tablet to the Buffalo community. It contained guidance from

'Abdu'l-Bahá that would bring light and unity back to Buffalo:

> O ye friends!
> Thank God that the Light of Truth shone in that city, the bounty of guidance was granted, the fire of the love of God was ignited and the veil of superstition was burned away.
> Some souls have arisen who have unsealed their eyes, unstopped their ears, witnessed the great signs and heard the eternal melody of the Supreme Concourse. Each of them became a faithful tree in the orchard of the love of God and a shining luminous star in the horizon of the knowledge of God. This is from the eternal bounty and the everlasting gift.
> I entreat and supplicate in the Threshold of the Almighty and ask for your confirmation and assistance, that you may be born wholly out of the physical world into the Realm Divine, to seek after the eternal life and wish for the everlasting gift, so that you may shine down upon ages and cycles like unto the morning star![42]

This encouraging Tablet was also sent to Henrietta Mills, who responded on 6 November:

> Alma dearest sister in the heavenly kingdom. The tears fall as I read the blessed Tablet you have forwarded to us – and while I do thank God that the Light of Truth shines in this beloved city and the bounty of guidance [has] been granted unto the believers and feel more than ever my own unworthiness and weakness and utter helplessness and nothingness and yet when the gracious lord says that He will supplicate for us in the Threshold of the Almighty and ask for <u>confirmations</u> and <u>assistance</u> that we may be born into the realm divine, I feel that I must put away my doubts and fears and strive with gladness to do His Will.[43]

The following day, Henrietta wrote about the condition of the Bahá'í community in Buffalo:

Dear Alma, I became lost in the contemplation of that wonderful Tablet and could write no more last night. We have had no letters from you dear Alma . . . how precious they are, I do not like to have you write much on account of your eyes. I told someone over the phone that I thought you had gone home . . . Your letter confirmed my thoughts and I hope you will be able to rest much . . . I am sure Margaret would enjoy a letter from you, will ask the Dr first if we may take her a letter – Our Friday meetings are not attended. I think I must go and see the people . . . It seems so very little I do and yet when I am writing to tell of what has been done in Buffalo, I feel the glory of confirmation . . .[44]

On 9 December 1906, Amalie Knobloch received a Tablet from 'Abdu'l-Bahá in which He asked her to convey 'greetings and praise' on His behalf to her daughter Alma, and assuring Amalie that Alma would become 'wholly illuminated and spiritual'. He told Amalie to pray for Alma's progress in the Kingdom of God.[45]

Another Tablet arrived on 12 December 1906, to Alma:

O thou kind maid-servant of God!

Truly, I say, thou art worthy of the service in the Kingdom and art meriting to be a maid-servant in the threshold of the love of the realm of Might. Rest thou assured upon the bounty and favors of the Lord of Hosts, who will undoubtedly confirm thee.

Restrict all thy time to the spreading of the fragrances of God and be thou engaged in the guidance of souls. I associate with thee in spirit at all times and am thy friend and helper.

Ere long thou shalt behold that innumerable centers are going to be organised in America for the purpose of the promotion of the Cause of God and hearing the speeches of the maid-servants of the Merciful and the believers of God. Consider thou the days of Christ, how they were a very few, yet in a short space of time they caused a clamor and acclamation throughout all regions.

Convey my greetings to Mrs. [Williamson] and say: 'These seeds which are scattered here and there are spreading strong roots in the bosom of the earth and these will develop and grow until many harvests are gathered. Rest thou assured.'

O thou maid-servant of God! Show the utmost affection and love towards Mrs. [Sprague] . . .

O thou maid-servant of God! Strive thou in Buffalo so that perfect and lasting spiritual assemblies may be established and the souls be trained and progress spiritually

Convey my respectful greetings to Mr. and Mrs. [Mills] and say: 'A most great gift is prepared and made ready for you in the universe of the Kingdom and the invisible realm. Display an endeavor and show ye an effort, so that ye may attain to It and become eternal and everlasting.'

O thou maid-servant of God! Praise be to God that thou hast become famous throughout the regions as a Bahai. This favor is worthy of the utmost thanks and praise.

O thou maid-servant of God! Whenever thou art intending to deliver a speech, turn thy face toward the Kingdom of Abha and, with a heart detached, begin to talk. The breaths of the Holy Spirit will assist thee.

. . . Exercise the utmost kindness to [Fanny Knobloch] and say: 'Whatsoever is thy desire is found in the Cause of Baha'o'llah. If thou art asking for confirmation and assistance, be thou faithful, firm and steadfast.'[46]

In addition, 'Abdu'l-Bahá sent a Tablet to Henrietta Mills in which He emphasizes the importance of her relationship with Alma:

> . . . Know thou the value of Miss [Alma Knobloch]. Truly I say, she was an angel of heaven and a light beaming and sparkling. Endear thy beloved daughter [Margaret Sprague]. Entreat God that she and [Alma Knobloch] may

become two shining lamps in the assemblage of the world and the cause of the grandeur and promotion of the divine teachings.

. . . I prayed in behalf of all the family, that they may be confirmed with the most great guidance and sacrifice their abilities, talents and possessions in the Path of God.⁴⁷

Ahmad Sohrab wrote to Alma on 24 February 1907:

> My beloved sister in the cause! The Master loves you. He showers his mercy upon you. He encircles you with the Light of His Bounty. He protects you from all outside influences. He empowers you with the confirmation of the Holy Spirit. And now he has revealed for you the enclosed beautiful tablet, commanding you to arise in his service, to spread the teachings; to promote his cause; to awaken those souls who are asleep and to make mindful those who are heedless. This is indeed a crown of glory and majesty of Heaven . . .⁴⁸

The Tablet enclosed instructed Alma to give various messages to the friends and contacts in Buffalo. This inspired many believers in Buffalo, who wondered how 'Abdu'l-Bahá knew all of their names and their spiritual conditions! 'Abdu'l-Bahá encouraged Alma with loving words, telling her that she was confirmed in service to the Kingdom and had been the cause of guidance for souls; she should thank God day and night for the help and assistance she was receiving. 'Abdu'l-Bahá continued with a personal message to each of the 22 new believers and seekers in Buffalo, and then again addressed Alma, telling her to return to Buffalo again to teach and assuring her that the breath of the Holy Spirit would 'descend and impart eternal life'. She should live and act in accordance with the teachings – if the American Bahá'ís, He said, would conduct themselves according to His advice, the region would become the 'Paradise of Abhá' in a short time.⁴⁹

In obedience to the Master, Alma returned to Buffalo.⁵⁰ Leone St. Clair Barnitz, a close friend and believer from

Washington, stayed with Amalie so that Alma could go. 'Abdu'l-Bahá mentioned Alma again in a long letter to Ahmad Sohrab, translated on 6 March 1907, asking him to tell her that she should 'unquestionably' deliver 'wonderful' public talks, and reiterating that He Himself would be her helper.[51]

Once again Alma lived with Henrietta Mills in Buffalo. Henrietta wrote to Ahmad Sohrab, 'We are most happy that our dear Alma has returned to us and will work again in our beloved city. She has seen our dear daughter Margaret Sprague who is recovering as best as it is possible.'[52] Alma happily served the community in Buffalo, visiting friends, giving talks, arranging meetings and visiting Margaret and reading Tablets to her.[53]

In the early Spring of 1907, Alma had a strong spiritual experience, as she recalled in her notes:

> One evening when retiring, had a most marvelous experience. A powerful outpouring of the spirit permeating the entire body and heard a voice speaking and realized that it was not that of Abdulbaha [sic]. [I] remembered hearing that it was to come through Ahmad and that blessings and assistance were assured.[54]

Change was in the air. Shortly afterwards, an important letter from Fanny arrived.

8

DR EDWIN FISHER

To understand Fanny's letter to Alma, one must become acquainted with another early Bahá'í: Dr Edwin Fisher. The next two chapters will follow his life up to the historic moment when he crosses paths with Alma for the first time.

Alma was not the first Bahá'í to travel and teach in Germany, although she is often regarded as the founder or builder of the German Bahá'í community. In 1905, through Ahmad Sohrab, the decision was made to send Edwin Fisher from New York City to settle in Germany to begin teaching the Bahá'í Faith in that country. Fisher arrived in Stuttgart at the end of April 1905.[1] He spent two years teaching the Bahá'í Faith in Germany, by himself, except for a brief visit from Carl Scheffler from Chicago after his pilgrimage in the Spring of 1907.

Edwin Fisher was born on 10 June 1861 in Ludwigsburg, Germany, just north of Stuttgart. The famous Templer movement had begun at the Ludwigsburg Salon of 1854. It is not clear if Fisher or his family had contact with the Templers directly, but he surely knew about them.

In 1877, Fisher's family emigrated to the United States, settling in Trenton, New Jersey. Trenton was a manufacturing centre with a large iron industry and production industries including pottery, clothing, cigars and rubber.[2] Fisher found work as a dental assistant supporting Dr Kniffin in his work. Life working for Dr Kniffin was tough. He was involved in many local scandals and known as a parsimonious employer who treated his employees and his wife miserably.[3] For the first six months of work, Fisher did not get paid. He was employed by Dr Kniffin on three occasions; the last time during his studies at dental school,⁴ an experience that left him with strong negative memories.

Dentistry was a new and emerging medical field. The world's first Dental College had opened in Bainbridge, Ohio in 1821. In 1884, Fisher set up his private dental practice in Trenton.⁵ He also served on the faculty of the Pennsylvania College of Dental Surgery, where he had studied dentistry,⁶ and was highly respected as one of Trenton's leading dentists.

On 11 August 1887, Fisher married Josephine Dickinson (1866–c.1946) in Ewing Mance, Mercer, New Jersey.⁷ She was the only child of Lambert Cadwalader and Elmira Dickinson, a prominent Trenton family. The Cadwalader park in Trenton was named in honour of the family.

The Fishers lived a lavish lifestyle. They sailed on the North German Lloyd Steamer *Aller* to Bremen, Germany on 7 July 1888, where Dr Fisher established an operating clinic on painless dental procedures used for teeth separation as practised in the United States. He introduced a new filling technique involving the combined methods of German and American practices to place gold fillings into cavities. He also visited various dental colleagues in Germany, Switzerland, Italy, and France.⁸ The Fishers' travels were of great interest to the Trenton local newspapers. 'Sea Jewel' medicine was recommended by Dr Fisher in a newspaper advertisement, because it had cured his wife of seasickness.⁹

After returning to the United States, Fisher's following years were filled with dentistry conventions in Niagara, New York, Asbury Park, New Jersey, and vacation trips to Cape May, New Jersey, Virginia and other resorts. The Trenton newspaper reported, 'Dr. Fisher is the proud owner of a black Kentucky thoroughbred horse and rides well. His skills are praised in the newspaper in an attempt to encourage others to get involved in horseback exercise.'¹⁰ In 1893, Fisher travelled to Cuba and Mexico.¹¹ These trips were probably related to Josephine's father, Lambert Cadwalader-Dickinson, who was a cigar manufacturer.

Edwin and Josephine Fisher had two children: Olga Wilhelmina born on 17 May 1889,¹² and Edwin, born on 1

October 1892. Unfortunately, little Edwin died after 12 days.[13]

Things had been going well for those living in Trenton at this time, and by 1890 it was a large city with a population over 57,000.[14] But tough times began rather abruptly when the iron and pottery industries were exposed to European competition through the Cleveland Tariff of 1893.[15] To make matters worse, the most serious economic depression in United States history (to that point in time) began.[16] Trenton suffered greatly. Economic contraction and financial difficulties persisted throughout the next decade.

This must have had a negative effect on Fisher and his dental practice. Dentistry was a luxury for those who could afford it. Fisher's world deteriorated quickly after 1892. While working out in the gymnasium at the Y.M.C.A., his gold watch and chain were stolen,[17] reflecting the economic hardships endured in Trenton. By 1895 Fisher and his family were living with his wife's parents.[18] Things reached an all-time low. On 30 June of that year, the *Trenton Evening Times* headlined: 'The Well-Known Young Dentist Suddenly Bereft of His Reason while Seeking Health'. The article reads as follows:

> Dr. Edwin K. Fisher, dentist, of 216 East State Street, was removed yesterday to the State Hospital, near this city, having suddenly become bereft of his reason. He is 32 years old and son-in-law of L. Cad. Dickinson, cigar manufacturer. He was born in Germany, has been in this country about seventeen years and is highly respected both socially and professionally.
>
> Dr. Fisher has been very successful, and his present affliction doubtlessly was brought about by too close application to his practice ... During the last few months, upon the advice of his physician, a noted Philadelphia specialist, he has endeavoured to regain his strength by carefully following a prescribed treatment, but without perceptible improvement in his condition.
>
> A fortnight ago Dr. Fisher went to Milford to remain during the summer at a water cure establishment to which

he was recommended. At the time of his departure, he showed no indication of mental aberration, but shortly after being received at the sanatorium began to act queerly. Last Tuesday night he suddenly became violent and leaped through a high window to a shed below and received several painful wounds. Shortly afterward he was placed in charge of special attendants and his relatives in this city were notified of his condition. As indications of insanity have never before been manifested by him, his physician believes that his malady is only temporary, and that he will soon recover.[19]

Dentists were confronted with many working hazards in the early days of dentistry. Mercury was often mixed in tooth fillings, and in the 1820s the proportion of mercury used in dental fillings was increased to improve binding at room temperature. Nitrous oxide and cocaine were used by dentists for their anaesthetic properties, where cocaine was especially preferred, but it was difficult to dose and caused addiction for many dentists and doctors as well as patients. Novocaine, a non-addictive substitute for cocaine, was discovered and became available sometime after 1905. Still, some dentists continued to work with cocaine.

After treatment, Fisher returned to his family in Trenton where he sought spiritual relief from his troubles as a devout member of the Christian Scientist Church. His faith was tested in late 1896, when his seven-year-old daughter Wilhelmina came down with typhoid. It is not known whether he sought medical care for her condition, as Christian Scientists were not fond of medicine and used only prayer for healing. On 1 January 1897,[20] the Fishers were devastated when their daughter passed away. Her funeral was held at Fisher's practice.[21]

Overcome with despair, in March of 1897 Fisher retreated to the mountains of North Carolina to regain his health.[22] By the end of 1897 he had opened a new dental office in Asheville, North Carolina. The local newspaper announced the opening, stating that Fisher had studied dentistry in Switzerland and Germany where he had worked in the laboratory of Dr Klein, the royal court dentist of the King of Württemberg. The article explains that he 'had a fine office in Trenton, New Jersey which he was obliged to give up on account of nervous prostration, from which he had now recovered'.[23]

In 1900, the Federal census lists as 'single' Josephine Dickinson living alone with her parents, not 'divorced' or 'married'. She lived in New Jersey until she passed away in 1946. Interestingly, the last mention of Dr Fisher in the Trenton newspapers was on 26 August 1903 when he came to Trenton from New York to visit his mother Mrs F. Fisher on South Clinton Street.[24]

Things in North Carolina also came to an end, and in 1902 Dr Fisher moved to New York City, where he learned about the Baháʼí Faith. He formally accepted the Faith in 1903, when he sent his first letter to ʻAbduʼl-Bahá and received his first Tablet in return.[25]

It is not clear who taught the Baháʼí Faith to Edwin Fisher. During his early days in New York City, he had contact with various early believers including Louise Gibbons, a Baháʼí in New York and a former Christian Scientist 'who claimed to receive Tablets from ʻAbduʼl-Bahá through "spiritual telepathy"'. The authenticity of her 'telepathic Tablets' was a source of disunity until 1912, 'when ʻAbduʼl-Bahá, while in New York, apparently told her to stop showing the "Tablets" to people'.[26] The issue of individual spiritual power was one that fascinated many early Western believers. Gibbons and Fisher mutually influenced each other during these years, and in 1910 a similar situation was to arise in his community in Germany.

Like the Knoblochs, Fisher communicated closely with Ahmad Sohrab. Sohrab, formerly a clerk for Ahmad Yazdí in Port Said, had been brought to the United States to cook and care for Mírzá Abuʼl-Faḍl at the request of Alí-Kuli Khan in 1901.[27] He quickly learned English and helped with the translating work. He was acquainted with most of the early Baháʼís in the United States and on his return to the Holy Land served for many years as translator of correspondence between the Master and the Western Baháʼís.

Fisher probably met Ali-Kuli Khan and Mírzá Abuʼl-Faḍl in

June 1902, while they were in New York preparing for the publication of Mírzá Abu'l-Faḍl's book, *The Baháʼí Proofs*, which was translated by Ali-Kuli Khan and published in New York on 14 September 1902.[28]

Howard MacNutt, who became a Disciple of ʻAbdu'l-Bahá, lived in New York City and knew about the large personal donations made by some early Baháʼís to sponsor Baháʼí teachers in America. Fisher was struggling financially and longed for a life free of the toil of everyday work. He wished to become one of these teachers and dedicate his life to teaching the Faith. He was considering setting up an independent practice in New York but was hoping, rather, to become a travel teacher with financial support from the Baháʼís. On 19 September 1903, Fisher wrote to Ahmad Sohrab a somewhat disjointed and confusing letter:

> I wish to tell you that my visit to Mr. MacNutt came to naught. After going to his house twice and once to his business and not being able to meet him, I finally received word to meet him at his house any evening I choose. I then met Mr. MacNutt alone in the parlour, but he astonished me with his rather brusque advice, which was this: 'Go and take the bit between the teeth and go to work for any dentist' . . . I was astonished, disappointed and am thoroughly convinced that he is in no way the man for this. ... I am glad I tested him.
>
> I wish you would communicate to the Master what is written on this sheet and the next one, namely by that I would like to be situated so that I could prepare thoroughly and unassailably to go traveling to spread the message especially in this country and finally in other English-speaking countries, eventually perhaps also in German speaking countries . . . I know I will leap for joy when I shall be so situated that I can give my whole energy and time for the preparation of this alone without spending any more energy in the temporal pursuit . . . I prefer to make my own living during this preparation to be independent . . . Therefore, I

want to be situated in my own practice in dentistry to have this opportunity for preparation, as I could not prepare to amount to anything, working all day for some other dentists . . .

Would it not be best for me to get the Master's sanction for this and perhaps one of His prayers to bring this matter to a focus guidance perhaps then it might otherwise come to pass?

. . . it has been mentioned to me also by Mrs. Gibbons and one other, to ask you for the address of Mrs. Hearst [Phoebe Hearst, a wealthy American believer], that I may put my case before her personally by writing to her, as well as to ask you to put this proposition before the Master to see whether he will think it advisable to write to Mrs. Hearst concerning me. I have been told that Mrs. Hearst not only wishes to do a great deal but is also able to do and preliminary preparation of the right person and doubtless would only be too glad to find the right people. I wish to spend my whole life traveling for the spreading of the message and other things pertaining thereto and to spend all of my energy for that cause alone; but to be independent in the preparation, I would prefer to be able to step up in the practice of dentistry until the time comes to go traveling rather than to be exposed to the misdirection of such a person and winding up stranded somewhere and then being forced to build up a new practice somewhere years after having gotten my hand out of practice for a long time and missed many new inventions in dental practice . . .

Do you care to write to Mrs. Hearst concerning me? I am occupied day and night with the thought of the message and am really very often unfit to occupy myself with anything else in spite of my material necessities.

After reading this letter at least twice and understanding it thoroughly, please interpret it to his honor Mr. Mirza Abul Fazl and tell him that some day when I am able and do not need the money, I would like to print all his truth in the finest possible shape for cost . . .[29]

Fisher wrote to Ahmad Sohrab again a few days later explaining how he would prefer to give up dentistry completely. In another long letter, he continuously expresses his confusion about his future, himself and various personal issues as follows:

> If you have not yet written to the Master concerning me, I wish you would add this: That I should like to put my complete (full) deliverance into His hands, if He does not mind, and if it pleases God . . . I think it would be well since the realization came to me through the writings of His Father as well as His own writings, also through my knowledge of 'Christian Science'. My desire is to be concerned about the message only . . . this is by far the foremost in my mind, so foremost that it weakens concentration in dentistry, and the realization of spreading the message and doing philanthropy largely on a large scale, because the Father does not do these things on a small scale, therefore the small retail like profession of dentistry begins to look so increasingly smaller in comparison with the other necessary work that I can no more hold myself down to it and yet there is no evidence of the absolute material necessities . . . still this battle returns occasionally that I have to do dentistry for my necessity and I have seen clearly and repeatedly now . . . that I do not have to do dentistry any longer for my support and that God is abundantly able to give me all I need for carrying on this much greater work and I suppose the Master through His prayer for me has helped me to realize it. But from some unknown quarters comes back the thought that I have to do more dentistry. I say, I know this to be false and though I do not believe that this can return many times, I would like the Master to deliver me permanently from this . . . Also, the lie of poverty is making its last desperate kicks and I have spiritually put the sword into the heart of that lie also . . . I wish the Master to deliver me completely . . . for I cannot tell how much harder and longer I alone might have had to work . . . What paralyzes activity is my being split up between the things for the message alone and

the dentistry and 'Christian Science'. When I can come out into the things of the message alone, for that deepest, greatest Cause, my activity would be much greater . . . I feel like letting the Master know to make sure of complete deliverance . . . I do not insist in the least that He should be my complete deliverer, but I would prefer Him to be. Any one whom God choses, suits me . . .
    Yours in Truth,
    Edwin Fisher[30]

Wealthy Western Bahá'ís, including Laura Clifford Barney, Helen Goodall and Phoebe Apperson Hearst, financially supported Persian teachers who came to America at the bidding of 'Abdu'l-Bahá between 1899 and 1905. Some Western Bahá'ís, including Edward and Lua Getsinger, also received financial support at times to allow them to concentrate on teaching activities. From the above letters, it is clear that Fisher was hoping for financial support.

In the Bahá'í religion, work is elevated to the level of worship. Bahá'u'lláh writes, 'It is enjoined upon every one of you to engage in some form of occupation, such as crafts, trades and the like. We have graciously exalted your engagement in such work to the rank of worship unto God, the True One.'[31] Thus, teaching and earning one's living are inseparable parts of a coherent Bahá'í life.

In 1903, only a few Bahá'í writings were translated into English. We do not have 'Abdu'l-Bahá's response to Fisher's letters, but most likely it was similar to the advice He gave to others who were asking for the same thing at that time. In the papers of Thornton Chase we find that on 3 October 1905 a Bahá'í on the West Coast was asking other Bahá'ís for money so that he could serve the Faith full time. Chase replied, 'AB ['Abdu'l-Bahá] discourages this and forbids asking for funds. The House of Spirituality has consulted on the matter.' When Mason Remey asked 'Abdu'l-Bahá whether he could give up his profession to serve the Faith full time, 'Abdu'l-Bahá responded that he should not.[32] Some Bahá'ís who longed for a life of teaching found other ways to provide for themselves. Chase noted, 'Mac Nutt has sold his business and will devote all of his time to the Faith.'[33] Since Dr Fisher was a trained professional, it is likely that 'Abdu'l-Bahá would have encouraged him to continue in dentistry.

Fisher understood this, and on 5 June 1904 he wrote to Ahmad Sohrab that he was working and still broke.[34]

9
EDWIN FISHER RAISES THE CALL IN GERMANY

In 1871, the concept of individual basic religious freedom was incorporated into the Constitution of the German Empire. From that point onwards, new forms of Christian belief entered Germany from America, such as Christian Science in 1894 and Mormonism in 1900.[1] The concept of individual investigation of truth and the responsibility to actively choose religious identity was just emerging.

As we have seen, Dr Edwin Fisher was the first Bahá'í teacher to move to Germany. He arrived in Stuttgart at the end of April 1905[2] and rented an apartment from Julius Grünzweig,[3] who probably then became the first Bahá'í in Germany. Later, the ground floor became Fisher's dental practice.

An American Bahá'í of German background, Carl Scheffler, visited Fisher in mid-1907 on his return from his pilgrimage to 'Akká,[4] and taught several people the Bahá'í Faith.[5] Fisher had shared the Bahá'í teachings with various members of the Christian Science Church in Stuttgart, whose services he attended.[6]

Alma recalls in her memoirs how Dr Fisher had been fervent in spreading the Faith even when he was ill in New York, where the Bahá'ís

> thought he would be better in his parents' country and give the message to his people. They were from Lutwigburg [Ludwigsburg]; his father was a doctor. He was very earnest in spreading the cause, and had a number of people

interested, and several believers when I arrived. Several of these were high standing, among these were Frau Med – Rat – von Burckhardt, several countesses and some men of influence and high standing. Not being well, he had a hard time, some of his patients asked me, please to tell the dear Doctor not to talk religion to them while in the dental chair, it was too nerve straining, but he would always say, I must give them the message right away, or they may not come again and I would have lost the opportunity. So much of his efforts were lost, but he did give forth the message at all occasion [sic], convenient or not convenient, loose [sic] his patients or not, he never missed the chance. He had made many friends for the Cause. The believers were very kind to him in every way, unfortunately he was always hard up and in need of financial assistance all the time.[7]

Another young person who learned about the faith from Fisher was Margarethe Döring, a young, tall, attractive blonde woman who worked in the fashion industry as a seamstress. She was the first woman to accept the Bahá'í message in Germany.

Teaching the Faith in Stuttgart was hard work and the progress was very slow. In the Spring of 1907, Fisher asked for assistance in the teaching work, and also for permission to visit 'Abdu'l-Bahá. 'Abdu'l-Bahá replied that he could come the following year, and that with regard to his request for help in Stuttgart, He would think about it 'and command it'.[8] On 8 July 1907 Fisher thanked Ahmad Sohrab for his translation of the Tablet from the Master:

Most beloved brother,
    . . . Appreciate your being in Washington in a Bahai Center for the U.S. by far the freest country; I feel these things are very lonely at times and hoping to live in that country again when my work is done here. Am looking forward with great joy to my visit at that White Spot and Holy Land in 1908. I do hope it will be next Jan. Feb. etc. because winters are very hard on me nowadays. I wish I

could stay as long as Mrs. Getsinger to become a considerable star of a teacher.

One thing I would like to impress on you and the rest of the believers is this: do remember that I am far away from a Bahai Center and would like to know more of what is going on in America, therefore, so send me plenty of literature in the future to give to the interested ones, without expecting me to acknowledge receipt each time or often, for my correspondence in the Cause is now extending over four continents and I have to cut out all correspondence that is not necessary.

I feel greatly honoured when I think it over that the Master would be so kind as to send someone to me to help me in answer to my wish and need. Of course, there would be work for a hundred Baha'is in Germany.[9]

Edwin Fisher brought the Bahá'í Faith to Germany. He was the first to break the ground there, he suffered loneliness and isolation, as the Germans were devoted to their churches which provided most people with their primary social network. Fisher needed support and encouragement, someone who could explain the Bahá'í teachings from a Biblical scriptural perspective to the church-going German people.

10

ALMA'S CALL TO GERMANY

Amalie Knobloch loved the Faith with all her heart. Her deepest wish was that the message would reach Germany. Alma recalled:

> There are some experiences in life that one never forgets. Running upstairs one day to speak to our saintly Mother, I stopped at the threshold of her door with awe – Mother was praying [for Germany]. This heavenly sight was indelibly impressed upon my heart, and there was no need for questioning. Quietly withdrawing, I, from that time on, never became deficient in the one great hope that Germany might become illumined with the Light of Truth, and be permitted to take her place in establishing it in the world.[1]

The memory of Amalie praying for the German people left a strong impression on her daughter Alma. Love for the Faith and love for the fatherland were to be joined and expressed in a unique act of service through the love of all of her daughters, and their sacrifice for and devotion to 'Abdu'l-Bahá.

As we have seen in the last chapter, Edwin Fisher had written to Ahmad Sohrab that he wished 'the Master would be so kind as to send someone to me to help me'. 'Abdu'l-Bahá had replied to Ahmad Sohrab, requesting him to find 'an attracted and severed soul' in America to go.[2]

Now, Fanny wrote to Alma in Buffalo:

Dear Alma, at the meeting last night, Ahmad called me aside, and in the most profound manner assured me, 'A glorious crown, a most brilliant crown, awaits someone, and it will be one of your sisters.' Oh, Alma how my heart leapt with joy, and instantly I replied: 'That must be my <u>sister</u>, yes it <u>must</u> be.' Then showing me the letter written by the hand of Our Lord Abdul Baha, Ahmad explained that the Master requested that someone able to teach, qualified to do so, known to Ahmad, shall assist Mr. Fisher in proclaiming the glad tidings in – Germany – . . . [Alma, I] will eagerly await your reply. Mama and I are both happy – Lovingly your affectionate sister Fanny

[at the bottom of the letter] This trip to Germany is to be made late in the summer or Fall – so you will have time for all things.[3]

Fanny sent Alma a copy of the Tablet, emphasizing that if Alma was willing, Fanny would pay for her trip! Alma wrote in her memoirs that she felt as though she already knew about it and wrote to say she would go, overlooking the tremendous sacrifice Fanny would be making on her behalf.

Fanny's spontaneous and selfless reaction is a tremendous sign of both her love for 'Abdu'l-Bahá and her dedication to the Faith of Bahá'u'lláh. Bahá'u'lláh teaches, 'Be ye as the fingers of one hand, the members of one body. Thus counselleth you the Pen of Revelation, if ye be of them that believe.'[4]

Alma was not surprised by this turn of events or Fanny's offer. She could feel their destiny unrolling before them and reacted with no surprise. Not knowing about Alma's spiritual experience (see Chapter 7 above), Fanny expected Alma to be surprised and thankful in response to her letter. Instead, Alma's cool reaction hurt Fanny, who felt that Alma had taken her offer for granted.[5] This misunderstanding was cleared up through the love of Pauline, who wrote to Alma:

> . . . new and wonderful work has been prepared by God for you and Fanny that is wide deep and grand as the ocean. In

a Tablet received recently, the Master speaks of the lack of time to answer the many letters sent. That He must take the time to answer the most important ones in the Face of this, it would seem to me that since the Beloved Abdul Baha saw fit to send a special Tablet written with His Own Blessed Hand, just on this one subject, that the only thing for you is to turn about face to go at once. If need be get things to wear on the other side and go as quickly as steamer and trains will take. Alma, my soul is crying out to you now! Go. Go. Go . . .

Please do write to Fanny <u>at once</u> without delay, for she was very, very disappointed at the matter-of-fact way in which you accepted her self-sacrificing offer to you. Dearest Alma, it is with an anxious but loving heart that I venture to tell you her feeling in order that without delay you may make it up to her in some way . . . You do appreciate most sincerely Fanny's great work in sending you, paying for your expenses, I mean this is as great and grand a work on her part, as you're [sic] going, both are links in the great chain of the Cause of God and cannot be separated.

Dearest Alma forgive me if I have spoken too plainly but can't do otherwise. I am so anxious that all the work done by you two wonderful sisters of mine be done in perfect love and harmony.

Now a little damper has fallen upon this grand work, and you alone can lift it. Tell Fanny how much you love her and how eager you are to do the Master's work at once, that you will leave the moment she says the word. You understand me dearest Alma, don't you? I am not dictating, but it is all meant as a suggestion. But hurry up and do something in the matter, if you have to borrow the money and come in person and surprise her into joy and happiness again.

Could you have seen her joy at the news, you could understand it better.[6]

Alma cleared up the misunderstanding with Fanny. But when Alma showed the Tablet to the friends in Buffalo, they said,

"'Abdu'l-Bahá has sent you to us!' They felt that this service was not for Alma and requested that someone else be found for the task. Ahmad Sohrab wrote about the sisters' offer to 'Abdu'l-Bahá, Who responded:

> Thou hast written about Dr. Fisher, that praise be to God, thou hast found a helper for him and ere long she will start for Germany. Truly I say, the beloved maid-servant of God, Miss Alma Knobloch, is very much acceptable for this service – thou hast done well to choose her. She is accepted by all means, but regarding her stay in Germany, she must stay as long as possible. Forward to this land a copy of every tablet translated into the German language. I hope that the endeavors and exertions of these two sisters, may display all-encircling effects.[7]

To Amalie, Fanny and Alma 'Abdu'l-Bahá wrote:

> He is God!
> O ye beloved maid-servants of God, the bounty of the True One hath elected you from among the maid-servants in order that ye may engage yourselves in the service of the kingdom, spread the Verses of the Lord of the Realm of Might, become the cause of guidance of the souls.
> Truly, I say, Miss Alma Knobloch will show forth and demonstrate on this trip that she is a beloved maid-servant in the Threshold of Oneness, is wise and intelligent and spiritual in the Kingdom of the True One.
> A great service is this, for it is conducive to the descent of the eternal outpouring and the cause of everlasting life. All the affairs of the world, though of the utmost importance, bring forth results and benefits for a few days, then later on they disappear and vanish entirely, except service in the Divine Kingdom, attraction to the fragrances of Holiness, quickening of the souls, vivification of the hearts, imparting joy to the spirit, adjusting characters and the edification of the people. I hope that ye may become assisted and confirmed to this.[8]

Alma's programme was quickly rearranged, keeping as many appointments as possible; cancelling those she could not reschedule. She returned to Washington to say goodbye to her mother and her sisters; she had only about one week to get ready before her departure for Germany![9]

Alma was heading back to far-off Germany with no plan for return. At the time, the family did not know how long she would be gone or what exactly 'Abdu'l-Bahá had meant when he wrote that she should stay 'as long as possible'. Alma left two months before Amalie's 70th birthday. The sacrifice for Amalie was great; she and Alma were extremely close. Neither knew that these would be Alma's last days in the physical presence of her saintly mother. 'Abdu'l-Bahá's confirmations were the steady focus: a new opportunity had opened for Alma leading her back to her roots, casting her name into the Tablets of the Divine Plan and thereby immortalizing her in the annals of Bahá'í history.

11

UNUSUAL CONFIRMATIONS

> Likewise, Miss Knobloch travelled alone to Germany. To what a great extent she became confirmed! Therefore, know ye of a certainty that whosoever arises in this day to diffuse the divine fragrances, the cohorts of the Kingdom of God shall confirm him, and the bestowals and the favors of the Blessed Perfection shall encircle him.
>
> 'Abdu'l-Bahá, *Tablets of the Divine Plan*[1]

Alma's time in Washington was short and intense. She had about one week to pack her things, organize her affairs, arrange her passage and bid farewell to those she loved. Great excitement filled the family during these days. Ahmad Sohrab came to visit the night before her departure. He was excited to see her actual ticket, which she had put in a special book for safe keeping. After they all marvelled at the ticket, the ticket was lost! Shortly before departure, luckily, they were able to get a reissue of the ticket. Years later, the ticket was found in a book at home, to everyone's great surprise.[2]

On 17 July 1907, Fanny, Amalie, Pauline and Joseph and their son Carl, Edward Struven and Ahmad Sohrab brought Alma to the port in Baltimore.[3] Fanny escorted her with various gifts including a chain to wear on board the Norddeutscher Lloyd steamer for Bremen. In her first letter home Alma remarked, 'God grant that the reunion may be brighter for the parting was painful.'[4]

Three of the pastors from Baltimore were also on board the ship. They were friends of Pastor Menzel from the Concordia Church and had been involved in her dismissal from the church. Alma's seat was on the upper deck, where she made new acquaintances. One of the women asked Alma about her mission to Germany. As she began to explain, one of the pastors pulled up his chair and started to refute all. Unfortunately for him, he 'tumbled all over himself' as Alma quietly maintained her calm composure. A gregarious lady stood by the pastor, and this was also no hurdle for Alma, who 'with great care won her friendship and invited her to visit her in Stuttgart'.[5]

The dining room on board was arranged with two special tables in the centre and all the others around them on the outside. One of the centre tables was headed by the Captain of the ship. Alma was uncomfortable upon entering the dining room the first night. She noticed that all the other passengers had red tickets with their seating on them. Hers was yellow and had no seating on it. Embarrassed, she thought it was because she was travelling without her original ticket and she wondered what to do. The pastors observed her as she entered to see where she would sit. To her great surprise, the ship personnel escorted her to her seat at the head of the long middle table next to the Captain's table! Her yellow ticket placed her at a distinguished table with 'selected passengers'. Having such a prominent seat made her the object of curiosity. Everyone was interested in who she was and why she was on board, enabling her to share the message and her mission with interested people right from the start.[6]

Word spread about Alma being on board to take the Bahá'í teachings to Germany and a growing number of people grew interested and wanted to hear about it. So she gave her first Bahá'í talk on board the ship in the Ladies Salon.

Some of the Concordia Church members were also on board, including Olga Krunke, an old friend from Alma's Bible study group at the church. She asked Alma about her work and Alma 'explained it for the benefit of all on upper deck, over two dozen passengers'. Miss Krunke, Olga's daughter, accepted the

Faith and asked Alma to mention her name to the Master. They accepted Alma's invitation and later were Alma's first guests to visit her in Stuttgart.[7] Mrs Krunke became a believer and sent a message to 'Abdu'l-Bahá declaring her faith.[8] After returning to Washington DC, the Krunke family joined the Bahá'í community there.

Alma was an extroverted happy person who made friends easily. She shared a stateroom with a Miss von Scheuerle who had relatives near Stuttgart. She accepted the Teachings while on board and invited Alma to visit her in Freudenstadt in the Black Forest. Together they spread the teachings in Pfadelbach near Stuttgart.

After having had such marvellous confirmations on the ship, Alma arrived in Bremen where she visited her old friend Hannah Bredemeier who had been 'so kind and cordial to me on my former visits to Germany'.[9] Hannah introduced Alma to her brother Herman. Alma shared the 'Glad Tidings' with them both and Hannah 'gratefully accepted' them and hoped that Alma would establish these teachings in Bremen. She told Alma that Bremen was ready for it, that the teachers of the schools in Bremen had 'succeeded in their requests not to be compelled to give religious instructions in school, as they no longer believed in the old explanations of the Bible, it being contrary to science, and had nothing to give in its place'. Although Alma promised to return to Bremen, if possible,[10] a return never happened. Years later in July 1922, after Alma had returned to the United States, she received a letter from Hannah's older brother George Bredemeier who had accepted the Faith and was immersing himself in German Bahá'í literature.[11]

After Bremen, Alma visited Uncle Wilhelm and Aunt Mina in Leipzig. She described her visit:

> My uncle listened to the explanations that I gave concerning the teachings of Baha o llah and Abdul Baha, and about the fulfillment of prophecy in the Latter Day. He was profoundly touched, and a few days later, made known his desire to serve the Cause. My heart leaped with

joy, although outwardly I remained calm. I knew that his mother had been a very saintly woman and also a Templar [sic]. This sect was founded on the Bible verse, Malachi 3:1, 'And the Lord whom ye shall seek shall suddenly come into His Temple.' This faith spread throughout Germany and the founders thereof settled in Haifa, at the foot of Mt. Carmel, expecting the Coming of the Lord, in 1863. Both my uncle and my aunt were most kind and helpful in introducing me to their circle of friends. These I found to be sincere and progressive in their attitude toward the Principles of Baha o llah and they all developed a greater consciousness of the Oneness of Mankind.[12]

Wilhelm Knobloch was a retired professor. His mother had told both him and Alma's father Karl to watch out for the return of Christ. Wilhelm found the Bahá'í teachings to be the fulfilment of that prophecy, especially the teachings about universal peace and universal language. He arranged for Alma to visit clubs and talk to other professors who were surprised to hear that a new religion from the East was teaching the equality of men and women! Mina arranged for Alma to share the message with her friends and various professors' wives.

On 9 August 1907, Alma arrived in Stuttgart.[13] She received a warm welcome at the Stuttgart train station from Dr Fisher, Margarethe Döring and Julius Grünzweig.[14] Prior to her arrival, Fisher had written to Ahmad Sohrab:

> Please go and give Miss Alma Knobloch my heartfelt thanks and greetings and best wishes to herself and family and that I will make it as pleasant for her as I can and avoid hardships. Stuttgart has a much better climate than Washington and beautiful surroundings.
>
> I have not had the time to do much translating on account of my profession. I hope the time is close at hand when I can give all of my energy and time to the Cause. I am praying for it now and will talk it over with the Master next winter, I hope. It would be very much easier to me to

spread the Cause in English than in German. I don't feel near as much at home in mediaeval German countries, also when one reads the revealed things in English, one is full of it and can talk it like a gusling [sic] fountain, but to talk it in German with criticising ears around you is not near as easy to me. However, I have it to do now until the work is done here. Miss Knobloch will be amazed what barriers we will meet with, at first it will look easy and it will be easier if Miss Knobloch has no business to attend to.

Please tell Miss Knobloch to write to me and to let me know about when she expects to get here as I hope to take two- or three-weeks' vacation in August. If I know when she is coming, I will see to it that I am here when she gets here.[15]

At this point in time, the little Bahá'í community of Stuttgart was made up of five members: Edwin Fisher, Margarethe Döring, Miss Frey, Alma Knobloch and Julius Grünzweig, who was Fisher's landlord and the first Bahá'í in Germany. Miss Frey was the first believer to receive prayer beads, which Carl Scheffler had given her after his visit to Abdu'l-Bahá.[16] Margarethe was born in Dresden and grew up in Leipzig, Saxony, the part of Germany where Alma was born. She had met Fisher at the Christian Science Church in Stuttgart. Alma described her as 'very good and kind, something like Aunt Ella in Richmond, her way or no way . . . very quick and active, up to date and very dressy. If you could see her sitting next to me, smiling so sweetly, you would also think you had never met anyone quite so lovely . . .'[17]

Alma and Margarethe quickly became close friends, but Alma wanted to be sure that their friendship would be based on service. In September Alma wrote to Fanny that Margarethe 'is very fond of me of which I am glad, but I have given her full sway until now and have told her that the phase is over and now, I must have my way in the Cause and all personal affairs must end'.[18] This was Alma's way; her focus was always on teaching. She did not let personal issues or obligations dilute that. Alma saw herself as a Bahá'í teacher, fully aware that Fanny's sacrifice made her independent of others, so that the focus was on spreading the teachings and building up the Baháʼí community. Each believer was responsible to ʻAbduʼl-Bahá, He was the centre that drew them together and united them. Although this may have been strange or awkward in the beginning, it proved wise and effective.

Alma stayed with Margarethe Döring in her room. Fisher had offered Alma a room in his place because he had a large apartment with many rooms, but Alma did not accept his offer because she wanted to have a place where she could receive ladies to teach.[19] She arranged to look for a place with Fisher, but when she awoke the next morning, she heard a distinct voice, which she believed to be ʻAbduʼl-Bahá, telling her to 'stay where she was'. As Fisher waited for Alma, Alma talked with Margarethe's landlady, Mrs Anna Palm, who continuously replied, 'I only wish I had a room for you so you can stay here' and then, to Alma's surprise, mentioned that she had a room used for storage. Alma asked to see it and was happy to take the room. Alma wrote to Fanny, 'I was told to stay and stay I did. Mrs. Palm bought a new iron bed and fixed up the room. In a few weeks, I found out why I had been asked to stay and now we are beautifully fixed, everything is fine style, and we are very happy.'[20] So Alma rented the small attic room on the fifth floor and lived with Margarethe in Mrs Palm's house. The room was only large enough to sleep in, so Alma spent the days with Margarethe.

Alma had a lovely spirit, but she was not a physical beauty, and she knew this. After meeting Alma, Fisher encouraged her to pay a little more attention to her appearance. Fisher was conscious about outward appearances. He lived in a large apartment and was concerned with how he dressed. Upon first meeting Alma, he encouraged her to visit the Air Bath (a spa) and Summer Health Gardens in Degerloch to 'get red cheeks so that she would look fine to meet his contacts' after the summer vacation.

Fisher spent his summer break in Bad Homburg v.d. Höhe, an expensive spa resort, where he shared the message with wealthy Germans. While he was gone, Alma went to the local Air Bath where she met many local working women with whom she shared the Faith. Soon this group grew quite large. They found a special place on the lawn of the Air Bath where they gathered to discuss the teachings.

Ten days after her arrival in Stuttgart, Alma held her first unity meeting on 19 August 1907. Mrs Palm kindly offered her sitting room to host the event. Alma invited some of the ladies she had met at the Air Bath. Miss Bowman, a French Bahá'í friend visiting from Chicago, came to visit Alma and they shared the teachings with Mrs Palm. It was a great conversation and Mrs Palm accepted the teachings. Two years later, in 1909, she became the first Bahá'í teacher in Tübingen.

Encouraged by Mrs Palm's response, Miss Bowman invited Alma and her contacts to visit her the following night, since Alma's room was too small. Unfortunately, only one of the ladies came. This turned out to be a blessing since they could focus on this woman and her questions. The friend was very excited to learn more about the Faith, and she invited Alma and Miss Bowman to her home the following week to share the message with a number of her friends.[21] So the teaching process had begun. The women Alma met at the Air Bath included Julia and Elise Stäbler, Rosa Schwarz and Mina Diegel, an art student from Lake Constance.[22] All these women became active Bahá'í teachers and rendered valuable services to the German Bahá'í community.

Alma spent all her energy teaching and was not interested in marriage or social distractions. She felt that Miss Bowman's visit was more social in nature and not supportive for community building or teaching activities. After some time, Miss Bowman decided to return to Paris. Upon her departure, she told Alma that Georgiana d'Astre was planning to visit her from Paris. Alma wrote to Georgiana declining her offer to visit, replying that she was 'in Stuttgart to work'![23]

Alma and Margarethe had rented rooms that had no kitchen access, as was common for many single women at that time. This inconvenience served as an important steppingstone in their community-building work. They ate in budget restaurants or at the Frauen Club, where Alma made many new friends. The Frauen Club was the only club that admitted women and provided food for unmarried working women at an affordable price. Marion Jack, inspired by Alma's success, used a similar approach at the Chaushev Coffee Shop in Bulgaria. She recalled, 'Our dear little Alma Knobloch used to haunt the restaurants of girls in her early days in Europe. God grant that there may be as much success in this corner of the world as she had in hers.'[24] Later 'Abdu'l-Bahá said that the Frauen Club would be blessed and remembered.

Outreach to Freudenstadt, Pfadelbach and Heilbronn

Alma wrote, 'To accept the message is not difficult but the hard times come in afterwards.'[25] Communities are built on authentic friendships. During the summer vacation in September 1907, Alma and Margarethe focused on friends outside Stuttgart. Alma and Margarethe celebrated Alma's birthday with Alma's roommate from the ship, Miss Scheuerle, in Freudenstadt, Black Forest.

The following week they shared the Bahá'í teachings with Margarethe's friends in Pfadelbach. A week later, on 23 September, Alma and Margarethe visited Miss Schaefer, an art student Alma had met through Mina Diegel at the Air Bath. Miss Schaefer invited Alma to share the teachings with her parents in Heilbronn; her father was very interested.[26] From Heilbronn, they travelled back to Pfadelbach to give the teachings to Miss Scheuerle's family. In Cannstatt, they shared the Bahá'í teachings with some friends of Dr Fisher and made new contacts.[27] They returned to Heilbronn and Pfadelbach on 2 October.

Alma was very busy. Miss Frey's family was interested,[28] Mrs Palm shared the teachings with her aunt, and invitations came from Basel and Munich.[29] Alma and Margarethe began looking for new accommodation with space to host Bahá'í gatherings.

Finally, in October, Fisher returned from Bad Homburg. Alma and Fisher were invited to the elaborate home of Mrs Med. Rat von Burckhardt to share the message with a few of her guests.

She was impressed with the explanations and invited Alma to give a talk about the Bahá'í teachings at the Frauen Club. On 27 October, Alma's talk entitled 'The Sun of Truth is the Word of God'[30] was the first public talk on the Bahá'í Faith in Germany and was announced in the newspapers.[31] Alma wrote home, 'The talk was a great success. We met opposition from one side and how beautiful to find the young students [Miss Schaefer and Mina Diegel] had taken an Oath to the Flag of Truth as they put it.'[32] Fisher was very happy and told Alma, 'The first cannonball has been fired and its explosion made a great commotion.' Alma continued in her letter, 'I received several invitations that evening by very highly cultured and refined people . . . I made my mark, and I am progressing and I'm working hard.'[33]

On 1 November Margarethe and Alma moved to Olgastrasse 102, where they shared a large, portioned room and a veranda.[34] The new landlady, Mrs Sassenburg, was kind and brought them coffee in the mornings. Alma was relieved after living for three months in a storage attic with just a bed! Like their former landlady Mrs Palm, Mrs Sassenburg was also attracted to the Bahá'í teachings.[35]

Alma and Margarethe met another art student, Miss Riehmann, from Lake Constance, Austria, at the Palace Park.[36] Afterwards they met up with Miss Schaefer, Miss von Struten, Ms Frey, and Dr Fisher. Miss Riehmann declared her belief in the Faith and decided to take the message home to her family in Austria at Christmas.[37] Alma wrote to Fanny, 'I teach every day and I have arranged to have Bahá'í gatherings every Thursday evening and have been holding meetings Sunday mornings. We are making headway you see. At the Frauen Club where I take dinner the ladies that have accepted the Message stay after their meal and we talk [and] have made friends with a number of ladies.'[38] In December Mrs Scheuerle, the mother of Alma's roommate from the ship, who lived in Pfadelbach, visited Alma in Stuttgart to hear more.[39] So the seeds were planted and nurtured, and the Faith began to grow.

While Alma and the German believers taught the message of unity, other forces were at work in Europe. On 31 August

1907, Britain and Russia signed an agreement in St Petersburg which led to the creation of the Triple Entente, consisting of Britain, France and Russia. The Triple Entente treaty provided mutual aid guarantees if any members were attacked by the Triple Alliance (Germany, Austria-Hungary and Italy). This was the final piece of the alliance system and a major contributing factor to the outbreak of the First World War.[40] Instead of bringing peace, these bilateral treaties encouraged heavy military investments.

12

RAPID EXPANSION IN STUTTGART

In 1894, Hans Eckert, a surveyor who had emigrated to America, returned to Stuttgart (Cannstadt) and was the first Christian Scientist in Germany.[1] Ten years later, he founded the Christian Science Society of Stuttgart which held regular Sunday services in English with German translation.[2] The Christian Science scriptural book *Science and Health* was not available in the German language until 1912,[3] therefore, most Christian Science believers were at least partially bilingual.[4]

Edwin Fisher, as a former member of the Christian Science Church, attended their Sunday meetings in Stuttgart, where he made acquaintances and dispersed pamphlets about the Bahá'í teachings. In the summer of 1907, while Fisher was recuperating in Bad Homburg, Margarethe Döring brought Alma to the Christian Science meetings and introduced her to some of the members.[5]

It was here that Alma met Adolf Eckstein, who was to become the spark of the Stuttgart Bahá'í community. The Eckstein family had a fine reputation and was well known. Eckstein was a well-read sincere seeker of truth with a very good knowledge of the Bible. He was retired from work, fluent in English, and actively involved with the Swedenborg Society and the Christian Science Church. He was intrigued by Alma's excellent understanding of the Bible and its relationship to the Bahá'í Faith. The people Eckstein brought to hear the new teachings, together with the women Alma had taught that summer, formed the core foundation of the Stuttgart Bahá'í community for the next decade. Their names will never be forgotten.

It started on 12 October 1907, when Alma and Fisher visited the beautiful Eckstein home. Alma recalled that Eckstein had invited a number of guests who were very refined and highly educated people of high standing and all were interested in the Bahá'í teachings. Teaching at the Ecksteins was easy since everyone understood English and Alma and Fisher provided them all with Bahá'í books.[6] Two of Eckstein's friends, Mr Rieger and Mrs Hauptman von Sonntag, quickly accepted the Bahá'í Faith and asked Alma if they could work on circulating the Bahá'í books. Mr Rieger was a Government Inspector of Buildings in Stuttgart[7] and the head of the United Swedenborg Organization, whose publication needs he had provided for years.[8]

Already on the following morning, regular Sunday morning Bahá'í meetings began at the Eckstein home. Eckstein invited many friends, and the meeting was a great success. Alma wrote to Fanny, 'Dr Fisher spoke very well, he is going to become a teacher something like Joseph [Hannen, her brother-in-law].'[9]

In December 1907, Sydney Sprague, an American Bahá'í, arrived in Stuttgart to help with the teaching work. Alma wrote:

> I arranged an evening at the Frauen Club for the friends and those interested to hear Mr. Sprague and become acquainted. I say, I arranged it, for I had to do it all alone, Margarethe not approving the English and the Dr not knowing what to expect and very busy. It proved very successful indeed, I had invited 30, of these a large number turned out. Mr. Sprague spoke plain and beautiful and Dr. F translated a greater part of it. Miss Julia Stäbler sang grand, she has a magnificent voice.[10]

The Frauen Club offered the Bahá'ís use of their rooms as needed, and many talks were given there. In late January 1908, Hippolyte Dreyfus, the first Bahá'í from France, joined their teaching efforts. Sprague, Dreyfus and Eckstein gave lectures and Fisher and Eckstein translated into German.

At the beginning of 1908, Mr Rieger surprised his close friend Wilhelm Herrigel by telling him that the Bahá'í Revelation is the 'Highest of all religions and will unify all other creeds into this great religion'.[11] Herrigel recalled having met Dr Fisher at the Christian Science Church, but 'either Fisher was not convincing, or they could not understand the English writings – for some reason they did not become Bahá'í'.[12] On 1 February 1908, Eckstein visited the Herrigels and invited them to a Unity Meeting on 3 February. Three lectures were given in three languages that night: Dreyfus in French, Sprague in English and Eckstein in German. There was no translation, in order to demonstrate the need for a universal language.[13] Alma recalled:

> It was a glorious proof to see how this Great Truth unites the Hearts of man, forgetting entirely the differences of Nationalities and Creeds. England,[14] France, Germany and America, united and grasping hands in fellowship and love. On the following evening, Feb. 3rd, a public Lecture was given by Mr. Sprague in English and Mr. Dreyfus in French and Mr. Eckstein in German . . . and it was a most impressive sight to see German, French, English men clasp their hands in union and love . . . Mr. Sprague after some music had been rendered closed the meeting after greetings had been extended from London and thanking the friends for all their kindness. Miss Stäbler also sang the New Jerusalem . . . Perhaps you would ask which I liked best? Both the English and French speakers spoke with spirit and eloquence; yet Mr. Eckstein, an elderly venerable gentleman, a new believer scarcely a half-year-old, also spoke with conviction and made my heart leap with joy and gratitude, I was overwhelmed with astonishment at the power and greatness of Abdul-Baha, for Mr. Eckstein being very spiritual his expressions were also sincere and filled with love and unity. I shall never forget this afternoon, four countries united in love and fellowship.[15]

It was at this meeting that Wilhelm Herrigel accepted the Bahá'í Faith. He later recalled that unforgettable night, when over 100 people filled the Bürger Museum to hear the lecture 'Universal Peace, Universal Religion and the Bahá'í Movement'. Many signed a letter written by Sydney Sprague and addressed to 'Abdu'l-Bahá. The next evening, 20 Christian Scientists went to the Riegers' home to ask their questions.[16]

Herrigel was attracted to the teachings and wanted to find out more. He invited Sydney Sprague to his home where 30 or 35 people, mostly Christian Scientists, came to hear about the Faith. After that he held weekly meetings which were led by Alma. At some point, Herrigel led the meetings and translated the English himself.[17] The new German community showed their appreciation by covering the travelling expenses of Dreyfus to France and Sprague to Vienna and later London.

Alma became even more busy. She wrote, 'a number of classes have been formed. I teach three evenings a week and two afternoons, also some mornings, receiving callers and making visits, there is very little or no time for myself.'[18]

From this early group of Christian Scientists, many joined the Stuttgart Bahá'í community and were simultaneously members of the Christian Science Church, including: Professor Braun (Secretary, Christian Science Church), Wilhelm Herrigel (Treasurer, Christian Science Church), Adolf and Agatha Eckstein and her sister Helina Pfankuche, Friedrich Schweizer, Emil and Babette Ruoff, Otto Rieger, Annemarie Warnke (later Schweizer), Mrs von Burckhardt and her daughter.[19] At some point in 1908, these early believers were told at a Christian Science business meeting that they had to choose a religion, either Christian Science or Bahá'í. All the Bahá'ís quit the Christian Science Church except Helina Pfankuche. It was a big setback for the Christian Science Church in Stuttgart. Even six years later, the Stuttgart Christian Scientist Society consisted of only 20 members.[20] In April 1908, Alma wrote, 'We have almost all of the gentlemen of the Christian Science and their Reader is not very much pleased, after having worked so hard for a number of years and now we come along and swipe their best members.'[21]

In 1900, the Mormon Church sent twelve missionaries to Heilbronn, Karlsruhe, Mannheim and Stuttgart. They held 450 meetings, were invited to present their beliefs to 5,000 people and distributed 17,000 brochures. The result of their efforts gave rise to a community of 35–65 members.[22]

When Alma had arrived in Stuttgart on 9 August 1907 there were only four Bahá'ís, but by 3 February 1908 far more than 100 people had heard the message in Stuttgart and a community of about 50 dedicated active believers had formed. Teaching was at the heart of the community and everyone was learning and sharing the message with the people in their lives. The community included a large portion of the congregation from the Christian Science Church, those who attended the talks at the Frauen Club, the women from the Air Bath, and all the friends, family members, landlords, and other contacts of the Bahá'ís.

13

BAHÁ'Í IDENTITY, COMMUNITY BUILDING AND CONSOLIDATION

The next challenge was to build a united community with all these diverse new believers. Various groups had entered the Bahá'í Faith in a short period of time, including art students, working single women, and socially elite men and their wives. Many of them had been Christian Scientists, and many had had prestigious positions in the Christian Science Church. Each person and each group brought in their own ideas, talents, understanding and ambitions. The challenge was to become a united Bahá'í community, a living example of unity in diversity. They needed to accept their new Bahá'í identity as individuals, as a group and as a community. What did that mean? They themselves knew so little about this new religion.

As it is not possible to teach Christianity without the Bible, or Islam without the Qur'án, so it is with the Revelation of Bahá'u'lláh, which is so vast that it has still not been completely translated into English. By 1907, rough English translations had been completed of the following Bahá'í scripture: the Kitáb-i-Aqdas (1900), Hidden Words (1900–1903), the Seven Valleys (1906) and the Kitáb-i-Íqán (1904). The Faith of many Western believers was built upon their personal relationship to 'Abdu'l-Bahá and His Tablets, which were largely written in response to their personal letters and petitions.

Bahá'u'lláh's Holy Words are His Revelation which transforms the individual and collective behaviour of the members of the Bahá'í community. Faith is fortified by prayer and meditation and sharing the Bahá'í teachings with others. Ultimately, through the power of the Word, the whole world is renewed, and the Kingdom of God will be established on earth. The exact words are important to extract the power and the concepts that they enshrine.

Printed materials were scarce as the Faith quickly spread in the West. Printing was expensive and distribution was complicated; many believers shared handwritten personal copies of some of the writings of Bahá'u'lláh and the Tablets of 'Abdu'l-Bahá. This was even more so on the European continent. German and French translations were derived from English translations of the Persian or Arabic originals. When Fisher began teaching in Germany in 1905, there were no German materials. He tried to make some rough translations. 'Abdu'l-Bahá praised Fanny Knobloch for translating 'Abdu'l-Bahá's Tablets into German in 1906.[1] Her translations were sent to Fisher and he had the first German pamphlets printed in 1907.

To compensate for the shortage of printed prayers and writings, many early believers kept journals in which they transcribed by hand the letters of 'Abdu'l-Bahá and some of the writings of Bahá'u'lláh for study, prayer and meditation. As the German Bahá'í community grew quickly, there was a great need for printed prayers and writings as well as for a location to hold public meetings. Due to limited financial resources, neither of these came easily.

Early believers shared the message and invited their friends, acquaintances and families to come together to pray, read and share Tablets. In this way, they started to build the German Bahá'í community.

The time had come for the new believers in Germany to discover what it really meant to be a member of the Bahá'í Faith; they needed to find a common understanding of the Bahá'í teachings and to let go of old concepts that did not belong to it. There is only one power that can accomplish this task: the Covenant of Bahá'u'lláh. For the Covenant to release its power, all had to focus on the Centre of the Covenant: 'Abdu'l-Bahá.

Many of the early Stuttgart Bahá'ís had served in the administration of the Christian Science Church and had organizational talents. In February 1908, four months after Eckstein and Rieger had accepted the Bahá'í teachings, the Stuttgart Bahá'ís organized the first Working Committee or Assembly consisting of Rieger (Chairman), Herrigel (Treasurer), Eckstein (Librarian) and Alma (Teacher).[2] The role of the Teacher was to explain the Bahá'í religion, answer questions and teach the community. The Librarian was to translate, publish and distribute Bahá'í scripture, prayers and Tablets. Lack of German materials made the consolidation work in the fast-growing community particularly challenging. Eckstein had been head of the Swedenborg Society of Europe for years and had handled their printing and publications. He bought all Fisher's Bahá'í books and organized several groups to translate the writings. Professor Braun, Emil Ruoff and Herrigel translated the Hidden Words at a rapid pace. In addition, Mrs Med. Rat von Burckhardt helped to arrange for the publication of the Hidden Words in German. Alma wrote, 'The gentlemen come to me with their translations to compare them with English and read them to me . . . I can tell you I have to be wide-awake to keep up with them, for there is nothing slow about them.'[3]

In the spring of 1908, regular Bahá'í activities were held at the Herrigels, the Ecksteins, the Bürger Museum, the home of Alma and Margarethe, and the Frauen Club (occasionally).[4] The first regular public meeting at the Bürger Museum was on 9 March 1908; 38 people attended. It was quickly followed by another large event on 13 March.

On 21 March 1908, the first Naw-Rúz Festival was celebrated in the Frauen Club in Stuttgart. Unfortunately, the attendance was low. Alma realized that celebrating the new Holy Day was awkward for the new Bahá'ís.[5] The believers liked the community and teachings, but they identified more with their traditional religious holidays which they were reluctant to replace. Bahá'í identity developed gradually, each at their own pace. Professor Braun was quick to use Bahá'í prayers on a regular basis and became a fine speaker. He felt that the quicker everyone could give up their old teachings and step into the 'Bahá'í movement', the better it would be for them.⁶ The Eckstein family decided not to confirm their youngest son Otto in the Church. They wanted him to be a Bahá'í and learn the Bahá'í teachings instead. This was a great step to take for a German family. At that time in Germany the Church played a strong role in community life.⁷

All of this did not go unnoticed. The Lutheran churches in Stuttgart warned their members about the Bahá'í teachings from their pulpits over Easter 1908, but the new believers remained firm. Alma wrote:

> I can't thank God enough for this, they are willing to step out and become teachers and work for the Cause and do not care what the ministers are preaching against us, Easter was a great time and they used the opportunity to denounce our Truth from the pulpits, saying that people have always run after fortune-tellers and mediums; but now the Mohammedianism [sic] has found it in Stuttgart & also finds listeners, they put us down for Mohammedians [sic] and are not very much pleased that we have our meetings.⁸

The believers remained under social pressure. Alma wrote,

> The believers here . . . are really holy souls and sincere and I only wish and hope the tests do not come too severe that they may remain firm. It means work and hard work for every movement is closely observed and they are so often told that many swindlers come from America that I have to be very diplomatic . . . We have taken the larger part of the Christian Science. Miss Nemmens [Christian Scientist] could chew my head off if she could get hold of it, but I will take good care, I can't prevent her and her little flock sending mental arrows, which fill the air and sometimes tire me very much for they use thought transference.⁹

In May 1908 Sydney Sprague returned to Stuttgart for a few days, and on 19 May a special teaching meeting was held for him. The format of the event was designed, 'so that they could go on without' Alma, and omitted the role of a central teacher, including the writings only. Alma found that method 'quite satisfying',[10] and it confirmed that the community could continue without her. She wrote home about the harmonious atmosphere. She received an abundance of invitations, and they sent her cake and fruits and flowers. Alma wrote to her family that when she returned home, she would not eat cake any more for a long time![11] The German tradition of cake and coffee in the afternoons is still alive today, and considering the number of home visits she made she must have enjoyed plenty of it! She was cautious in her interactions with the men, a formality that some of the men found backward or old-fashioned. Still, it was important to Alma not to seem 'forward', so she 'went slow' to 'win the men as friends'. They supported each other and expressed their wish that she should 'remain in Stuttgart longer'. [12] This of course meant she would need support from Fanny for a longer period than initially planned.

After Sydney Sprague's departure, Fisher invited nine men to meet in his office and form a men's working committee. They did not invite Alma, Margarethe, or any of the other women in the community.[13] This committee was formed by Fisher's individual initiative without the support of the community; therefore, it did not last long.

In 1908, decentralized meetings were organized in the Stuttgart city districts of Degenloch and Zuffenhausen, and in Esslingen. In Degerloch, Julia and Elise Stäbler's friend Rosa Schwarz started a weekly afternoon meeting with interested friends. In Zuffenhausen, Annemarie Warnke (later Schweizer) invited Alma to share the teachings with her friends and family. One of her close school friends, Anna Köstlin, the Herrigels' niece, was very interested in the Bahá'í teachings and she also wanted to learn English. Anna asked Alma to give her English lessons and help her translate the writings in her home. Anna's mother, Mrs Eger, and Max Bender joined for the second class. Mr Köstlin asked Alma, 'does it make sense for you to come here for so few participants?' The answer was a resounding 'Yes!'

Within a short time, there were too many people coming to fit into the small room! The Esslingen community hosted hiking trips where groups hiked into nature and then rested at beautiful locations to read and deepen and talk about the teachings. Many learned about the Faith this way.

Further confirmation of the strong Bahá'í identity was celebrated at the first Bahá'í marriage in Germany between Annemarie Warnke and Friedrich Schweizer on 30 November 1909. The wedding took place in Fisher's office. According to the wish of 'Abdu'l-Bahá, they repeated Bahá'í vows after Fisher and Alma read some prayers. Anna Köstlin was the witness. Alma gave the bride prayer beads from 'Akká and the groom received black prayer beads from 'Akká from Mason Remey. All the prayer beads had been blessed by the Master.

The Schweizers moved to Zuffenhausen. Later they were blessed with the first German-born Bahá'í children and their home was personally blessed in 1913 by 'Abdu'l-Bahá during His historic visit. They donated their home to the German National Spiritual Assembly, which serves as a Bahá'í centre up to today. The Schweizers were a model Bahá'í family and the first Germans known to pay Ḥuqúqu'lláh. Years later, Annemarie Schweizer endured imprisonment for her Faith by the Nazis. Annemarie Schweizer and Anna Köstlin both served on the National Spiritual Assembly of Germany after the Second World War.

Although she did not have the financial means, Alma started to plan a teaching trip to Leipzig, Bautzen and Zittau, the area where she had been born. She consulted about it with Fanny,[14] who generously sent extra money for Alma to travel and financed a shipment of teaching books. But there were two other issues which prevented Alma from travelling East.

Her first concern was about the steadfastness of the Stuttgart believers to maintain their Bahá'í identity. The new believers felt a lot of social pressure from their friends at the Christian Science Church and others in Stuttgart.

The private Bahá'í lessons Alma offered constantly attracted new seekers and new believers. The importance of this consolidation work cannot be overestimated. For example, new believers such as Mr Imhoff[15] and Mrs Forester[16] (who later offered her home for a party for the freedom of 'Abdu'l-Bahá) spent much time with her during this period.[17] Once Alma came home and found Miss Scheuerle from Pfadelbach and Mr Haigis waiting at her door for more than an hour to hear about the teachings! Upon leaving, Mr Haigis expressed his gratitude and told Alma he would do his best to work for the Faith.[18] Whenever Alma talked about going to Leipzig, the friends in Stuttgart discouraged her.

Alma's second concern was that none of the petitions sent to 'Abdu'l-Bahá by any of the new German believers had been confirmed. At that time, when a person became a believer, they sent a petition to 'Abdu'l-Bahá declaring their belief in Bahá'u'lláh and asking to be accepted. 'Abdu'l-Bahá always sent back a Tablet of confirmation. Such Tablets were sometimes addressed to individuals directly or to an entire group of new believers with the names listed individually. In this case 'Abdu'l-Bahá had not sent anything! Throughout 1908, Alma wrote home about her deep concern that the petitions from the German believers had not been answered. She asked that her family write to Mason Remey and ask him to ask the Master.[19] Nobody knew why 'Abdu'l-Bahá was silent towards the German believers. This was a great test for them; they had left their Church to join the Bahá'í Faith and they felt unsure about whether they had been accepted.

Of these days, Shoghi Effendi later wrote, 'I recall the slow eastward spread of that infant Light which led to the gradual emergence of the German and Austrian Bahá'í Communities, during the darkest period of 'Abdu'l-Bahá's incarceration in the prison-fortress of Ákká.'[20] In July 1908, Alma wrote that the believers

> found they could not go on worshiping in their old place of worship for it was made unpleasant for them and they are not strong enough to stand alone and not having but a few of the Tablets, that means but a little of the teachings

in German. You can see that they feel as though they have been thrown into the sea and swim as best they can . . . They come regularly and put themselves out very often as to come and they also keep up their extra meetings and make appointments with me for private talks, so I am sure they are earnest. I do hope the Master will reveal a Tablet for them.[21]

When Mason Remey travelled to 'Akká in September 1908, the believers asked him to find out if their petitions had reached the Master or if they had ever reached 'Akká. On 2 October 1908 Alma wrote, 'it may be that the believers may wish me to go to Acca at once as Mr. Remey says that no doubt our letters and petitions have not arrived, he has asked our Lord'.[22] Remey thought that they might have been sent to the United States for translation into Persian. Marion Jack, on her arrival from 'Akká, explained that some of the mail did not make it and that the Master was flooded with mail and could not answer all of it every day.

But Alma had another concern about leaving for Leipzig: difficulties with Dr Fisher.

14

ALMA AND EDWIN FISHER

Dr Fisher was not in good health. His constant suffering worried Alma and Margarethe and they tried to care for him. In November of 1907 Alma described the situation to her family:

> He was examined a short time ago and the doctor told him he must gain strength for about a month and then be operated. He has been spending all his money for the cause and often would spend his last money and then live on bread and tea, I am sure that since I am here, he has had but few good meals . . . he suffers greatly not having a suitable place to eat restaurants he does not like . . . the food does not suit him. I have offered to cook dinner twice a week . . . it is hard to help and help is so much needed and he is so greatful [sic].[1]

When Fisher wrote to 'Abdu'l-Bahá asking for a helpmate, his incentive and expectations were beyond assistance with teaching. In reality, he was looking for a personal helpmate, a wife who could support him, his lifestyle, and his wish to be able to be free of dentistry work and devote himself full time to studying and teaching the Faith. In contrast, Alma at age 43 was too old to be anything but practical about the prospects of marriage. At that time, marriage entailed financial and legal implications for the wife far beyond the concept of romantic love. Once married, a woman lost the right to own property; to work, a woman needed written permission from her husband who bore the sole right to manage her salary if she earned money. After losing her fiancé and subsequently finding the Faith, Alma had consciously dedicated her life completely to teaching the Faith. She did not want to marry.

The gap between Fisher's and Alma's expectations gave rise to a social disaster which began in August 1907. The strain on Alma's relationship to Fisher developed into a seed of disunity in the Bahá'í community. Here is Alma's perspective of the story as it unfolds in her letters home. On 16 October 1907, she wrote to Fanny:

> Dr. F. is looking for a helpmate to assist him in every way. And all I can do for him is help him try to find one and that is what I am doing, and I hope dear mother [Amalie] may be settled soon for I am tired of hearing about marriage, and he needs one with means . . .[2]

About two weeks later, she wrote:

> I am getting along with everything beautiful but with Dr F he talks about marrying all the time and places me in such an ocward[sic] position . . . it is only that one subject, he has asked the Master for the right one and Oh I do wish she would come along and have this matter settled, for I hope he does not think Abdul Baha has sent me for that.[3]

Alma's efforts to help Fisher were not successful. Caring for him was too time-consuming. Alma wrote, 'I have given up trying to cook, time is to [sic] precious.' The more he tried to persuade her that he needed her, the more she realized that she could not help him. Alma explained further, 'I can't see how I can work in the cause and nurse a sick man without means . . .'[4]

Fisher wasn't just looking for a wife, he was looking for an American wife, and although he received much attention from the German women he was focused on Alma. He said he 'would carry out great plans and she could do his housekeeping and typewriting and answer the telephone, etc. and he considered marrying her, as that would be the best way to bring things about for his comfort'.⁵ Alma did not find the offer attractive!

> ... he has found more love and attention here than anywhere in his life, the only trouble, the ladies that he has given the teachings to, all are in love with him and he does not wish to marry them, and they are all so very fond of him and they are beautiful, refined ladies. I have to help him straighten matters out and teach them the Bahá'í Truth, please do not think this is easy, I am glad that I am not good looking, for I would have a time. I can understand why he has asked our beloved Abdul Baha to send him the right one, and I hope she will come.⁶

> Margarethe is still very fond of him. Also, Miss Frey, but he wishes an American . . .⁷

Fisher and Alma had very different approaches to teaching the Bahá'í Faith. He aimed at the upper class with means and titles, while she focused on teaching the middle class. Alma wrote:

> Dr. Fisher wrote from the elaborate Kurort [Spa] in Homburg v.d. Höhe that he had 'broken ice there and there would be a great deal of work in the Cause for me to do there'. I would like very much to go and follow up his work but the trip is most expensive for me at present, it is a fine resort, the water is very healthful, he was so disappointed last year that I did not go, I know that it would be excellent for me, but it takes a great deal and fine clothes, for Dr F.'s aim is for people of rank and position, others tire him and he has no time for them, that is why I have taken so much pain with them, and they really make the best believers and do not take it up as a fad.⁸

Regarding her appearance, Alma once wrote to Fanny: 'I had a good laugh about your description of my hair, Margarethe had always been scolding me about my poor way of dressing my hair, Well I will try my best to improve and please you both if possible . . . although I am not good looking and have no charms, still I manage to attract people after all.'⁹ On another occasion, she wrote, 'At first glance, I do not make much of an impression, but in a very short time win the hearts of those I meet. This is what I am told and no doubt it is true.'¹⁰

Once Fanny complained about a photograph of Alma that Alma had sent her. Fanny did not like it. Alma explained that it was taken in a studio run by a woman who told her to 'look earnest because that woman likes to make her portraits reflect the brain'. She wrote, 'So you don't like the brain photograph. Well next time I will have my picture taken by a man, they in general don't think women have any brain.'¹¹

Alma felt that Fisher 'needs a wife with money and one that would devote herself to his welfare'.¹² When he returned in June, he looked splendid, but that summer he only attended the meetings in the hall once. Alma wrote, 'his feeling towards me is anything but pleasant and is hard to bear. He likes me and hates me at the same time.'¹³ By August 1908, Fisher had given up. Alma wrote:

> I am really sorry, he had written the Master a long-detailed letter telling Him what he wishes and needs and made up his mind that I was the one that Abdul Baha has sent him and that is why he repeated and repeated his proposal and told me in a thousand and one ways he wished to marry and I would tell him he wishes too much.¹⁴

Alma and Dr Fisher had different expectations of their relationship right from the start. Knowing the legal and social loss of independence that marriage entailed for women at that time, it is easy to understand why Alma never married. At her age, she had little to gain and was unlikely to have children. Fisher, as the husband, would have had a different position, but he never found a new wife after he left Trenton. Those days had passed.

15
INVITATION TO THE HOLY LAND, AND THE PASSING OF AMALIE KNOBLOCH

By the end of August 1908, things had calmed down. Edwin Fisher was once again attending the meetings.[1] After a very beautiful and successful unity meeting in August, Alma considered leaving for Leipzig. Eckstein warned her, 'you won't have it as nice in Leipzig'.[2] But after a successful unity meeting, she was confident that the time was ripe for her to go.

Marion Jack was a steadfast and knowledgeable Canadian Bahá'í who had accepted the Faith at the turn of the century in Paris. In the Spring of 1908, she had been privileged to visit 'Abdu'l-Bahá while He was living in 'Akká under the greatest tension and forbidden to leave the city. During that time, she served as a secretary to 'Abdu'l-Bahá and managed His correspondence with the Western believers. In addition, she was an artist, and He gave her permission to paint the Holy Tomb and the interior of the prison so that she could keep in good practice. By the end of July, 'Abdu'l-Bahá was free to leave 'Akká again. He told Marion Jack to return to London by way of Germany so that she could meet the German believers.[3]

Marion's arrival was Alma's opportunity to go East. She could trust Marion to accompany the new believers and Alma would be free to travel. Interestingly, she did not feel she could leave the new believers with Dr Fisher. Alma secretly hoped that

Dr Fisher would become interested in Marion Jack and wrote, 'perhaps Miss Jack will like Dr Fisher so he will be happy . . . he is coming to the meetings now and is getting used to the believers and learning to like them'.[4]

After leaving the Holy Land, Miss Jack visited Laura Barney and Hippolyte Dreyfus in Switzerland. Alma was looking forward to meeting Miss Jack, especially since it was the 'Master's wish for her to meet or visit the believers'.[5] Alma went to Switzerland to meet Marion in September 1908.

Alma and Marion travelled for two weeks in Switzerland, and Margarethe joined them for the second week. The women visited Nidwalden, Kersetten on the Fürwaldstetter Sea, and Luzern, travelling as tourists. While visiting Kersetten, their hostess Mrs Hensteckel became interested in the Bahá'í teachings and later Alma visited her to tell her more.[6] While Alma, Margarethe and Marion were travelling, Ahmad Yazdi from Cairo visited with the other German believers. When they returned, Alma prepared to visit her family in Bautzen and Leipzig.

The sisters had written to the Holy Land asking for permission to visit the Master. On 9 June 1908 Fanny and Pauline received a Tablet in which 'Abdu'l-Bahá told them that although their longing to go on pilgrimage was an indication of their faith and their firmness in the Covenant and that he would have been pleased to receive them, it was too difficult at that time and that Ahmad Sohrab would explain to them why this was so. 'Abdu'l-Bahá however reassured them that firmness in faith was conducive to true nearness, a nearness that was constant and eternal, unending and uninterrupted. He expressed the hope that heavenly confirmations would encircle them, that they might develop spiritually and travel in the worlds of the Kingdom – and also that they would be able to come to the Holy Land later.[7]

The dramatic political events in the summer of 1908, including the Young Turk Revolution, would grant freedom to all Iranian political and religious prisoners and usher in long-awaited freedom for 'Abdu'l-Bahá. On 2 October 1908, Alma sent the happy message home that a letter had arrived from the Holy Land with permission for the Knobloch and Hannen families to visit. They were told to be careful not to come together, but rather one by one.[8]

Before departing for 'Akká on 6 October, Alma went to Bautzen and Leipzig to visit her father's brother, Uncle Wilhelm, and his wife Mina. She also met Uncle Bruno Rössler's eldest daughter Jennie Scholz and her husband, and their two children aged 5 and 4, as well as Jennie's brother Arthur. Uncle Wilhelm and Aunt Mina invited their friends to meet Alma and hear more about the Bahá'í teachings. Unfortunately, the unhappy news of Amalie's death arrived while Aunt Mina was preparing for their guests.

Amalie Knobloch had passed to the Abhá Kingdom on 30 September 1908. Both Amalie and Alma had known, when Alma left for Germany, that they might never see each other in this world again, but for Alma the loss of her mother was a shock. She was the only one in her family who did not share the precious last spiritual moments with the mother she loved so dearly. She had just received a letter from her mother telling her how happy she was about the upcoming pilgrimage, and how Amalie looked forward to taking care of the grandchildren while Pauline and Joe travelled. Alma did not expect that she would pass away so suddenly! She wrote home:

> Your letter reached me yesterday morning, can you imagine my surprise? For I can't realize, I cannot think, could not sleep last night and feel dazed. My comfort to you all is my earnest prayer and at least I will pray, for until now I could not and it seems hard and yet how beautiful it was for dear Mama to go to sleep so sweet as she had wished. I will not wish her back but only hope we may be able to join her . . . If I only knew what my future would be! I was so homesick the last 3 months. When I was in Buffalo, I wished to be nearer to home so as to be nearer to Mama and how often did she write that she wished that Abdul Baha would send me to work somewhere nearer home, I well knew it

was hard when I left and that changes could take place, but when it comes it is terrible. Mason Remey's visit was a great comfort but I fear to ask too many questions about the dear ones not trusting myself, no I am not so strong but to the contrary a weakling. It is only that I cannot forget the commanding request and words of Abdul Baha three months before I knew anything about going to Germany, that I have to obey and do his work and do it as bravely as I can.[9]

When Mina heard the bad news, she had immediately wanted to cancel their dinner guests. Alma felt Amalie would not like that, so she convinced Mina to keep their plans. Alma joined them towards the end of the evening. She wrote home, 'I told them of my experience, erasing the tears and all were bright as could be expected. But I do not think any of them slept all night. Uncle Wilhelm always did admire Mama and recalled the past.'[10]

In her last letter to her mother on 2 October 1908, Alma had written, 'All those who see your picture immediately say that I look just like you! I must have changed because I did not look like you before. I am so happy that I always carry your picture with me!'[11] Alma considered her mother to be a saint. She was always concerned about Amalie's well-being and had asked 'Abdu'l-Bahá to comfort her mother in Fanny's absence, should their pilgrimage request be approved. She felt that her mother's passing shortly before Fanny's departure was an answer to her prayer, and that Amalie would now be comforted in the presence of the Master, as well as the Blessed Perfection, Bahá'u'lláh.

The passing of Amalie Knobloch was a dramatic spiritual event which Pauline recorded in detail in a handwritten account which was personally delivered to Alma, the only family member who was not present. Pauline recalled how her mother, gasping for breath, painfully shared the Bahá'í message with her nurse in her last hours. The nurse in turn recalled, 'I do not understand all your Mother said to me, but this I do know: it was the truth of God. Never in my experience as a Nurse have I ever witnessed or even heard tell of such a glorious death scene; to see such a pure soul leave this world with such joy and great peace, and to see the transfigured faces of you and your sister when you would repeat that name [Allah'u'abhá] for her. I shall never, never forget it as long as I live and <u>I shall use that name</u> too.'[12]

Although Alma was not physically present, Amalie told those at her bedside, 'Alma is here. I see her. Dear Alma, she is doing the Master's work.' Later, with both Fanny and Pauline kneeling by her side, Fanny asked her mother, 'Have you no message for Alma?' Pauline recalled that Amalie 'looked so pityingly and replied, "Alma will become wholly spiritual. She is entirely under the care and protection of Abdul-Baha. What can <u>I</u> say more than this? She is blessed."'[13] Fanny recalled:

> Abdul Baha who in one of His Holy tablets to Mamma wrote: I am her Guide and Protector be ever near unto you – also declared by Tablet: 'your daughter Miss Alma <u>has</u> been confirmed, verily I say she will become wholy [sic] spiritual' – when the last moments were drawing near and I asked Mamma – will you give me a message for Alma – Mama repeated those words of our Lord – and I felt there was a silent reproach in her look – and naive as she added <u>Is there anything more I can say</u>?[14]

On 14 October 1908, a memorial service for Amalie Knobloch was held in Washington DC. Pauline recalled, 'When my mother died, the pallbearers were both races.' It must have been very sad for Alma to miss this occasion. On 10 November when Alma and Fanny were on pilgrimage, 'Abdu'l-Bahá told them, 'If you could see the glory in which your mother now dwells you would not care to live another day – you could not live. I will write a Tablet for your mother, which you shall read at her grave. Through this Tablet her name will be known through all eternity.'[15]

Thus, 'Abdu'l-Bahá revealed in His own handwriting a Tablet of Visitation for those who visit Amalie Knobloch's grave. Lua Getsinger, Roy Wilhelm and the Kinneys were among the many Bahá'ís who visited her grave at Prospect Hill Cemetery in Washington DC and read the Tablet in her honour.[16] This blessing has been passed on through the many generations of friends living and serving in Washington DC since that time.

Visiting Tablet
Revealed for the Attracted Maid-Servant of God, Mrs. Amalie Knobloch, who has Ascended to the Kingdom of God!

He is God!

O, thou Pure Spirit, Amalie Knobloch! Although thou didst soar away from this terrestrial world, yet thou didst enter into the immeasurable, illumined Universe of the Almighty. While in this life thou didst hear the Divine Call, beheld the light of Truth, became alive by the Breaths of the Holy Spirit, tasted the sweetness of the Love of God, became the Maid-Servant of the Lord of Hosts and the object of the Bounties of His Highness the Desired one. Thou didst lead the erring ones into the Path of Truth and bestowed a portion of the Heavenly Food to those who are deprived. Thou didst consecrate the days of thy existence to the Service of His Highness the Clement and spent thy time in the diffusion of the Fragrances of the Paradise of Abha. There are many souls perfumed and many spirits illumined through thy services!

O, thou divine, beloved Maid-Servant! Although thou didst disappear from the mortal eyes, yet thou didst train and educate thy daughters, each of whom has arisen to serve the Kingdom like unto thee and is engaged in the guidance of souls. In the Assembly of wisdom they are the lighted candles; they sacrifice their lives in the Path of God; they are gardening in thy orchard and irrigating thy rose-garden. Happy is thy condition, for thou art enjoying Eternal Life in the Kingdom of Everlasting Glory and hast left in this world kind and loving Remembrances. Happy are those souls who visit thy luminous resting-place and through thy commemoration receive and acquire spiritual Powers![17]

16

PILGRIMAGE

Alma's trip to Leipzig and Bautzen had lasted ten days, but she had to return to Stuttgart, since she had promised the believers there that she would start for her pilgrimage from their city. This was the first pilgrimage from Germany to 'Akká. Alma's family was surprised that she did not take the direct route from Leipzig to Haifa.

Alma was concerned that the believers could lose their faith if they were not confirmed by 'Abdu'l-Bahá. Having not heard anything, she wondered, 'Will Abdul Baha be glad to see me? I know He will be pleased to see you all, but I am not so sure about myself, can't understand that all of our letters should not have reached him. I do so long for message from Him and will again feel happy when Fanny and I will be permitted to present ourselves.'[1]

An important Tablet arrived in Stuttgart after Alma's departure for pilgrimage. Although it does not mention the new German believers or their petitions to 'Abdu'l-Bahá, it indicates that He had answered the letters she had forwarded to him.[2] Now all she had to do was to find His response to their petitions!

The Stuttgart community arranged two farewell parties to see her off, one at the Eckstein home and one at Margarethe's.[3] The next morning Alma spent some hours with Mr Eckstein and his sister as they travelled by train together to Zurich. Alma continued on through Milan to Rome and visited St Peter's before going to Naples, where she met Fanny and Ida Finch at their ship on 23 October. They had a joyous reunion. They visited Pompeii and other sights around Naples and took the next steamer to Alexandria en route to 'Akká.

In Alexandria, they met Mírzá Ḥusayn and Mírzá Muḥammad Yazdí, whose faces 'shone with the Bahá'í light'. The Yazdi families had been sent to Egypt by Bahá'u'lláh where they had set up a business and served the Faith in many heroic ways.[4] One of their tasks was to meet the Western pilgrims on their way to 'Abdu'l-Bahá. Alma was impressed by the devotion and purity of these Bahá'ís; although they came from different cultures, looked so different from each other, and had never met before, they felt like one big family. The Bahá'ís in Alexandria told them to empty themselves of everything before arriving in 'Akká, so that they could take as much with them as possible when they left. Alma and Fanny spent the next days in quiet prayer to prepare themselves for this journey. They realized that there was a great difference in the spirituality of the Oriental believers and themselves. They wondered if they would be happy in 'Akká or if the light would be too powerful for them to take?

On the steamer to Haifa, they met some Germans who were travelling to Jaffa to wait for the return of Christ, and who were very surprised to learn that the Knoblochs were travelling so far just to meet a special teacher! After the stop in Jaffa, the ship sailed on and anchored at Haifa. The three women climbed down a ladder on the side of the steamer and at the bottom a 'large strong arab' picked them up and carried them to a rowboat as a Cook's agent brought their baggage.[5]

A group of Persian believers met them in Haifa and escorted them to the Mount Carmel Hotel. They were invited to have dinner at the home of the Ruhi [sic] family, where they met Munírih Khánum, the Master's wife. She lovingly advised them, 'Become like dry leaves so as to be wafted by the breezes; to be moved by the spirit with no will of your own.'[6]

Alma was privileged to be with 'Abdu'l-Bahá in 'Akká from 7 to 13 November. She recorded her first impressions of 'Akká:

> Reaching the city gate a caravan with a number of camels had settled down for the night and the men in their accustomed religious devotions a most picturesque sight. We had

passed several trails of camels leaving for the desert packed with merchandise, disappearing between date palms. Reaching the City Gate of Acca, which was guarded by soldiers who asked something of the men who drove our carriage. They answered in reply, 'Abbas Effendi!' and we drove through the gate into the ancient city. Such narrow streets – the men stood close up to the walls and the carriage drove through and into the courtyard of Abdul Baha's house . . . Our expectations were high, perfection in a human body, the surroundings reflected His divinity, His followers the superhuman, given for the light and spreading the fragrance of God's love. His family purified from all dust of the world, beautiful flowers in the garden of the Abha Kingdom. Heavenly home of peace in a prison town, Acca was inhabited by only state prisoners of a very low type, surrounded by a high wall and soldiers guarding the entrance city gate.[7]

Munírih Khánum, her granddaughter and Amin Fareed (her nephew, the son of her brother Mírzá Asadu'lláh) accompanied them to 'Akká. Dr Fareed was fluent in English and had studied medicine at the University of Chicago and spent at least six years working with the House of Spirituality in Chicago starting in 1901.[8] They crossed three streams on the way to 'Akká, and as the water covered the carriage wheels, Munírih Khánum told them the story of how she had come to the Holy Land and married 'Abdu'l-Bahá. As they drew closer to 'Akká, they saw merchants leaving the city for the desert with a caravan of packed camels. They saw a number of Arabs kneeling in prayer beside their camels at sunset just outside the 'Akká city gate. Alma recalled that it was like a fairy tale that would suddenly disappear.[9]

Soon they entered the inner courtyard of the house of the Master. Three of the surrounding sides were occupied by 'Abdu'l-Bahá and the fourth side by two Christian missionaries. Fanny and Alma were led to their room, in the corner next to the dining room. 'Abdu'l-Bahá had the room next to theirs and

Ida Finch had the room on the other side of His room. That night, 'Abdu'l-Bahá was having dinner with the Governor; they were told they would meet Him in the morning. In her memoirs, Alma wrote:

> The next morning, we were up bright and early. His daughter came and told us that we could come to the living room. We had been looking up at the roof in hopes to see Abdul Baha, having been told that he frequently goes up here and spends hours in meditation. We found all the ladies siting [sic] on the devan [sic] that was along two sides of the room and saw the Greatest Holy Leaf for the first time a marvelous Saint. A woman from India on the floor at Sameviour [sic: a samovar] serving tea in small glass cups we sat down facing the door and all of a sudden were heard quick footsteps and Abdul Baha was in the room – all stood to greet Him – Welcome – Welcome – glad to see you Welcome – Welcome – how are you? I was the last one to shake hands – He seemed most powerful – like a powerful magnet if one is in tune with Him – or one would be far from Him although near. He took His place in the corner, Fanny next to Him and Miss Finch and next to me on the other [side]. He asked if we had a pleasant journey how we had left the friends – if they were well and united – if we were well and happy – Then He inquired about the different assemblies and our friends at home.
>
> The room was large, flooded with light and the birds came in and hopped on the floor and picked up the crumbs of sugar or just picked and hopped about and flew out again, there was an air of perfect freedom, no depression, or strain whatsoever, an atmosphere of heavenly bliss, one felt as though we had come home after a long, weary journey, every breath seemed to inhale this sweet balmy air of love and freedom.
>
> One realized that Abdul Baha knows one's very thoughts, of the past and present and that He also knew how we would work out our future. All this we felt – that

our shortcomings were clear before Him and still we felt happy – and perfectly willing to be read, even to our depths of our souls.

Our main desire was to be empty of all former thoughts and be filled with this spiritual gift, this outpouring, that would permeate our entire being, longing to be worthy to become an inmate of this heavenly home, having been told that it was our eternal residence, it depended on us what station we would attain.

When Abdul Baha arosed [sic]to leave, He said He had made a program for every day of our stay.

We were taken to the dining room and had breakfast – walking along the wide portico, with marble . . . our steps seemed to rebound . . .

I also had a little caller who came about every morning with his slate. Fanny and Miss Finch had no time and I thought it must be included in the program so gave him the greatest attention and courtesy. He would hand me his slate and say 'Springlsh' or at least that is what I understood – my letters were rubbed out – also the figures and words . . . Shoghi continued to come with his slate and one morning when kneeling on the floor beside him with his slate on the table, Abdul Baha opened the door and stepped in – feeling embarrassed I arose instantly. Abdul Baha looked pleased and said, 'Khali Kub', it seemed like a flood of light and spirit filled the room, and He left without another remark. From that time on I felt sure that the calls of this little grandson were included in the program He had made and that sometime I would be able to understand.[10]

The 'little caller' was Shoghi Effendi, the future Guardian of the Bahá'í Faith, the 'priceless pearl' or 'little child' foretold in the Bible.

While in Haifa they met many older believers, who had served the Faith during the life of Bahá'u'lláh and who 'gave brilliant accounts of their experiences, how they had been put in prison, tortured with their eyes sparkling with mirth and telling jokes of one another'. These believers showed them the scars around their necks and ankles from the heavy chains they had worn. They told how they had been chained together and when one moved all suffered.

On behalf of the German believers, Alma told 'Abdu'l-Bahá about the new Bahá'í house which had been built by Mr Eckstein. The German friends wished 'Abdu'l-Bahá to give it a name. He asked, 'A German or a Persian name?' She responded that the friends would like a Persian name. 'Abdu'l-Bahá named the house 'Anjomani Rahmani' (Merciful Assembly).[11]

Fanny asked 'Abdu'l-Bahá if Alma should return to Stuttgart, and He answered, 'Why not? Yes, she has been confirmed in her work there by the Holy Spirit, why should she go elsewhere? When a tree in the forest is ablaze the others will be ignited.' He said: 'If you make Stuttgart a strong center, it will be of great benefit for other cities, for they can refer to it.'[12]

Alma and Fanny normally saw 'Abdu'l-Bahá at mealtimes and took notes about what he told them. He stressed unity, emphasizing the privilege they had to serve the Faith and the importance of the time in which they lived. He said:

> For every great cause which is to appear, God will prepare some means. For instance, when the season of spring is at hand, before that season appears there will be snowstorms, rain and thunder and a great many things will happen. This is a preparation for the coming of the Spring. If preparation should not precede, the Spring would not appear.
>
> The greater the storms, the more abundant the fall of rain, the more beautiful and splendid is the Spring.[13]

In addition, He shared this insight:

> In the world of existence, one must look in everything to the capacity and ability. For instance, if a man wishes to attain the art of writing, he must look to himself to see whether he has the ability or not. If a man wishes to teach, he must feel sure that he has the ability. So it is with a captain; he

must first realize in himself whether he is fitted for that work or not. In short, every work depends upon capacity and ability, that is man must first see whether or not he has the ability for working in some profession, or not; without regarding this matter he would at last be disappointed. But in the work of the Kingdom of God, that is exceptional: In this place or station one should not consider capacity or ability; the confirmation of the Spirit will descend; because we hold that the weakest souls through the confirmation of the Holy Spirit become the most powerful. Some souls who were outwardly ignorant, through this gift become learned ones. The weakest souls become the strongest.[14]

With regard to teaching, Alma recalled: "Abdul Baha said, "He was nearest to those on the front lines – like a King – He is most interested and most concerned with the soldiers in the fronts of the battle.""[15]

Alma, Ida and Fanny enjoyed a visit to the Riḍván Garden where Bahá'u'lláh had spent peaceful hours under the mulberry trees less than two decades earlier. When they returned to 'Akká, their carriage entered the gate and 'there stood Abdul Baha and several of the old teachers at a respectful distance. The attitude was so unspeakable [sic] reverent – as the carriage passed. One of the most impressive pictures that has been printed on my soul.'[16]

Alma shared an interesting experience she had one night at dinner with the Master. On the table, there was a bowl with long, hot peppers. 'Abdu'l-Bahá looked at Mírzá Asadu'lláh, his brother-in-law, and told him to eat one of the peppers. Looking at the Master, Mírzá Asadu'lláh slowly reached out to take a pepper, looking as if he hoped the Master would just excuse him from the table. But the Master did not, instead, He said, 'eat, they are good, eat . . .' Mírzá Asadu'lláh held the pepper up, hoping the Master would excuse him, but the Master again repeated, 'eat, they are good, eat . . .' As Mírzá Asadu'lláh ate the pepper, the tears rolled down his face. 'Abdu'l-Bahá had him eat the whole pepper. The atmosphere at the table was tense. Alma recalled, 'All at the table felt the severe strain and seriousness of the position and realized that Abdul Baha wished to teach us a lesson of complete obedience no matter how severe to overcome difficulty, victory comes through obedience, is what I saw in this illustration, a lesson never to be forgotten.'[17] Mírzá Asadu'lláh and his son Dr Fareed both became Covenant-breakers in 1914, after accompanying 'Abdu'l-Bahá to America.

Other memories include touching descriptions of receiving gifts from the Holy Family, including five stones with the Greatest Name, a silk scarf, and a white silk scarf with soil from the Shrine of Bahá'u'lláh, nine candles which the Greatest Holy Leaf lit inside the Shrine of Bahá'u'lláh and white pearl prayer beads from the Holy Mother, Munírih Khánum. Alma found these gifts so overwhelming that she almost fainted.[18] Other highlights included seeing the pictures of the Báb and Bahá'u'lláh and praying in the Shrine of Bahá'u'lláh.

At the end of the pilgrimage, the pilgrims visited the Shrine of Bahá'u'lláh. Alma recalled in her notes that it was

> an experience that will be remembered throughout all Eternity. The Holy Mother, Monever [sic] and Dr. Fareed took us, we visited a relative who served a glass of tea – then we passed through a court with trees and flowering bushes and removing our shoes stood at the threshold, the heavy portier being put aside we entered after a most [sic] chant of the Holy Mother, we were transformed into another world – every fiber of our being seemed to vibrate and penetrate our whole being. All I could do while here was to breath and inhale the heavenly atmosphere that was lifting me far beyond my bounds. I heard the sweet beautiful tones of the chant, it filled my soul . . . There was a rich Persian rug over the remains of Baha ullah – lamps and handsom [sic] candle holders around the edge, here seemed to be flowers, for the air was filled with perfume . . . We were surely going through a new birth and longed to become worthy of all these blessings . . . An increase of longing to be able to serve filled our hearts, no matter how humble the servers may be,

it was serving humanity that we could in a way show our gratitude for these boundless blessings.[19]

'Abdu'l-Bahá said, 'You have been here nine days, in reality it was nine years.'[20] The lessons Alma learned while in His presence were the wisdom of a lifetime! Later Alma, Fanny and Ida Finch printed their pilgrim notes in the small book, *Flowers Culled from the Rose Garden of Acca*. Remembering her pilgrimage, Alma later wrote:

> I had no worldly wish or desire, no longing for joy in this world, my only prayer was to improve daily that Abdul Baha would be pleased. These were the most precious moments of my life before leaving when He told us that He was well pleased with our advancements. We were His real daughters and that He was our Home for all Eternity and with tears in His eyes He said several times the bounties during our stay had been perfect. These words cheer me during my hard times, which are a blessing and I can stand a great deal of unkindness and injustice.[21]

Leaving Haifa, the three women returned to Port Said. Here they met Siyyid Taqíy-i-Manshádí, at the store of Ahmad Yazdi. He was a physically dark man and told them that he was the spiritual child of Lua Getsinger, the Mother Teacher of the West. Alma and Fanny told him that they also had a number of dark spiritual children, although they were not even married! Everyone laughed a lot. They gave 'Abdu'l-Bahá's message to the believers of Port Said, 'That the light seen in Alma, Fanny and Miss Finch was 'Abdu'l-Bahá's love for the believers of Alexandria and Cairo!'[22]

In Port Said they were blessed to meet Mírzá Abu'l-Faḍl once again. He came to see them although he had been ill in bed. He said he had many letters from the friends in the United States, but he could not answer them all.

17
DISTRACTIONS

The teacher, when teaching, must be himself fully enkindled, so that his utterance, like unto a flame of fire, may exert influence and consume the veil of self and passion. He must also be utterly humble and lowly so that others may be edified and be totally self-effaced and evanescent so that he may teach with the melody of the Concourse on high – otherwise his teaching will have no effect.

'Abdu'l-Bahá[1]

Although the Bahá'í Faith began to spread in the United States in the last years of the nineteenth century, by 1908 only a handful of 'teachers' in the West truly understood its concepts and could apply them to the field of teaching and community building. It seems that most of the Bahá'ís who did understand this were trained, as Alma was, by Mírzá Abu'l-Faḍl. He was her role model and had given her a solid knowledge of the Faith which she used her entire life. He accompanied her into the field of service in small steps. He started by including her in his Bible study classes, then he supported her early teaching meetings and prepared her to explain the Bahá'í truth to friends from church and at church. He introduced her to the concept of devotionals by bringing the community together to pray for 'Abdu'l-Bahá and he inspired the Washington community to arrange their first Bahá'í celebration, the Declaration of the Báb, in May of 1904. When Alma finished his course, he asked her to support teaching meetings in Baltimore and to write to 19 believers who no longer attended meetings.

Before Alma left for pilgrimage, she was hoping that an experienced, dedicated Bahá'í teacher would come to Stuttgart to accompany the new believers while she was in the Holy Land. The large community of new believers had not yet celebrated any Bahá'í Holy Days. She felt that they would benefit from steadfast support as they developed their Bahá'í identity. 'Abdu'l-Bahá sent Marion Jack to Germany to support the new believers while Alma was on pilgrimage.

Alma and Marion Jack met in Switzerland in the summer of 1908 for a short vacation before Alma's departure. After Marion arrived in Stuttgart in September, she invited her friend Jean Stannard, whom she had met in 'Akká, to visit and teach in Stuttgart without first discussing the idea with Alma.

Jean (Jane) Stannard (1865–1944) was an Englishwoman who had been a psychometrics practitioner and a writer for the Psychic Press, a well-received lecturer, and a delegate to the 1900 Psychological Congress in Paris in 1900.[2] Earlier in 1908 she had learned about Sufism in India, where she first heard about the Bahá'í Faith. Shortly afterwards she proceeded to 'Akká to meet 'Abdu'l-Bahá to learn more, and while she was there, she met Marion Jack. 'Abdu'l-Bahá advised Jean to read the Hidden Words and to return to the West. At first, she did not want to accept His advice, but she finally read the Hidden Words, which had a great effect on her.[3]

When Marion informed Alma that she had invited Jean to teach in Stuttgart, Alma asked her, 'What does Mrs Stannard teach?' Marion answered, 'She has the latest information about the Sufis in India.' Alma responded, 'What do we have to do with the Sufis?' Alma and Marion did not agree on Jean's possible role as a Bahá'í teacher in Germany. Alma was uncomfortable with a new believer coming to Stuttgart to teach the German friends; the other Western teachers who had visited Stuttgart were experienced Bahá'ís, and many new Bahá'ís in Stuttgart had been believers longer than Jean, who had joined the Faith only five months earlier.

Jean Stannard arrived in October 1908, while Alma was in Leipzig. When Alma returned to Stuttgart to repack and depart for her pilgrimage, Marion introduced Mrs Stannard to Alma at the Ecksteins' farewell party celebrating Alma's departure on this first pilgrimage to the Holy Land. Mr Braun's kind speech of gratitude for Alma's services as a Bahá'í teacher in Stuttgart impressed Miss Jack, but surprised Mrs Stannard, who seemed uncomfortable.[4]

Before leaving Stuttgart, Alma had asked Mr Eckstein to serve as the Bahá'í teacher for the community while she was gone, and he had accepted.[5] From their conversation, Alma felt that Mrs Stannard supported teachings from esoteric schools of thought, not purely the Bahá'í teachings. Afraid of the confusion this might cause the German believers, Alma asked Wilhelm Herrigel and Margarethe not to visit or invite Mrs Stannard while she was gone. Although she meant to keep the new believers focused solely on Bahá'í concepts, instead she left them feeling suspicious. Unintentionally, Alma had planted a seed of disunity, especially since Marion Jack and Dr Fisher were in support of the idea of Mrs Stannard as a teacher for the German friends. It was a critical phase of community building. The believers still had not yet received any response from 'Abdu'l-Bahá to their petitions, they had had no personal contact with Him, and translated Bahá'í material was scarce.

Fanny and Alma returned to Stuttgart from their pilgrimage in December 1908. Fanny was eager to meet the Stuttgart community, and Alma was very anxious to finally deliver 'Abdu'l-Bahá's answer to the supplications of the German believers. When the two sisters arrived at the 'Regular Meeting' they were surprised to find 'a non-Bahá'í Doctor giving a strange talk with surprising contents' at the request of Mrs Stannard. Alma and Fanny, anxious to change the topic, shared with the believers their first Tablet from 'Abdu'l-Bahá, which had been 'revealed during our stay in that Sacred Place' on 12 November 1908 and translated by 'Abdu'l-Bahá's 'youngest daughter' Munavvar Khánum:

O ye Daughters and Sons of the Kingdom!
    When the proclamation of God was exalted and spread in the East and West and the souls became attracted to the

words of God and heard the call with perfect devotion, joy, happiness and gladness, all the veils of doubt were torn and they were saved from imitating their fathers and ancestors; they beheld with their own eyes and not with those of others; they heard with their own ears, and not through the ears of others, and they comprehended with their own minds and not through the minds of others. Such souls were the Lovers of Light and when they beheld the Morn of Reality and the Light of the Divine sun, they became attracted, enkindled and believed in the Kingdom of God. They became the receivers of Benevolence and the manifestors of Light, because of the Rising Point of the mysteries.

They chanted the verses of Righteousness and turned unto the Kingdom of Abha. Blessed are such souls who have recognized the Promised Beauty and have entered under the shadow of the Lord of Hosts.

Such souls are today the Army of Salvation, they are the Hosts of Light, they are occupied with heavenly victories in the East and West and are engaged in dominating the hearts in Asia and America. At every moment, they receive assistance from the Kingdom of Abha, and every day an Army will descend to them from the Supreme Concourse; this is why you see that when a single person will reach a country or city and begin to teach, he will at once see his words having great effect in the Holy Souls and the light of assurance and belief will shine in splendor.

The call of the kingdom is like a spirit, it produces sudden effect in the nerves, arteries, hearts and souls and regenerates the people; baptizes them with Water, Spirit and Fire; the second birth will be produced and new people will be raised; but other souls are like those Christ mentioned in the Gospel, saying that they have hearts but do not comprehend, and I cured them.

In short, I say that these souls were awakened and quickened by the Proclamation of God, but the others are still in ignorance, doubtful and deprived from the Sea of Life, and are deprived of the Benevolence of the Lord of Signs, have become shareless from the Heavenly Blessings; portionless and remote of the Heavenly Beauties; they have soiled themselves with the things of this perishable world and neglected the Everlasting World and Eternal Life.

They satisfied themselves with a drop and became shareless from the waves of the Sea; they attracted their hearts to a ray of the sun and became remote and indifferent to the Sun of Reality.

It is a source of great regret that a man in this enlightened age and Divine Century will become deprived from the heavenly blessings.

If a tree will not become fertile and green through these Life-giving Breezes of the Spring Season, and will not bring forth blossoms and fruits and leaves, then in what season may it become verdant and fertile and at what time will it bear fruit.

Be assured, it will be forever deprive, and for all eternity hopeless.

Now you ought to give thanks to God that you have attained to a share of the effulgences of the Sun of Reality and have had a portion from the Heavenly Grace.

Having heard the Call of God, you have attained to Life through the Breezes of the Holy Spirit, and have entered into the Eternal World and received Everlasting Mercy.

You have attained to such favors that you are able to shine forever, like unto the Morning Star, through Centuries and Ages. Like the life-giving breezes of the Paradise of Abha, you will become the Cause of Eternal Life for many people.[6]

After listening to this Tablet revealed by Abdu'l-Bahá, some believers remarked that it was strange to be addressed as 'Daughters and Sons of the Kingdom'.[7] Perhaps such words were not familiar to them, or they had expected to receive individual responses to their petitions. In any case, Alma was disappointed at their response. She attributed their cool attitude to the effect of the teachings brought by Mrs Stannard. She felt that the community was no longer focused on the Centre of the Covenant.

After the meeting, Jean Stannard looked very uneasy as Alma gave her a personal message from 'Abdu'l-Bahá. She replied that she would leave and that she knew that Alma did not wish her to stay. Alma explained that she was 'only giving her the message that 'Abdu'l-Bahá asked her to give'. Mrs Stannard left shortly afterwards for Paris, where she kept up a correspondence with some of the Stuttgart believers.

Esoteric spiritualism was very popular at the turn of the century, especially amongst the upper-middle and upper classes of white Western society. It attracted people who were interested in esoteric spiritual powers, contact with the dead, healing through solely spiritual means, etc. Because of their deep interest in spiritualism and psychic powers, most of the large group of new Bahá'ís in Stuttgart had been members of the Swedenborg Society and/or Christian Scientists before accepting the Bahá'í Faith. Both the Christian Science Church and the Swedenborg Society focus on the powers of individual spiritualism. Christian Science teaches that sickness can be healed by the power of prayer alone, while Swedenborg claimed to have spiritual powers and contact with spirits.

Alma taught that Bahá'u'lláh fulfilled the Biblical prophecy of the Day of God. She intended to turn the focus from personal powers to the power of faith in Bahá'u'lláh and 'Abdu'l-Bahá to bring the promised Kingdom of God on earth. Her teaching method relied mostly on Biblical scripture and prophecy. She taught others, as she herself had learned from Mírzá Abu'l-Faḍl, to focus on the Manifestation and the powers He had released for the regeneration of all mankind.

This was a critical moment in German Bahá'í history. It was an opportunity to join the people together from the different perspectives to find the one true spiritual light. Spiritual paths start at many different places, but they all lead to the Covenant. Unfortunately, personal preferences and personalities distracted the friends and made it difficult to find unity. From Paris, Jean Stannard encouraged the Stuttgart friends to continue the esoteric meetings that she had started, and Alma wrote home in late December 1908:

I have some real hard work to do after Miss Jack and Mrs. Stannard later wrote to the believers here that Miss Barney approves the circles and they have organized them there. I am sorry for her soul, the Master spoke very severe and hard or rather earnest.[8]

The letter implies that certain esoteric meetings or circles were not uncommon in the Paris community. Alma believed strictly in the power of 'Abdu'l-Bahá alone, and she felt sorry for any believer who could not share that perspective.

It is interesting to note that at this point Jean Stannard was a new believer and eager to teach her understanding of the Faith. In time, she developed into a strong Bahá'í and made important contributions to the Bahá'í Faith throughout the rest of her life. In 1925, she rendered a valuable service by establishing the International Bahá'í Bureau in Geneva at the request of Shoghi Effendi, to facilitate expansion of the Bahá'í Faith in Europe.[9] The Bureau also maintained Bahá'í relations with the League of Nations and later the United Nations, and so in some sense could be seen as the forerunner of what is today known as the Bahá'í International Community, although with a much more limited scope. This illustrates how each Bahá'í was special in their own way and each had their own contribution to make.

This was a time of transition and learning; the very early days of community building. There was a lot to learn about unity and how personalities must not distract us from our purpose. In January 1909, these clashes shed darkness on the teaching work. Soon Sydney Sprague also encouraged opposition towards Alma, who wrote home:

> Don't worry about me, Mr. Sprague nor Mrs. Stannard cannot harm me much, they both only hurt themselves and prevent their own spiritual development. Both write to the believers here and do all they can to belittle me and why? –The Master is with me so I do not worry at all – it only makes the work a little hard...[10]

Bahá'u'lláh teaches that absolute truth exists only with God. Truth leads to unity when it is obtained through honest and sincere collective search using prayer, consultation and the Bahá'í writings to guide it. If in the process, conflict or contention arises, 'the truth will remain hidden'.[11] There was only one power alive that could bring such unity: 'Abdu'l-Bahá. Only He could guide with the balance needed to maintain unity and bring the diverse perspectives into a peaceful solution.

At the end of 1908 or the beginning of 1909, Alma finally received the long overdue translation of a Tablet from 'Abdu'l-Bahá through Ahmad Sohrab in Washington: it was the Master's answer to the personal supplications and petitions of the German believers! It had been lost, awaiting translation in Washington for more than nine months. In this special Tablet Abdu'l-Bahá emphasized those things that create a united Bahá'í community:

> O Thou beloved maidservant of God.
>
> Thy letter was received. Praise be to God thou hast become the cause of the diffusions of the Fragrances in the countries of the north. The guidance of the people is greater than presenting one's self in the Blessed Spot; for any soul who sacrifices his life (serves faithfully) for the promotion of the Word of God, his real country is the Blessed Spot and he is near to it with his heart and soul, nay, rather, he is its Eternal dweller. I hope that thou mayest be assisted to visit the Holy Land. Abdul Baha is always thy Companion and thy Confident; He sings the same melody and chants the same songs with thee. He beholds the services of the friends and thanks them with gratitude for their hardships and troubles. The great feast that you celebrated on the occasion of the appearance of His Highness the Bab, likewise the feasts of nineteen days produced great rejoicing in the hearts of the believers. Whenever the friends and the maidservants of the Merciful gather together, read the Tablets and the words, interchange ideas and deliver eloquent speeches the heavenly blessings descend, the spiritual

food becomes present, the celestial bounty is unveiled, the confirmations of the Holy Spirit descends [sic] uninterruptedly, spiritual development is attained and attractions of heart realized.

Convey respectful greetings to Miss Doring [Döring] on my behalf and say, 'The Supreme Concourse praised the Feast that thou didst celebrate and the melodies of Miss Staebler [Stäbler], Miss Betzold and Mr. Brown [Braun] were heard by the Angels of Heaven.'

Announce yearning greetings to Mr. and Mrs. Herrigel and say, 'Indeed ye have celebrated a Bahai Feast and have sought for Supreme Bounties. I am very pleased with you and ask confirmation and assistance in your behalf so that that household may become ready to receive the Graces of the Lord and its good name descends to future generations and cycles and be encircled with the help of the Kingdom of God.'

Declare greetings and salutations on my behalf to Mr. Eckstein and say, 'I ask God that thou mayest crown thy Head with the diadem of servitude – to the Beauty of Abha and become conducive to the progress of the Cause of God.'

Convey on my behalf the wonderful Abha greetings to Dr. Fisher.

O thou beloved maidservant of God! Whereas innumerable people enter the meeting and ask difficult questions turn thy face to the Kingdom of Abha, ask assistance, open thy mouth and speak with perfect courage and strength the Holy Spirit shall confirm thee.

O thou beloved maidservant of God! With heart and soul, I am with thee. Rest thou assured thou shalt be assisted in such wise that you will stand astonished . . .[12]

In this manner, Miss Stäbler, Miss Betzold and Mr Braun, Mr and Mrs Herrigel, and Mr Eckstein were first mentioned in a Tablet revealed by the Master, followed by the Tablet Alma brought with her from her pilgrimage which addressed the Stuttgart community as 'Sons and Daughters of the Kingdom'.

These words confirmed how much the Master knew about the spiritual capacity of the friends, although they had not yet met. And His words 'Like the life-giving breezes of the Paradise of Abhá, you will become the Cause of Eternal Life for many people' unveiled their glorious future ahead.

Subtle diversions are challenges that sometimes have unexpected outcomes. The less one knows about the Bahá'í teachings, the more one is inclined to mix personal ideas with them. The great Bahá'í teacher Mírzá Abu'l-Faḍl told his students to put their notes aside once they understood who 'Abdu'l-Bahá was, and to turn to Him only. This was challenging in 1908, since the early believers did not have access to an abundance of Holy Writings. True knowledge is acquired solely through the Holy Writings, the source of prosperity for mankind.

18

GERMANY 'AS LONG AS POSSIBLE'

When Ahmad Sohrab asked 'Abdu'l-Bahá if Alma Knobloch could assist Dr Fisher in 1907, He had replied, 'Truly I say, the beloved maid-servant of God, Miss Alma Knobloch, is very much acceptable for this service – thou hast done well to choose her. She is accepted by all means, but regarding her stay in Germany, she must stay as long as possible.'[1] But how long was 'as long as possible'? Alma may have felt that she might not see her mother again, but Fanny was not planning to financially support Alma for 13 years!

Reflecting on the speedy growth of the Faith in Stuttgart between 1907 and 1908, the sisters began to consider the duration of Alma's stay in Germany. Several times the question arose, 'is Alma needed in Stuttgart?' Alma felt that it was her calling to support the new believers so they could become strong in their faith; consolidation, the most important phase of the community building process, was just beginning. Also at that time, Alma was so busy with meetings and organizing community activities, travel teachers, visitors and teaching that she could scarcely imagine leaving.

Meanwhile, back at home in the United States the financial pinch was a challenge for Fanny, who was working full time for the Viavi pharmaceutical company. Of course, Fanny had generously offered to support Alma's efforts in Germany, but indefinite support was not what she was thinking of! When the family at home heard that Dr Fisher wanted to marry Alma, they initially wondered if that could relieve them of their financial obligation for her. Alma assured them that this was not a solution.

One of the secrets of Alma's teaching success had been indeed that she was financially independent. She reflected on this in a letter to Pauline, saying she was trying to 'strengthen all and especially the weak and not let people of means and position have any influence on one, of course this I am able to do through the kindness of Fanny. I am under no obligation and can work easy in that direction which is really the secret of my success, relying on God and the guidance of Abdul Baha, you have been helping us most wonderfully.'[2]

Alma prayed for financial relief for Fanny in her Viavi sales work.[3] Her prayers were answered in February 1908, when Fanny's boss, Mr Sharp, increased Fanny's salary. Alma had also considered the possibility of opening Viavi sales in Germany or whether Amalie could come to Germany so Alma could care for her. Alma wrote to Fanny, 'I often wish for dear Mama, the air is so different here, and it would be grand to have her here if I am to teach as long as possible, I wonder how long that means; there are so many that need Viavi, but if I start that topic it is the end of spiritual talk and I hear of nothing but pains and what their grandmother had. So, I don't like to talk about it very much.'[4]

As we have seen, during their pilgrimage in late 1908, Fanny asked the Master, 'Shall Alma return to Stuttgart?' and He replied, 'Why not? Yes, she has been confirmed in her work there by the Holy Spirit, why should she go elsewhere? When a tree in the forest is ablaze others will be ignited.'[5]

Realizing that Alma's work in Germany would be long-term, the sisters seriously considered alternative ways to make her service financially sustainable. Since 1902, Fanny and Alma had invested in real estate in Washington DC and the greater DC area, which they rented to generate extra money.

Alma contacted Mary Stuart Glassford, Head of the London Viavi Office. In July 1908, she decided not to work for the Viavi office in London, as the salary conditions were not attractive. Although she was a firm believer in and a heavy user of the

Viavi products, she decided to order Viavi products for those interested through Fanny instead. Alma and Fanny generated some income from selling them, but shipping to Europe was a challenge.

In December 1908, Alma asked Pauline to ask 'Abdu'l-Bahá on her upcoming pilgrimage whether she, Alma, should work for Viavi in Germany to relieve Fanny.[6] Pauline's letters on this have not survived, but after Pauline's pilgrimage in May of 1909, Alma wrote to her that she was hoping to open Germany for Viavi, but Miss Glassford had not yet arrived.[7] Later Miss Glassford invited Alma to visit her in London[8] and in 1911 Alma and Marion Jack met her there. She offered Alma 30 per cent on investment if Alma invested 500 pounds. But Alma did not have money to invest. She considered giving Viavi lectures to raise money.[9] In the end, she never worked for Viavi and Fanny supported Alma with her salary and the income from the Washington properties for her entire stay in Germany.

The sisters wondered if the German Bahá'ís would be willing to cover Alma's expenses to support Alma's work in their community. Alma responded to Pauline,

> Later on the people will be very glad to assist and pay expenses for the Bahá'í teachers, at present I am only glad that I am able to break ice get them to accept the truth. It costs many trips and earnest labour; it is very fine simply to give the beautiful teachings, but it means hard work to make believers of them with the help of God and this has been favoured me and words fail to express my joy and thanksgiving. You, as our mother in the truth, know what it is. Therefore, you can appreciate the result and success of the labour here traces its benefactors to Fanny and you our dear spiritual mother and provider, for what could I do without Fanny?[10]

Alma often wrote to Fanny and thanked her for her financial sacrifices. She acknowledged that she could not 'serve as she does' if it were not for her freedom and material independence.¹¹ Alma taught people regardless of their financial success and enjoyed relationships to people, with no obligations.

Apart from the financial challenges, there was the question of citizenship and the right to German residency. Citizenship was an issue because when Alma had left, as a child, she was a citizen of Saxony. In 1871, when she was living in the United States, Saxony became part of the new country of Germany. In December 1908 Alma wrote, 'Please write at once about my papers in America or if I should remain a German. Dear Papa never wished to become an American so perhaps it would please him if at least one of his girls remained one [German].'¹²

Because 'Abdu'l-Bahá had asked her to remain in Germany, Alma began to process the necessary papers to become an official German citizen.¹³ Her landlady, Mrs Beiswanger, referred her to someone for help. The process became complicated, and the police got involved.

By the end of May 1909, Alma still could not get her papers legally processed. She wrote to 'Abdu'l-Bahá asking Him to give her work in America. 'Abdu'l-Bahá's daughter Munavvar Khánum responded that Alma 'should be very thankful to be called to work in His new field!'¹⁴ The German government began an assessment process to be sure that Alma would not become needy or rely on the German social system.

In August 1909, Fanny sent legal papers from the United States confirming that their father was not and had never become an American citizen.¹⁵ At last Alma could write to Zittau, where her birth was registered, to request the German papers regarding citizenship. She wrote to Pauline, 'I had to make a number of statements to find out if I am still a Saxon, or whether they will consider I belong.'¹⁶ Emil Ruoff translated Alma's official documents from the United States.¹⁷ In September, after nine stressful months, Alma was called to court where she learned that the papers from Bautzen confirmed that both Alma and her father were still Saxons. The next step was for the court to decide if she would be accepted as a German citizen from Saxony, which they did. They told her she would no longer have any trouble with the police.¹⁸

Later Alma discovered that her landlady had withheld the important letter from Alma's attorney that proved that she and her father came from Zittau.[19] Faith in 'Abdu'l-Bahá had helped her make it through these uncertain times. Alma wrote, 'All the time I thought Abdu'l Bahá is helping me and I tried not to think about it, but it was hard.'[20] Alma was now an undisputed German citizen and would be able to extend her stay in Germany as long as needed with no further trouble.

19

BEYOND STUTTGART

From the very beginning, the German believers shared their new religion with friends and family outside of Stuttgart. In mid-February 1908, Adolf Eckstein, the librarian in the Working Committee, travelled to Frankfurt, where he shared the Bahá'í teachings with a friend who offered to make copies of all translated Tablets.[1] By March 1908, Mr Alfred Morstadt, Alma's 'first spiritual son', had also left for Frankfurt planning to 'spread the message'. Unfortunately, he is never mentioned again.

Throughout 1908, Alma and Margarethe visited the believers in Heilbronn, Weinberg and Pfadelbach.[2] Miss Scheuerle and Miss Scheiling and their families formed a Bahá'í group in Pfadelbach,[3] while Miss Schaefer's family accepted the Faith in Heilbronn.

At the beginning of 1908, Alma and Margarethe visited the Döring family in Gera. Margarethe's brother Kurt accepted the teachings of Bahá'u'lláh,[4] and his fiancée wrote a letter to Abdu'l-Bahá.[5] Later in the year, she accepted Bahá'u'lláh while visiting in Stuttgart.[6]

Mrs Palm, Alma's first landlady who had hosted the first unity meeting in her home in the summer of 1907, moved to Tübingen, the home of the renowned Theological Ministries of Europe. She invited Alma to come and share the teachings there.[7] Alas, no community emerged in Tübingen; instead, in 1910 a young Pastor from there printed articles in the Stuttgart newspaper labelling the Bahá'í Faith a 'Muslim sect in Stuttgart' and calling for steps to be taken against its spreading.[8] The articles warned about Alma and her charms!

The First Bahá'ís in Bohemia, Austria (now Czech Republic)

Margarethe Döring's friend Miss Rosa Kosky became a new believer in Stuttgart in 1909.[9] Soon afterwards, while she was on vacation in Saaz, Bohemia, Miss Kosky met Mr Karl Krüttner.[10] After listening to Miss Kosky, Mr Krüttner quickly became the first Bahá'í in what is today's Czech Republic, which was at that time part of the Austro-Hungarian Empire. The first Bahá'í from Austria was Miss Riehmann, whom Alma had met in 1907.

Mr Krüttner was a teacher who had lost faith in the Catholic Church and was searching for truth. The Bahá'ís in Stuttgart sent him Bahá'í literature, and his heart was touched. He and Alma exchanged letters and Alma was amazed at how 'advanced' he was. By December 1909, two of his colleagues in Bohemia had accepted the Bahá'í teachings and formed a little Bahá'í centre to study the teachings of 'Abdu'l-Bahá. Alma wrote, 'It seems that 'Abdu'l-Bahá has prepared the souls of all these seekers, he received some wonderful tablets from 'Abdu'l-Bahá.'[11]

In Bohemia, after the churches warned their congregations about the Bahá'í Faith, Mr Krüttner had a rough time. Alma wrote to her family, 'In Austria we are successful through Mr. Krüttner and there will be more to arise and spread the Cause.'[12] Krüttner spread the teachings amongst other teachers and taught three new believers,[13] starting a 'little' Bahá'í assembly.[14] He wrote to Alma that his 'circle is most enthusiastic and the different teachers have written most spiritual letters, telling how their souls leaped for joy when studying the teachings, how very happy they are to find kindred'.[15] Mr Krüttner wrote an article in a teacher's newsletter which closed with the names of other Bahá'í books printed in Germany and giving Wilhelm Herrigel's address. From this article, Herrigel received more than a dozen orders for the Hidden Words and for his translation of Sydney Sprague's book about his trip to India.[16] Mr Krüttner wrote beautiful letters and sent a long list of names of teachers who were interested in Saaz. He planned to visit Stuttgart in the summer of 1910.[17]

Mr Krüttner was mentioned in a Tablet to Alma in March 1910 in which 'Abdu'l-Bahá asked her to give him greetings and the following message: she should tell Mr Krüttner that those who have come to the light of truth and found the way to the Kingdom of God are happy indeed; that he had advanced into the straight path and heard the call of the Lord of Hosts. 'Abdu'l-Bahá expressed the hope that Mr Krüttner would take such strides in the Cause as to attain his ultimate hope, and would act according to the teachings of Bahá'u'lláh.[18] In another Tablet, the Master wrote, 'Convey my greetings to Herr Krüttner . . . I supplicate to the Divine Glory, and ask for them bright hearts, merciful spirits, seeing eyes and hearing ears.'[19]

20

THE STUTTGART BOARD OF COUNSEL

Just as the potential of the individual believer unfolds by the power of the Word of God, so the Bahá'í community and its institutions are generated gradually over time through a dynamic and interactive process. The Bahá'í Administrative Order is a gift of God given to mankind through the Revelation of Bahá'u'lláh. It unfolds through the power of the Covenant which cleanses and protects the Bahá'ís and their communities.

When Alma arrived in Stuttgart in August 1907, there were only five active Bahá'ís, including Alma. That month, Alma and Margarethe began actively teaching the Faith and the community grew quickly. Alma's landlady and her new friends from the Air Bath joined that summer. The first believers from the Christian Science Church joined in October. By the end of 1907, a petition was sent to 'Abdu'l-Bahá signed by 31 believers in Stuttgart,[1] and by the end of February 1908 there were at least 50 active believers and at least another 50 who participated in Bahá'í meetings. New believers naturally brought with them their friends, family members, and the organizational concepts and structures they were familiar with.

An intellectually strong core group of men (Eckstein, Rieger, Herrigel and Fisher) emerged who had previously served in various administrative functions at the Christian Science Church. They quickly began to consider ways to systematically organize the believers and make the Holy Texts available. As the group grew, so did the need for organization. The Word of God would be spread through translations, publications, lectures, teaching activities, and celebrations, all of which would be guided by some sort of committee. In Stuttgart, that committee would inevitably consist primarily of new believers, who themselves were still learning about their new religion. The word committee is used here because in 1908, the word 'assembly' was often used to indicate a group of believers and was not an institution or a formal organizational structure.

Most of the members of the Stuttgart Baháʼí community had entered the Faith in one of two main groups. The first group was composed of the women who had heard about the Baháʼí Faith through Alma and Margarethe Döring at the Frauen Club, the Air Bath, and through other women. The second group consisted of mostly socially and financially well-established men with their families, primarily from the Christian Science Church. The challenge to unify these people from their diverse social, economic, and religious backgrounds was further complicated by the underlying personal tensions between Alma and Dr Fisher. The only way to emerge united was to focus on the Master's teachings and writings and the power of prayer. Many prayed for their success. On 27 February 1909 ʻAbdu'l-Baháʼs wife Muníríh Khánum wrote to Alma that she had been praying in the Holy Shrines for the unity of the German Baháʼí community:

> Most loving Bahai greetings from this Blessed Mt. of God to the dear maid-servant in His Holy Vineyard in Service Miss Alma Knobloch
>
> Beloved Sister in His Love!
> ... Earnestly I supplicate the divine threshold to remove from among the beloved ones of God whatever most affords ground for discord and disagreement.
> The fundamental basis of the Bahai Revelation, as you know, is love. Hence upon no other foundation can any Bahai edifice long stand. May you ever be a means for this longed-for end.
> We often think of you ... [2]

To foster unity, Alma focused on increasing participation during meetings. She encouraged men who had not read before to read at the Friday meeting, and organized the Feast on 21 March 1909 so that the young ladies could read out loud for the first time. This meant a lot to them and they practised for it.³

'Abdu'l-Bahá surely wanted the two American teachers to accompany the new Bahá'ís to build a united community. Having given Alma considerable attention while she was on pilgrimage in November 1908, 'Abdu'l-Bahá now turned His attention to Dr Fisher. He greatly honoured Dr Fisher by inviting him on pilgrimage for eleven days in the Holy Land to witness one of the most dramatic and important moments in Bahá'í history: the interment of the sacred remains of the Báb in the Shrine on Mount Carmel on 21 March 1909.⁴ The Master told him that it was a great favour for him to be present and would be the cause of spiritual upliftment for him.⁵

Upon his return to Germany, Dr Fisher shared little information about his pilgrimage. He recalled only that 'Abdu'l-Bahá 'wore a blue robe under his coat' and 'he heard him warn-groan' [sic].⁶ Not long afterward, Mírzá Munír Zayn, one of the Master's secretaries, sent Alma a detailed account of the ceremony at the request of 'Abdu'l-Bahá.⁷ This account was later published in *Star of the West*.

Fisher told Alma that 'Abdu'l-Bahá wanted him to travel to London to learn Persian and that He had also said the day would come when she would regret not having married him. Alma was puzzled and could not believe that 'Abdu'l-Bahá would have ever said anything like that; she accepted it as a sign that Dr Fisher was still hurt.⁸

In the winter of 1908/09, Alma realized that Mr Eckstein and Mr Rieger were no longer attending the general community meetings.⁹ At the beginning of 1909, Dr Fisher invited them to the home of Mr Imhoff to build a network called the 'Board of Counsel' to arrange for the publishing and distribution of translations. Soon afterwards, this self-proclaimed Board of Counsel informed the community that they would control all finances and circulation of Bahá'í literature.¹⁰ This was a great surprise to many community members, who did not accept it at all. Since it lacked the support of the community, the Board of Counsel collapsed.

After the failed attempt to form the Board of Counsel, Mr Eckstein 'lost interest' and spent his time with Mrs von Sonntag, his teacher at the Christian Science Church. She no longer liked the Bahá'ís and encouraged him to keep away from them.[11] In the summer of 1910, Mrs Eckstein sent Alma a card and a box of chocolates, but not a word about her husband.[12]

Two of the early believers, Mr and Mrs Imhoff, returned their Bahá'í literature to Alma at the beginning of May, with a note saying they were sorry for her and prayed that her eyes would open and she would accept that she was following a 'false prophet'.[13] Despite their withdrawal, Mr Eckstein and Mr Imhoff continued to attend the weekly translation meetings at the Herrigel and Ruoff homes.[14]

Things seemed fragmented, but then these beautiful words from 'Abdu'l-Bahá arrived and brought confirmation and light and hope:

To the favored servant in the threshold Margaret Döring

He is God!

O thou candle of the love of God!
 Thy letter was received. Its contents emanated from a spiritual heart and indicated advancement toward the Kingdom of God. Ye must be infinitely thankful and grateful to Miss Knobloch for she became the cause of guidance and directed from the darkness of the world of nature and became enlightened by the illumination of the Kingdom which is supernatural. Love greater than this is not possible. As ye remain firm and steadfast, the confirmation of the Holy Spirit shall descend, The Hosts of the Kingdom become triumphant and the symphony of the Supreme Concourse reach the ears.
 Praise be to God that the voice of the Divine Trumpet

has moved the East and West; spiritual emotions are stirred; the meetings of the Kingdom uninterrupted; the bounties of the True One overflowing; the doors of the Kingdom open, and the Spring of the water of Life bursting forth. Therefore, engage yourself in rendering thanks to the Lord of the Kingdom for He has bestowed such Mercy and Bounty . . .

. . . The two garments sent by thee were accepted.[15]

This was the first Tablet directed to Margarethe, and when she received it she was surprised, cried, and read it over and over again. She became increasingly steadfast and was of great support to Alma.

In June, Alma received another Tablet from 'Abdu'l-Bahá in which He expressed his joy that 'in every place you have visited you have beheld the signs of confirmation'. He asked her to convey greetings to Mr Braun, Mr Ruoff and Mr Herrigel and to tell them on his behalf: 'Happy is thy condition, for thou art engaged in the service of the Kingdom and are heralding the appearance of the Realm of Might.' He also asked for the booklet by Mr Sprague to be translated.[16]

Having realized that only 'Abdu'l-Bahá could restore unity to this diverse group, Dr Fisher told Mr Herrigel to ask the Master for consent for the Board of Counsel. 'Abdu'l-Bahá's response arrived at the beginning of August of 1909 in His first Tablet to Wilhelm and Marie Herrigel:

July 3, 1909
Through Mírzá Ahmad Sohrab to Mr. William Herrigel and Mrs. Marie Herrigel

He is God!

O ye two seekers of the Kingdom:-
    Thy epistle was received. Thou hast written that Dr Fisher arrived suddenly and conveyed to you the Greetings of Abdul-Baha.

THE STUTTGART BOARD OF COUNSEL

> The Friends of Stuttgart must be so attracted by the Fragrances of God that the spiritual Glad tidings may descend uninterruptedly upon them from the city of Acca, that the hearts may communicate with each other and the souls may gladden and rejoice with each other . . .
>
> The time has not yet come for the election of a Counsel Board in Germany. Should you desire to translate any epistle you may translate the Words of Paradise, Tarazat, the Glad tidings.
>
> Thou hast asked permission to visit Acca. Wait thou a little while the proper time will come.
>
> I hope from the bounty and favor of the Blessed Perfection that day by day ye may increase your love for God and exert yourselves to display unity and harmony among each other.
>
> Upon ye be Bahá El Abhá[17]

Since Abdu'l-Bahá wrote, 'The time has not yet come for the election of a Counsel Board in Germany', and did not give the Herrigels permission for pilgrimage, this must have been as disappointing to them as it had been for Alma back in 1904. Unfortunately, Marie and Wilhelm Herrigel never made a pilgrimage to the Holy Land.

Alma wrote, 'Mr. Herrigel's Tablet made a deep impression on him, not having a word of praise and telling him to work for unity and harmony.'[18] Herrigel translated Mr Sprague's booklet during his vacation in Switzerland during that summer of 1909.[19]

At the end of September 1909, Mírzá Ahmad Yazdi, whose brother Alma and Fanny had met in Alexandria, visited Stuttgart for a few days.[20] The believers arranged a large reception for him at the Herrigel home. Alma was honoured that the Herrigels asked her to translate at that event.[21] The Herrigels were working towards unity, and the Master wrote to Alma: 'You have written that the beloved ones are daily progressing and will soon each become a teacher. I hope it will be so. Give glad tidings of Help and Assistance from the Divine Majesty and my part to Herr Herrigel. Let him know for a certainty that he will be confirmed.'[22]

In this way, 'Abdu'l-Bahá, the Master, illumined the path and guided the community. Those who emerge from crisis to victory become stronger and share the joy of confirmation.

21

THE ROLE OF WOMEN IN THE COMMUNITY

At the turn of the century, women lacked full citizenship rights in Germany, France, Great Britain, and the United States.[1] The first efforts by women to influence state policies in these countries were in the area of maternal and child welfare.[2] Indeed, the concept that 'a woman's place is in the home' had a notion of morality to it. In general, married women enjoyed a higher social status to those who were unmarried and earning wages. 'Maternalism' emerged successfully before feminism as a political movement to gain rights for women on behalf of their children. In those times, the interests of children came before the rights of mothers and women were 'expected to subordinate their gender-specific demands to male-controlled political and economic agendas'.[3] Nonetheless, as economic and political awareness grew, reform efforts began to expand.

Within a week of Alma's arrival in Stuttgart on 9 August 1907, the first International Women's Conference was held in that city, prior to and in conjunction with the first International Conference of Socialist Women which started on 17 August. The International Women's Conference focused mainly on winning voting rights for women workers. To coordinate this effort, a permanent secretariat was established in Stuttgart.[4] This had an effect, and in 1908 women obtained the right to belong to political organizations in Germany, but they were still subordinate to men and had no voting rights.

Married women in Germany were completely dependent on their husbands. Husbands took ownership of their wives' property at marriage, and they alone had complete decision-making power regarding residence, finances, property and custody of children until 1958. Married women needed written permission from their husbands to work in Germany until 1977! In Stuttgart, state law required female civil servants to give up their positions when they married. In contrast, unmarried women held the same legal property rights as men, but they earned poorer salaries and their contracts could be immediately terminated. Many working women could only afford to rent a single room with no kitchen to live in, hence the Stuttgart Frauen Club was a very important meeting place for working women to obtain their meals at an affordable price.

The Frauen Club was a main location for the teaching events in Stuttgart right from the start. It was where Alma gave the first public talk on the Bahá'í Faith in Germany on 27 October 1907.[5] After the Frauen Club relocated to a beautiful modern building in July 1909, the first social event that was held in the new building was a Bahá'í Unity Meeting hosted by Margarethe Döring and Rosa Kosky.[6] Many well-known Bahá'ís, including Louis Gregory, visited the Frauen Club. In 1913 'Abdu'l-Bahá spoke there at a Nineteen Day Feast.

The concept of gender equality was a major challenge for the early Bahá'ís, men and women alike, everywhere. It is one of the fundamental teachings of Bahá'u'lláh; however, its far-reaching implications are still unfolding. In August 1908, Mason Remey invited Alma to teach in Munich but, she wrote, 'as all here tell me I cannot go there alone, having the old idea that a girl cannot go anywhere alone, I will leave this work for the believers here, for several of them are fully able to teach and give the message in a very interesting and intelligible way and give the Bahá'í proofs'.[7] Alma turned down this exciting opportunity so as to conform with the expectations of the new Stuttgart Bahá'í community. From the start, she did not want to be provocative.

In April 1909, Wilhelm Herrigel offered to accompany Alma when she travelled to other places to help her teach. She was happy that he wanted to also teach people outside of Stuttgart. But during these times, Alma did not need an escort since she was mostly accompanied by her nephew Carl, Pauline and Joseph's 14–15-year-old son who lived with her in Stuttgart from March 1909 until 6 June 1910. Herrigel repeated his suggestion to her in May, saying that it was 'inappropriate for a woman, a girl, to travel to a city to teach alone. It would get people talking.' Alma felt that this comment was a further attempt by the men in the community to take control and 'crowd her out'.[8]

From the start, in the summer of 1907, Alma taught the faith to many single women who invited her to share the Bahá'í teachings with their families, friends and neighbours. This group included Margarethe Döring, Rosa Kosky, Mina Diegel, Anna Köstlin, and Julia and Elise Stäbler. Mrs Rosa Schwarz, Elise and Julia Stäbler were early believers whom Alma taught at the Air Bath in 1907. In August 1909, Elise Stäbler shared the teachings with friends on her holiday at a vacation home for working women in Thüringen.[9] In November 1909, Alma and Margarethe visited with the Stäblers in a recovery home for women in Bucherhof, Lorsch and shared the teachings with some of the women there. Rosa Schwarz and Alma taught a large group of Rosa's friends in the Stuttgart district of Degerloch.

Anna Köstlin lived in Esslingen with her mother, who was a sister of Marie Herrigel, Wilhelm Herrigel's wife. Anna never married; it seems that the community in Esslingen was less concerned with the married status of women. Together Alma and Anna taught many families and friends in Anna's neighbourhood, including Gustav Eger and his family, Max and Hugo Bender, Heinrich Schwab, Richard Kohler and Friedrich Schweizer. They also taught Annemarie Warnke, Anna's friend from school. Annemarie and Friedrich Schweizer married, the first Bahá'í marriage in Germany; their home in Zuffenhausen continues to serve as a centre for Bahá'í activities today. Annemarie Schweizer referred to Alma as her 'spiritual mother'.

Alma understood that the changing roles of women in the world were a challenge for the men. Her compassion enabled her to overlook mistakes, to forgive, and to give her whole heart for unity. Despite their disagreements, she continued to help

Fisher when she could. For example, by 4 December 1909, Fisher could not repay Herrigel the money he had borrowed for his pilgrimage in March. Fisher was angry, he felt that he had, 'sacrificed his business for the cause and was now getting pushed out'. Alma tried to restore unity by giving Fisher some of the money she received from Fanny.[10] But when by the end of December, Fisher's troubles had not subsided, and he still needed more money, Alma wrote,

> Regarding Dr. Fisher . . . I am almost afraid of him, but I know that I will be protected, he has a very hard time, he told me his conditions shortly before Christmas but I really have no money to give him and he says all the believers only give him nice words, but he has told me the same thing so often, thinking I could get money from America . . . too bad that he is always in such a condition for he really can be very nice, when he's cross he is horrid, can't see how he can be helped . . . my trying has proven a failure; he can't bear to give in to a girl and his ideas are so very different than mine.[11]

It is a tribute to her unfaltering faith and tenacity that Alma once more tried to help Dr Fisher. She wrote to Pauline:

> . . . my tests have been severe, but they were the cause of my growth, although they crushed me at times, it was only physical and not one moment spiritual, not wishing to be a stumbling block for the weak by venting my feelings, I master them and I use the first opportunity to prove true friendship and fellowship.[12]

The unresolved differences between Alma and Dr Fisher, and the underlying different social status and position of the women in the community, combined with the diverse understanding of gender equality, set the stage for the challenges ahead.

22

TWO DREAMS, TWO MEETINGS

At the end of December 1909, Alma wrote about a dream she had: 'The coming year will be a successful one, had a beautiful vision, a pillar of fire clear and bright and its flames reaching into the heavens. Fire always means for me that I will be successful in giving the teachings.'[1] But the early months of 1910 were to bring severe difficulties.

In the summer of 1909, Alma had been taking care of her young nephew Carl from Washington. The weekly translation meetings at the Ruoffs' house were well attended and provided the fountain of life for the community. It was the place where the Bahá'ís worked together to focus on the deeper meanings of the Word of God to faithfully express them in the German language.

Wilhelm Herrigel wanted to move all meetings to his home; he felt that the Ruoffs' house was too small to host the translation meetings. Alma knew that the translation meetings were important to the Ruoffs. As Alma was taking care of Carl, it was not easy for her to attend two meetings each week. Alma and Edwin Fisher divided their support responsibilities: she attended the meetings at the Ruoffs and Fisher attended the translation meetings at the Herrigels.[2]

Emil Ruoff was a good-hearted believer and was dedicated to the translation meetings. In late 1909 'Abdu'l-Bahá revealed a special Tablet for Babette and Emil Ruoff and advised the believers to publish this Tablet before any further publications:

To the Maidservant of God Mrs. Babitt [sic] Ruoff and Mr. Emil Ruoff
Upon them be Baha'o'llah!

He is God.

O ye two ignited candles of the Love of God!
    The country of Germany is like unto the glass and the beloved of God are like unto illumined lamps; it is assured that that country will become illumined.
    The letter ye have written was received and it indicated firmness and steadfastness in the Covenant and Testament. I hope that day by day you may increase your devotion, find a new power, and like unto a firm mountain, resist the trials and persecutions, and day by day ye may become more enlightened, receive more and more of the confirmation of the Kingdom of Abha, and be quickened through the breath of the Holy Spirit.
    Upon ye be Baha El Abha[3]

Unfortunately, the publication team led by Wilhelm Herrigel did not see the urgency of publishing this short Tablet. Instead, they were working on the publication of a book that Herrigel had written.

In addition to the weekly translation meetings, the community rented a hall at the Frauen Club for public meetings once a month. All the believers contributed to it, and all the friends who attended meetings at the Herrigel and Ruoff homes also attended the successful Frauen Club meetings. In January 1910, the Frauen Club unity meeting hosted by Alma and Professor Braun was the largest ever given.[4]

Then, at the beginning of February 1910, Alma had a second dream. In it, she was in a garden with her mother and a flower caught fire. Her mother stepped on it to put it out but burned her leg. Alma tried to prevent her from burning it further and told her mother she wished her own leg would have burned instead. Her mother looked at her lovingly.[5]

A few days later, on 7 February, Alma attended the Monday translation evening at the Ruoffs' home. The atmosphere was tense from the start; Alma noticed when she arrived that Professor Braun and Mr Ruoff did not come to meet her as they usually did. She felt something was out of place and began to repeat the Greatest Name quietly to herself. That night, Edwin Fisher was at the meeting and had brought with him a friend of Wilhelm Herrigel, from Zurich, Mr Schneebeli. Mr Schneebeli was not a Bahá'í, he was a medium. He announced to the friends that he could communicate telepathically directly with 'Abdu'l-Bahá. He offered to communicate with the Master on their behalf and answer their questions directly, telling them that they did not even need to ask him their questions out loud, as he could read minds. [6]

The first person to ask a question was Professor Braun, followed by Mr Ruoff. Alma was shocked, and told them, 'There is no such thing as a medium in the Bahá'í religion!' Mr Schneebeli proceeded to write down the answers to their questions. Alma's protesting against all this did not have much effect, for Mr Schneebeli was very persistent. Fisher asked questions out loud calling on God. Alma began to tremble from head to foot. Fisher finally asked if 'he would receive acknowledgments for his work done here?' and Mr Schneebeli wrote, 'The Master wishes to speak to Miss Knobloch. He has something to tell her.' Fisher urged the men not to listen to Alma, at which point Mr Schneebeli wrote, 'It was not right for any soul to be uneasy and annoyed when He wishes to speak to us.'

Again, Alma refused to participate. Mr Schneebeli responded, 'If you do not wish to be in the circle, then lay your hand on mine.' 'To keep peace', Alma placed her hand on his. Schneebeli then asked her to think of God, moving his hand about as he had done before and then reading the answers to questions out loud. Alma repeated the Greatest Name. Finally, Alma told those gathered, 'If people comprehend what the words of Bahá'u'lláh and 'Abdu'l-Bahá were, they need nothing else . . .'[7]

Later Alma learned that Mr Schneebeli had attended the Herrigels' translation meeting previously on 30 January, and that the men had been delighted and believed the Master spoke to them through this man. Alma convinced Professor Braun and Mr Ruoff that telepathy was not part of the Bahá'í teachings. Fisher said, 'Mr Schneebeli could tell them how to conduct meetings.'[8]

The effect that Mr Schneebeli had on the community was great. While the believers still needed to wait for translations of Tablets from the Master, Mr Schneebeli's 'telepathy' offered them a more immediate response. In addition, 'Abdu'l-Bahá often wrote in an indirect poetic language which some found difficult to understand. Furthermore, sometimes His answers or instructions were not the answers the members of the community wanted to hear. For example, 'Abdu'l-Bahá had asked the believers to publish His short Tablet to the Ruoffs, but Mr Schneebeli wrote that 'Abdu'l-Bahá wanted them to wait, so it was not published for a long time.[9] M. Schneebeli was actually confirming instructions from Wilhelm Herrigel and Edwin Fisher.

Alma was quite alone and looked for authoritative support to help the believers understand that the only way forward was to follow the instructions of 'Abdu'l-Bahá. On her pilgrimage in 1909, Dr Fareed, the Master's nephew and translator in Haifa, had told her that he would like to teach in Germany, so Alma had asked 'Abdu'l-Bahá if Dr Fareed could come to Germany to support her.[10] In 1910, Dr Fareed and Lua Getsinger passed through Europe on their way to the United States, but they did not stop in Germany.[11] On 24 July 1910, Sydney Sprague married Dr Fareed's sister, Farahangiz Khanum, the niece of 'Abdu'l-Bahá.[12] Neither Fareed nor Sprague supported Alma. At the time it may have been disappointing for her, but soon both Fareed and Sprague would leave the Faith.

Perhaps the relationship between Sydney Sprague and 'Abdu'l-Bahá's niece inspired Fisher in some odd way. When Fisher returned from 'Akká in 1909, he told the believers that 'Abdu'l-Bahá had given him permission to marry His youngest daughter Munavvar Khánum. Indeed, Fisher had been writing many letters to Haifa asking 'Abdu'l-Bahá if he could marry her.[13] Almost one year after Fisher's pilgrimage, there was no result. 'Abdu'l-Bahá 'supposedly speaking through Mr.

Schneebeli' confirmed that He desired the two to be married.[14] The Stuttgart believers felt that out of respect to 'Abdu'l-Bahá they must believe Fisher. Mr Schneebeli told them terrible things about Alma, encouraging the disunity in the community. To settle the situation, the believers asked Alma to write or even place a telegraph to Haifa to find out the truth.

On 21 February 1910, Munír Zayn, 'Abdu'l-Bahá's secretary in Haifa, wrote to Alma:

> My dear spiritual sister:
> Some days ago a precious Tablet being revealed on your behalf, will be sent to you very soon.
> Will you please advise and admonish our brother Dr. Fisher to stop any further writings or letters ful [sic] of confused and nonsense subjects to the holy presence of the Master; in fact, the contents of his letters are awful and quite absurd. We do earnestly pray for him to be delivered and released from such vain and void desires and passions.
> May God cure and heal him!!!
> We receive excellent news regarding the promulgation of the Cause on different parts of the world, they are delightful, charming and beyond expression!
> The Master is well and happy, at present He is staying in Haifa, and most of the members of the Household have gone to Egypt.
> Our love and greetings to all of you dear sisters and dear brothers.
> Yours faithfully,
>   Moneer Zaine[15]

Dear Sister, again I want you to make Dr. E. Fisher entirely free from such thought and let him become completely delivered from this imagination. It is impossible, absolutely impossible. Please make him clearly understand and precisely informed that the matter of marriage which he bears in mind shall never take place, it is an impossibility.

I was really ashamed to translate his letters which we

received succeedingly one after the other. 'If the world is to be destroyed, such thing shall never be accomplished,' said the Master. I think this is sufficient and there is no need of any more elucidation.

    Yours truly,
       Moneer Zaine[16]

Fisher never received a response to his letters on this subject. A message to Alma written on stationery from the Grand New Hotel, Haifa, states, 'A message to Alma Knoblock [sic] from Mirza Moneer. He said your letter of great importance was received . . . regarding the marriage of Abdul Baha's daughter, Abdul Baha says this is impossible. Mirza Moneer said he could not reply to Dr. Fisher's letter.'[17]

The two groups of believers now met at different meetings: those who supported Fisher's perspective and the work of Mr Schneebeli, and those who did not (Esslingen, Degerloch, Zuffenhausen groups in particular and some from Stuttgart). The Ecksteins no longer attended either meeting, preferring to return to the Christian Science Church.

Alma wrote to Fanny: 'It takes all I have to teach; it is a great strain to train souls believe me. To train them for business is difficult, but my word it takes so long to see what has been done, so much patience and love is required, really to love one's enemy, a self-sacrificing love and knowing and feeling that others are working against you.'[18] A month later she wrote, 'I am so thankful for your loving letters and those of Pauline, could not stand the pressure were it not for your kind lines, for I almost feel crushed and keep reading the Holy Tablets over and over again . . .'[19] And on 30 March:

> Mr. Herrigel had a large attendance at the hall, he gave the lecture by Mírzá Abu'l-Faḍl: to know God through love. I could not attend on account of a severe cold but had done all I could to advance it and made many calls to invite the friends. You know how much work there is that no one sees, still it must be done if we wish success. I am looking forward

to the time when our believers will give lectures in the surrounding cities and towns, that will give me great joy, for I will feel that I have not laboured in vain. To train souls is indeed a gift from God and I try to be truly thankful . . . Mr. Schneebeli failed to cure Mrs. Herrigel, they don't feel quite so happy now and she was in bed the last time I was there.[20]

During this time of test and trial a Tablet arrived from 'Abdu'l-Bahá to Alma, dated March 1910:

> O dear servant of God!
> Your detailed letter has arrived from Stuttgart, but on account of lack of time, my answer will be short. As much as you can, be firm and steadfast in the Cause of Baha'u'llah, and thus, be sure that you will receive the greatest confirmation and attain to what is the ultimate desire and hope! When the tree is well rooted, the building becomes elevated.
> O dear servant of God! The Cause of Baha'u'llah is like the rain of Spring and the shower of Nisan: There is no doubt that when it falls orchards and rosegardens blossom, the wilderness and the deserts become green and blooming. The Friends of God are husbandmen: They must sow the seed, the growing of which depends on the Lord of signs . . .
> Upon you be Baha'u'llah[21]

Alma felt much better after reading this Tablet. Also, after this, Mr Schneebeli left Stuttgart and returned to Switzerland. 'Abdu'l-Bahá continued to shower His blessings on Alma, writing on 2 April:

> O Daughter of the Kingdom
> Your letter of February 27, 1910 arrived, and it became evident from its contents that night and day you are busy in serving the Kingdom occupied in spreading the teachings of God.
> . . . All that is contrary to the teachings of Baha'u'llah is wrong, and you must never accept it. What has taken

place was a test: the friends must be firm and steadfast in the midst of tests. If an angel would manifestly come down from heaven, and if a word contrary to the teachings of Baha'u'llah would proceed from his lips, it would be wrong, and you should not heed it.

You have written that the Friday meetings have been organized: this news caused me joy, and I pray for that sick one.

For the present, it is not permitted for anyone to come to the Holy Land, for the summer is near, and in these regions the heat becomes very severe in that season . . .'[22]

And in a Tablet to Fanny translated on 5 May 1910, He wrote: 'The Maidservant of God Miss Alma is displaying the utmost magnanimity in the Cause of God in Stuttgart.'[23]

But Alma was disappointed to learn that some of the believers still kept up correspondence with Mr Schneebeli, believing his claim that 'Abdu'l-Bahá wrote through him. Alma read 'Abdu'l-Bahá's Tablet at a meeting and afterwards remained silent so that the effect and the weight would be on the words of 'Abdu'l-Bahá's words and not on her own. Although she tried her best to help them to focus on the Master, she felt that part of the community was not touched. Alma wrote to Pauline, 'My worst troubles have come . . . for they do not accept Abdul Baha's words . . .'[24]

Shortly after 21 May, all the Stuttgart believers were invited to a meeting where Herrigel renounced his position as Treasurer. This caused some confusion because Herrigel had previously said that he needed to add some money to the Fund. After considering the situation, Miss Stäbler offered to take the position, greatly surprising the men. They later said they realized that they had lost an opportunity to have a man take the position.[25]

Alma realized that in the aftermath of all the confusion, the community had not organized a celebration for the Declaration of the Báb on 23 May, so in the name of 'Abdu'l-Bahá she sent cards to all. Knowing that it would be a difficult situation for Herrigel, she went to his home to invite him personally. He responded that he 'would not speak for or against it but he did not think that he would come'. Alma reminded him that unity was the main thing. After Alma left, Herrigel sent out exclusive invitations to some members of the community to celebrate at his home. The friends Alma described as the 'plain, working people' were not invited to the Herrigels and they celebrated in a loving atmosphere. Alma wrote, 'I am so glad I made this effort for God surely blessed us.'[26] She described the desperate situation in Stuttgart:

> There was no message to the assembly. It means that we few will have to work hard to stand firm and steadfast, the others have the money, books, homes for meetings and everything apparently, but Abdul Baha promised His help and assistance so we will succeed in the end, for we have His assurance.[27]

In November 1910, Herrigel sent an invitation to Alma and the women who had been meeting at the Frauen Club to meet at his home. Unfortunately, in the invitation, he told the women in what spirit they should attend. None of the women accepted, as they felt they had been 'treated like slaves and did not wish to have that experience again'.[28] The main disagreement was that those who attended the meetings with Fisher and Herrigel followed whatever Schneebeli wrote for them to do and Schneebeli wrote whatever Fisher wanted him to write.[29]

The Stuttgart community was obviously being tested. The believers themselves felt that differences were of both a socioeconomic nature and also gender-related. The gap drew the friends apart geographically, with prosperous men living with their families in Stuttgart and hard-working women and their friends and families living outside in Esslingen/Zuffenhausen. To overcome the barriers, each was tested at the level of their inner motivation. There was no way around it, the only way to emerge as a united Bahá'í community would be for everyone to turn to 'Abdu'l-Bahá and truly strive to live according to the teachings.

23
STEADFASTLY BUILDING COMMUNITY

Relying on the unifying power of the Covenant, Alma redoubled her efforts at community building. For this there were three main processes at work: public information in the newspapers, Bahá'í celebrations and meetings, and continuously striving to apply the Bahá'í teachings in individual life. The believers needed to avoid the pitfalls of slander and backbiting and keep the light of love and unity shining. This was Alma's greatest wish.

Publicity in 1910 for the Stuttgart Bahá'ís was mixed. Some pastors in Stuttgart warned their communities of 'a sect who called themselves Bahá'í Vereinigung', with a 'Mohammdian [sic] Missionary coming from America', while at the same time, a local newspaper published a favourable article about the Bahá'í Faith.[1]

Alma wrote to newspapers and other organizations about the Bahá'í teachings. In this way she met Albert Lutz from St Gallen, Switzerland, who became one of the first Swiss Bahá'ís living in Switzerland. Their exchange of ideas proved fruitful. He travelled to Stuttgart to visit her for a few days to learn more about the teachings. Afterwards he travelled to Ernsee to share them with a small group of interested people.[2]

The year began with the third Naw-Rúz celebrated in Stuttgart, held at the Frauen Club. Although not everyone attended, the meeting was blessed with a Tablet received from 'Abdu'l-Bahá, emphasizing the spirituality of such an event:

O sons and daughters of the Kingdom!

Your letter which was written on the Day of Naurooz in the assembly of the friends, has arrived. Its contents told of spiritual happenings and feelings of attraction. Its reading brought me the utmost happiness, for – Praise be to God! – in Germany, the servants and the maid-servants of the Rahman [Merciful] have adorned a gathering of friendship and love in the Day of Naurooz, have perfumed their nostrils with the vivifying breezes of the divine garden, and have been mentioning the King of the Kingdom and the Lord of Hosts.

Therefore, Abdul-Baha has been praying and supplicating to the Word of God that these servants and maid-servants of the Rahman may day by day become more brilliant and make greater progress, penetrate the mysteries of the Kingdom, become the cause of the diffusing of the principles of human unity, call every one to the Shade of the Tent of harmony and instruction of mankind, become the cause of enlightenment of these regions, make the hearts filled with the love of the bountiful Beloved, and attract the people to the divine Kingdom, so that during the coming year they may make still greater progress.

The flowers which were inside of your letter were exceedingly sweet, delicate and perfumed; it told of the sweetness of your countenances and characters.

Upon you all be the glory of God.[3]

The same issue of *Bahai News* includes a letter from the Bahá'ís in Stuttgart, signed by M. Schweizer, 'To the dear friends in America':

> Our assembly remembers with love all the friends, especially those in America, to whom we owe such boundless thanks for sending to us a teacher, who with great love and patience led us to the True Path. Through our beloved Miss Knoblock and the Bahai News we know that, also in America teachers are necessary, yet, nevertheless, a teacher

decided to acquaint her old Fatherland with the joyous Message. The Lord be thanked, therefore, a thousand times!

Our constant prayer in that we may become more and more worthy of our Great Teachers, Baha'o'llah and Abdul-Baha. We, therefore, beseech the friends to support us in this our prayer as we also remember them in our prayers.[4]

Following the difficult first months of 1910, in July Howard Struven, one of the American Bahá'ís who had brought Alma to the New York Port back in 1907, visited the Bahá'ís in Stuttgart and stayed for a week. He attended the meeting in Zuffenhausen at the home of Mr and Mrs Schweizer. Since Howard was visiting Alma, Fisher and the other men did not choose to meet or invite him to their meetings.[5] All of this was painful, and Alma wrote:

> I have never been so homesick as I am now. But I must do Abdul Baha's work and perhaps He will permit me to come to you later. Was dreadful not to have been here with Mr. Remey, but he was overworked, and it was good for Mr. Strueven to have the experience and I could not have stood it if they had snubbed Mr. Remey it would have made one ill. Mr. Strueven felt it, but he is young, and he had not met the others before to know the difference so much as Mr. Remey would.[6]

Throughout this time, teaching in the Stuttgart area continued on both sides of the divide, despite the animosity. In July Alma wrote Pauline that the stories that Fisher and Herrigel were telling people about herself and Margarethe had caused some of the Bahá'ís to act 'as though they were afraid of' her and that it would 'hurt the cause for some time'.[7]

Despite this, Alma sent six new 'petitions' (declarations of faith) to 'Abdu'l-Bahá.[8] Alma and Rosa Schwarz taught Rosa's two sisters in Degerloch, and both accepted the Faith. In addition, Rosa's other sister, Sudovika Spiedel in Ludwigsburg, also joined the Faith through correspondence with Alma and organized a small Bahá'í group in that city.

Fanny Weigle also joined the Degerloch group. Initially, this upset Fanny's husband Richard, who had been born in Jerusalem where his parents were early Templer pioneers. His parents had known 'Abdu'l-Bahá. After Richard listened to the Bahá'í principles and teachings, he became a very enthusiastic new believer, and said, 'I wish you would read our books, they are somewhat alike but this is better!'[9] At the same time, Mrs von Steiner became a new believer in Stuttgart.[10]

In September, Alma was happily surprised to receive several very kind lines from some of the 'Schneebeli-crowd'. Alma remarked to Fanny, 'How queer they must feel? Not any of them have a word to say about the beautiful Tablet for the Assembly.'[11] Alma and about 25 others kept up the meetings in the public hall over the summer, while others travelled to Zurich where they held meetings with Mr Schneebeli.

After his visit to Germany, Howard Struven met the American lawyer Mountfort Mills in Paris. He told the Bahá'í friends there about the awkward situation in Stuttgart and Mountfort wrote to Alma that he would like to visit. Alma was happy to hear this; she had met him in Switzerland and liked him very much. She wrote to Fanny that he was 'straight forward and no queer thoughts and ideas that people call spiritual, and I really think he can help a great deal to straighten matters some . . .'[12] Mr Mills visited and the Bahá'í community gave him a large reception at the Frauen Club. Alma wrote that it was 'a most excellent spiritual meeting and felt that his visit will be of great benefit to the cause',[13] and she also sent a report to *Bahai News (Star of the West)*:

> The believers wish me to extend hearty thanks for the highly appreciated *Bahai News*, which is always translated into German, bringing welcome breezes from the Kingdom of Abha . . .
>
> Mr Mountfort Mills, of the New York Assembly, spoke to us at a social Bahai gathering held Sunday evening, Sept. 11th, giving interesting and very helpful notes taken at Acca. The spiritual fragrances from the powerful Words

of Abdul-Baha were highly instructive and deeply felt by all. Recognizing the importance of coworking in this Most Great Cause, whereby the bonds of unity are strengthened, his visit will ever be remembered...[14]

We are now sending Bahai literature to different cities and towns in Austria, Switzerland and Germany. We pray that God may bless the seeds that have been sown.

At the end of 1910, Mr Schneebeli returned, and his daughter moved in with the Herrigels to work as their housekeeper. In January 1911, Herrigel and Fisher rented a five-room apartment for meetings; Schneebeli and Mr Sehn also lived there, with one room used for Mr Sehn's massage practice. A sign on the door read 'Bahai Home'.[15] The meeting room was decorated with the Greatest Name embroidered with gold.[16] Herrigel was angry when his niece Anna Köstlin, in Esslingen, refused to have anything to do with Schneebeli and told him that she did not think it was right. Mrs Herrigel told her sister, Anna's mother, many bad things about Alma, but Alma was not deterred. She patiently visited the family throughout this uncomfortable phase and showered them with love until Mrs Köstlin became more kind towards her.[17] For Alma, patience, love and understanding were the only way to pass through these times. She held fast to the teachings.

This attitude was successful. Anna Köstlin hosted a harmonious Feast of the Covenant on 26 November 1910.[18] In the following year Anna wrote to John Bosch, 'Our dear Miss Knobloch always tried her utmost to bring about unity and now she can see the blessing of her labors. We are all extremely thankful for her love and sacrifice...'[19]

Unfortunately, after his return Mr Schneebeli continued to write negatively about Alma at the large meetings he held. Alma was surprised and saddened at the number of people who approved of that.[20] Furthermore, because Sydney Sprague had encouraged Fisher to continue the meetings with Mr Schneebeli, Professor Braun continued to attend and continually tried to convince Mr Ruoff to come back and join the

Herrigel meetings.[21] Alma wrote, 'What Mr. Sprague means I cannot understand, I am sure of one thing and that is that *he does not know anything about the conditions here.*'[22]

Alma's letters home at this time express her concern regarding the spiritual effects which this behaviour had on some of the naïve believers who were under the influence of Mr Schneebeli. She genuinely cared for them and missed seeing them at the meetings she attended. She wrote, 'How very hard it is . . . I know that the right will come out victorious in the end.'[23] How wise she was. Tests are a necessary part of purification for the human heart. It is only when we are tested that we find out who we really are.

She focused on the teachings and studied them with the believers to find new ways to apply them to their lives. After reading Bahá'u'lláh's teaching that if one raised a child, it would be the same as if they had raised a child of His, Mrs Stäbler and her daughters took in their niece, a little girl of 12 years, to raise and train, despite their financial difficulties. To this end, the Schweizers in Zuffenhausen, despite the birth of their own first child in August,[24] took in a young blind girl.[25]

The summer of 1910 brought changes for Alma's family in East Germany. Aunt Mina passed away in Leipzig in August, leaving Uncle Wilhelm sad and lonesome.[26] Alma went to Leipzig to visit them in August. Uncle Wilhelm and Cousin Martin invited Alma to come to Leipzig to manage their household. Although they had not made much headway teaching, Martin promised Alma to help her share the message if she came. In addition, Margarethe's brother Kurt and his wife had moved to Leipzig.[27]

Alma considered moving to Leipzig, but she wanted to keep her room in Stuttgart, to be able to return at any time. Many of the believers wanted her to stay in Stuttgart. Margarethe and Alma finally moved into a home with a kitchen so they could entertain and eat at home. Teaching work continued successfully. Whenever Alma did not feel well or was lonely, Margarethe took care of her and comforted her.[28]

News of another change came in a letter. Sydney Sprague wrote to Alma: 'Our beloved Master is in Egypt.' This was a great surprise to the friends, since no one had known of his intentions until one hour before his departure. Ahmad Sohrab wrote that this 'fulfilled prophecies' concerning Egypt, and 'will be great help to the Cause for all the world will now be turned towards Egypt'.²⁹ But Alma felt insecure, worrying that it would now become more difficult to communicate with 'Abdu'l-Bahá. In fact, the Master was moving closer to Europe.

24

TABLETS TO THE GERMAN BELIEVERS

On 6 February 1911, Alma wrote to Fanny that the Herrigels happily invited her to attend their meetings again, stating, 'I do not know what he [Herrigel] wrote to Abdul Baha but he is very happy.'[1] On 1 March 1911, new Tablets in English arrived in Germany from London.[2] These Tablets were sent to many individuals including the Herrigels, Mr and Mrs Ruoff, Anna Köstlin, the Schweizers and Alma. Additionally, a Tablet addressed to 'the Friends of God and the Maidservants of the Merciful in Stuttgart' foretold things that they would need to know for the difficult days that would soon encompass Germany:

> O Sons and Daughters of the Kingdom!
> Your letter arrived, and by its significances it was conspicuous that you are all approached to the Kingdom of God
> Blessed are you who in such a day have heard the Heavenly Melody and found out the Everlasting Father.
> I have prayed for you that you may be favoured in promulgating the new Teachings and with intense longing engage yourselves in the service of the world of humanity. To become Physicians for every ill one and most kind to the oppressed. To comfort those troubled, and be the cause of joy for the afflicted ones and exert yourselves with all your souls that you establish love and kindness amongst the individuals of mankind.

To be loyal and faithful to the local government and most useful in the service of the State and that you pray for the happiness of the Emperor . . .³

In this Tablet the Schweizers received a name for their new baby: Khurshed – meaning 'sun'.⁴ Anna Köstlin joyfully received her first Tablet⁵ and it was a great blessing for all in Esslingen.

From this point on, the Bahá'ís in Europe no longer had to wait for translations from Ahmad Sohrab in Washington. The Tablet to the Herrigels explained new procedures for communication with the Master:

> O two Lights of God's Love!
> Your letter arrived and its significances brought the feeling of heart. I hope that you will ever be Bahais and firm and faithful in this greatest Revelation. I love you exceedingly verily.
> Mírzá Dawud is firm and faithful in the Cause, therefore I will send the letters for Stuttgart to him to translate and send them on to you. Always write to Mr Thornton Chase and send my greetings to him; I love him very much.
> Read those Tablets and Books of this Revelation among the friends, but do not publish them in the public, for thus wisdom requires at present time.
> Convey My greeting to Dr Fisher.⁶

Unfortunately, the initial euphoria did not last. Some members of the community had expected a more personal response. In particular, some felt that the specific questions they had asked were not answered in any of the Tablets they received. Furthermore, these Tablets were all signed through Mírzá Yuhanna Dawud, London. Although Yuhanna Dawud had visited Germany and the believers had given their questions to him to take to the Master, nonetheless, the German believers had not expected to receive 'Abdu'l-Bahá's response from Mírzá Dawud. They were not familiar with Mírzá Dawud's handwriting and did not believe these were 'Abdu'l-Bahá's answers. In addition, the envelopes were labelled differently than they had been previously, and it was the first time that the Tablets were sent to Wilhelm Herrigel's address with instructions for Herrigel to disperse them instead of Alma.[7] Unfortunately many, including Wilhelm Herrigel, grew suspicious. They claimed that Alma had forged these Tablets.[8]

Once more, Anna Köstlin's mother became more sympathetic to the group at the Herrigels, and it became very difficult for Alma to visit the Köstlin family. At first, Anna and Annemarie Schweizer also thought that the Tablets were forged, since their questions were also not addressed.[9] Alma again relied on patience and love to gain back trust and serve in this environment. It is truly a sign of her spiritual greatness that she was able to endure!

Mr Schneebeli had told many of the believers that he had spoken 'His wisdom' before they received the Tablets, and of course, 'Abdu'l-Bahá knew that.[10] Alma believed that it was the wisdom of the Master that He did not discuss with them the things they were discussing with Mr Schneebeli. She repeatedly visited many of the friends and patiently explained to them until they understood that their Tablets were authentic and truly written by none other than 'Abdu'l-Bahá Himself. Alma sent the Persian originals to Ahmad Sohrab in Washington for verification. There were many reasons for 'Abdu'l-Bahá's decision to send the Tablets to the Herrigels' address. Alma wrote to Pauline that one reason was her own 'wish that a change should be made, and it has already proven that it was wise'.[11]

Despite the challenging atmosphere, Alma continued to meet the believers, study the Bahá'í teachings with them, and help them to develop their Bahá'í identity. For the first time, Alma and Margarethe kept the Fast while the other believers held the 'spiritual fast'. The Esslingen/Zuffenhausen group grew firmer in their faith. Friedrich and Annemarie Schweizer were the first to pay Ḥuqúqu'lláh by counting out and donating 1/19th of their income to the Cause; other friends followed.[12] This Bahá'í law is not calculated this way, and would not be binding on Western Bahá'ís until eighty-one years later, but these actions demonstrated their strong love and devotion. The Bahá'ís in Zuffenhausen and Degerloch were able to keep up the monthly meetings at the rented hall, although the wealthier part of the community had split off and no longer provided financial contributions. The Schweizers opened their home for the Naw-Rúz festivities and invited the entire Stuttgart community,[13] but sadly, Professor Braun declined and the others who attended Herrigel's meetings ignored the invitation entirely.[14] Many youth attended the celebration including Gustav Eger, Hugo and Max Bender, Heinrich Schwab, Richard Kohler and Franz Pöllinger.

A ray of light reached Stuttgart on 13 May 1911 with the arrival of the saintly Louis Gregory, an African-American lawyer who had learned about the Bahá'í Faith from Pauline in 1908. He was returning home after his remarkable pilgrimage to the Holy Land where he met the young Shoghi Effendi, 'Abdu'l-Bahá's grandson, and to Egypt where he was in the presence of 'Abdu'l-Bahá. 'Abdu'l-Bahá asked Louis to visit the friends in Stuttgart.

Before Louis had left for pilgrimage, Pauline told him that he would never again be the same. After his visit to Germany, Margarethe received a Tablet from 'Abdu'l-Bahá attesting to the fulfilment of that prediction. 'Abdu'l-Bahá wrote:

> Mr. Gregory, by visiting the Blessed Tomb, hath received a new power, and obtained a new life. When he arrived at Stuttgart, although black of color, yet he shone as a bright light in the meeting of the friends. Verily, he hath greatly advanced in this journey, he received another life and obtained another power. When he returned, Gregory was quite another Gregory. He hath become a new creation.[15]

Louis spoke in the Frauen Club about his visit to 'Akká and meeting 'Abdu'l-Bahá in Egypt. The following day, a grand meeting was arranged for him in Esslingen, followed by a large dinner served at the Stäblers' home.

Alma and Margarethe invited Louis to join them for dinner at the YMCA. One night, a waiter approached their table and told them that a famous artist who was dining in the large hall would like to meet them. The artist was quite excited to meet Louis and showed him the entire building. The little children in the streets, having never seen a person with such dark skin colour, would pass Louis very slowly, looking intently at him when they passed and then run back to pass and look at him again. Alma told Louis that he had received more honour than his two Bahá'í brothers Mason Remey and Hippolyte Dreyfus during their last visit. Louis laughed and told her that they were very attentive to him at the hostel where he was staying. He remarked that in Germany the children were very polite to him, but in Paris they had thrown stones at him. This is interesting, considering the future racism that would later grasp the German population under the Nazis.

Alma and Louis travelled to Strasbourg to visit the sister of a new believer, Mrs Kusterer. She was so impressed, despite the language barrier, that she came to Stuttgart to learn more about the Faith and became a devoted Bahá'í.

Alma also took Louis to meet Wilhelm Herrigel, who spoke with them for 'fully ¾ of an hour on the street'.[16] Herrigel asked Louis if Sydney Sprague was coming to Stuttgart that summer.[17] Then he spoke only to Alma regarding the different meetings in Stuttgart. Herrigel wanted to have only one meeting place, the 'Bahá'í Home' which had been rented for Mr Schneebeli. The friends who were not comfortable meeting at that location had rented a hall for their public meetings. He was concerned with the impression it made on people who were interested in the Faith to hear that there was more than one meeting place in town.[18]

Anna Köstlin kept a book in which she asked special guests who had touched her heart when they visited Stuttgart to sign. Louis Gregory wrote a lovely message in this book which is today in the German National Archives.

After Louis's visit, the issue of the two meeting places needed to be sorted out. It was difficult for the believers to finance two meeting locations. Alma wrote, 'Herrigel and his friends find it difficult to meet expenses, they have rented out their guest chamber and they are beginning to lose faith in Mr Schneebeli and wish us to give up our Hall and come over to them. Dr Fisher has lost his hold entirely.'[19]

Everyone agreed that something needed to be done to find unity. Alma and Mr Schweizer, with about ten others, visited Herrigel's meeting. Herrigel read from the Bible and Mr Schneebeli explained the contents; then they read the teachings of 'Abdu'l-Bahá, among them a part of Alma's 'Akká notes. After this Herrigel cordially invited Alma to come again and the Herrigels promised to visit the group at Anna Köstlin's home on the following Sunday. He then escorted them to the door while Mrs Herrigel and the others remained in their seats.[20] Unfortunately, for reasons unknown, they did not manage to come to Anna Köstlin's Sunday meeting.

Herrigel told Alma that 'it was not often that those present at the meeting go to him [Schneebeli] and that he had grown more spiritual'. Alma 'advised him to give up the writing [from Schneebeli] entirely', and encouraged him to work in direct communication with 'Abdu'l-Bahá who had given him the 'assurance that he would be confirmed, what more could he wish?'[21]

The basis for the two meetings was essentially Schneebeli's writings versus 'Abdu'l-Bahá's Tablets. Alma believed that Bahá'ís must rely solely on the Writings of Bahá'u'lláh and the Tablets of 'Abdu'l-Bahá for their spiritual guidance. She did not want any person to step in the middle of that. As long as Herrigel could not commit to that, she felt there was no other way but to keep the meetings separate. She wrote, 'You see my darling sister, Abdul-Baha is guiding us and we are earnestly striving to do His will, sacrificing everything if necessary, so as to have them realize that Abdul-Baha does as He wills and that it is His meeting not ours.'[22]

On 25 May 1911, at the close of the Friday evening meeting, Mr Haigis, who had been attending the meetings with Herrigel, came and asked that they all work towards unity. He pointed out that Friedrich Schweizer and Alma had made a start by attending meetings at the Herrigels' home. Alma suggested, 'they all pray "the remover of difficulties" for 19 days and they could set the date we are to be one in spirit and considered in meetings as Abdul-Baha's meetings.'²³

Despite the confusion over the two meetings and by Schneebeli's interpretations, the Faith was still growing and spreading. Alma always ensured that new believers understood the position of 'Abdu'l-Bahá as the Centre of the Covenant. At the weekly Sunday coffee meeting held by Rosa Schwarz, new believers, including the Weigles and the Sanders, joined the Degerloch group. Rosa's sister in Ludwigsburg, now a Bahá'í, had started to share the teachings with friends in Mannheim. Mrs Kusterer's sister from Strasbourg came to learn more about the Faith.²⁴ Anna Köstlin was busy teaching many of her young friends and Alma accompanied her to explain the Bahá'í Faith. In June 1911, Anna Köstlin taught Klara Krieger and her parents in Aalen.²⁵ Her father, the Mayor of Aalen, arranged a large meeting where the message was shared with many friends and the nobility.²⁶ This opened teaching activities with the nobility in Munich. Four believers moved to Berlin: Mr Otto Stäbler, his friend Mr Fisher, the sister of Miss Schweizer and the girl the Schweizers had raised for one year.

Some friends had begun rumours that Alma had not sent the believers their Tablets. Of course, this was not true. Recent Tablets sent through Hippolyte Dreyfus had arrived without being registered and with no return address, so Alma could not track them to prove that she had not withheld anything.²⁷ No longer surprised at such accusations, Alma had decided not to trouble 'Abdu'l-Bahá with it.²⁸ Instead, by the end of May, Alma sent the Tablets to Anna Köstlin and the Schweizers for translation and authentication to Ahmad Sohrab.²⁹ By July, Alma worried that they were lost.³⁰ Unfortunately, even by December 1911 Alma had still not yet received the translations of these Tablets!³¹

In August 1911, a Tablet arrived through Yuhanna Dawud. It emphasized the importance of community gatherings:

> Thanks be to God! that you have been gathered together and celebrated the birthday of the Bab with much joy and amity and were engaged in remembering God.

> From the rose-garden of that meeting a beautiful fragrance has reached to the nostrils of these friends, and the light of God's love hath shone; therefore, it was a cause of delighting the hearts of these friends. I ask God, by His infinite mercy, that such meetings may be held often.
>
> Likewise, that the entertainment every nineteen days may become current among you; so that the friends and maidservants of the Merciful may be engaged in praising and remembering God and singing to Him, and may become the cause of guiding the people.[32]

In the summer of 1911, Sydney Sprague returned to Stuttgart. Unfortunately, he only found time to visit Herrigel and his friends.[33] Alma felt very sorry about this, as it did not support any concept of unity.

In Leipzig, Stuttgart and Germany in general, times were changing in 1911. In Leipzig, Alma's family became smaller when Uncle Wilhelm passed away. In Stuttgart, an important new believer, Alice Schwarz, began to attend the Bahá'í meetings and shared the Faith with her husband Consul Albert Schwarz. She had learned about the Faith in 1909 as a patient of Dr Fisher.[34] Although she had been warned by her friends not to listen to the things that Dr Fisher talked about while he worked on her teeth, she was surprisingly moved by his stories.

In all of Germany, intense nationalism was on the rise and the growing military was increasingly visible. On 23 August 1911 Alma wrote home: 'just now a regiment passed by, what a splendid mass of humanity it is looking down and seeing them pass and still one's heart aches knowing how much strife it will still take before the military is put aside'.[35] But even as the clouds of war began to gather around Europe, the sun broke through! Two days later Alma received an important message: "Abdu'l-Bahá is at Hotel Parc, Thonon les Bains, Chablais, France, on Lake Geneva. He expects to stay 2–3 weeks.'[36] From August to 3 September the Master was in Thonon-les-Bains, France and visited Geneva and Vevey, across the lake in Switzerland.

25

THE GERMAN BAHÁ'ÍS MEET 'ABDU'L-BAHÁ IN LONDON AND PARIS

'Abdu'l-Bahá was invited to give a speech at the first Universal Races Congress held at the University of London, where more than 2,100 individuals from fifty different countries gathered

> to discuss, in the light of science and the modern conscience, the general relations subsisting between the peoples of the West and those of the East, between the so-called 'white' and the so-called 'colored' peoples, with a view to encouraging between them a fuller understanding . . . and might, in friendly rivalry, further the cause of mutual trust and respect between Occident and Orient, between the so-called 'white' peoples and the so-called 'colored' peoples.[1]

When Alma heard this, she wrote to 'Abdu'l-Bahá in Paris asking for permission to visit Him in London. In her memoirs, Alma recalled that she received permission to meet 'Abdu'l-Bahá in London the week after the Universal Races Congress ended and that 'Abdu'l-Bahá 'sent a Tablet which was read at the opening with regrets that He could not be there'. He wrote:

> This Congress is one of the greatest events. It will be forever the glory of England that it was established at her capital . . . O ye people! Cause this thing to be not a thing of words, but of deeds. Some congresses are held only to increase

differences. Let it not be so with you . . . Let brotherhood be felt and seen among you; and carry its quickening power throughout the world. ²

The Universal Races Congress of 1911 was unable to promote the concept of the unity of humanity. Instead, it 'had the unintended effect of reinforcing racial identities and idioms, especially in the context of challenges to colonial rule'.³

Later, 'Abdu'l-Bahá said,

> The Universal Races Congress was good, for it was intended for the furtherance and progress of unity among all nations and a better international understanding. The purpose was good. The causes of dispute among different nations are always due to one of the following classes of prejudice: racial, lingual, theological, personal, and prejudices of custom and tradition. It requires a universal active force to overcome these differences. A small disease needs a small remedy, but a disease which pervades the whole body needs a very strong remedy. A small lamp may light a room, a larger would light a house, a larger still might shine through the city, but the sun is needed to light the whole world.⁴

Alma arrived in London on 3 September 1911, and called on Lady Blomfield, who was very busy organizing things for the Master's arrival on the following morning. The next morning, Alma walked to the train station where she met Marion Jack and another friend. They said, 'You have come just in time!' and Miss Jack handed her a white rose. Alma ran off with them, hand in hand, Alma in the middle, so as not to get lost in the crowd. A large, long train pulled into the station. Mírzá Asadu'lláh, the Master's brother-in-law, was the first to emerge from the train, followed by Hippolyte Dreyfus. The crowd was so intense that Alma felt it would be easier to get by alone and let her hand slip free . . . a few moments later she saw a white turban at the far end! Alma ran to the Master and upon reaching Him, He grasped her hand firmly and said, 'Welcome, welcome!'⁵ An official pointed to the gate where all the passengers were leaving the station. 'Abdu'l-Bahá walked past as all the people respectfully cleared the way for him. Alma wrote, 'Coming from His 40 years of imprisonment, this was very impressive.'[6]

It is quite remarkable how 'Abdu'l-Bahá was able to keep such a busy daily schedule throughout His travels in the West. During His stay in London, He resided at the home of Lady Blomfield where he gave talks and received visitors from early morning until late at night. One morning Alma arrived at the regular time for one of His talks to find the room filled with people and the Master already talking. When she opened the door He immediately welcomed her and pointed to the chair next to Him, the only free chair in the room. As she moved to sit she saw 'the deepest sorrow, pains and distress in His glorious face' as her eyes welled up with tears. That morning He shared His experiences of being a prisoner in 'Akká. Alma wrote, 'There was no doubt left in the minds of anyone presence [sic] that the Holy Family and believers suffered beyond all human comprehension.'[7]

Archdeacon Basil Wilberforce from St John's church at Westminster wrote to 'Abdu'l-Bahá regarding the unity of mankind saying, 'We are one behind the veil.' 'Abdu'l-Bahá responded, 'The veil is very thin and will soon disappear.'[8] Archdeacon Wilberforce invited 'Abdu'l-Bahá to speak at St. John's on 17 September 1911. The talk was described in detail in the newspaper *The Christian Commonwealth* under the heading 'The Vanishing of the Veil'.[9] Alma described this, saying that Wilberforce:

> Prepared his congregation saying that a very distinguished guest was in their midst, the Spirit of God was with them and that they should receive Him with a prayerful heart. He then walked down the aisle the choir boys preceding him and returned with Abdul Baha and His secretaries, Lady Bloomfield [sic] and M. Dreyfus – A.B. ['Abdu'l-Bahá] delivered His address in Persian which was read in English by the Bishop [Archdeacon Wilberforce] then was asked to

give a prayer. The Bishop [Archdeacon Wilberforce] knelt at His side. A.B. ['Abdu'l-Bahá] with hands extending upward offered supplicated – it was heavenly – one realized that this prayer went out into the universe and would have a great effect upon mankind. We were overwhelmed by the powerful spirit that prevailed - A.B. ['Abdu'l-Bahá] and the Bishop [Archdeacon Wilberforce] passed down the aisle and the Persians followed before the congregation arose to leave the church. Our party gathered without speaking a word, there was a quietness that no one wished to disturb.[10]

This intense, 'theatrical' event, although described in detail in *The Christian Commonwealth*,[11] went largely unnoticed by the public, in contrast to 'Abdu'l-Bahá's address at the Church of the Ascension in New York, which was described in the newspaper *The Church Times* as 'A Shocking Affair'.[12] After His trip to North America, 'Abdu'l-Bahá's renown was not appreciated by the Christian clergy, perhaps causing Wilberforce to maintain a distance when He returned to England.[13] Years later in 1935, Alma was working as a guide at the Bahá'í temple in Wilmette where she had the honour of guiding a group which to her delight included members of the Wilberforce family.[14]

The friends in Germany had asked Alma to give the Master some roses on their behalf. Alma begged the Master's secretary for an audience with Him where she could fulfil this task, and received a card inviting her to meet 'Abdu'l-Bahá. She gathered her 19 beautiful roses and set out for the Master's residence, only to find that the Master was not there! She realized she must have made a mistake, because 'Abdu'l-Bahá would never miss an appointment He had made. Then she looked again at the card with the invitation, and realized it had a different address. She quickly found a taxi and showed the driver the card – the driver drove quickly to the nearby house of Mrs Cropper where she found 'Abdu'l-Bahá waiting for her at the head of the staircase with a hearty welcome.

On another occasion, Alma was invited to meet the Master privately:

A.B. [sic] was sitting by a window reading some letters as I entered and quietly advanced and placed a bunch of rosebuds before Him in silence. He gave a signal and all His secretaries entered and stood silently at the rear of the room, one advance [sic] and acted as interpre [sic] . . . After a time, it seemed about 20 minutes Abdul-Baha gave the sign and they filed out, they were about 8 or 10 Persians. Then He spoke in general of the work in Germany, unity, the most essential for growth and firmness in the Cause, this must be at any cost, no sacrifice is too great. 'Serve **all!**', emphasizing **all** – Christ said, 'He who serves the most is most beloved. **Serve all!**' I had had a wish to devote all my time to training the women in the teachings, but had not mentioned it to anyone, Abdul Baha gave the answer.[15]

'Abdu'l-Bahá told Alma, 'I want you to go out and give the teachings.' Alma promised Him she would strive with all her heart to bring about unity in Germany.[16] She wrote to Fanny and Pauline, 'I was told twice by Abdul-Baha, "I want you to go about and give the teachings," and left no doubt that He wishes me to feel that Germany is my field of work.'[17]

Although 'Abdu'l-Bahá had told Alma to return to Germany and spread the teachings, she longed to remain near Him, so she disobeyed Him and remained in London. When 'Abdu'l-Bahá saw her, He asked, 'Have you been to Stuttgart? How are the friends?' Of course, she had not! And she replied, 'I will leave this evening!' Alma knew very well that He had expected her to leave at once after their last conversation. In London, 'Abdu'l-Bahá reminded her not to fear opposition. He said, 'No one tries to put out a lamp that is not burning. No one throws stones at a tree with no fruits to come down.'[18]

'Abdu'l-Bahá also granted permission for three other German friends, Mr Haigis and Mr and Mrs Herrigel, to meet Him in London. Wilhelm Herrigel recalled that he 'tried to talk to 'Abdu'l-Bahá about the disunity and problems in Stuttgart' but 'Abdu'l-Bahá always told him, 'Be steadfast. Be happy.' Herrigel wrote that 'Abdu'l-Bahá could 'see in his face that he would bring unity to the friends in Stuttgart'. 'Abdu'l-Bahá encouraged the believers to teach the faith 'far and wide'. Mr Haigis and the Herrigels returned to Stuttgart determined to teach the Faith.[19] Back in Stuttgart, the friends held a united Unity Meeting on 8 September for the first time.[20]

On 4 October, 'Abdu'l-Bahá left London for Paris with Mrs Stannard and two of the 'Persian brothers'.[21] A very large crowd watched Him depart at 11 a.m. from Victoria Station. His parting words were, 'Be kind to all the people in the world, be children to the childless parents; parents to the orphans and kind to the poor.'[22]

Many Germans who had not been able to meet 'Abdu'l-Bahá in London travelled to see him in Paris. Mr and Mrs Eckstein arrived in Paris on 30 September. Mr and Mrs Häfner (from Fellbach) and their little boy left for Paris on 6 October and Margarethe Döring travelled there on 7 October.[23] Julie Stäbler, Anna Köstlin, and Friedrich and Annemarie Schweizer arrived on 17 October. Symbolically, Anna Köstlin departed for this trip from Alma and Margarethe's apartment.[24]

Margarethe visited 'Abdu'l-Bahá for nine days, until 16 October. She had the honour of living in His house in Paris, fulfilling her wish to sleep under the same roof as 'Abdu'l-Bahá.[25] She ate with Him on several occasions. Once He heaped bread upon her plate and when it was full, He took it from her plate and gave it to others.[26] From 16 October to 16 November 1911, 'Abdu'l-Bahá gave some of the famous 'Paris talks' at 4 Avenue de Camöens. They were recorded for humanity by Lady Blomfield, a true and dedicated English believer.

A famous photograph was taken of 'Abdu'l-Bahá with Mr and Mrs Eckstein and Mr and Mrs Häfner and their little boy Otto, by a Paris reporter. Alma wrote, 'Abdul-Baha holding the little boy in His arms . . . I am very thankful that the Germans are on this photo, how very wonderful it all is.'[27] Indeed, in these times Germany and France were already preparing for war, and yet the European Bahá'ís met as one united family in Paris under the loving protection of 'Abdu'l-Bahá. Unity was the Bahá'í standard. Alma wrote:

. . . Our goal is to become united. Margarethe asked ['Abdu'l-Bahá] if we should give up our assembly and join them and He said no there can be many assemblies, but they must come together once a month. He told us to have double unity meetings every 19 days. During the Ecksteins' visit Abdul-Baha gave Mr. Dreyfus a Tablet to read and requested him to arise to read it. They were very much impressed with this. Abdul-Baha told Herrigels that their meeting would become very large and that they would become bright lamps . . . Herrigels asked Him to stay in their home and He said if He came, He would . . . then He said He is not coming! It matters little where He stops to me if He would only come . . . England and France have had the teachings for many years and many English and French friends have visited Abdul-Baha in Acca. Our friends are having this provision now, visiting Him in London and Paris.[28]

Anna Köstlin, Julie Stäbler and Annemarie Schweizer were received six times in private audience during their three-day visit.[29] They also accompanied 'Abdu'l-Bahá on His walks. Alma wrote to her sisters that when they asked 'Abdu'l-Bahá if He would come to Stuttgart, He said,

When the wisdom of God guides me, I am always with you. I have never been in Tehran & they have many firm beautiful believers. I have seen you; it is just as though I have seen Stuttgart, one thing is missing & that is unity between the believers & he laughed heartily saying that was very little – of no importance that separated them. He will pray that they will be united. He is sure that they will be united. He will send a talk that He gave in London to the Theosophical Society, if they follow the Teachings all difficulties will be removed.[30]

Annemarie and Friedrich Schweizer, Julie Stäbler and Anna Köstlin visited 'Abdu'l-Bahá and gave Him a letter with questions from Alma which were translated for Him. He told Julie to write down His answer, which He then signed, saying (according to a letter from Alma):

> I have no time now but will send an answer through words and messages. If I had time, I would write a long answer. But as I have no time at all, therefore I send the answer through (looking at Mr. and Mrs. Schweizer, Miss Köstlin and Miss Stäbler) for you are speaking letters. My wish is that you love each other very, very much & be united. I am glad that you attended the other Assembly. I will pray to Bahá'u'lláh to bless you for going there. Strive with your heart and soul that the Believers there be extremely united & love each other. The love & unity will be the cause of spreading His Holy Cause. You must not only be the cause of unity among each one of you, but the cause of unity in the whole world. This is a long letter. You are the writer Miss Stäbler. (signed) E.E. Abdul-Abbas.[31]

The Schweizers asked for a name for their little girl, and He gave her the name Nur (Light). 'You can imagine everyone so transformed, they are so happy that they really can't contain themselves, laughing all the time and when they read their notes their eyes are filled with tears although their faces are beaming with delight.' Alma attended the other assembly and invited them to the Unity Meeting. Mr and Mrs Eckstein had returned and showed the photo taken with 'Abdu'l-Bahá.[32]

The Master sent further guidance to the Stuttgart Bahá'ís and love and confirmation to Alma in two Tablets sent through Yuhanna Dawud on 27 November 1911. He advised the friends in Stuttgart to ask God to make them manifestations of great firmness and steadfastness, to become able to resist 'fierce temptation', and to live together in perfect union and concord.[33] To Alma, he wrote that he noted that

> you have been gathered together in one place, and with perfect love, you were engaged in praising God.

> Union and concord between the Friends and the Maidservants of the Merciful are the causes of extention [sic] of God's Kingdom, and receiving the help of the Holy Spirit.
>
> I hope that all the friends at Stuttgart to be favoured with those. That is the intense desire of the people of the Kingdom.
>
> If there should be no unity, then the basis of God's religion will fall to pieces.
>
> However, it is my hope that you may be of one spirit, one heart, and one opinion. I am very pleased with all the friends at Stuttgart and exceedingly love them.[34]

Once again, Alma's hard work had paid off. Later, she wrote, 'A few years ago, I only wished to serve the women and work for their development, but 'Abdu'l-Bahá told me in London, "That he who serves all is the greatest." And as I wish to attain the good pleasure of God, I will have to continue to do the best I can and trying to serve all . . .' The women then focused on teaching both men and women. Alma wrote to many prominent men from a list Fanny sent her, and Anna Köstlin and the others also reached many men. Their success was reflected in the characteristics of the Esslingen community in 1913 in which two-thirds of the participants were young men and Anna Köstlin's room was always filled.[35]

26

LADY BLOMFIELD AND THE STUTTGART BAHÁ'Í COMMUNITY

In late 1911 'Abdu'l-Bahá sent Mírzá Asadu'lláh, Lady Blomfield, Ahmad Sohrab and Mrs Earle from England to visit Stuttgart at His behest with a special message for the German Bahá'í community. On 2 December, Mr Eckstein, Mr and Mrs Herrigel, Professor Braun, Dr Fisher and Alma Knobloch met them at the train station.

Lady Blomfield and Mrs Earle stayed at the Herrigels' home, while Ahmad Sohrab and Mírzá Asadu'lláh stayed with the Eckstein family. On Sunday 3 December Lady Blomfield invited Alma to meet her at the Herrigels' house to receive a personal message from 'Abdu'l-Bahá. She told Alma that the Master sent Alma His loving and affectionate greetings and deep appreciation for Her work in establishing the teachings in Stuttgart; furthermore, He would be very much pleased if Alma would go to Leipzig to build up a community there as she had done in Stuttgart.[1] Alma expressed her concerns: if she herself were to leave, erroneous teachings might spread in the Stuttgart community. On the other hand, of course she would go to Leipzig if the Master wished it. Lady Blomfield asked Alma to announce her departure at the large reception at the Bürger Museum that night, to which Alma replied that she would prefer to have time to consider how and when she would announce her departure.

Alma and Lady Blomfield were interrupted by Wilhelm

Herrigel who invited them to lunch, where Dr Fisher joined them. At lunch, they discussed the Master's work in London and Paris, sharing their opinions about the disunity in Stuttgart with her. They explained that some of the believers, being knowledgeable in Christian Science and mystical Christian interpretations, had received most spiritual messages by 'automatic writing', and they showed her some of these messages.[2]

The messages that were shown to Lady Blomfield were very spiritual in nature. She recalled that with all her experience in such matters, she was convinced that 'personas of great dignity and sanctity must have vouchsafed to employ that means of guiding these pure, unselfish souls to whom these messages were conveyed'. The Herrigels believed that because some souls were more spiritually developed, they had these spiritual experiences and that other less spiritually developed souls could not understand this automated writing and therefore they rejected the spiritual meetings where automated messages were made. Lady Blomfield recalled, 'No mention was made of any knowledge of an element of disunion in Stuttgart, it seeming wiser to avoid any reference to personalities – rather giving out the Teachings of the Master from a wide impersonal standpoint, which, from its very grandeur would cause personal likes and dislikes to melt away as too trivial to obtrude themselves!'[3]

That afternoon, when Lady Blomfield met the families in the community at the Bürger Museum, she delivered the Master's message in English and Mrs Earle then read the German translation. 'Abdu'l-Bahá's message was:

> Rejoice! Rejoice! Because of the Glad-tidings! You have attained to the light of the Kingdom. The glory of the Sun of Truth penetrates all regions.
>
> Rejoice! Rejoice! Glad-tidings I send unto you. The doors of the Kingdom are open. The heavenly manna has descended upon you.
>
> Rejoice! Rejoice! There were many holy messengers sent into the world; they came one after another, and all diffused the breath of the Holy Spirit.

Praise God! Praise God! That you have turned your faces toward the Kingdom. The rays of the Sun of Truth are illuminating you.'

Strive with heart and soul that the Heavenly Light may descend upon all people and that through it every heart may be enlightened and that the spirit of the human race may partake of Its glory. Work and strive until all regions of the world are bathed in this Light. Fear not when trouble overtakes you. You will be criticized; you will be persecuted; you will be cursed and reviled. Recall in those days what I tell you now: Your triumph will be sure; your hearts will be filled with the Glory of God, for the heavenly power will sustain you, and God will be with you. This is my message to you.[4]

The meeting was a grand success and Lady Blomfield embraced and kissed all the children in the name of 'Abdu'l-Bahá. The Stäblers' little nephew, Wolfgang Sturm, whom they had adopted upon the death of his mother in the previous year, was especially moved by Lady Blomfield and laid his head upon her shoulder, not wanting to let go.[5]

Mr Eckstein invited all the believers to a Unity Meeting in the large hall at the Frauen Club at 7:30 p.m. that evening. People attended from Stuttgart, Esslingen, Zuffenhausen, Aalen, Fellbach and other places. Ahmad Sohrab and Mírzá Asadu'lláh spoke and again Lady Blomfield read the message from 'Abdu'l-Bahá, everyone sang a hymn and Miss Stäbler sang the Greatest Name.[6] All the believers were happy and the concept to unite all believers in one community was accepted. Lady Blomfield was surprised that although both groups attended this event, there were no signs of disunity from those who were closely associated with Alma. Alma wrote that Ahmad Sohrab told Lady Blomfield that the Unity Meeting was the second most spiritual event he had witnessed in Europe and that 'she should try to establish Spiritual unity meetings in London like the ones in Stuttgart'. Lady Blomfield was 'rather surprised and answered that they have Unity Meetings in London; Mrs

Cropper, Miss Rosenberg and I give a unity meeting'.[7] As Lady Blomfield, Miss Rosenberg and Mrs Thornburgh-Cropper were of the wealthy and educated class, Ahmad Sohrab may have alluded to the fact that the Unity Meeting in Stuttgart included all levels of society.

On 4 December, Lady Blomfield was invited to have tea at the Schweizer home in Zuffenhausen. In the evening, they were invited to return to the Frauen Club to meet again with Mírzá Asadu'lláh and Ahmad Sohrab, since they would be leaving on Tuesday the 5th to meet 'Abdu'l-Bahá. All rose as Mírzá Asadu'lláh entered the room. Alma opened the meeting with a prayer about the 'Day of God', Mírzá Asadu'lláh and Ahmad Sohrab both spoke and once more Lady Blomfield read 'Abdu'l-Bahá's message. Mr Schweizer closed with a prayer. Mr Herrigel announced that his Sunday and Thursday meetings would be held as well as Alma's Friday meetings so that the friends could attend whichever meeting they wished.

On the morning of 5 December, Eckstein, Herrigel, Ruoff, Schweizer, Braun, Margarethe and Alma accompanied Mírzá Asadu'lláh and Ahmad Sohrab from the Eckstein home to the train station, where the pair departed to meet the Master in Marseilles.

The Herrigels and Lady Blomfield visited Mr Haigis, who was ill and passed away shortly afterwards. That night many people from both 'groups' attended a meeting at the Herrigels. They read the Master's message again and there was an enthusiastic discussion about unity and how different souls being at different developmental stages approached the Writings from their respective understandings, but that the Writings brought unity to all.[8] It was at this meeting that Alma asked Lady Blomfield to announce to everyone that she (Alma) would be leaving for Leipzig. Alma then invited everyone to attend the meeting at the Schweizer home the following evening.[9]

On Wednesday, 6 December 1911, Lady Blomfield, Mrs Earle and Wilhelm Herrigel visited the Schweizers' for tea and attended a large gathering at the Köstlin home in the evening. Lady Blomfield talked about how 'Abdu'l-Bahá had spoken with the clergy in London. They also discussed the story of the famous Bahá'í heroine Ṭáhirih and the strength of women. At the end of the meeting, to her own surprise, Alma kissed Lady Blomfield![10] On Thursday, 7 December, Lady Blomfield departed from Stuttgart for Switzerland. She promised to send the names of some of her contacts in Leipzig to Alma to visit and teach.[11]

In her letters, Alma described Lady Blomfield's elegant disposition, as well as Alma's own hope that her visit would bring unity to the Stuttgart friends so that Alma could leave for Leipzig.[12] In addition, Alma hoped that Lady Blomfield would help the friends find a way to reorganize into a joint united assembly.

Alma was surprised to find that contrary to her own understanding, Lady Blomfield's report of this journey to Stuttgart did not mention the formation of a Working Committee or a joint assembly consisting of members of both groups. Rather she recommended that the community be entrusted to the Herrigels, to whose 'wise and devoted hands may safely be left the conduct of the teaching in Stuttgart, possessing as they do much knowledge and a wide tolerant sympathy with all forms of belief, and other methods of work'.[13]

Lady Blomfield reported that Dr Fisher had been 'perhaps more enthusiastic than wise', and that 'Mischievous reports were spread abroad with an opposing force, born of lack of knowledge rather than of a desire to persecute! But great harm was done!'[14] Lady Blomfield believed that Dr Fisher suffered financially because he had lost patients when they found out about the disunity in Stuttgart and he was starving, as he had no financial means. In her report to 'Abdu'l-Bahá, she asked Him if Dr Fisher should continue teaching in England and offered to start a fund for him, which Herrigel kindly offered to manage. 'Abdu'l-Bahá, in His wisdom, did not choose to send Dr Fisher to England. Interestingly, there was a wealthy Reverend named Dr Fisher, also from Brooklyn, New York, who did start teaching the Bahá'í Faith in England at this time.[15]

Friedrich Schweizer wrote about the progress Stuttgart had made in just two years:

The work of spreading the Glad-tidings in Stuttgart is progressing. At the close of the year 1910, there was only one Bahá'í meeting; but now, at the close of 1911, we have meetings five times a week at four different places in this city and vicinity – the number of participants having increased considerably.[16]

In December, 'Abdu'l-Bahá sent love and encouragement to all the Stuttgart friends:

> O My true friends!
> The friends on their return from Stuttgart are praising all the friends of the Merciful in that city, saying: Praise be to God! that the friends are in utmost attachment and are ignited by the Fire of the Love of God. They are occupied in naught but the Divine commemoration. And also the contents of your letter proved your great love.
> It seems that the Light of the Sun of Truth will shine powerfully in Stuttgart and all over Germany; the Breath of the Holy Spirit will show forth a great result, and the Bounty of the Word of God will spread over all.
> I give you the Glad-tidings that your advancement in the Divine Kingdom will be great and that the Doors of the Kingdom are opened to all the people of Germany.
> Who will embrace it first? I hope that the called ones of Germany may become the chosen ones.
> Therefore, you should seek no rest; nay rather endeavour day and night to guide the people, to give sight to the blind, to give life to the dead and to grant Everlasting Life.[17]

And on 19 December He shared His happiness with Alma, sent messages for all the friends who had come from Aalen, Esslingen, Zuffenhausen and Fellbach, and to Gustav Eger, Anna Köstlin and Margarethe Döring – saying of the latter that 'her services are accepted by the Kingdom of Abhá' – with encouraging words for Alma to strengthen her confidence for Leipzig:

O dear Handmaiden of God!

Thy letter has been received. Its contents brought happiness, for it was an indication that Praise be to God, real unity has been established among the friends. Today the greatest work is the establishment of unity and love among the friends of God, so that they may become examples for all mankind. The Friends of God and the handmaidens of the merciful must endeavor to unite all the world, for if they themselves are not united, how can they be the means of uniting others.

His Holiness the Christ says: Ye are the salt of the earth, but if the salt has lost its savor wherewith shall it be salted? However, my hope is this that the deepest love and unity may be established amongst you all . . .

O dear handmaiden of God, thou art confirmed, therefore be assured that thou wilt be the means of the Exaltation of the Word of God; and wilt spread His fragrances in Leipzig as in Stuttgart . . .

I beseech and supplicate the Heavenly Father and always wish for all of you new Blessings and Confirmation.[18]

After reading these Tablets, Alma wrote home:

It does not depend upon the praise of man but that our services are accepted by God and to have Abdul-Baha say, 'Our service is accepted', is worth more than everything man can say, in fact there is no comparison . . . How thankful we can be for the opposition and oppression, for if it were not for them, I would not have received the praise.[19]

Alma now began to plan her move to Leipzig. She set up appointments to meet all her contacts in Stuttgart before she moved.[20] She wrote to her cousin Jennie Scholz and to Margarethe's brother in Leipzig asking help to find a room or a boarding house. The Scholzes offered Alma a sunny room in their home, which 'she can have at once & all other arrangements can be made after Alma arrives'. Alma told them upfront that she was coming because it was 'Abdu'l-Bahá's wish that she spread the teachings in Leipzig as she had done in Stuttgart. It was important to her that the Scholzes knew what to expect.[21]

Lady Blomfield wrote to Alma from Switzerland that she was planning to return to Stuttgart in February for a few weeks.[22] Alma was to depart for Leipzig after Fanny's money arrived and after Lady Blomfield's visit.[23]

When Lady Blomfield arrived, she called for a meeting to discuss the organization of 'a working committee' composed of men and women from both circles. The goal was to consider how to unite the two assemblies. Alma hoped they would be united into one assembly. People from both groups attended the meeting, but unfortunately Herrigel himself did not attend. Alma wrote to Pauline, 'It was rather a hard task for him to invite his friends at his meeting to come to our meeting and plan a working committee.'[24] The friends decided to leave the topic for the Sunday evening meeting at the Herrigels.[25]

On 21 February, Herrigel invited the community to an event at the large Hall at the Bürger Museum, where Lady Blomfield read the following message from 'Abdu'l-Bahá to the Assembly at Stuttgart:

Oh, Sons and Daughters of the Kingdom!

Be thankful to God the Heavenly Father is extremely kind to all!
He has opened the doors of Heaven to you. He has sent down His Kingdom for you. He has ignited a brilliant lamp in your heart. He has breathed in you the breaths of the Holy Spirit.
He has baptized you with the Water of Life, the Fire of the Love of God and with the Spirit of His Kingdom and bestowed upon you eternal life!
Glad Tidings! That the Lights of the Sun of Truth have dawned from the Horizon of the East!
Glad Tidings! That the Heavenly Powers are set in motion!
Glad Tidings! That the Earthly Powers are quaking!

Glad Tidings! That the sun of prejudices and the moon of superstitions are eclipsed!
Glad Tidings! That the stars of worldly honours are falling!
Glad Tidings! That the Divine Spirit and the Host of Heaven are attacking!
Glad Tidings! That the angels of heaven are sent throughout all regions!
Glad Tidings! That the fragrances of the Holy Spirit are wafted!
Glad Tidings! That the Morn of Exhilaration has appeared!
Glad Tidings! That the Sun of Truth is shining![26]

Alma and all the friends who were not part of Herrigel's circle were informed about the event at short notice with little time to invite people, but even so the room was filled. Lady Blomfield and Mrs Earle came, dressed exquisitely. Herrigel was the Chairman of the evening. Lady Blomfield read the message, Mrs Earle read the translation in German and Herrigel gave a talk. Lady Blomfield shared her notes and Alma closed with words from a Tablet she had recently received from 'Abdu'l-Bahá. Although it was common for believers to share new Tablets when they received them, all were surprised about Alma's Tablet, because it was new and it had not come to her through Herrigel, and the contents were not what they expected. Alma had not previously had a chance to share the new Tablet from 'Abdu'l-Bahá because there was consultation regarding the programme.

The following evening, Alma was invited to dinner at the Ecksteins to discuss how to unite the two centres in Stuttgart. Lady Blomfield explained that the Master desired three things: the unity of the two centres, that Dr Fisher should leave for California where his relatives were living, and thirdly, that the believers would organize Dr Fisher's return for him. Alma was concerned that although Dr Fisher often spoke of doing this, he would probably find it hard since he did not expect his departure to come about in this way. Fisher's friends were getting tired of financing him.[27]

At the Herrigels' Thursday meeting on 29 February, the idea

of creating a Working Committee to organize a united meeting was presented and everyone was invited to the Schweizers' home in Zuffenhausen on the following evening.[28]

Lady Blomfield, Mrs Earle and a large number of believers attended the meeting in Zuffenhausen, where they consulted about the Working Committee consisting of both women and men from both groups. Herrigel did not come to the meeting. Several gentlemen said that although they also believed it was the only right way to proceed, it would be wise to once again postpone the discussion of the issue until Herrigel's Sunday meeting, so that he could be present. On 1 March at the Sunday meeting, Herrigel presented a list of 18 names (including women) of which nine were to be elected and at least two should come from the Schweizers' meeting. Professor Braun arranged a Unity Meeting for 3 March at the Frauen Club to take the next step.

At the Frauen Club, they planned to elect a committee to organize the teaching work. Alma wrote, 'All the believers are strong and active, and I hope splendid work will be accomplished with this working committee . . . As soon as our believers are united and work together my work is finished here and with the help of God will do the same in Leipzig.'[29]

Later that day, Mrs Eckstein visited Alma and shared her ideas about how Alma could be successful in Leipzig. She told Alma which of Herrigel's books to use when teaching in that city. Alma replied that she would primarily use the Tablets from 'Abdu'l-Bahá and showed her the Tablets which Professor Braun and Mr Ruoff had printed at His request. These were the Tablets that 'Abdu'l-Bahá had requested to be published as a priority in the summer of 1909. Now, three years later in March 1912, Herrigel still had not done so because Mr Schneebeli had written that Herrigel's books should be published first.[30] Alma wanted to be sure that any new believers she taught in Leipzig would turn solely to the Master.[31]

Alma asked Mrs Eckstein to kindly look after Margarethe while she was in Leipzig. She was particularly concerned about Margarethe being left alone to work with the men in Stuttgart.

After the meeting with Mrs Eckstein, Alma attended the funeral of Mrs Sophie Stäbler,[32] the first Bahá'í funeral in Germany. After four and a half years of teaching and community building, Alma had seen many Bahá'í Holy Day celebrations, the first Bahá'í wedding, the birth of two Bahá'í children, and now the first Bahá'í funeral.

Unfortunately, there was still no common basis for unity. Mr Schneebeli attended the meetings at the Herrigels and when the two groups came together to elect the Working Committee or adopt a united approach, Herrigel's group insisted again that the others must join them since they were the larger group. In this way, as Alma had feared, the concerns of the Esslingen/Zuffenhausen friends were not considered. The Bahá'ís in Esslingen/Zuffenhausen did not believe in automated writing and could not submit to the programme the others enjoyed on the basis of the size of the group.

Alma had made plans to leave for Leipzig on 10 March, provided the two groups agreed on fair terms for unity.[33] Since that goal had not been reached, she postponed her trip and stayed in Stuttgart for the Eger family's Naw-Rúz Feast. It was the first Naw-Rúz celebration in Esslingen and 23 people attended.[34] It was a source of unity for Esslingen and strengthened the group; that would be all she could accomplish before her departure for Leipzig.[35]

Louise Bosch, a Swiss-American Bahá'í who had learned about the Faith from Lua Getsinger in the early days in America, asked Alma if any believers would like to correspond with her in German. Alma gave her address to Anna Köstlin, and their correspondence began in the Fall of 1911. In a very touching letter on 18 March 1912, shortly before Alma left Stuttgart, Anna Köstlin wrote to Louise:

> Miss Knobloch, our dear teacher who has been working in Stuttgart for 4 years is moving to Leipzig in the next days to spread the heavenly words there as she has done in Stuttgart. She was a real mother to me. Despite many disappointments and bitterness that she had to experience

through me, she has not given up her love and conquered me with it. I ask God that I gain power and become ever more worthy of my spiritual mother.[36]

A few weeks later Alma wrote home that Anna's mother 'Mrs Köstlin has changed so much one can scarcely believe she is the same person. Never have I seen one change so much in such a short time.' Alma believed that Mrs Köstlin, being Mrs Herrigel's sister, could build unity in Stuttgart.[37] Indeed, the Köstlin family filled that unifying role.

From outside the community, new doors were opening in Stuttgart as various outside organizations invited the Bahá'ís to speak at their venues. The Stuttgart community received many invitations to give lectures on Islam, unlike the early days where lectures had been held *against* Islam. There was a demand in Stuttgart for those who could shed light on the favourable aspects of Islam, and so Bahá'í teachers were invited by the Christians.[38] It was an interesting change of *Zeitgeist*, since about two years later, after signing a secret treaty, Turkey entered the First World War on the German side. In any case, this was a great opportunity for the Bahá'ís, who had been teaching that all religions came from one God. Alma was confident in the ability of the Stuttgart believers to give good public talks. Friedrich Schweizer worked hard to translate more of the Writings into German.[39]

As she left for Leipzig, a Tablet from 'Abdu'l-Bahá summarized her services in Stuttgart:

> O Faithful to the Covenant!
> Thy letter arrived, as well as the letters from the friends. I will answer all of them. Thou hast written that the Assembly of Esslingen is progressing. This news was the cause of a great joy. I hope that Esslingen will be a great center for Bahá'ís.
> May the Cause of God progress in it day by day, and the light of unity of the world of humanity shine forth.
> May the light of the kingdom radiate forth and fill all men with delight and joy . . .

> Thank God that the Assembly of Stuttgart is also progressing. Do thank God, because thou hast been the cause of diffusing there the Breath of God . . .[40]

At the beginning of March 1912, the Stuttgart Bahá'ís had made an appointment with a photographer who was to take a photograph of the entire community. Shortly before the photograph was taken, Herrigel and the friends who attended his meetings cancelled. As it was too late to cancel the photographer, the picture was taken, but to the disappointment of all it did not show the whole community. Margarethe Döring sent this photo to Albert Windust in the United States.[41]

'Abdu'l-Bahá wrote to the believers in Stuttgart:

> Through the maidservant of God Miss Alma Knobloch
>
> To the Friends of God and the maidservants of the Merciful . . .
>
> O ye real divine friends!
> Your letter was like unto a torch which was enkindled with the fire of the heart and the spirit. Therefore, it displayed great effect upon the hearts.
> You have written regarding the Feast of the Declaration of His Holiness the Bab, that you have celebrated a banquet and arranged a blessed gathering. If you sensitize your ears you hear the commendation of the Supreme Concourse and the Praise of the dwellers of the Kingdom of Abha . . .
> If in the world of existence a meeting is organized, the attractions of consciousness surround, and the attention is completely turned toward the Kingdom of Abha, immediately the Supreme Concourse will photograph that gathering and that meeting will become the image and the likeness of the Kingdom of Abha. Strive by all means that your meetings become as such. Read the Tablets of His Holiness Baha o llah with a good melody, peruse them with the tone of the heart and of the spirit. It will confer life; it

will quicken the dead and it will grant the power of flight to every broken-winged bird and cause it to sing and chant.[42]

Herrigel sent Alma a handwritten copy of a message 'Abdu'l-Bahá had sent him through Lady Blomfield.[43] It is only available in German; Alma wrote that it was translated by Herrigel.[44] In it, 'Abdu'l-Bahá confirms that Mr Herrigel is indeed encompassed by difficulties, tells him to wait and be patient, and expresses His hope that the odour of selfishness in Stuttgart will be dispelled.[45]

Lady Blomfield's support fund for Dr Fisher did not raise enough money for his return trip to the United States.[46] Alma wrote, 'The believers in Stuttgart did not wish to give Dr. Fisher several thousand marks in his hands' and he was not 'anxious to leave now that he is asked to leave'.[47] Alma hoped that the Ecksteins might be able to start a new centre when they returned from their trip to Italy and in this way they could combine the two groups into something completely new and not polarized.[48] Lady Blomfield wrote to Alma expressing her sadness that after all her efforts no unity had been found. She sent Alma the original English translation of 'Abdu'l-Bahá's first message to Stuttgart from 19 February, addressed to the 'Sons and Daughters of the Kingdom'.[49] Alma thanked Lady Blomfield for her efforts and wrote, 'Every kind word and thought done in the service of Abha will bring results in due time.'[50]

It was difficult for Lady Blomfield and many of the other Bahá'ís who visited Stuttgart and stayed at the Herrigels' home to maintain neutrality at this time. Most visitors stayed only a short time and their agendas and exposure were largely controlled by Herrigel while they were in Germany. Furthermore, Herrigel himself was quite charming and he and his wife were experts at hospitality. 'Abdu'l-Bahá had sent Lady Blomfield to accomplish one of the most challenging tasks in Europe at the time. No one knew Herrigel's true motivation, which would only become apparent in 1928.

27

LEIPZIG AT LAST

United or not, it was time for Alma to leave. Her last days were spent visiting and teaching the Eger and Bender families. On her last night, there was a grand good-bye party where Mr Schwab and other men shared funny poems in memory of Alma.[1] Many Bahá'ís brought their friends to the party and all were interested in the Bahá'í teachings. On 10 April 1912, Alma finally left Stuttgart. Margarethe, Anna Köstlin, Julia and Elise Stäbler, Mrs Kusterer and Mina Diegel brought flowers to the station to see her off. Alma left with a heavy heart full of love.

History would never have clearly illustrated Alma's talent for community building had she not been sent to Leipzig. Whatever role the Bahá'ís felt she had played in Stuttgart would now be vacant. The Bahá'ís in Stuttgart would have to find their own way to bring the community together.

It was hard for Alma to relocate and start all over again, but fortunately she had some family contacts who would help her to get started. Her first stop was a two-day visit to Mrs Metzeroth and Aunt Clara in Hildburghausen.[2] Alma felt that Aunt Clara and Cousin Priska accepted the teachings.[3]

Mrs Metzeroth and Aunt Clara took Alma to visit other relatives.[4] Mrs Metzeroth's son Fritz, who had once been interested in marrying Alma, had remained single. The two women mentioned the situation to Alma, but she was not interested. She wrote to Fanny: 'to become a German housewife would mean several thousand marks for a dowry and would take up all one's time. I do not know what will become of me when I am older, there is no need worrying, will have to take things as they come.'[5]

Alma arrived in Leipzig on 12 April. Cousin Jennie and her two children picked her up at the Leipzig train station and brought her to their home.[6] She was given a lovely room with a window from which she could see the then almost completed Völkerschlachtdenkmal of Leipzig, a monument commemorating the defeat of Napoleon at the Battle of Leipzig, near the site where Napoleon had stood and watched the battle. Leipzig was expecting 6,000 German and American guests to come for the opening ceremony in the next year.

In August 1912 'Abdu'l-Bahá sent strength and confirmations to Alma from the United States, referring, as he often did, to her height:

> . . . Thou shalt arise to thank God fully when thou shalt stand before the mirror and behold how a little girl as thyself is so wonderfully confirmed that the tall and great women have not attained to one drop of this ocean. This is the Power of Baha'o'llah! This is the Might of the Kingdom of God. Thank thou God! Thank thou God![7]

After her arrival in Leipzig, Alma visited Margarethe's brother Kurt Döring and his wife who had already shared the Bahá'í teachings with many of their friends.[8] Cousin Jennie's husband Fritz shared the teachings with his friend who was the Leipzig Chief of the Police.[9] Alma gave the Police Chief private English lessons and taught him more about the Faith, which he found interesting.[10] The Frauen Club in Leipzig gave her a hearty welcome and offered her use of their rooms for meetings.[11]

Alma worked to build strong friendships between those she had started to teach. She invited Kurt Döring and his wife to visit the Völkerschlachtdenkmal and spend a day together with the Scholz family. On this day, Alma did not talk much about the Faith, rather she helped the friends to become better acquainted with each other.[12]

Alma visited her cousin Martin every week.[13] In May 1912, Jennie and Fritz Scholz accepted the message and started to help Alma make contacts,[14] although their circle of friends was small.[15]

On Wednesday 12 June, Alma was invited to join a group of 19 members of the Frauen Club on a tour to Oberholz. All the women were very progressive intellectual ladies who did not mind listening about the teachings but preferred no 'heavy topics'.[16] On 18 June, about two months after Alma's arrival in Leipzig, two Bahá'í gatherings were held, one at Jennie's and the other at the Dörings'.

Unfortunately, the contacts from Lady Blomfield and the other Stuttgart friends did not live in or near Leipzig, so Alma's family and Margarethe Döring's family were her only contacts in the beginning. Alma approached her work in a spirit of devoted detachment: 'Will do the Master's work to the best of my ability and let the future take care of itself. Abdul-Baha is my guide and my helper and it is wonderful . . . to accept the message is not difficult but the hard times come afterward.'[17]

Although Alma was far away, she was still on Wilhelm Herrigel's mind. His letters to the American friends did not speak very well of her. In addition, he wanted to control the agenda when 'Abdu'l-Bahá came to Germany. During 'Abdu'l-Bahá's visit to America, Herrigel wrote to John Bosch on 7 June requesting him to ask 'Abdu'l-Bahá whether He was really going to visit Stuttgart and if so, about what time? He explained to John that in London 'Abdu'l-Bahá had accepted his invitation to stay at his home.[18]

'Abdu'l-Bahá responded to Herrigel in a Tablet revealed for John Bosch and Luther Burbank from Montclair, New Jersey on 24 June:

> Write long letters to Herrigel and lead him to firmness and steadfastness, and say that 'Miss Knobloch, though a weak woman, remained firm and steadfast. Is it not a pity that thou art a man, with power and might, yet thou hast remained behind?' Verily this is a strange affair.[19]

After Alma left, the Bahá'ís in Stuttgart continued to have separate meetings throughout the summer of 1912.[20] It was expensive and inefficient to pay rent for two halls and doubled the expenses for the copying of materials. Margarethe was not comfortable at the Herrigels' meeting and focused on her teaching work, while Herrigel prevented his friends from associating with the Esslingen group. Dr Fisher did not leave, thereby continuing to cause trouble. The situation remained the same, whether Alma was in Stuttgart or not.

28
SUMMER OF 1912

Alma's cousin Jennie and her children were invited to visit Uncle Bruno in Bautzen for the summer. Bruno could not accommodate so many people and Jennie was concerned about Alma being alone in the house,[1] so she spent her summer visiting friends in Stuttgart.[2] She was relieved that she did not have to go to Bautzen, because she 'did not like their drinking and eating'.

Karl Krüttner, the first Bahá'í in the Austrian Empire (today Czech Republic) planned to visit Alma in Leipzig on the way to his summer vacation at Wilhelmsbad on the North Sea.[3] Jennie decided to lock up the house when she left, so Alma had to go too early, and missed Karl's visit by a week.[4]

Upon her arrival in Stuttgart, Alma found that Margarethe was ill and took care of her until she was well.[5] Her summer vacation was quite busy. She joined her old friends in their teaching and consolidation work. There were five new friends in Esslingen who were grateful to hear the message. The Egers had moved into a new large home with a 'Bahá'í room'; the Schweizers' home was filled with new friends and seekers. In July, Mayor Krieger's family invited Anna Köstlin, Gustav Eger, Margarethe and Alma to meet their friends from some of the best families of Aalen at Café Bär to discuss the teachings. Mr Schwab was translating *The Seven Valleys* and Alma helped his parents understand his new beliefs.[6] They organized the first public meeting in Esslingen with many new seekers. There were six young men about the same age who worked harmoniously with Anna Köstlin to spread the teachings: Mr Eger, Mr Schwab, Mr Bender, Mr Kohler, Mr Aeckerle and Mr Beg. Mr

Eger's father had become a strong believer and when his new belief caused trouble for him at his job, he remained firm and did not waver. Alma also helped Rosa Schwarz, who was organizing a Bahá'í Centre in nearby Degerloch.[7]

'Abdu'l-Bahá kept close contact with the German Bahá'ís during His journey in North America in 1912. When He visited Dublin, New Hampshire, with Alma's sisters and Joseph Hannen, they discussed Alma's teaching work in Germany several times. On 31 July 1912, 'Abdu'l-Bahá told them: 'Anyone whom I send to a place is confirmed; anyone. One of them is Miss Alma Knobloch. God has confirmed her. In the beginning, she was teaching in Stuttgart. Now she is in Leipzig.'[8] Shortly after this He sent Tablets to Germany reminding the friends of this. To Julia Stäbler He wrote, 'O Thou Maidservant of God! Thy letter was received. I am much occupied; therefore, brevity is befitting. Be very grateful to Miss Alma Knobloch and Miss Anna Köstlin, for they became the cause of thy guidance.'[9] To Mr Schweizer He wrote:

> O Thou Seeker of Reality
> ... When the Maid-Servant of God, Miss Knobloch, was sent to that country, I supplicated from the threshold of his Highness Baha Ullah that Confirmation may descend upon her, and I am yet with all my heart and soul praying for her, that she may become more assisted. This is the cause of her Confirmation, for she was thus able to carry out the Glad-tidings of the Appearance of the Blessed Perfection to that region. The manner she was confirmed is a sufficient demonstration and evident proof that the support of the Kingdom of Abhá is the Protector and the Guardian. Every person becomes the eagle of the apex of Glory and thus captures the blessed souls. Therefore, strive ye that each one of you may become a real hunter, just as his Holiness the Christ says: 'Come and be ye the fishers of men.'[10]

'Abdu'l-Bahá also reminded the friends of the importance of unity, the Nineteen Day Feasts, and Bahá'í celebrations:

Praise be to God that, on the Day of the Declaration of His Holiness the Bab, you celebrated the Feast with the utmost beauty. The nineteen days'[sic]Feast has the utmost importance, that the beloved ones may gather in a meeting, be occupied with the utmost love and fellowship in mentioning the name of God, and speak about the glad tidings of God, deliver the proofs and evidences of the appearance of Bahá'u'lláh, mention the praiseworthy deeds and the sacrifices endured by the Believers of God in Persia, talk about the severance and the attraction of the martyrs and remember the cooperation and the mutual assistance of the friends, Therefore this nineteen days'[sic] Feast is most important.[11]

Mrs Kusterer attended the Herrigels' meeting at the end of August. Dr Fisher arrived at the meeting with Bruce Nagel, a 28-year-old man who had moved to New York years previously and was visiting his mother in Nuremberg.[12] 'Abdu'l-Bahá had sent Bruce to Stuttgart with a message for the believers.[13] That evening the Herrigels made unfavourable remarks about Alma and her friends, prompting Mrs Kusterer to speak up. One of the men suggested that they all visit the other friends the following evening at a peace meeting.

The following evening, a reception was held for Bruce in a large hall decorated with flowers. Mr Stäbler sang and Bruce shared his stories and brought copies of 'Abdu'l-Bahá's talks in America. He did all he could to unite the friends and told them that 'Abdu'l-Bahá confirmed that He 'will come to Stuttgart if it is God's Will'.[14] Bruce noted that most Bahá'í communities had a Working Committee composed of nine members and he was surprised that in Stuttgart the Working Committee had been elected but was not functioning since Alma had moved away. Therefore, he asked Margarethe if she would accept Alma's now vacant spot and be the ninth member? When she agreed, he rushed over to her and thanked her, saying that she had, 'taken a great stone off his heart'. Herrigel described the committee work and the prayerful spirit he hoped all would bring to the meetings. Alma shared Pauline's letter describing her experiences in Dublin, New Hampshire with the Master and Mr Schwab closed the meeting with a message from Lady Blomfield.[15]

Herrigel could not envision that Stuttgart could find unity. After Bruce Nagel's visit he wrote to Thornton Chase to thank him for his advice on dealing with the disunity and added, 'Of course, we would be very happy to meet Our Lord here in Stuttgart. And yet how very sorry I am to think He will come, and not find what He is preaching throughout the world, namely peace and unity; this is a drop of wormwood in the cup of my joy. For I know what He is suffering and what He has suffered and all this for peace and unity in the world.'[16]

Despite this, the Stuttgart community boasted an active agenda with activities six days a week:

Tuesday: evening at Esslingen (Miss and Mrs Köstlin)
Weds: Zuffenhausen (Schweizer home)
Thursday: Bürger Museum Stuttgart (Herrigel and friends)
Friday: Kanzleistr. 24 Hall of Frauen Club (Assembly)
Mondays and Sundays: Neue Weinsteig 23 (Margarethe)

In addition to those events, Anna Köstlin arranged several meetings in Schaffhausen, Annemarie Schweizer was teaching the Frank family, the Esslingen Bahá'ís gave a talk at the Esperanto Conference and the Esslingen Esperanto Institute had started translating and publishing Bahá'í materials.[17] Mrs Eger, herself a new believer, visited her family in Eningen (50 kilometres south of Stuttgart) and they all became Bahá'ís.[18] She and Anna Köstlin started children's classes in Stuttgart based on 'Abdu'l-Bahá's talks to the children in Washington and New York which Pauline Hannen had sent her.[19]

Alma was happy to hear that 'Abdu'l-Bahá had assured Fanny that Alma was working, 'for I am really trying my best, keeping right on no matter what others think or say, knowing well that Abdul-Baha will support me, and in the end all will be explained without my doing so. All who serve for a material gain or to become known will wither and die out of the arena of Abha.'[20]

By 1913 the German Bahá'í community was the largest in Europe. Success can be attributed to at least four factors: Alma was an effective teacher, the converts were native Germans (the community in Paris was mostly American expatriates), teaching was a central part of Bahá'í community life involving all Bahá'ís, and finally, many of the converts came from the middle class.[21]

29

ALMA'S FAMILY IN LEIPZIG

Having enjoyed such an eventful summer full of confirmations in Stuttgart, Alma returned to Leipzig on 4 October 1912 hoping to build up a stable Bahá'í community with her family members, their friends and contacts. The Bahá'í community in Leipzig consisted of the Scholz family, Kurt Döring and his wife and a few contacts.

Alma visited her mother's brother, Uncle Bruno Rössler, his wife Aunt Emma and their 19-year-old daughter Melanie in Bautzen. Melanie served as Uncle Bruno's housekeeper and was engaged to a Catholic. Uncle Bruno and Aunt Emma were not very interested in the Faith, but Melanie was! She wrote to Alma that she was 'strangely affected when she read the Bahá'í writings' and that she wanted 'to serve humanity'. She fully accepted the teachings and asked for prayers so she would 'become a true Bahá'í'.[1]

Alma hoped that the friends in the east would travel to Stuttgart if 'Abdu'l-Bahá visited Germany. She wrote, 'If Abdul-Baha comes to Stuttgart, Uncle Bruno will also go to Stuttgart, Cousin Arthur [Jennie Scholz's brother] will pay for Melanie to go with his sister and her father.'[2] She wrote that cousin Priska Wagner, her husband, and her mother Aunt Clara from Wermsdorf near Leipzig had accepted the teachings.[3] Mr Wagner said he would go to Stuttgart to see 'Abdu'l-Bahá if He came.[4] Alma hoped that 'Abdu'l-Bahá would even come to Leipzig![5]

In December of 1912, Alma finally met Karl Krüttner, the

first Austrian (Czech) Bahá'í, in Leipzig. He had married a young woman from Kassel and was in Germany to meet her family. He shared with Alma stories about his troubles with the Catholic priests in Böhm and told her he had begun to learn Esperanto to better serve 'Abdu'l-Bahá.⁶

At the end of the year, Alma took a smaller room and a rent increase at the Scholz house.⁷ Of course, it was Fanny who had to bear the weight of this. Alma consoled Fanny for all her sacrifices:

> ... our beloved Abdul-Baha ... sees you equal as much as us (Alma and Pauline), our services are different, but both are necessary and He appreciates your sacrifices. It is really great to understand the fullness of it, be assured there is no one who knows me who does not admire you ... you are making it possible so that I can accomplish something, for it seems like slow work, we always want to see a great deal at once, therefore one is never contented with oneself, one longs to do so much.⁸

The Scholzes knew that Fanny struggled to pay for Alma's stay in Germany. Fanny was disappointed that the family tried to get so much money out of her, Fanny. Alma began looking for alternatives. Later, Alma wrote to Fanny: 'It has always been my experience that to stay with relatives is very much more expensive than elsewhere.'⁹

On 19 December 1912 'Abdu'l-Bahá returned to the United Kingdom and stayed until 22 January 1913. Ahmad Sohrab wrote to Alma from London that he believed that 'Abdu'l-Bahá would be visiting Stuttgart at the end of February or the beginning of March.¹⁰ Friedrich Schweizer postponed his vacation, hoping to use it when 'Abdu'l-Bahá arrived.¹¹ In December, Margarethe wrote to Alma asking her to return to Stuttgart, which she did in January 1913.¹²

In February 1913, Mr N. George Enzlin of Holland wrote to Alma asking her to beg 'Abdu'l-Bahá to visit Blaricum, Holland, where there were some believers who wished to introduce 'Abdu'l-Bahá to the Dutch public.¹³ The Bahá'ís in Europe were happy – the Master had returned from America, and everyone was looking forward to hosting Him.

30

PETITIONS TO THE MASTER

When 'Abdu'l-Bahá returned to Paris from 22 January to April 1913, He sent two messages to the friends in Germany, one through Alma addressed to the 'people of the Kingdom' and the other through Herrigel addressed to the 'believers in God'. In these letters He said He was longing to see the German believers. He hoped to go to Stuttgart but would not be able to stay more than two nights; so, if any of them wanted a longer visit they had permission to come to Paris. Then, he said, he would go to Stuttgart later.[1]

In response to His invitation, Alma, Gustav Eger, Annemarie Schweizer and Anna Köstlin departed for Paris on 11 February 1913. Not having the money for the trip on such short notice, they were financially sponsored by other Western believers. The following day they visited 'Abdu'l-Bahá at rue St Diviers 30[2] in the reception room and were greeted by Ahmad Sohrab. Immediately Alma recognized Dr Fisher in the room, 'who looked up rather surprised'. They brought nine long stem roses for the Master. 'Abdu'l-Bahá greeted them saying, 'very welcome, you are very, very welcome'. Laura Dreyfus-Barney translated, and Ahmad Sohrab recorded what was said. Alma wrote that 'Abdu'l-Bahá looked at her and said, 'You have a very good sister, a very, very good sister. You are a good teacher. Bravo!'; then He turned to Annemarie, Anna and Gustav, and said, 'You are burning torches!' Alma was surprised that He looked 'very ill and weak and yellow and his eyes were sunken'. He had had a 'prison chill' (a sickness he developed while in prison) a few days before He arrived.[3]

The second morning the four friends arose early and brought a very pretty pot of lilies of the valley to 'Abdu'l-Bahá. He was still quite weak but looking somewhat better, and He welcomed each one with a firm grasp of the hand. He said:

> I am longing to see the Bahá'í friends in Germany. I am very anxious to meet the German believers. The Germans are firm, it is their natural characteristic to be firm and steadfast. It will be through you that the teachings will spread through Germany. I hope it will be through you that the teachings will take a firm root and the blessings of Bahá'u'lláh be spread throughout the land. The German Bahá'ís are pure in heart. I hope to hear that you are all happy, and that you were all united in one assembly, the spirit will then assist and give great power, if there remain two assemblies, they will both fade away, but if they unite they will receive power.[4]

He gave each one prayer beads. They removed their gloves and He anointed them with attar of rose from Persia, putting some in each one of their right hands. 'Abdu'l-Bahá said, 'The Balkan Commission in London did not accomplish their task, I hope you will. Your mission is easier, for it is done through love.'[5]

The friends from Germany were invited to many events while they were in Paris, including an Esperanto banquet given in honour of 'Abdu'l-Bahá followed by a reception, as well as a reception at the Theosophical Society. One day a lady invited them to have tea with another German lady and the president of the German society in Paris. Alma recalled, 'There were always many gatherings, all seats were taken. I was told they were mostly Americans, Canadians, English, and Elsass-Lothringen Germans. There were many Persians, Arabians, also some from Bombay and Egypt.' Elsass-Lothringen or Alsace-Lorraine is the area on the German-French border which France and Germany fought over in the 1871 Franco-Prussian war and World War I. They had only two French believers.

While in Paris they attended a talk 'Abdu'l-Bahá gave at the home of Laura and Hippolyte Dreyfus-Barney. He told them that wealth is one of the bounties of God and if it is used wisely and for the benefit of uplifting humanity man receives great blessings. As He spoke, He paced back and forth touching the knob of Alma's umbrella three times. This umbrella had a special meaning to Alma; it had been a gift from Margarethe Döring. In 1928 Alma left it at the home of the Ripley family who were raising up the community of Orlando, Florida. The Ripleys felt it was a blessing and kept it for some time stored safely in a trunk. Years later, Alma asked to have it back and everyone was surprised to find that the silk of the umbrella was still in perfect condition, without a break or a hole despite the warm climate and the age of the umbrella.[6]

On the last morning, Anna, Annemarie and Gustav brought 'Abdu'l-Bahá another nine perfect red roses and Alma gave him a huge bunch of violets. 'Abdu'l-Bahá looked much better, and said, 'It gives me joy to see the German believers; Germans have pure hearts. They are firm, and they are steadfast, they are the illumined ones. It is like a tree; if the tree is well rooted it will give forth its branches and fruits.' He asked if it would be possible for them to take Dr Fisher back with them to Stuttgart. Alma answered, 'If You said so, [so] it is.' But that morning Dr Fisher did not come to the reception and they did not know where to find him. Returning in the afternoon, they found him with 'Abdu'l-Bahá and the Persian friends. The Master asked Alma to come to sit with Him, and after a while the Persians left, and He arranged four chairs in a row for Alma, Annemarie, Anna and Dr Fisher. He asked Alma when they were planning to leave. She answered that they would leave that evening and had come to invite Dr Fisher to join them. Then 'Abdu'l-Bahá said, 'Very good. You can join them Dr Fisher, you go tonight.' Fisher was surprised and answered that he intended to stay. 'Abdu'l-Bahá asked him why he wanted to stay. What for? Dr Fisher responded that he had not seen some of the friends. The Master asked him whom he wanted to see. To this Dr Fisher answered, 'If the Master wants me to leave, I will leave.' Then

'Abdu'l-Bahá took Alma's hand and joined her hand with Fisher's hand and holding them together He said, 'Now there is peace between you!'[7]

The atmosphere was beautiful. Alma, Annemarie, and Anna told Him how happy they were to hear that He was planning to visit them in Stuttgart. 'Abdu'l-Bahá told them He did not want any newspapers to publish anything about His visit. Before leaving them, 'Abdu'l-Bahá gave each one two stones with the Greatest Name on them, a small photo of Himself, and a delicious piece of cake. All were in tears, including Hippolyte, who had translated for them.

As Dr Fisher was unable to leave that evening, the group planned to leave the next morning, after a successful visit to the German Association in Paris. While waiting for the train, Dr Fisher suddenly decided to return to 'Abdu'l-Bahá. But when he arrived, 'Abdu'l-Bahá sent him once more back to the train station to depart with the others.[8]

In Stuttgart, Alma immediately began to work on the task the Master had given her. She organized a special event for the friends to come together to sign a petition inviting 'Abdu'l-Bahá to visit Germany. The usual discussion began regarding the location for the event: should they meet at the Frauen Club in Esslingen or the Bürger Museum in Stuttgart? Although the large room at the Frauen Club was available, Herrigel's group insisted that the Bürger Museum was larger. But Alma knew that the large hall at the Bürger Museum was booked for that night and was afraid that they would be cramped into the small room which was not large enough. Herrigel insisted that the Bahá'ís could use it. Not wanting to cause disunity, Alma gave in and invited everyone to come to the Bürger Museum. As expected, the large hall was being used for a loud dance and the Bahá'ís overfilled the small hall. The programme began with the announcement that the Herrigels had received a letter to leave for Paris immediately to meet 'Abdu'l-Bahá. Everyone cheered! The rest of the community signed the following petition:

2 March 1913
Petition to Abdul-Baha in Paris

We the undersigned believers wish to express our most heartfelt appreciation for the many favors and Bounties which we have received during the past, and the renewed blessings and precious words for the Germans through Thy Great Love.

With earnest efforts, we are endeavouring to prepare ourselves for the much longed-for visit from Abdul-Baha. So that the Believers be united in love and harmony.

We therefore supplicate at the Threshold of God to accept our prayers and grant us to be able to attain the true Bahá'í spirit and favour us with the visit of our Beloved Abdul-Baha, that through the same Stuttgart and the entire German nation be honoured and blessed,

In deepest reverence,
Your humble and submissive servants and maidservants
Stuttgart 2 March 1913[9]

Alma later recalled that this was one of the happiest evenings of her life, to have been able to accomplish the task 'Abdu'l-Bahá had asked of her. There were 105 signatures on the petition. All were praying for 'Abdu'l-Bahá to visit.[10]

In June, Herrigel wrote about this event to Louis Gregory as follows: 'On February 27, 'Abdu'l-Bahá sent me the message that I should visit Him in Paris as soon as possible, Therefore, my wife and I left on 1 March for Paris . . .' Herrigel further explained that in Paris the Master said that 'there must be complete unity' and that Herrigel 'should admonish (the friends) seriously' and write 'Abdu'l-Bahá 'a letter that all Stuttgart Bahá'í would have to sign that they were all agreed, then He will hurry to come to Stuttgart'. Herrigel wrote, 'Our dear Miss Alma Knobloch was already in Paris about 10 days before us and the Master gave her the same task . . . but she was not able to fulfil it to His satisfaction . . .'[11]

Years later, in 1926, Herrigel asked his secretary to send his 1913 memoirs to Mason Remey. In them, he recalled that

'Abdu'l-Bahá asked him many questions about the friends in Stuttgart and their meetings and that He had already asked a group of Stuttgart believers (Alma, Anna, Annemarie and Gustav) who had visited Him earlier to send Him a petition declaring the unity of the friends. After that, Herrigel's memoirs tell a different version of the story. Due to 'various circumstances', he wrote, their letter had been signed by only half of the community, and therefore, 'Abdu'l-Bahá turned to Herrigel and told him, 'Now you have the task of writing this letter and returning it to Me signed by all the believers in Stuttgart and the surrounding area.' He told Herrigel to take care that the promise of unity would happen. 'When I have this letter and my health is better, I will come to Stuttgart.'[12] Of course, had Herrigel been supportive of the attempt made by Alma, Anna, Annemarie and Gustav, allowed them to organize their signing event at a suitable venue, planned to attend himself and encouraged others to attend it, they would have been successful.

Furthermore, Herrigel recalled that on his trip to Paris he asked 'Abdu'l-Bahá about a prophetic dream he had had, in which he was five or six meters away from 'Abdu'l-Bahá who was digging up a field with a hoe. In his dream, Herrigel also had a hoe in his hand and was frantically digging, trying to catch up with 'Abdu'l-Bahá, but no matter how hard he tried he could not; 'Abdu'l-Bahá was faster and, seeing that Herrigel was struggling, He called out encouraging words to him to keep him from getting discouraged. 'Abdu'l-Bahá smiled at Herrigel and told him, 'This was not a dream.'[13]

Herrigel wrote, 'There was something else in the dream. As 'Abdu'l-Bahá worked there were two cats that coaxed 'Abdu'l-Bahá around the feet to stop Him from working. Suddenly 'Abdu'l-Bahá forcefully (vigorously) sent one of the cats away. The cat hesitated and finally left, always looking back to see if it could return. 'Abdu'l-Bahá said, 'Also this was not a dream, but reality.'

Remembering his visit, Herrigel said that 'Abdu'l-Bahá asked him lots of questions about how he would teach the Faith and answer certain questions, especially relating to Islam and the

Bahá'í Faith. When Herrigel responded, 'Abdu'l-Bahá would reply to him, 'Sehr Gut, Sehr Gut!' (Very good, very good!) [14]

'Abdu'l-Bahá was trying to rescue Herrigel from his own self. The Herrigels stayed in a quiet room in Hotel Oxford and Cambridge. On the last night Herrigel woke up during the night with a strong feeling of happiness which left him in a state of bliss for about two hours with tears streaming down his face. The following day, before their departure 'Abdu'l-Bahá told him, 'I have filled your heart with love, and you must take this love back to the believers!' Herrigel believed that this referred to what had happened to him the night before. The whole way home he was in noticeable bliss. [15]

The Herrigels returned on 4 March and invited everyone to come to their home on the 6th to hear the message 'Abdu'l-Bahá had given to them. Alma was so happy. On 5 March she wrote to Fanny, 'I am sure 'Abdu'l-Bahá will be pleased!'[16] At this meeting, everyone signed the united petition drafted by Herrigel inviting 'Abdu'l-Bahá to visit their united community. Alma did not care who wrote what petition, she was only happy that the community was united and the Master finally could visit Germany!

> My first commandment was to train souls, now I am to spread the teachings in all the cities in Germany. When I have trained one who is attracted, he will make 10 Bahá'ís in one year. That's wonderful. In asking 'Abdu'l-Bahá if he can give any advice as to who to teach or how to go about it, He says, 'No, do as you have been doing.' That means sacrifice oneself for others, train them in the Teachings, don't think of oneself and rejoice over the advancement and good fortune of others. This is not always easy.

The Stuttgart Naw-Rúz Feast was celebrated in unity at the Frauen Club with 80–100 people attending, each donating to cover the expenses as they wished. Also, a united meeting was held at the Herrigels' house every Sunday morning.[17] The Esslingen group abandoned their Friday night event to encourage united participation in the Sunday meeting. Some believers asked Alma to remain in Stuttgart until 'the putty that holds them together is dry'.[18]

The friends anxiously awaited 'Abdu'l-Bahá's arrival in Stuttgart. Cousin Arthur paid for Melanie to travel to Stuttgart, but unfortunately, she arrived too early. While she was staying at the Stäblers' home, Uncle Bruno became unhappy that she was not caring for his household and called her home before 'Abdu'l-Bahá arrived.

On 29 March 1913, after visiting his daughter Rúhá Khánum who was in hospital in Paris, 'Abdu'l-Bahá gave Siyyid Aḥmad Báqiroff, Mírzá Maḥmúd-i-Zarqání, Mírzá Asadu'lláh and Ahmad Sohrab instructions to pack and prepare to travel to Germany. He 'told them to change completely from Eastern garb to Western dress and to discard their oriental headgear'.[19] 'Abdu'l-Bahá wanted His arrival in Stuttgart to be a complete surprise. It was.

31
'ABDU'L-BAHÁ IN GERMANY

I recall the slow eastward spread of that infant light which led to the gradual emergence of the German and Austrian Bahá'í Communities, during the darkest period of 'Abdu'l-Bahá's incarceration in the prison-fortress of 'Akká. I am reminded of His subsequent epoch-making visit, soon after His providential release from His forty-year confinement in the Most Great Prison, to these newly-fledged struggling communities, of His patient seed-sowing destined to yield at a later age its first fruits, and constituting a landmark of the utmost significance in the rise and establishment of the Faith of Bahá'u'lláh in that continent.
Shoghi Effendi[1]

On 1 April 1913, at the request of 'Abdu'l-Bahá, Siyyid Aḥmad-i-Báqiroff, Mírzá Maḥmúd-i-Zarqání, Siyyid Asadu'lláh and Ahmad Sohrab changed from their Eastern garb into European dress,[2] and they all departed for Stuttgart from the Paris train station crowded with friends saying goodbye.

On the train, Ahmad Sohrab read Him the news that J. P. Morgan had passed away. In late November 1912, 'Abdu'l-Bahá had visited Morgan's library where He had left a benediction for him in his album. The event was recorded in many newspapers.[3] Now Morgan's life had closed and 'Abdu'l-Bahá said regretfully, 'He would have been well, had he breathed one breath in the Cause of Bahá'u'lláh! He has left all that wealth which he accumulated during his lifetime, and which now will serve him no purpose!' Ahmad told Him that they closed the New York Stock Exchange for five minutes to pay homage to the financial genius; 'Abdu'l-Bahá replied, 'Only five minutes?!'[4]

'Abdu'l-Bahá originally planned to spend two days in Germany, but when He travelled, anything could happen. The Master moved when He was inspired to move; the timing was almost always a surprise. In 1910, after having been a prisoner in the Holy Land since 1869, 'Abdu'l-Bahá had suddenly in one hour departed the Holy Land for Egypt. On 2 September 1911, an article in the populist British newspaper the *Daily Mail* explained that 'Abdu'l-Bahá's movements were kept so secret that 'even those who know him' did not know when he would arrive.[5] On 25 March 1912, 'Abdu'l-Bahá boarded the S.S. *Cedric* heading for the United States. The ship stopped in Naples where some fellow passengers departed to join the transatlantic maiden voyage of the *Titanic*, asking Him to do the same. 'Abdu'l-Bahá had declined, later saying that His heart did not 'prompt Him to do so'.[6] During His travels in America, Edward Getsinger wrote to Mrs Parsons: "'Abdu'l-Bahá said, "I cannot be bound to any place or arrangement before the day arrives." The spirit arranges to send the contingencies.'[7] One time while in the United States, the Master took His time and thereby missed the connecting train he needed to be on time for an appointment in Kenosha. The disappointed believers found themselves quite thankful later when they heard that the missed train had collided with another train.[8] The Master moved with the Will of God, under the protection of Bahá'u'lláh; no man could understand, control or capture that, it is impossible.

Before arriving in Germany, 'Abdu'l-Bahá said, 'This is the best thing; we will arrive in Stuttgart, take our rooms in the hotel, settle down and call up the friends. How surprised they will be! Is this not a fine plan? We are going to surprise them. Then when they come, they will find us in their midst, and knowing nothing about it at all. Yes! This is the best plan.'[9] He arrived quietly in Stuttgart at 8 p.m. on 1 April 1913 and proceeded at once to the Hotel Marquardt. He took room 150 on the second floor overlooking the broad avenue.[10]

Returning from Esslingen that evening, Alma was surprised to find Margarethe at the Depot waiting for her. Margarethe asked, 'Guess why I am here?' Alma replied, 'To show your kindness to me as you always do.' Margarethe answered, 'No! 'Abdu'l-Bahá is here staying at the Marquardt, here is a letter from Ahmad!'[11] They went directly to the hotel. Sohrab told them that 'Abdu'l-Bahá was resting and asked them to return early the next morning to arrange their meetings, to avoid confusion or conflict.

During His stay in Stuttgart, 'Abdu'l-Bahá received the friends at the hotel daily from 9 to 11 a.m. His engagements and meetings were planned for the afternoons and evenings. The German believers communicated with 'Abdu'l-Bahá through double translation, Herrigel, Eckstein, Fisher or Alma translating Sohrab's English translation into German.[12] As 'Abdu'l-Bahá requested, the newspapers were not informed about His visit to Germany.[13] The reason for this remains a mystery, although the friends were often curious about it.

Early the next morning, Alma woke up and began planning. She went to an art store owned by two believers and asked them to place telephone calls to the rest of the Stuttgart friends. Already early that morning, Bahá'ís gathered at the Hotel wanting to see the Master.[14] When Alma and Mina Diegel arrived at the hotel, the Herrigels, Margarethe, and Emil Ruoff and his son were just leaving.[15]

Alma flew into 'Abdu'l-Bahá's open arms and began to weep. He asked, 'Are you happy now? How is everything?' She replied, she had worked so hard her hair had turned grey and He countered, 'If your bones had melted it would also be well for such a Cause . . .' 'Abdu'l-Bahá then spoke about the importance of love between believers. Alma recalled that He said:

> It is very necessary that love and unity exist between the believers. In New York there were 800 believers at one time and when I arrived there only 80 on account of disunity, petty quarrels. When I left, they were in perfect unity and love, there must be unity amongst Bahá'ís. When the

believers are not united the people will say, 'If there's no unity among you, how can you teach unity for the whole world?'[16]

In his letters, Ahmad Sohrab recalled Alma's visit to the Master:

> Miss Alma Knoblock [sic] came and the Master arose from His seat and greeted her most unusually! Oh, Miss Knoblock! Oh! Miss Knoblock! She was very welcome. He loved her very much! His heart was attached to her. In reality, she was the blessed of the Kingdom. Her heart was pure and attracted, otherwise she could not serve the cause so well. Her sincerity confirmed her in the service of the Cause. While in America, He always remembered her, He never forgot her. He was greatly attached to the severed friends who are selfless. Let her thank God that she has attained such a bounty! God willing her heart will become more illumined day unto day. He will ever pray for her and all the German believers so that the confirmations of God may descend upon them. If she taught one soul in a city and he was attracted, after one year he would make ten Bahá'ís. And so on and so on. I can write many more pages but there is no time.[17]

Alma remembered what 'Abdu'l-Bahá told her that morning:

> I asked if I should return to Leipzig soon & Abdul-Baha said: yes. You must go to many cities & teach. All over Germany, when you have made one good believer in a place, they will then spread the teachings. You must always be the means of keeping the Stuttgart Assembly together, be their support & strengthen the others. When mentioning Leipzig, He said many pure souls will arise who will serve the cause of God in Germany, simply for the love of Bahá'u'lláh. The teachings will be spread all over Germany, the Holy Spirit will illumine this country. The Germans are very susceptible, they are very religious.[18]

At 3 p.m. Herrigel took 'Abdu'l-Bahá for a drive in the Royal Park and then brought Him to his home where He was received by more than 100 people.[19] When He entered the room, all arose with tears in their eyes, rejoicing for the greatness of that long-awaited moment. 'Abdu'l-Bahá addressed them: 'How attracted and enkindled are the German Bahá'ís! How full of love they are! Love does not need a teacher.'[20]

In the car ride back to the hotel, 'Abdu'l-Bahá told Herrigel, 'You must thank God that you are sitting in this car with the Centre of the Covenant. The importance of this event cannot be fully appreciated at this time.'[21] After a short rest at the hotel, Consul Schwarz brought Him back to the Herrigels' for the evening programme. After that 'Abdu'l-Bahá was transported with Consul Schwarz's auto and driver during His time in Stuttgart. Before His visit, the Schwarzes had had little contact with the Bahá'ís. Alice Schwarz wrote that she had previously attended meetings occasionally; it is not clear if her husband had attended them at all. The profound relationship between 'Abdu'l-Bahá and the Schwarz family began with His visit to Stuttgart. Alice recalled,

> As far as I am concerned, I often found myself in front of the hotel, driven there by my great devotion and respect for my beloved Master, watching the window, hoping to have the good fortune to get a sight of the blessed Face, because an account of the rush of so many friends, a certain shyness prevented me from disturbing Him. Sometimes I went home with a sad heart, but sometimes I was irresistibly driven to his Presence, and I found myself in front of His door and it sometimes happened that He opened the door Himself and welcomed me in inexpressible kindness with the 'Greatest Name' and invited me to come in with benevolent signs of His blessed hand.[22]

In addition, she wrote,

> When I was in the presence of the Master, the radiant

Aura of the Beloved caused me to feel as though I must pass away, I had the feeling that new, unknown forces were forming inside of me, as if my soul was blossoming like a lily. The inner needs, what struggles are to endure, what suffering is to bear, until the inner person has changed. It is hard to describe, but every true Bahá'í must experience it.[23] (my translation)

Alice Schwarz's diary begins on 1 April 1913, the day they first met 'Abdu'l-Bahá, who 'for the first time taught them about Bahá'u'lláh and His Revelation'.[24] On the long car rides through the German countryside in the Spring of 1913 Consul Schwarz enjoyed close contact with 'Abdu'l-Bahá and became a pillar of strength for the German Bahá'í community. In 1919, he served as a delegate to the first Universal Peace Conference at Bern, Switzerland where he presented a paper on Bahá'í principles. Alma wrote of Consul Schwarz's noble character in her memoirs, recalling that he had reorganized his bank to permit clerks to become partial owners.[25] He was later named a Disciple of 'Abdu'l-Bahá.

'Abdu'l-Bahá returned to the Herrigels' on the evening of 2 April, and addressed the community:

> This evening I am united with those souls of God, with people, who have really learned to listen to the call of God, with people, whose faces are enlightened by the rays of the Sun of Truth . . . All nations of this earth have been waiting until this day for the Promised One to appear.
>
> The Promised one of the Old Testament was Jesus Christ. The Jews waited anxiously day and night for Him . . . But when His Holiness Jesus Christ appeared, they were deprived of the blessing to understand him. They tormented him with persecution and ill-treatment and at last they crucified him . . . They are still awaiting their Saviour . . . The Saviour appeared 2000 years ago, but up to the present day, they have not yet recognised him . . . They

waited 1500 years for this Saviour and when he came, they denied him.

. . . We must really thank God that we are to-day aware of the vast importance of the coming of Baha'o'llah. The veil is removed, and you have opened your eyes and sought for truth. Therefore, the light of understanding shines in your hearts . . . you have heard His call. This is the greatest mercy. God hath chosen you for His service. Whilst all others are asleep, you are awakened, the greater number of mankind, are blind, but you are seeing . . . If you thank God a thousand times an hour for this mercy, you are nevertheless unable to thank him enough.[26]

The next morning, 3 April, 'Abdu'l-Bahá began to receive visitors at 8:30 a.m. He talked about the great bounties bestowed upon Stuttgart. He told the friends, 'I hope that our happiness will be eternal, I hope we will be together in all the spiritual worlds. We will find refuge and shelter under the protection of the gifts of Bahá'u'lláh. There is a union which has no end, a life which is not followed by death.'[27]

That afternoon, 'Abdu'l-Bahá drove with Consul Schwarz to Schloss Solitude,[28] a rococo palace which had once served as the strict military academy in which Friedrich Schiller had been confined. In 1782 Schiller secretly left his regiment to attend the premier of his first play *The Robbers*. For this he was imprisoned, after which he fled to Weimar where he became one of the most famous German poets and thinkers of all time; he is the author of the famous chorus of Beethoven's Ninth Symphony 'Ode to Joy', which is today the European Union anthem.

They returned to the Schwarz home where 'Abdu'l-Bahá addressed several prominent men and women. Alice Schwarz knew that in the Orient dogs were not permitted inside the homes, so she locked away the family Dachshund. Despite all her efforts, the dog pushed through a half-opened door and ran into the room where he jumped on her in front of the Master! She begged the Master for forgiveness, to which He replied,

Stuttgart, 12 March 1912. Standing, left to right: Katharina Eger, Henrietta Kusterer, four people unidentified, Anna Köstlin, Max Bender standing behind her, unidentifed, Friedrich Schweizer, Annemarie Schweizer, Gustav Eger, Heinrich Schwab, unidentified. Seated, left to right: Helene Eger, two unidentified women with children, Julia Stäbler, Elise Stäbler, Margarethe Döring, Alma Knobloch, Mrs Wanke with her grandchild Khorshid Schweizer, Rosa Schwarz, unidentified. This was planned to be a photograph of the entire community, but shortly before it was taken, Wilhelm Herrigel and the friends who attended his meetings cancelled (see Chapter 26)

© USBNA

The old train station in Stuttgart where 'Abdu'l-Bahá arrived and departed

'Abdu'l-Bahá in Stuttgart, 6 April 1913: (1) Lydia Bauer, (2) Rosa Schwarz, (3) Helene Eger, (4) Hede Jäger, (5) Alma Knobloch, behind her left to right: Julia Stäbler, Elise Stäbler, then Wilhelm Herrigel, unidentified, Siyyid Asadu'lláh, Siyyid Aḥmad-i-Báqiroff, 'Abdu'l-Bahá, Alice Schwarz. Back row: (6) Katharine Eger, Margarethe Döring in white hat, Heinrich Schwab holding the Greatest Name, Adolf Eckstein (holding the darker version of the Greatest Name), Ahmad Sohrab, (8) Maḥmúd-i-Zarqání, (9) Christian Haug, (10) Mrs Jäger

'Abdu'l-Bahá in Stuttgart, 6 April 1913: (1) Julius Grünzweig, (2) Dr Edwin Fisher, (3) Max Bender, (4) Karl Goll, Mr Häfner, (5) Heinrich Schwab, then following, left to right: Siyyid Asadu'lláh, Maḥmúd-i-Zarqání, Christian Haug senior, Siyyid Aḥmad-i-Báqiroff, Hugo Bender, (6) Adolf Eckstein, (7) Richard Kohler, (8) Mr Schneebeli, (9) Wilhelm Herrigel, then following left to right: Axel Schwarz, Consul Schwarz, 'Abdu'l-Bahá, (10) Gustav Eger, (11) Emil Ruoff, (12) Friedrich Schweizer holding the Greatest Name, (13) Aḥmad Sohrab, (14) Wolfgang Schwarz, (15) Otto Häfner

'Abdu'l-Bahá at the Esslingen Kinderfest, April 1913

Friedrich Schweizer

The Schweizer house, visited by 'Abdu'l-Bahá and today the seat of the Spiritual Assembly of the Bahá'ís of Stuttgart. 'Abdu'l-Bahá is reported to have said: 'In this house the call "Yá Bahá'u'l'Abhá" will always be heard and the teachings Bahá'u'lláh will be spread from this house . . .'

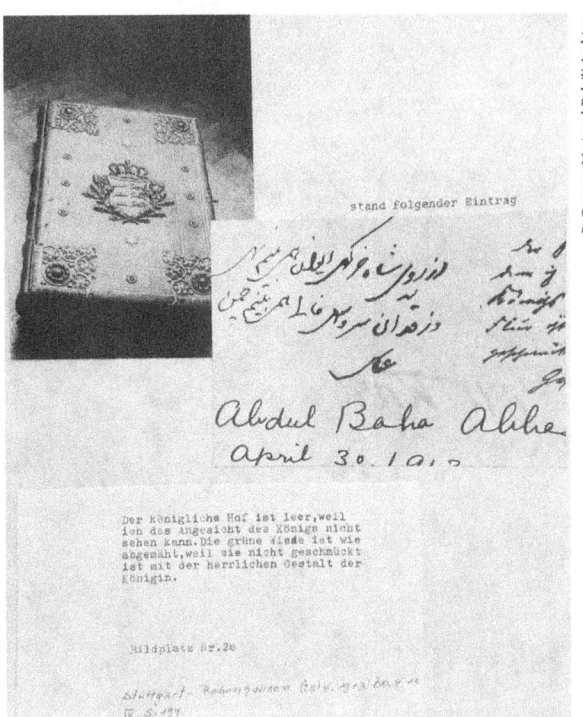

30 April 1913, the guest book in the Palace of Bebenhausen where the King of Württemberg did not come to meet 'Abdu'l-Bahá, so 'Abdu'l-Bahá wrote in the guest book: "The Imperial court is empty because I cannot see the face of the king. The green pasture is as if mown down, because it is not adorned with the glorious figure of the Queen" (see Chapter 35) After the First World War the King was forced to abdicate the throne and he fled to the palace of Bebenhausen where he passed away

The Stuttgart Obere Museum, where 'Abdu'l-Bahá spoke. Many Bahá'í talks were held here; it was destroyed in the Second World War

Alma in Stuttgart on Neue Weinsteig Strasse, where she lived with Margarethe Döring when they entertained Abdu'l-Bahá in 1913

*Fanny in Stuttgart
Stadtgarten, Spring 1913*

*Alma and Fanny in Stuttgart
Stadtgarten, Spring 1913*

© German National Bahá'í Archives

1914: Commemoration of 'Abdu'l-Bahá's visit to Stuttgart. Alma is in the back row (circled)

'There is no need for apologies, a dog has many attributes. It is loyal, affectionate, watchful, frugal and without wrong.'[29]

At 8 p.m. hundreds attended a public meeting held in the Bürger Museum. In his opening announcements, Herrigel gave some incorrect information. To everyone's surprise, 'Abdu'l-Bahá corrected him although Herrigel had been speaking in German.[30] 'Abdu'l-Bahá's speech was about the Balkan States which had 'become a volcano' and explained that 'all this ruin originated from the prejudices created by the different dogmas which arose from superstitions and racial prejudice'. 'Abdu'l-Bahá stressed the importance of transformation and change in the world.[31]

The following morning, 4 April, many visitors arrived at the Hotel Marquardt. 'Abdu'l-Bahá remarked, 'People thought they could extinguish the Light in Persia but however it begins to shine in every part of the world. This proves that if something is good it can never be extinguished. His Holiness Jesus Christ in His days only attracted 11 followers. At that time the Jews imagined that His light would be extinguished by His Crucification' [sic].[32]

That afternoon, Anna Köstlin organized a large meeting with the children and parents from the children's class in Esslingen. Rows of children stood in front of the building waving flower bouquets to welcome 'Abdu'l-Bahá. Ahmad Sohrab described the scene: more than 50 children, all dressed in spotless white with flowers, sang 'Alláh-u-Abhá' as 'Abdu'l-Bahá entered. He asked them, 'Are you happy?' The children answered by waving their flower bouquets in the air which amused 'Abdu'l-Bahá. Each child gave Him their flowers and He, in turn, gave each child a handshake and a box of chocolates. Sohrab wrote, 'It was the most beautiful, the most heavenly, the most artistic picture I have ever seen in all my life!'[33]

In the hall the Master addressed the audience talking about peace, civilization, and unity. He told them, 'I recognize my own face on your bright countenances . . . This assembly will be engraven on the book of my memory, it will ever be before me in my thoughts . . .' and as He walked out to the car the children arose to scatter rose petals at His beloved feet.[34]

In the end, the children crowded around 'Abdu'l-Bahá's automobile waving flowers. Sohrab continued, 'Oh, it looked really beautiful; I cannot describe it, so wonderfully sweet! The children waving their dear little hands, and 'Abdu'l-Bahá in the auto, covered with flowers, waving his blessed hands to them. 'Abdu'l-Bahá said that this event would go down in history.'[35]

April 5th began with the usual stream of visitors crowded into the hotel. Among the visitors was the Häfner family from Fellbach. Samuel Häfner was a banker and owned a shoe shop in Paris. In 1911, when his son, Otto Häfner, was three years old, his photograph with 'Abdu'l-Bahá had been published in the Paris newspapers. Little Otto was very excited that the Master was finally in Germany. Now aged five, he was an avid teacher of the Faith, and he taught all the other children in his neighbourhood! On this morning young Otto brought the Master a basket of red apples decorated with pink carnations. 'Abdu'l-Bahá was most impressed and said that 'It is most excellent to be a teacher in the Cause from childhood.'[36] He told Otto,

> It is well to teach the holy teachings in early youth, when I was the same age, I noticed that one of the friends, a most educated man, had a brother, who did not believe in the new Manifestation and whom no one could convince. Once when he came to see me he said: a great many people have spoken to me about this teaching, but no one can convince me, or fully satisfy me as to the truth of it. I replied to him: 'You have no desire for it, only a thirsty man is glad to be refreshed by a glass of water, but you are not thirsty. A man with seeing eyes beholds the moon and sunlight, but a blind man cannot be convinced of them, as he cannot see the constellations. If I tell a musical person to listen to beautiful melodies, he will harken, and thereby be made happy. But if I offer the most exquisite music to a dumb [sic] person, he will nevertheless not hear. Go hence and acquire seeing eyes and hearing ears, then I will speak to you again. He went and came back again. He understood

and became a good Bahai. This happened, when I was still very young. Behold the result of rain on trees, which are still able to bloom, they force blossoms and bloom. In a certain sense they respond to the rain. But rain may pour down a thousand years on a withered tree and it will not shoot forth. Plants will grow, if the earth is watered if the earth is salty, nothing will grow, in spite of the rain.[37]

Otto Häfner remained a strong Bahá'í throughout his life. After studying mathematics, he became the director of a large insurance company. Then he used his talents in service as the treasurer of the National Spiritual Assembly of the Bahá'ís of Germany and rendered valuable services for the construction of the European House of Worship.[38]

That afternoon, 'Abdu'l-Bahá visited the Royal Palace of Emperor Wilhelm, whose design was in Arabian style after the Alhambra in Andalucía, Spain. In the evening, 'Abdu'l-Bahá spoke to the Esperantists on the unifying influence of a common language.[39] Afterwards He said, 'I delivered an address to them according to their conception of truth . . . The Bahá'ís must always speak with the people from their own standpoint.'[40]

That night He ate dinner at the Ecksteins' with the Herrigels, Consul Schwarz and Mrs Susan Pollock, the sister of Mrs Ásíyih Allen from Washington. Pauline had asked Alma to contact Susan Pollock when 'Abdu'l-Bahá came to Germany.[41] Susan was an English teacher from Gotha and travelled ten hours to visit the Master. Afterwards she said, 'For seven years my sister tried to make me a Bahá'í, now I am one.'[42] After she returned home, she helped build the community of Gotha and spread the teachings in other parts of Germany.

After dinner, 'Abdu'l-Bahá looked at Mr Eckstein, Wilhelm Herrigel, and Consul Schwarz and said, 'You are three fine spiritual champions. I am going to let you wrestle with each other to see which one is the victor.'[43]

On the morning of 6 April, the Master received Anna Köstlin's cousin, Bertha Bahnmüller, with her fiancée Mr Bopp. He spoke to them about divine confirmations and wished that they would receive many.[44] Indeed, they were confirmed with a daughter Anneliese, who later served as a Counsellor at the International Teaching Centre.

That afternoon, 'Abdu'l-Bahá visited and blessed the home of Friedrich and Annemarie Schweizer in Zuffenhausen, but the detour made Him late for His visit to Villa Wagenburg where a photograph was taken of Him and all the believers in the park in front of the house. Alice Schwarz recalled that after the photographs were taken, 'Abdu'l-Bahá spoke with some friends about His visit to the Schweizer house and said,

> Thank God, that through the Bounty of Bahá'u'lláh we have been in every house where the Name of Bahá'u'lláh is mentioned; that house is blessed and will become prosperous, we bestowed the Divine Gift upon it, the light of God will shine upon it, the breath of the holy Spirit will be put in it, therefore it is my hope, that your house will be blessed and will become a heavenly one. In this house the call 'Ja Bahá' El Abhá' will always be heard and the teachings of Bahá'u'lláh will be spread from this house to many other houses. So I hope.[45]

The Schweizers had bought their house at Friesengasse 26 after their wedding in 1909. It served as a centre for teaching activities right from the start. Today the Schweizer house is the home of the Spiritual Assembly of the Bahá'ís of Stuttgart. One room dedicated to 'Abdu'l-Bahá is used for prayer and in it are many of His personal items. National and local teaching projects and events ever continue to be spread from this house.

The Villa Wagenburg was constructed in 1863 and owned by the family of Alice Schwarz. Unfortunately, it was destroyed in the air raids of the Second World War.

After the visit to Villa Wagenburg, 'Abdu'l-Bahá spoke to an audience of 250 people at the Stuttgart Obere Museum. The meeting was organized by the Bahá'í women. Alma said a prayer and Julie Stäbler sang as 'Abdu'l-Bahá entered the room. He spoke about unity, the abolition of religious prejudice, and the importance of the rights of women and love amongst all humankind.

This was the night Alma had been waiting for! Every evening 'Abdu'l-Bahá had spent His time with the other German believers, and she had not been invited, but this evening the Master would come to her home! Alma and Margarethe hired a car to pick up the Master at the Obere Museum and bring Him to their humble home for dinner. Surprisingly, when the car arrived, He preferred to ride in the Schwarzes' car, and upon arrival, He invited the entire Schwarz family to join Him for dinner!⁴⁶ Alma and Margarethe had hoped for the chance to serve 'Abdu'l-Bahá once privately, and they had not expected so many guests. The small table was set for three, but the Master reorganized the table, sat Consul Schwarz next to Him and organized chairs for the Consul, his wife Alice and daughter Olly. The Master continuously served many helpings to Consul Schwarz, telling him in English, 'Eat! Eat!'⁴⁷ 'Abdu'l-Bahá filled the room with love and friendship. Alice Schwarz recalled, 'It was but a small circle of friends He saw around Him, but He was full of kindest care for all of them and with His blessed hand personally helped those sitting next Him from the dishes and encouraged them to eat. It seemed to us to have a twofold significance, because He, as our physical father, looked after our bodily welfare, as well as He did after our spiritual welfare, in the capacity of our spiritual shepherd, Who nourished our souls with the water of life and the bread of Divine knowledge.'⁴⁸

Although 'Abdu'l-Bahá planned to leave on 7 April for Budapest, at the request of Consul Schwarz He postponed the journey by one day and visited Bad Mergentheim, a spa district built by the Consul.⁴⁹ In Bad Mergentheim, while sitting in the park, a handicapped child ran up to 'Abdu'l-Bahá and reached for Him. The friends were surprised at how lovingly 'Abdu'l-Bahá received and caressed the poor child. Later 'Abdu'l-Bahá explained to them that every agony is an angel sent to us by God to see how we receive it. These angels recount to God how we treated them.⁵⁰

Later, the famous sculptor Johannes Maihöfer made a bust

of 'Abdu'l-Bahá and a monument was erected in the park in 1915 to commemorate His visit. Years later, the Templers of Haifa were banned from the Holy Land and exiled to Bad Mergentheim. Imagine their surprise, banished from the Holy Land and exiled, when they were greeted in the park by the figure of the Master! The monument was demolished by the Nazis and re-established by the German National Spiritual Assembly in 2007.[51]

'Abdu'l-Bahá spent much of His time in Stuttgart visiting the Schwarzes, the Herrigels, and other believers and Alma had not been invited to attend many of the private events they hosted. She did not have an opportunity to host Him privately and it was difficult for her. She had waited so long for His visit, but since His arrival he had been quite busy without her. Then, on Tuesday afternoon 8 April, Alma heard her doorbell ringing several times. She looked out of the window to see what the trouble was and saw Anna Köstlin, who told her that 'Abdu'l-Bahá wanted to see her immediately at the Schwarzes' house.[52] Elation filled her heart and she went quickly to the Schwarz home. 'Abdu'l-Bahá received them in the hall, called for Ahmad Sohrab to translate, and brought them to His large, beautiful bedroom. He sat near the window. He patted Alma several times on her shoulder and cheerfully repeated, 'Very good, very good, blessed, blessed.' Then He said, 'I have come here to please you!' Alma fell on her knees before Him, placing her head on His blessed knees. He continued to pat her shoulders, repeating 'blessed'. Alma asked if He was pleased with the arrangement of His meetings; He said He was.[53]

Miss Köstlin told the Master that she knew a man whose wife had died, and who was unhappy and did not believe in God. She asked 'Abdu'l-Bahá to heal this man's sick daughter so that he could become a believer. 'Abdu'l-Bahá told her, 'A belief that is brought about through material ways would also go again the same way.' Then He laughed and told them about the many letters people sent him: 'A young man in love with a young lady, she has another admirer and he writes and asks Him to pray that the other man shoots himself so that he can marry the young lady . . . A young lady loves a man, but he is cold and loves someone else. She writes please pray that the other girl dies, she is ugly I am pretty so that I can marry the man I love. I never answer such letters. This is the same.'[54]

Then 'Abdu'l-Bahá told Alma, 'I wished to bid you goodbye, that is why I sent for you.' He left for the train station at 7 p.m. in the automobile with the Persian friends and Consul Schwarz. Alma, Anna Köstlin and Alice Schwarz walked 45 minutes on foot to the station. When they arrived, they saw that more than a hundred Bahá'ís had come to see 'Abdu'l-Bahá off, much to the bafflement of the railroad officials and other passengers. Just before the Master boarded the train, a huge bouquet of flowers arrived for him. Alma, Anna Köstlin, Mrs Schweizer, and Mr Sherman asked to join Him for the first part of the train ride to Plochingen and 'Abdu'l-Bahá agreed. They were alone in the first-class wagon; it was joyous, and He was happy. There was no translator, so they communicated with the few words they shared in common. All the others sat in the second class. The train departed Stuttgart for Budapest at 8 p.m. on 8 April 1913. He had spent exactly eight days in and around Stuttgart, six days more than originally planned.[55]

Anna Köstlin and the Esslingen Bahá'ís had arranged a surprise for Him. Shortly before the train passed through Esslingen, Anna asked 'Abdu'l-Bahá to look out of the window. Just then the Esslingen station platform came into view. It was filled with Bahá'ís waving white handkerchiefs and flowers in the air. Seeing them, His face lit up, 'radiant, surprised, happy' as He delightedly waved back. Within seconds, the train had raced through Esslingen, but everyone would remember this moment. 'Abdu'l-Bahá had surprised the German Bahá'ís when He arrived in Germany, but when He left, they surprised Him![56]

Wilhelm Herrigel had the honour of travelling with 'Abdu'l-Bahá and His Persian friends to Budapest and Vienna.[57] Unlike the visit to Germany, the trip to Hungary was widely publicized in the Hungarian newspapers.[58] There was a large Esperanto meeting in the old Parliament, at which 'Abdu'l-Bahá gave a speech which was translated first into English and then into

Hungarian. 'Abdu'l-Bahá's talk was lively and often interrupted by stormy applause. In the end, 'Abdu'l-Bahá stood between a Catholic priest and a Jewish Professor holding their hands in His while more than 600 people applauded wildly. Seeing this, Herrigel told a student, 'I hope that this symbolic handshake between East and West will soon become a spiritual reality.' His statement attracted a large crowd of students. As they gathered around Herrigel, they asked him the same questions 'Abdu'l-Bahá had discussed with him during his visit to Paris about one month earlier. Herrigel was so occupied with the crowd that he did not return to the hotel with 'Abdu'l-Bahá, but on his return 'Abdu'l-Bahá welcomed him warmly and seemed to know where he had been.[59]

From 18 to 20 April, 'Abdu'l-Bahá visited Vienna, thereby visiting all the European countries that would soon enter World War I: France, England, Germany and Austria-Hungary. On His first day in Vienna, He continued to receive visitors from Budapest. One of them, Mr Moore, brought a gramophone into which 'Abdu'l-Bahá chanted a prayer which Ahmad Sohrab translated into English. 'Abdu'l-Bahá gave an important talk at the Theosophical Society of Vienna, where He was asked: if the object of the Bahá'í movement and the Theosophical Society were one and the same, why should there be two names, two distinct organizations, or two modes of expression? 'Abdu'l-Bahá is reported to have answered:

> Well said. You have brought up a good point. According to our Faith, whosoever investigates independently the reality, he is a Bahai although he may not know this himself. We do not desire to add another name or words to the already many names . . . the Bahai movement is not an organization. It is the fresh breeze of the Garden of God. You can never organize the Bahai Cause. It cannot be located in one single place or centred in one individual. The Bahai movement is the spirit of this age. It is everywhere. It has no geographical limits. It is the essence of all the highest ideals of this century. A person may claim to be a Bahai or may

be known as a Bahai for all his life and may not know at all what a Bahai means. Another person may never have heard the name Bahai and they have the same time practice all attributes which are necessary to make one a Bahai. That is why his holiness Christ says, those who were not against us are with us. You must know a tree by its fruit. Now to answer your question, everyone knows that in a seed, there lay enveloped the young plants, the tree, the branches, the blossoms and the fruits. This simple knowledge is however not sufficient, there must be a gardener to plant the seed in a pure ground, to water it, take care of it till it reaches the stages of fruition. There must be the power of the Holy Spirit to put into practice the divine principles.[60]

'Abdu'l-Bahá linked the spirit of the age, the Zeitgeist, to the Manifestation, Bahá'u'lláh, He did not say that the Bahá'í Faith does not need an administrative order. Unfortunately, years later Wilhelm Herrigel used this talk to justify his rebellion towards the unfolding Bahá'í administration.

At 10 a.m. on 24 April 1913 'Abdu'l-Bahá left Vienna to return to Germany.[61] His train passed through Esslingen at 1 a.m., where Anna Köstlin and Friedrich and Annemarie Schweizer entered the train to join Him for the last hour of the train ride to Stuttgart.[62] Tired and physically ill,[63] 'Abdu'l-Bahá arrived in Stuttgart at 2:15 a.m. on 25 April after a 16-hour train journey during which the train had stopped for one hour in each city on the way.[64] He had a very severe cold.[65] Although it was way past midnight, more than a dozen Bahá'ís were waiting at the Stuttgart station to greet Him.[66]

Early on the morning of 25 April the Schwarz family went to His hotel. Uncertain whether to bother the Master so early, they finally decided to at least see how he was doing. 'Abdu'l-Bahá Himself answered the door with a big smile and welcomed them.[67]

The hotel was quite full when Alma arrived at 11 a.m. She asked Herrigel about his trip to Budapest. He was 'radiantly happy' and glad to talk about it, but his wife Marie did not want them to converse and beckoned him to come and sit next to her; quickly he got up and moved away from Alma. Shortly afterwards, 'Abdu'l-Bahá came and motioned that the party should leave. Naturally Alma got up to leave with the rest, but 'Abdu'l-Bahá held her back. Alma recalled:

> He took my right hand that he was holding very firmly and placed it into his left hand and held tight shaking hands and did not say goodbye to His guests but remained standing where he stood. Then he opened his arms and held me closely; I snuggling in his arms and he folded me closely to him, after some time it seemed long and heavenly I looked up and the guests were standing at the door spellbound – and others were looking in from the hall – he led me to the door and patted me and said, 'Blessed, blessed.' I will always feel thankful to Mrs. Herrigel . . .[68]

The Master told Alma:

> The love of Baha'u'llah is the essence of happiness. Any heart which will become the depository of this love is always happy . . . Therefore you must be very happy because you are living in the Day of the Blessed Perfection. All the prophets longed for this day. They yearned for one moment of this time. Appreciate the value of this age, the more you appreciate these days, the greater will be your blessings.[69]

Then someone asked Him, 'How can a person keep this in his mind all the time, especially when always in a hurry?' The Master replied, 'A real Bahai who acts and lives in accordance with the teachings of Baha'o'llah will never forget.'[70]

Although 'Abdu'l-Bahá had explicitly told the German friends not to publicize any of His talks in Germany, while He was travelling in Austria and Hungary the German Bahá'ís widely publicized that 'Abdu'l-Bahá would give a talk at the Bürger Museum![71] Consul Schwarz invited 'Abdu'l-Bahá to eat at his home after the talk, but 'Abdu'l-Bahá replied that He did not feel well and would not be able to attend either the dinner or the talk. Instead, the Master asked that Herrigel read the translation of the talk He had given at the Temple Emmanuel synagogue in San Francisco.[72]

Many expressed their disappointment that 'Abdu'l-Bahá was too ill to attend the talk that night. Alice Schwarz recalled,

> In the evening 'Abdu'l-Bahá said to His secretaries and several German friends: 'My poor health prevents me from speaking to the audience tonight, go and speak yourselves in my name, the blessings of the kingdom of Abhá will be with you.' He turned to a German Bahá'í and said: 'Be sure that you will have success in what you will say, if you confide and turn to His Kingdom. I never visited a school, but when I was still quite young, I spoke one day in Bagdad to a big audience. I talked to the people as they were in need of. Suddenly I saw the Vali (governor) come in. Instantly I felt that my words displeased him; therefore, I read a verse of the Koran saying that the spirit of God can only be seen in the Manifestation and that this spirit of God will be perceptible in a new Prophet. Also, from the Arabian language I recited a verse of the same sense. The Vali lingered and listened attentively. Afterwards he invited me to his house. On that account some of the scholars present became very jealous. I mean to say herewith that, if He helps, then we can have confidence. The help of Bahá'u'lláh always overcame the difficulties that I had before me. I shall stay here, and you go to the meeting and His holy assistance will be with you.'[73]

In retrospect, it is hard to comprehend that they planned and expected that 'Abdu'l-Bahá, who was quite ill after returning to Germany via a 16-hour train ride should then 17 hours later give a talk before hundreds of people! 'Abdu'l-Bahá told them, 'When I was in Paris, I caught a cold, in Budapest I caught another, in Vienna it accompanied me and while there I walked twice up 120 steps to the fourth floor to speak to the theosophical society and last night on the train I felt the chills. Now it is impossible for me to go to the meeting tonight. You express my apology and deep sorrow in not being able to come.'[74]

An enormous crowd of hundreds of people gathered at the Bürger Museum that night. When Ahmad Sohrab and Consul Schwarz saw this, they returned to the hotel and told the Master of the many who had come from great distances.[75] They asked the Master if He could at least come in the car to show Himself, saying that His 'appearance alone would have made a great impression'.[76] Abdu'l-Bahá finally succumbed for the sake of Consul Schwarz.[77] He arose and said, 'I have promised the doctors I would be careful, but I willingly offer My health for the holy Cause and for the service of Baha'u'lláh.'[78]

Back at the Bürger Museum, Herrigel had informed the audience that 'Abdu'l-Bahá had become ill and would not be present. He gave an account of the Bahá'í movement and just as he began to read the address that 'Abdu'l-Bahá had given at the synagogue in San Francisco, 'Abdu'l-Bahá entered the hall.[79] Everyone stood up and cheered, giving Him a warm welcome. 'Abdu'l-Bahá asked the audience about their health. Then He said,

> I was not feeling well, but I came for your sake. It is my greatest hope that you are all very happy and that the divine Bounties may surround you. I have a great love for you. I am exceedingly happy to be able to be here in this illumined assembly tonight. Not being well, I beg of you to excuse me in not giving a detailed talk. It is this! That in every age there is a great movement set in motion. The 19th century is marked as a cycle of Monarchy and Republic freedom. But the greatest cycle, in reality, is the cycle of Universal Peace. This century is the century of light. This age is the age of knowledge. Therefore, the results of this cycle should be international peace and perfection. Be assured, that the banner of international freedom will be raised in this century. Because the spirit of this age is to realize this great peace . . .[80]

And He ended His talk:

I ask God to strengthen me to be able to open your eyes to the truth. May I become the means of your happiness.

At a time when war was carried on in the Orient, when conflict among the different religions and hatred among the different sects took place, when there was a constant fight between the different communities, and nations fought against one another, when the nations of the East did not love each other, but hated one another, Bahá'u'lláh appeared like a sun.

He proclaimed the unity of men. He taught harmony among the religions and instructed them to be kind to each other. All the nations of the Orient, which have adopted the Cause of Bahá'u'lláh, are working to-day with the greatest love for the whole humanity. Jews, Mohammedans, Christians, Buddhists have forgotten their former hatred and have become good friends, always ready to sacrifice their life one for another. Persians and Arabians, Indians and Turks, who have adopted the doctrines of Bahá'u'lláh, are working together in greatest love in the service of humanity.

I don't feel well enough to say more than this, therefore I will finish this short address and state once more, that Germany – thank God – is a country of the highest purity and clearness. The government is very just. The nation stands for the highest culture and civilization. Therefore I hope that the light of universal peace will spread from Germany over the whole world. I shall pray for the German nation and for this government. I shall ask God to help them, so that every one of you may be a means for the happiness of humanity.[81]

Many were in tears by the time He finished speaking. Handkerchiefs were waving in the air and people were giving roses and other flowers to Ahmad Sohrab who walked behind Him gathering the flowers as He left.[82]

The next morning, 26 April, 'Abdu'l-Bahá addressed the believers and said:

'I was very ill yesterday evening; I knew very well how dangerous it was for me to leave my room, but nevertheless I went out to speak to the assembly and God's help was with me and protected me . . . I came to the assembly yesterday evening although I was hardly able to stand upright. I thought even [if] I was running a risk, I would willingly sacrifice my life for the holy Cause and for the friends of Bahá'u'lláh. There is nothing better than this, but praise be to God, all went well . . .'

Then He turned to a new group of friends with the words:

'You are people, whom God chose in His love, you must be very happy, that God placed such a crown on your heads. You don't yet know the value of it, but later you will recognise it. In the days of His Holiness Christ the importance of the apostles was unknown and they were laughed at and ridiculed by the people!'[83]

He said that He would stay longer than planned because He was ill, In a letter, Ahmad Sohrab wrote that 'Abdu'l-Bahá explained that this extended stay had a wisdom and would bring important results: the first would be the creation of love in the hearts of the friends in Stuttgart; the second would be the progress of the Cause in Germany; and the third would be the penetration of the Word of God.[84]

After hearing a newspaper report about His talk. 'Abdu'l-Bahá asked:

What did the people say about the talk last night? . . . Why has He come to Germany? Let peace be for the weaker nations but war is for the mighty! . . . This morning looking down from the window I saw a regiment of soldiers passing by in fine shape. They were ready to fight for the fatherland. How barbarous and foolish it is to send men who know not each other at all to the battlefield and order them to shoot down each other and cut one another's throats! But friends, let us talk about our own war. Our Grand Army consists of the invisible angels of the Supreme Concourse; our swords are the swords of light; our armaments are the invisible armaments of heaven. We are fighting against the forces of darkness . . . Ye shall scatter the sowers of ignorance! Your war confers life, theirs brings death. Your war is the cause of the illumination of humankind, theirs is the means of the darkness of the hearts.[85]

On 27 April, the Master spoke to large groups of people from different social strata. Alice Schwarz recalled that after the afternoon car ride:

'Abdu'l-Bahá rested for a short time. In the meantime, friends of the Schwarz family had come by invitation, but it was a great question whether the beloved Master would be able to address them as He had been requested to be present at a celebration of unity in the Women's Club and had promised to go. 'Abdu'l-Bahá was walking up and down in His room in deep prayer, when He was asked whether He would honour those awaiting Him with a greeting. And how overjoyed they were when the Master entered their midst.[86]

Among these friends of Consul Schwarz were many prominent men and women from the royal court of the King of Württemberg; Countesses and Counts; members of the King's cabinet. As all spoke English, there was no need for further translation into German.[87] 'Abdu'l-Bahá then departed for the Unity Meeting at the Frauen Club at 5 p.m.[88] Although the meeting was planned at very short notice, all four rooms were opened to accommodate the 150 guests.[89] 'Abdu'l-Bahá gave His last public address in Germany:

Consider how many meetings are held in the world. There are the different parties which gather in the political civilization, many such industrial institutions, commercial associations, many such movements are held, none of these meetings are eternal or last for 2000 years, but the Supper that was held by His Holiness Christ, the results of that meeting are eternal . . . strive that your meeting may be the meeting of the kingdom. Whenever you enter such a meeting, cleanse your hearts from every thought, be purified from all natural and physical emotion. In the utmost spirituality and sanctity with the greatest light and purity be engaged in mentioning God. Study the Holy books, hearken unto the teachings of Bahá'u'lláh, so that you may be free from all else save God. So that your spirit may fly, your thoughts be extended, spiritual susceptibilities may develop, and you may be entirely free from the abstruse form of the natural emotions and your susceptibility be enlarged, so that there may be room for the entrance of the Breath of God.[90]

At the end of the evening, Consul Schwarz begged 'Abdu'l-Bahá for one more public meeting, but He declined as He would have to leave for Paris.[91] 'Abdu'l-Bahá encouraged the Bahá'ís in Stuttgart to maintain regular correspondence with the friends in America; He said it would be of mutual benefit.

For the next couple of days, 'Abdu'l-Bahá met with the friends in His hotel. He spoke about marriage as 'a fortress of well-being' to the newly engaged couple Eugene Diebold and Helene Wieland.[92] He explained to Pastor Rohleder, 'Ordained ministers are many, confirmed are few.'[93] He said, 'In the time of Christ, there were many ministers (priests) that taught the Word of God, but from all of these, not one was confirmed but Paul . . . I hope that you will distinguish yourself amongst the pastors . . .'[94] The Master talked to the friends about the education of children:

> They cannot be taught through books. Many elementary sciences must be made clear to them in the nursery; they must learn them in play, in amusement. Most ideas must be taught them through speech, not by book learning. One child must question the other concerning these things, and

the other child must give the answer. In this way, they will make great progress. For example, mathematical problems must also be taught in the form of questions and answers. One of the children asks a question and the other must give the answer. Later on, the children will of their own accord speak with each other concerning these same subjects. The children who are at the head of the class must receive premiums. They must be encouraged and when any one of them shows good advancement, for the further development they must be praised and encouraged therein.[95]

'Abdu'l-Bahá told Mrs Eckstein, 'In this cause, there are two kinds of Bahais. The first is active and speaking; the second is inactive and silent. These two, although Bahais, yet they are widely different from each other. The former is more beloved than the latter. The lady has two hands, one is active, the other is paralyzed. Which one do you prefer?'[96]

When Alice and Ollie Schwarz inquired about the Beloved Master's health, He said, 'Complete physical health is to be enjoyed by the animals . . . The happiness of man is through his spiritual health and not bodily health.'[97]

On 30 April 1913 'Abdu'l-Bahá spoke to the friends on the equality of men and women. Afterwards He took His last ride with the Schwarzes to visit Bebenhausen.[98] At that time no one could imagine that the palace of Bebenhausen would become the final residence of the King of Württemberg after his abdication at the end of the First World War. Here 'Abdu'l-Bahá wrote in the guestbook, 'The royal court is empty because I cannot see the face of the king. The green pasture is as if mown down, because it is not adorned with the glorious figure of the Queen. (sig.) Abdul Baha Abbas'.[99]

Later they drove by the royal park and the palace of a Baron. Consul Schwarz said that it was the best residence in the city, but the Master contradicted him, saying that the Consul's home was the best because He had been there, and they had raised the mention of God. Then the Consul spoke of the nobility of the Baron's family. Again, 'Abdu'l-Bahá contradicted him, saying

'The noble family will be the one which you will start, because you are a believer in Bahá'u'lláh.'[100]

The end of His historic visit to Germany had come. Alma wrote:

> Our beloved left on 1 May at 10:55 AM for Paris. At 10:30 AM our beloved came to the station ... Oh, such a beautiful sight, our Beloved came out of the center aisle of the depot like – well words fail to express the King of the Universe, majestic and powerful and looking so large and handsome, His oriental robes giving a royal aspect, slowly with a kingly bearing. He advanced several steps behind Him was followed by an immense crowd ... All of a sudden, He began to speak, and I translated it into German: 'I hope you will become trained in the teachings of Baha'o'llah. I hope the heavenly blessings may descend upon you! That you love each other more, that the Heavenly confirmation may descend upon you! I have sown pure seeds, it depends upon you, what the results will be. It is my hope that they will grow, they will give forth many harvests, I will pray that you may become confirmed in the divine path.' He then asked if the train was ready and a few moments later passengers began to file out and He arose, and the believers formed 2 rows and He passed through. He then got into his car, almost all were crying a sight never to be forgotten. Here we stood for about five minutes. Consul Schwarz, wife and daughter, Dr. Faber and a number of young men from Esslingen and I stood back against the building and all the many believers in front of us and Abdul-Baha at the large window, the Persians in back of him and Mirza Mahmood with an immense bunch of followers which He saved. How glorious Abdul-Baha looked so pleased, so happy. And as the train moved out, He turned His blessed face toward the front of the train, for all were crying.[101]

This was the last time in her life that Alma saw her beloved Master.

Eight months later, at the end of 1913, Alma reflected on the Master's visit and how it had affected her. He had spent most of his time with the wealthier group of Bahá'ís from Herrigel's meetings and that had been a test for Alma, who had been excluded from many of their events. Typically for Alma, she made the best out of her difficult situation and learned a 'great lesson' from this: she realized that her only mission was to simply train souls for the kingdom, being ever alert to give the message and to accept that what the people do is for them to 'account for'.[102] Alma was happy to hear that her letters had given 'Abdu'l-Bahá some pleasure: 'what more' could any mortal wish for?' But there was one command He gave her that she did 'not fulfil' to her satisfaction. He told her: 'Pray at night and weep.' She wrote,

> It was rather difficult for me at the time to understand just what He meant. I understand now, I think, it is the condition of the people in the world, how very few really understand His station, they commit every little trifling thing to prevent them from going forward and obtaining a higher spiritual station. In fact, the world is still very dark and submerged in worldly things, having no interest for real spiritual truth, if there is no personal worldly gain for them to obtain![103]

'Abdu'l-Bahá had showered Alma and all the believers with love and taught them through His example. What more could any mortal wish for?

32

FANNY'S ILLNESS AND RECOVERY WITH ALMA AND 'ABDU'L-BAHÁ

In the spring of 1913 Fanny suffered a nervous collapse – mentally and physically overworked, the financial burden of supporting the family had become too much for her. Alma longed for Fanny and wished she could do something for her, but she lacked the necessary financial capacity. A Bahá'í friend, Josephine de Lagnels,[1] realized that Fanny needed a break and offered financial assistance for her to recover in Europe with her beloved Alma. Suddenly, Fanny was on her way to Stuttgart! Fanny arrived as fast as she could at midnight, 3 May 1913. Unfortunately, it was two days after the Master had departed for His last visit to Paris, from 1 May to 12 June.[2] Alma wrote to Pauline:

> Oh, I am so happy and only regret that precious sister did not come a few days sooner. He ['Abdu'l-Bahá] asked me if I have news from my sister? When I told Him that I expected her to arrive by the end of the week He inquired how far is Bremen from here? How long does it take? Tell her to come to Paris I want to see her. I have a great love for her. Tapping me on the shoulder He said you have a good sister a very good sister a firm and sincere Bahai. Take good care of her, she is very dear to Me. How long will she stay?[3]

Shortly after Fanny arrived in Stuttgart, 'Abdu'l-Bahá sent a telegram inviting her to visit Him in Paris. As she reflected on whether she was too weak to make the trip, He sent a second telegram, so she quickly departed for Paris on 19 May.[4]

'Abdu'l-Bahá greeted her with much love and affection and her days in Paris regenerated her spirit.[5] He said, 'How is your sister? Is she happy? She has done wonderful work, for she has established a great assembly.' He told Fanny that Alma had led many souls to the Kingdom and that her work was confirmed by Bahá'u'lláh. The Master said, 'tell her to have no fear, to be confident, very confident, she will be assisted by the heavenly concourse.'[6] On many occasions, He told Alma to be confident.

In addition to Fanny, the Schwarzes also accepted an invitation to visit 'Abdu'l-Bahá in Paris in May 1913.[7]

Fanny was still weak. In June, Alma and Fanny met in Flüelin, Switzerland for her to recover.[8] Fanny was too sick to climb any mountains. Instead, they visited the monument of Wilhelm Tell in Altdorf and then walked to where he had lived. Fanny wrote Pauline that Alma had regained her peace of mind, but that she day-dreamed a lot. Together they also visited Lucerne, as well as Albert Lutz and his sister in St Gallen, who were so impressed with the teachings that they planned to meet again at the city of Constance on Lake Constance. By July, both Alma and Fanny felt better and stronger.[9]

Alma and Fanny then shared an emotional trip to Carlsbad. Alma wrote to Pauline:

> My heart had been aching for some days and tried my best not to let her know, but oh to be separated again, I did not think I could stand it. Everyone loves Fanny, she is so very good and makes everyone happy . . . You asked if I was run down? My dear I did some hard work before Abdul-Baha's coming and had no one to talk about things . . . and after Abdul-Baha left, the strong light had effect and there was also much to bear, really more than before He came. Yes, I felt it very much and to know that Fanny was not well, and I knew that for some time dear, precious, glorious soul, my heart was aching all the time, also after she arrived, and I did the best I could not to show it. I really wish she would

not work so hard and am very thankful that she is so much stronger . . . Thank heavens I am in excellent health now; the trip was most glorious.[10]

Before she left Stuttgart, Consul Schwarz and his family gave Fanny a grand farewell dinner.[11] Nobody at that time could imagine that it would be nine long years before Fanny and Alma would see each other again.

Fanny was a selfless heroine. Imagine a member of your family moving to a foreign country to teach the Faith full-time, completely financially dependent on you for thirteen years. Would you struggle to your financial, physical and mental breaking point to support a sibling with joy and happiness?

33
THE STUTTGART BAHÁ'Í COMMUNITY 'ABDU'L-BAHÁ CREATED

Immediately after He left Germany, 'Abdu'l-Bahá sent Mírzá 'Alí-Akbar and Mírzá Luṭfulláh Hakím from Paris to assist with the follow-up work in Stuttgart. They arrived on 10 June with the following Tablet:

> I send to those parts his honor, Mirza Ali Akbar, and his honor, Mirza Lotfullah, that they may associate with the friends, convey to them the yearnings of the heart of Abdul-Baha and explain the degrees of the power of the Covenant and the importance of the Center of the Testament. These two persons are very blessed.
>
> Assuredly the believers shall obtain joy and happiness through meeting them. Know ye this, that *today the greatest of all affairs is obedience to the Centre of God's Covenant, the power of The Covenant shall stir the regions, and the spirit of the Covenant shall rejoice.*
>
> Therefore, all the believers, in all the meetings and gatherings, must mention the Covenant and raise the Song of the Covenant.[1]

Six large meetings were held for these Persian friends at the Bürger Museum, the Frauen Club, and in the hall of the 'Home of the Good Templers' in Esslingen. In addition, there were a number of smaller gatherings held in the private homes of the

Jaegers in Degerloch, the Häfners in Fellbach, the Schweizers in Zuffenhausen, and at the Herrigels and the Schwarzes in Stuttgart.[2]

While these meetings were being held in Germany, the Master concluded His journey to the West. On 12 June 1913 He left Paris for Marseilles and on 13 June departed from Marseilles for Egypt, where He arrived on 17 June. Thus, the holiest soul to visit these Western countries in the known history of religion had returned to the East.

As a result of His visit, the German Bahá'í community was now united and focused and Tablets to Stuttgart were sent to Consul Schwarz for distribution.[3] The unity meetings at the Herrigels' were so well-attended that they had to be divided into two meetings.[4] In July, the Schwarz family started to attend the meetings in Zuffenhausen and Esslingen. New friends declared their Faith in the Schweizers' home,[5] fulfilling 'Abdu'l-Bahá's promise to Annemarie Schweizer that the circle in Zuffenhausen would grow and become large and firm. By September 1913, the Esslingen assembly had outgrown the Köstlins' home and their meetings were moved to the Home of the Good Templers.[6]

German Bahá'ís entered the arena of travel teaching. 'Abdu'l-Bahá chose Margarethe Döring as the first travel teacher from the Stuttgart assembly to teach the Faith in Nice, France in September 1913.[7] Margarethe was surprised because she could not speak French, but she used all her savings and went in obedience to the Master and as a tribute to Alma.[8] While in Nice, Margarethe overheard people speaking in German and joined their conversation. When the Germans left, she spoke to their German-speaking friend who then invited more people he knew to hear about the Bahá'í Faith.[9]

Mrs Köstlin visited and strengthened the friends in Aalen;[10] Lydia Bauer visited Margarethe's contacts in Gmünd.[11] Julie Stäbler opened a boarding house where she taught the Faith in Degerloch.[12] In October 1913, Mr Schwab took a new position in Bern, Switzerland.[13]

On 18 April 1914, 'Abdu'l-Bahá revealed the first Tablet of Visitation for a German Bahá'í:

A visiting Tablet for the Maidservant of God, Mrs. Babette Ruoff.

Upon her be Baha'u'l-Abha [sic]!

He is God!
O Almighty! Endear thou this maidservant of Thy Threshold, Frau Ruoff, in the Kingdom of Thy Holiness, and submerge her in the Ocean of Light. Overlook her shortcomings; confer upon her Thy Grace! Vouchsafe her Thy Purity in the Court of the Paradise of Abha! Bestow upon her Eternal Life and suffer her to become the manifester of infinite bestowals in the meeting of transfiguration.

Verily Thou art the Generous, the Pardoner, and the Compassionate.[14]

So by 1914, the German Bahá'í community was united around the Centre of the Covenant, expanding the number of its communities and sending its first teachers into the world.

34

THE 'AMERICAN GIRL' TEACHES THROUGHOUT GERMANY

'To accept the message is not difficult but the hard times come in afterward.'[1]

On 6 May 1913, 'Abdu'l-Bahá sent Alma her final mission in Germany, telling her to travel throughout all the German cities to raise the call of God, and to be assured that the 'invisible confirmations' and 'divine powers' would be her helpers and assistants. He also asked her to associate with 'the utmost amity and union' with the Herrigels, and that this would be conducive to the progress of the Cause.[2]

In August 1913, 'Abdu'l-Bahá sent a Tablet to Fanny describing the confirmation of Alma's efforts in Germany:

> Consider how thy sister has been confirmed in Germany. This is purely through Heavenly Confirmations, otherwise, how could an American girl go to Germany and become the means of the guidance of many people. This is self-evident that it is through Confirmation. If the greatest philosopher of the world went there assuredly, he would not have been so confirmed and would not have gained such an influence. Therefore, know this, that all successes are made possible through Divine Confirmation and assistance.[3]

THE 'AMERICAN GIRL' TEACHES THROUGHOUT GERMANY

'Abdu'l-Bahá surprised everyone by calling Alma an 'American girl'. Alma wrote to Pauline, 'I am really very thankful that 'Abdu'l-Bahá has called me an American girl, since I am not a woman, it is rather a compliment to the American girl and who knows what 'Abdu'l-Bahá wished to convey in these words . . .'[4] She wrote to Fanny that she did not understand why 'Abdu'l-Bahá called her an 'American girl', but 'I don't mind being called an American Girl at all – I am told that pure girls are few . . . In this case, it was a pure girl from America who came to Germany and trained a number of beautiful souls as teachers for the Cause.'[5]

The tests of her first years in Germany had raised a new consciousness in Alma. She wrote,

> Had Dr. Fisher been a well man, others who came on a visit could not have had such an influence and made such troubles among the believers, it was really very difficult. I never would have received such glorious Tablets had everything went off smooth and I would perhaps only have been an assistance to someone else had they not tried to shove me out but I was too much of an American girl for them and could always look them square and straight in the face and had no thought of leaving until Abdul-Baha saw fit.[6]

The strong bond between Alma and 'Abdu'l-Bahá gave her strength and certitude. He accompanied her every step. In a Tablet to Alma in August 1913, written on the same day as His Tablet to Fanny, He described it as follows:

O thou herald of the Kingdom of God!
    I was thinking of thee and praying on thy behalf that God may increase thy assistance and confirmation day unto day; because truly I say thou art the Maid-servant of the kingdom and art favored at the Holy Threshold of his Holiness Baha'o'llah. At this juncture, Mirza Ahmad entered carrying with him your letter. I told him I desire to write a Letter to Miss Knobloch. He said a letter has just been received

from her. Then he read it to me and I occupied my time in writing the answer. Consider how much thou art before my sight that before the receipt of thy letter I was thinking of thee and intended to write thee a letter. Thank thou God. Thou hast written concerning the attraction of the hearts of the believers and the maid-servants of the Merciful. It became the cause of great rejoicing. I beg from his Holiness Baha-ollah to confirm and assist thee under all conditions and circumstances; so that thou mayest become the cause of the guidance of many people. I write a letter for thy dear sister so that thou mayest forward it to her.[7]

Alma was honoured that 'Abdu'l-Bahá had instructed her to go to every city in Germany and teach, but she had no means to finance such an undertaking. In addition, many friends in Stuttgart wanted to travel-teach and the community had many expenses to carry including rent for the halls, printing costs, and financial support for Dr Fisher and another Stuttgart friend; they could not possibly provide financial support to Alma as well.[8]

To lighten the financial pressure on Fanny, Alma and Fanny sold their Takoma property lot. The sale was profitable, and the money was placed in an interest-generating account. They maintained ownership of an additional investment property which they rented 'without making much loss for future investment'.[9] Alma asked Pauline to sell her furniture at home to the tenant, to raise more money.[10]

> I deny myself everything possible for I have extra expenses in serving others. My work has been personal and so far, it has been successful, and the friends are becoming more interested in the teachings . . . At present, I have no one to go ahead and make arrangements or invite those who are interested and so it falls on me and the expenses also, but I am sure that in a short time there will be many who will work for the Cause, for Abdul-Baha has said so and therefore I am very hopeful.[11]

When Alma first went to Leipzig, she focused her teaching efforts primarily on her relatives. She had been disappointed when they did not come to meet 'Abdu'l-Bahá in Stuttgart. She returned to Leipzig in late summer 1913, stronger and more focused. But Fanny could no longer bear the burden of the increased rent at the Scholzes, so to save money Alma moved out and rented a shared room in a guesthouse.[12] Years later, she was still comforting Fanny about the fact that their family in Leipzig had tried to make her pay an unfair price for her room: 'We have done for our relations what we could . . . True they are materialists and not inclined, therefore there is little attraction they do not understand us . . . It has always been my experience that to stay with relatives is very much more expensive than elsewhere.'[13]

Although it was difficult to move out of cousin Jennie's house, the move increased Alma's independence and she became more focused and productive in her teaching work.[14] The rent was considerably cheaper, and that was very good for Fanny. Alma's new landlady, Mrs Von der Fange, accepted the teachings and asked Alma to teach her son and her sister.[15]

At age 50, sleeping and living with a stranger in a shared room with no private space was difficult for Alma. In October, she moved into a large sunny room in the home of Mr and Mrs Hochkirch. Mr Hochkirch was hard of hearing and worked as a bookkeeper in a large firm.[16] Like most of Alma's landlords, Mr and Mrs Hochkirch also accepted the teachings. The Master confirmed Alma's work and more than 11 new believers[17] in Leipzig, telling her that since the 'heavenly confirmations' and the Holy Spirit were supporting and helping her, and the bestowals of Bahá'u'lláh were the 'vanguards' of her army, she became 'victorious' in any city she entered. He was praying for the believers in Leipzig, so that day and night they might engage their time in teaching so that the love of Bahá'u'lláh would so fill their hearts and minds as to leave no place for anything else.[18]

Alma wrote, 'Oh, Fanny I am so thankful to you for all your kindness . . . Just think how much has been accomplished during six years. Three assemblies have been confirmed by our Lord and Aalen and Leipzig mentioned of which the latter have received most glorious words from Abdul-Baha.'[19]

Through the Dörings, Alma met Miss Södel and Eugenie Böttger who were interested in the Faith.[20] These women introduced Alma to their friends in the best circles of Leipzig. She attended the English circle at the Frauen Club. In October Alma sent two more petitions (from new believers) from Leipzig to 'Abdul-Bahá.[21] Leipzig was growing.

Alma improved her teaching abilities by overlooking the shortcomings of those who did not value the role of women. Miss Södel introduced Alma to Professor Steinmetz and young Dr Pitzer and his wife who lived in an elegant home. They did not accept the Bahá'í message, but Dr Pitzer invited Alma to join their Bible study group. Alma was not offended when they studied texts and discussed how women must be subordinate to men. Instead, after all she had been through, Alma found it amusing. She had learned how to deal with such comments and remain completely undisturbed and friendly. Nothing they said upset or surprised her at all! Professor Steinmetz was of a high calibre, his concerns were not meant to be insulting, they were rather of a genuine nature. To her surprise, he became a Bahá'í. Alma wrote to Fanny, 'If you hear of some of my hardships that I am having here, be assured that it is a sign that I am very successful. 'Abdu'l-Bahá said, "They throw stones only at a good tree."'[22]

Soon Alma arranged a weekly social event on Sundays for her new contacts. Each week she gradually added more Bahá'í content to these meetings. After a while, the conversations on Sunday were only about the Faith and the new believers themselves organized the meetings.[23] Mr and Mrs Hochkirch invited Alma to teach the Faith to their mother. On 16 November, Mr Glitz from Chemnitz visited a Unity Meeting in Leipzig where nine people attended. Alma did not have enough space to invite more people. Mr Glitz planned to return with his cousin.[24]

Alma exchanged letters with newspaper contacts, most of whom were men who had published articles touching on Bahá'í themes. Two of them invited her to visit them in Langenbrück (near Dresden), but Alma was uncomfortable meeting them alone.[25] In December 1913, Eugenie Böttger accepted the Faith and invited Alma to travel with her to Dresden to meet her friend Mr Schröder and his friends who were interested in the Bahá'í teachings.[26] The trip strengthened their friendship.[27]

Leipzig held its first Naw-Rúz celebration in 1914. Afterwards, a letter from Ahmad Sohrab dated 7 April 1914 reached them with a message from 'Abdu'l-Bahá:

> ... tell them: 'I am always thinking about them, and praying in their behalf, wishing for them spiritual success and prosperity.
>
> These days are the days of service and the time for the proclamation of the Glad-Tidings of the Kingdom of Abha!
>
> Whosoever teaches one soul, it is as though he has quickened through the Breath of the Holy Spirit a community. All other thoughts must revolve around this one Supreme Ideal! If we drop into the pure soil one seed, it will yield a hundredfold.
>
> The Cause needs many soul-sacrificing teachers and those who arise to teach, the Confirmation shall surround them.'[28]

Alma wrote home, 'What do you think of the message He has sent to the friends in Leipzig? It is the hardest thing for me to get them interested in the Bahá'í teachings and still 'Abdu'l-Bahá expects them to become teachers. Do you think I will be successful? I will do my best; they tell me that if I speak of religion all the time, they will drop me quickly and take me for a fanatic. I jolly them along and watch for my opportunity.'[29] Not concerned with first impressions, Alma was confident that in time, with prayer and perseverance, people would become interested.

By the summer of 1914, the new Bahá'ís in Leipzig had begun to teach. Cousin Jennie Scholz brought her friend Mrs Rohr with her children to visit Alma and hear about the Faith.

Mrs Rohr was ready and eager to hear more. Alma arranged to make weekly teaching visits at the Rohr home.[30] The Rohr family became a vital part of the Leipzig Bahá'í community. Mrs Von der Fange's sister, Mr Max Staub and his wife and children joined the Faith.[31]

Alma attended church services at the Leipzig English Church, a church in Schlenzig, and the American Sunday Services held in the Gewerbe (vocational) School in Leipzig to meet new people and share the message.[32]

Susan Pollock arrived in Leipzig to help Alma with the teaching work for several weeks. As previously mentioned, Susan had met the Master in Stuttgart at the Eckstein home and was eager to teach. She introduced Alma to her contacts.[33] In August, Alma visited Susan in Gotha. Susan had told her friends that she had met 'Abdu'l-Bahá in Stuttgart and invited Alma to explain the Bahá'í teachings to them. A small group of Bahá'ís was formed including the Grimm family and Marie Plessner.[34] In mid-December 1913, they organized a public meeting in a large hall with an opening speech from the Mayor of Gotha. Alma was interviewed by the press, visited many new believers and people joined the Faith.[35] Susan told Alma that the Stuttgart believers finally recognized what Alma had done for them.

'Abdu'l-Bahá sent His confirmations and blessings to the ten new believers in Gotha. He wrote:

> O Ye sons and daughters of the Kingdom!
> The heavenly daughter Miss Knobloch has given the utmost praise about your faith and love, that Glory be unto God, when you heard the call of the Kingdom your spirits gained the capacity of flight, your spirits were illumined with the Light of Guidance, you drank from the cup of divine Knowledge and the Elixir of Bestowal and you became intoxicated with the Wine of the Kingdom.
> Thank ye God that He hath chosen you from amongst all the people of the world and obtained such an eminent Gift, so that each one of you may usher in the Kingdom of

God and you may shine and gleam like unto the stars. This Bestowal of the Most Great Guidance is not so apparent now but in the future ages it will illumine the East and West.

Consider that during the days of His Holiness Christ . . . The populace said, Ah! a number of insignificant souls who are the catchers of fishes have gathered themselves around a poor man and are talking foolishly, nay rather they were ridiculing them. They laughed even at the Blessed Personage of Christ and spat upon that radiant, luminous, and wonderful Countenance. But reflect, that afterwards, the guidance of those the catchers of fish became famous throughout all the regions and up to this time mankind is glorifying and praising them.[36]

Word spread; the community in Gotha had grown in a just few months to a small and stable community whose members all contributed to German Bahá'í history.

Raising up the first Bahá'í community in Chemnitz

On 24 August 1913, Richard Glitz had heard about the Bahá'í teachings through Lydia Bauer in Stuttgart.[37] He invited Alma to visit Chemnitz to teach him the Faith.[38] His new faith was a turning point for him, and he wrote to Alma, 'You brought me new life and I see the Earth as a symbol of the high and incomprehensibly beautiful spirit, our eternal, one God.' He made plans to visit Alma in Leipzig,[39] and in September was confirmed by 'Abdu'l-Bahá:

O thou respected youth!

How many holy souls in the past ages have longed most intensely just to hear the name of the Divine Kingdom and be living during the days of the Promised One of all the nations of the world; but they passed away and left this world with utter regret, because they did not attain to their wish. In this radiant Century God has so confirmed thee that thou may'st step into the Universe of Life . . .

Consider what a great Favour is this! . . . Therefore, loosen thy tongue in the glorification of this most great Bestowal and summon the people to the Kingdom of God so that others may receive a good portion from this Holy Cause! [40]

Through Richard Glitz, Alma made new contacts in the nearby villages of Oetzsch, Gautzsch, Wermsdorf and Bautzen.[41]

* * * * *

In the Spring of 1914, the Dörings moved from Leipzig to Gera. Kurt Döring quickly interested a friend in the Bahá'í teachings and they decided to start a group together.[42] In June, Alma visited the Dörings' new home and while out for a walk met Kurt's employer Mr Flässel and his family. The following day at work, Mr Flässel asked Kurt, 'What is your relationship to the woman you were walking with?' This allowed Kurt to explain the Bahá'í Cause. The next time Alma met Mr Flässel, 'his face shone with delight' and Kurt immediately brought him literature. The following evening the first Bahá'í gathering was held in Gera, and the many friends the Dörings had shared the teachings with 'fully accepted the Truth'. The party ended late after midnight. Alma recalled, 'one more city added to the list, Gera, no doubt it will become a Bahá'í centre & the Teachings will be promoted . . . Mr. and Mrs. Döring are a flame for the Cause & will use every opportunity to spread the teachings.'[43] While in Gera, Kurt also shared the teachings with his sister Hetwig Döring, who emigrated to South America shortly after that.[44]

The Master wrote to Alma that it was because she was confirmed in services to the kingdom of God and was self-sacrificing in the path of God that she had been 'reinforced' in Gotha and a number of souls advanced toward the Divine Kingdom.[45]

On 5 December 1913 'Abdu'l-Bahá had returned to Haifa, thus ending the greatest teaching trip in the history of the Bahá'í Faith. Although His journey had ended, He was ever present, guiding the Faith through His inspiring Tablets and prayers.

THE 'AMERICAN GIRL' TEACHES THROUGHOUT GERMANY

The German community He had built up and left behind was mature and steadfast.

Two weeks later, on 13 December, Dr Edwin Fisher boarded the *President Grant* steamer of the Hamburg–America Line en route to New York; his destination listed on the ship documents was California.[46] His sister Luitgard and her husband had moved from Trenton, New Jersey to Los Angeles, California and Dr Fisher went to join them. At this time, Alma was teaching in Gera and watching the seeds of her new efforts grow.

In June 1914, Alma wrote to Fanny, 'My dear sister, do not think that I ever slack in working for the Cause. Mr. Sydney Sprague was 2 years in London and could see no results from his efforts. Miss Jack said he did not make one Bahá'í during the time, but in his Tablet Abdul-Baha told him that in the future results will be seen. How gratifying it is to see results right away. Surely we have reason to be thankful.'[47]

History reveals confirmations and exposes the true motivation behind our actions in life. How sad the fate of Sydney Sprague, whose marriage into the Master's family brought about disastrous consequences for him. Sprague had married the Master's niece, the sister of Dr Fareed, who continuously disobeyed 'Abdu'l-Bahá and had caused much trouble while travelling with the Master in the United States. Dr Fareed even went so far as to challenge the position of the Master as Head of the Faith in the newspapers in California.[48] The Master was forgiving, but when Dr Fareed asked some believers to join him in opposition to the Master, he broke the Covenant. In July 1914 an important message arrived in Germany from the Master, telling the friends that Dr Fareed, his mother and relations intended to make a journey there, but that they were violators of the Covenant, and to warn all the friends not to associate with them, as such association was like poison.[49]

Years earlier, in late 1908, Alma had hoped that the Master would send His nephew Dr Fareed to Germany to help her with teaching,[50] but when Fareed passed through Europe two years later, he did not visit Germany.[51] Many of the early believers admired Sydney Sprague's marriage on 24 July 1910;

through it, Sprague had become part of the Master's family.⁵² Sadly, his wife chose to follow her brother and not the Master, and both Sydney Sprague and his wife left the Faith. After this none of the believers in Germany kept in contact with him. Alma wrote,

> Consul Schwarz received a tablet warning him against Dr. Farid and his relations . . . We will do all we can do . . . that Dr. Farid and his family will have no chance here whatsoever. They are in London where they did a great deal of harm and have planned to come . . . They are quite a pair . . . Dr Farid, wife and mother, Mr. Sprague and wife. Abdul-Baha has sent Mirza Asadollah, His brother-in-law to bring his wife [Dr Farid's mother] back to Haifa. Whether they will succeed is a question.⁵³

Unfortunately, Mírzá Asadu'lláh joined efforts with his son. He did not learn from the warning of the Master at the dinner table in Haifa years before when the Master had served him the hot pepper (see Chapter 16 above)! Neither Dr Fareed nor Sydney Sprague had any further influence on German Bahá'í history. Many, many years later, the elderly, lonely Sydney Sprague re-joined the Faith in California shortly before he died.

As the Bahá'ís worked to spread the teachings through Germany, the country was preparing for war. Everyone in Germany expected France or England to start a war. Already at the end of 1912, Alma had begun to look into ways to transfer money to Germany when the war started.⁵⁴ In May of 1914, she wrote to Fanny,

> The Red Cross has collected a great deal, all for the Great War preparations. Everybody seems to expect war within a year. What will become of me? War on your side & war expected on this side. The German Kaiser has been very successful so far to avert war, he rather took the insults & thereby displeased the nation; but he did not wish to go

into war. The people at large are not pleased, & the strain is almost beyond their strength.[55]

In those days, pomp and pageantry blinded the German people. Kaiser Wilhelm declared 1913 a 'Festive Year' of celebration simultaneously celebrating both the 25th anniversary of his reign and the Centenary of the Prussian victory over Napoleon at the Battle of Leipzig. His goal was to reinforce the identity of the German people with their Kaiser; to make that bond so strong that the German people would want to give their lives for him. The festival was designed to 'legitimatize the regime by invoking national unity, community and loyalty to the fatherland'.[56] Historically, the Festive Year 'advanced a new dimension of mass mobilization'. Increasingly, Europeans believed that war was inevitable, but most Europeans thought that it would be quick and that their nation would win.

Alma was moved by this spirit of nationalism and identity which rolled over Europe and culminated in the First World War. She was influenced by the newspapers and was a great believer in the Kaiser and the Fatherland. One of the biggest propaganda events in Germany was the Centenary Anniversary of the Battle of Leipzig on 18 October 1913. That morning Alma and Eugenie Böttger woke up early to find a good spot from which to see the great parade and the unveiling of the Battle of the Nations Monument. She recalled, 'There were 80,000 students, a most brilliant sight in their festive suits and patent leather boots about the knees, white pants, white gloves, and colourful coats and sashes with ribbons representing their various clubs, guilds, associations, and organizations . . . a sight never to be forgotten.' The entire procession was headed by Kaiser Wilhelm and the King of Saxony. In the evening, Alma and the Dörings saw all the houses in Leipzig illuminated.[57]

In these confusing times, German and American newspapers reported from quite different and contrasting perspectives. These were reflected in the letters and opinions of the Knobloch family members. The propaganda did not match, the truth was blurred. But Bahá'í identity and emphasis on unity were above all of this. The Bahá'ís read the Bahá'í news in the *Star of the West*. It focused on the Covenant of God and the unity of mankind. In 1914, Bahá'ís in Stuttgart, Esslingen, Zuffenhausen, Leipzig, Gotha and Hamburg subscribed to the *Star of the West* and shared their copies with the others. It included regular contributions about the Bahá'í activities in Germany. Even throughout the war, the *Star of the West* focused on Bahá'í identity. What a contrast to all other newspapers of that time! Although the countries were at war, the Bahá'ís called mankind to unity.

In July 1914, 'Abdu'l-Bahá met the German Consul in Haifa. The *Star of the West* reported Abdu'l-Bahá's recollection of their conversation as follows:

> . . . I had the pleasure of meeting the German Consul and discussing with him the ominous signs of the coming European war. He delivered himself of the opinion current among the statesmen, that a nation must go on increasing its annual military and naval expenditures if it desires to protect its growing commercial and national interests from the attack of its equally powerful and expanding neighbors or rivals; that the greater the military devices and paraphernalia, the more one is assured of the progress of the nation and its constantly developing resources. In that meeting, there were present a number of German and other nationalities. Strange to say, on this question they all agreed with the Consul, and concurred in his opinion as though he had voiced their hidden and most cherished thoughts. I said: "If the power of Love and Peace become predominant and supreme, their effects will be greater than the power of hate and Mars, the god of war. In the world of existence there is no power as efficacious and as penetrating as the Power of Love. Military power coerces and compels men through unnatural resort to force and violation, but mankind yields happily and willingly to the Power of Love.[58]

The *Star of the West* printed a talk given by 'Abdu'l-Bahá on 3

THE 'AMERICAN GIRL' TEACHES THROUGHOUT GERMANY

August 1914 on Mount Carmel, the eve of the start of the war, and recorded in the diary of Ahmad Sohrab:

> The world is at the threshold of a most tragic struggle ... Vast armies – millions of men – are being mobilized and centered at their frontiers. They are being prepared for the fearful contest. The slightest friction will bring them into a terrific clash, and then there will be a conflagration the like of which is not recorded in the past history of mankind.
>
> While in America I spoke before many Peace Societies, Churches and Conventions, and foretold the fearful consequences of armed peace in Europe. I said Europe is like unto an arsenal and one tiny spark will cause a universal combustion. *'O men! Come ye together and as far as possible try to extinguish this world-raging fire; do your utmost to prevent the occurrence of this general conflict; make ye an effort that this flood-gate of human butchery may not be set loose!'* I found no one to listen to my advice. I searched, but there were no hearing ears. I cried out at the top of my voice, I pleaded, I enunciated the evils of war, but people were self-occupied, self-centered. And now *this* is the *result* ...
>
> It is very strange to see how 'Illusion' has taken possession of the hearts of men, while 'Reality' has no sway whatsoever. For example: 'Racial difference' is an optical illusion! It is a figment of imagination, yet how deep-seated and powerful its influence! ...
>
> ... More astonishing than all these matters is this: These warring nations believe that the object of the religion of God is war and strife! This is the most preposterous idea that any man could let enter into his mind! ...[59]

Humanity did not listen. Turbulent times were on their way. The Bahá'ís kept busy spreading light and focusing on love and unity as the world order and the reigns of the Kings of Europe were being rolled up before their eyes.

35
THE WAR TO END ALL WARS

George Latimer had just finished college in mid-summer 1912 following his pilgrimage in 1911 when he met Mason Remey and they spent a long evening discussing 'the great work to be done' to spread the Cause in the world. They wrote to 'Abdu'l-Bahá about their wish to work together and they became a strong teaching team. First, 'Abdu'l-Bahá sent them to teach in Hawaii.[1] In 1913, 'Abdu'l-Bahá wrote to George Latimer's mother, 'If it be possible that these two be together it will become the cause of greater confirmation.'[2]

In 1914, 'Abdu'l-Bahá advised Remey to spend the winter wherever he liked, and then to visit Europe, especially Germany and France, the following spring. Remey and Latimer set sail on 27 March 1914 from New York to Cherbourg en route for Paris.[3] They planned to visit Germany as soon as they could leave the work in Paris.[4]

In Paris, Remey held a class on the Bahá'í teachings every Thursday afternoon at the Trianon Palace Hotel. He offered the same classes in French every Thursday evening at 8:30 at the studio of Mrs Hellock. Alma sent him the names and addresses of the believers in Holland and Remey and Latimer planned to also visit them.[5]

Alma looked forward to their support and the support of other American believers in Leipzig. In June 1914, Alma invited Agnes Alexander, who was in Rome at the time, to travel teach in Germany.[6] Unfortunately, all the summer teaching plans unfolded differently from planned. Alma wrote,

I just received a card from Remey, they expect to leave Paris on the 18th [of June] for London. This does not please me exactly, but I have learned to take things as they come. They expect to come to Leipzig now about the middle of July – from the 15th of July until September is Grosse Ferien [summer vacation period] and there is little or nothing during this time going on in any large city. Do not know whom they expect to meet at that time.[7]

While Agnes Alexander was visiting her aunt in Milan, Alma sent her several addresses in Stuttgart, but she preferred to visit Alma in Leipzig. Her visit was planned for the beginning of July and she asked Alma to meet her at the station.[8] The only thing that arrived in Germany, however, was Agnes's trunk, which arrived in Stuttgart in the end of July. Agnes herself got as far as Switzerland.[9] In September, Alma wrote that Agnes had been sent to Japan and might go to India and the Holy Land from there. With war coming, Alma surmised, 'Abdu'l-Bahá was turning his thoughts to Japan and India.[10]

On 28 July Austria-Hungary declared war on Serbia; on 30 July, Russia declared general mobilization. Germany immediately demanded that Russia demobilize.[11] And so the First World War had begun.

The Latimer–Remey teaching team arrived in Leipzig from Berlin on 31 July. They had not met any Bahá'í friends in Berlin due to the summer holiday and were thankful that Alma had arranged meetings for them in Leipzig.[12] These meetings proved very successful. Alma had personally invited Dr Hugo Vollrath, the editor of the *Theosophical Monthly*, who became very attracted to the teachings. Remey gave a talk and Alma translated it and answered the closing questions. Several meetings were held; one was advertised in the newspapers and the response was good, although the trains were interrupted due to military operations and Bahá'ís in surrounding areas could not reach some meetings.[13] Dr Vollrath was delighted, encouraged by the spirit of the words of 'Abdu'l-Bahá. He suggested that Alma stay in Leipzig to spread the Bahá'í teachings. It was through his efforts that Bahá'í children's classes began in Leipzig in 1914. Hugo Vollrath became 'a very spiritual enlightened young man of high culture and a beautiful Bahá'í'.[14]

On 1 August, Germany declared war on Russia for not demobilizing. The next day, Latimer and Remey took one of the last passenger trains to Stuttgart. After they had departed, a police officer questioned Alma regarding their nationality and destination. When their train reached Naumberg, they were taken off the train for questioning, after which they re-boarded and continued their journey. The train was seized for military purposes in Nuremberg. They continued via freight and omnibus train until they arrived, dusty and hungry, in Stuttgart. Once again, they were arrested briefly to have their identities verified. They were unable to notify any of the friends about their arrival.

Two other travel teachers sent by 'Abdu'l-Bahá had also arrived in Stuttgart: Dr Habíbu'lláh Khudábakhsh, a recent medical school graduate (Habíb Moayyad, whose diaries document his time with 'Abdu'l-Bahá) and 'Azízu'lláh Bahádur, a student at the American University in Beirut and one of 'Abdu'l-Bahá's secretaries. A couple of days later, Alma joined the teaching efforts in Stuttgart.[15]

The government called on all German citizens to house soldiers during the mobilization. In this way, the Bahá'ís taught many soldiers whom they otherwise would never have met. These young men participated in Bahá'í meetings while they were training, and when they left for the front, they took Bahá'í literature with them. Those who were sent into battle were replaced by others who in turn also came into contact with the Bahá'í teachings in these homes. Remey shared some stories told by wounded soldiers who had been in contact with the teachings and he reflected that it was not easy for the young Bahá'ís who believed in peace and who taught the unity of mankind to then serve in the army, but that there had been no way out for them, and they accepted it, as in the Bible it says, 'Render unto Caesar the things that are Caesar's, and unto God the things that are God's.'[16]

Alma introduced Remey and Latimer to Richard Glitz and

his mother from Chemnitz. Remey recalled the sad day when Richard, scarcely 19, was selected for war and sent to Strasbourg on the French border. The mobilization of troops began on 2 August. Two days later, England declared war on Germany.

The American Consul organized trains to evacuate more than 300 Americans out of Stuttgart via Rotterdam for passage to New York. Latimer and Remey were among the few Americans who remained in Germany.[17] They were waiting for word from 'Abdu'l-Bahá.[18] Habíb Moayyad and 'Azízu'lláh Bahádur stayed at the Ecksteins' home. Both the Eckstein boys, including the younger one who was only 20, were drafted into military service.[19]

Consul Schwarz was also called from civil life to army service. While Latimer and Remey were in Stuttgart, Schwarz was stationed at Ludwigsburg. Remey wrote about a widowed relative of the Schwarz family who was notified during a prayer meeting that her only son had been killed and buried in battle.

Many believers served in the Red Cross during the War. Wounded officers in the hospitals had Bahá'í literature and read it to the other patients. During the War, Consul Schwarz's daughter Olly served as a nurse and gave the Bahá'ís a tour of a hospital. The hospitals were clean and well-organized, with tidy white beds, fresh flowers and clothing for the soldiers when they arrived.[20] Melanie Rössler, Alma's cousin in Bautzen, passed the Red Cross examination and also became a nurse.[21]

On 22 August Remey described the situation in *Star of the West*:

> George Latimer and I were in Leipzig with Miss Alma Knobloch when the first hostilities began. There were some people in Leipzig who were attracted to the Cause, and the work bid fair to progress; but with the commencement of the war all was thrown into confusion and it was impossible to carry on . . . Therefore, we decided to come on here to our objective point in Germany – Stuttgart. After much difficulty we got through and were followed in a few days by Miss Knobloch.

Here in Stuttgart we found our Bahai friends in great material trouble, but in a state of great spiritual attraction and enkindlement. Their beautiful spirit has been a lesson and a blessing to us.

Although we are suffering humanly because of the suffering about us, yet our own difficulties are nothing compared with those of our German friends. There is hardly a household that has not a father, a brother or a son at the front, and each day brings the news of many killed and wounded – you may imagine the rest! Think of our Bahai brothers going thus to battle! They do not want to kill. They have only love in their hearts, but the conditions necessitate their sacrifice!

Yet despite all this human agony and misery, nowhere in Europe have we found such real spiritual warmth, peace and joy of soul as here in Stuttgart – here where the friends are all in the very vortex of material distress. Every night and every afternoon a meeting is held, and the spirit of the Covenant of God is always manifest in our midst. Through distress the hearts of the people are turned towards God, and many new faces are appearing in the meetings . . .

Pray for the Bahais in Germany, and pray for these multitudes who are soul-hungry and are seeking the peace of God's Kingdom.[22]

On the evening of 30 July, Alma and Susan Pollock were at a veteran's café when loud noises broke out and they observed thousands of men filling the streets. They had come from a meeting and were protesting against the War. Later, as Alma passed the city courthouse, they were passing by and just as she arrived were singing a prayer. She recalled, 'All were very quiet and indeed it was very impressive.' Indeed, not everyone in Germany supported the War, a fact that is often forgotten in the annals of history. In general, the newspapers spread propaganda to kindle fear in the people, promoting the belief that war was inevitable.

Things were getting worse every day. On 23 August, Japan declared war on China and entered the War on the side of the Allies. Across Europe, newspapers published stories to support their different governments and hype up national enthusiasm for the War. In reality, the War was not necessary or advantageous for any of those who died for it! It was exactly as the Master had warned many times during His European visits to England, France, Germany, Austria, and Hungary.

Alma and the other Bahá'ís in Germany believed that the 'war was for self-defense and the Germans are a peaceful people';[23] they felt that the Germans were victims and were forced to fight to protect themselves from their aggressive neighbours. On 27 September 1914 Alma wrote to Fanny in German, 'Germany did not declare war . . . it had to protect itself . . . the war will be short because of the advanced military technology . . .' The newspapers in Germany and America reported conflicting information. Alma wrote, 'I am sorry that the American papers do not publish fairly,'[24] she felt this was due to English influence.[25] Most Germans believed that they had been attacked but that they would be victorious. Alma sent German articles home for comparison. These articles reported that a bomb the English used splattered the bones and that the English, Belgian and French papers published fake accounts and shameful lies. She wrote to Pauline,

> Pray for our fatherland. The Germans do not want a war, they tried to live in peace with their enemy neighbours, but when they were attacked from both sides, they could not hold back anymore. It came like a dark cloud suddenly covering a clear sky. God will punish the deeds of those who spill innocent blood . . . The Germans are innocent.[26]

In August 1914, Alma sent a strange postcard home with photos of Belgian prisoners of war at the front. She wrote that it was no longer permitted to take pictures, but that 'all the prisoners are well treated and comfortable where they are stationed'. These postcards were meant to portray the image of German fairness in the war.

The atmosphere and propaganda on the streets of Stuttgart was dramatic. On 2 September, Alma returned to Stuttgart from a devotional in Zuffenhausen in an over-filled streetcar that unexpectedly stopped in front of the King's Palace. A great crowd had gathered, and they were singing with a band, 'Now Thank We All Our God'. Alma sang 'with her heart full of thankfulness'. Then King Wilhelm II of Württemberg spoke, and in the end, the band played once more, and the people sang again with excitement.[27]

Although reportedly King Wilhelm did not get along well with Kaiser Wilhelm because the King did not appreciate military life, nonetheless he gave moving speeches and from Alma's perspective he wholeheartedly supported the mobilization. It is reported that he had tears in his eyes when sending the troops to war. The King visited the trenches. One soldier told Margarethe that 'King Wilhelm shook his hand as though he was equal'.[28] After the war, King Wilhelm II of Württemberg was forced to abdicate, and he passed away in sadness in the castle in Bebenhausen, which 'Abdu'l-Bahá had visited in 1913.

Remarkably, Alma did not detect her own obvious contradictions:

> Our soldiers look so strong and their faces do not look warlike, they stay fearless with the words of Bismarck, 'We fear God and no one else in the world.' The Kaiser ordered that the churches use the following prayer in their services:
> 'Almighty merciful God! Lord of the Hearses! We thank you for humbleness and your almighty assistance for our German fatherland. Bless this gathered German war power and lead us to victory and give us grace to prove to our enemies that we are Christians. Let us quickly come to a peace that guarantees the honor and independence of Germany.'[29]

She also wrote,

> Germany did not declare the war, but only had to defend itself, until now the biggest damage up to now is in other countries . . . the German people did not realize that the others were already so prepared to use the first chance when

Germany declared it would support Austria. The latest news reports that Germany has moved forward and has taken over a fort near Paris, which is very advantageous for us. We hope and pray then we will be victorious . . . The fatherland comes first, how true and united we stand by each other. How glorious that empire is in every way.[30]

Generally, at the beginning of the century, conscription in Germany began for some men at a very young age. The 'Landsturm' (home defence units) took some at age 17, so many men were trained between the ages of 17 and 20; at 20 effective military service began. Half the German men in each age group were trained for two or three years between the ages of 20 and 23, then they were released as civilians but could be called up to active duty until the age of 45. Through this system, Germany had a large pool of trained inactive soldiers who could serve if war began. It took only 12 days in August of 1914 for the German army to expand from 808,280 to 3,502,700 soldiers.[31] Alma saw the Landsturm returning from training in Degerloch. She described their enthusiasm:

> They sing 'Wacht am Rhein' [Guard the Rhein] and 'Deutschland über Alles' [Germany above all else] . . . They sounded so firm and solid as they pass. Miss Döring and I pray at 12 at night and also at dawn for our country. Surely God will grant our earnest prayers. The War in 1870 brought the Germans together as one nation and now they feel as one nation . . .[32]

Bahá'í soldiers who joined the war effort left home protected with the Greatest Name and wrote from the battlefields describing the inhumane behaviour of the Belgians, French and English. In Stuttgart, Bahá'í meetings were well attended and held every evening and often in the afternoons. Alma and Margarethe prayed every evening and morning for the Kaiser and German victory. Alma sent home two prayers from Mírzá Munír Zayn in 'Akká that were translated into German.

The Bahá'ís focused on distributing the Word of God to as many as possible. Fanny's Tablets from 'Abdu'l-Bahá were translated and distributed amongst the army, Alma wrote, 'so my precious sister you are doing so much for your Fatherland'. Consul Schwarz distributed many Bahá'í books and pamphlets to his soldiers and officers. Alma remarked, 'How very excellent it is to have him as a Bahai . . .'[33]

In Gera, new believers joined the community, as the men left for the battlefield carrying Bahá'í literature with them. One of them took one of Fanny's books with a cover Mrs Kurt Döring made for it and placed it over his heart.

Regarding Leipzig, Alma wrote, 'Cousin Jenny [sic] Scholz received a stone with the greatest name and has found a true soul who comes every Monday to find strength in the teachings. Cousin Arthur cheered for the war and was accepted. And he also has a stone from Abdul-Baha. The Cause moves forward how wonderful it is to see this.'[34]

There were so many meetings in Stuttgart that Alma decided to stay and help their efforts. She wrote,

> I couldn't do anything but to come here where so many people are. Margarethe and I can so strongly pray together . . . we are certain that you also pray for us . . . There are always new ones in every meeting, and they are very excited. Every night and very often in the afternoons we meet and pray. We pray with pride for luck for the Kaiser that commands us. How wonderful it was that Abdul-Baha cared for us and prepared us for this difficult time. When it's a bit quieter again, the teachings will be spread quickly . . . I cannot say how things will come to pass. I will have to accept my possibilities as God provides them and hope that God protects me. It is amazing how different beliefs have developed, material and spiritual, one would not believe it's possible, but one sees God's blessing in so many different ways . . . On Tuesday I was in Esslingen, I visited Mrs. Kohler, and her husband also came. From there we went to the unity meeting, it was very nice, over 55 new seekers

... On Wednesday, we were in Zuffenhausen, the largest meeting, they also have new seekers, over 26 were present. On Thursday, we visited another meeting ... also new seekers. On Friday, Unity Meeting at Miss Stäbler's there were more than 28 ... with such a number of new people, one cannot invite all the friends, because it is too many ... Oh how I wish it would be like that in other locations. But we are thankful for what we have, that all are fest [firm] and steadfast and active. I hope that there will be spiritual meetings all over Europe so that through the spirit of attraction we can overcome all difficulties ... [35]

Already in September two Bahá'í soldiers returned wounded: Willy Schmand and one of Mr Braun's sons who had been shot in the leg.[36] For many weeks this son could not walk, so he did not return to the battlefield. He had distributed Bahá'í literature to his comrades and head Sergeant and felt he was under the protection of the Master. Unfortunately, before the end of 1914, Mr Braun's other son fell in battle.[37] All the Bahá'í soldiers used the Greatest Name for protection. All the women prayed 'that the satanic clouds will disappear'.[38]

Confronted with death, the community focused on their loved ones lost in the years before the War. They visited the grave of Sophie Stäbler, whose grave now boasted an elaborate tombstone; she had been the first in Germany to have a Bahá'í funeral.[39] In addition, they celebrated the birthday of Amalie Knobloch. About a week later, many believers including Alice Schwarz and her children, Eckstein, Herrigel, Dr Habíbu'lláh, Mírzá 'Azízu'lláh, Margarethe, Julia and Elise Stäbler, Gustav Eger, Richard Kohler, Max and Hugo Bender, and Mr Ruoff gathered at the grave of Babette Ruoff to read her Tablet of Visitation.[40]

Mason Remey wrote to Albert Windust and the friends in Chicago:

> Although there is in this troublesome time no material safety, rest or peace, and all humanity suffers terribly, yet the

friends of God are in the greatest activity, in spiritual tranquility and heavenly fragrance. They have meetings every day and their voices are raised in the song of the Covenant and hearts are illumined. The people are firm in the Center of the Covenant – they raise no questions in regard to the divine institutions of Abdul-Baha, hence their meetings are in a growing condition of joy and fragrance. The physical sorrow at present is causing the people, in general, to turn their thoughts to God and inquire into the reality of spiritual things. One sees new and hopeful faces in every meeting and while the country here is in such a deplorable condition, yet the people of the Covenant work continually in spreading the message of the Kingdom, and the result of their labor is apparent on all sides.

Dr Habibollah, Mirza Azizollah (the two Persians), Mr. Latimer and myself were called to Accá by Abdul-Baha. We are at present detained in Stuttgart on account of the passes of our two Persian friends, which had to be sent back to Berlin for correction. Just as soon as they come back, we shall start for the Holy Land.

All the friends here join in sending their love and greetings.

Miss Knobloch was kind enough to translate this letter into German because only German letters are allowed to be sent at this time, and they must be open.[41]

In Washington, the *Evening Star* reported:

Charles Mason Remey, George Latimer, and Miss Alma Knobloch are Washingtonians who are now in Stuttgart, Germany, and plan to remain there for some time. They are interested in the spread of the Baháʼí religious movement, and in a letter just received by Joseph H. Hannen, secretary of the moment here, Mr. Remey tells of their experiences.[42]

On 16 September, Mason Remey, George Latimer, Dr Habíbuʼlláh and Mírzá ʻAzízuʼlláh Bahádur departed from

Stuttgart for Haifa. Alma wrote home, 'The days [they] spent here were heavenly and will be a pleasure to recall always . . . The meetings were glorious. We will miss them very much . . .'

Regarding herself, Alma decided, 'The conditions are really very serious, but I will remain at my post unless I receive orders to do otherwise. Abdul-Baha in one of the Tablets [translated 13 July] says: 'Praise be to God it [her letter He received] contained the good news of thy health.'⁴³

Surprisingly, Alma did not become afraid of the situation. She was now a registered German subject and could remain to serve in Germany. She firmly believed that 'Abdu'l-Bahá would protect her. On 11 September, she wrote, 'Do not be worried about me, God will protect me, He has so far, and I will work for the Cause just as long as He wishes me to. To be united with our parents is also something to look forward to, and then there will be no more separations.'⁴⁴

And a week later she wrote, 'I am very well indeed and Abdul-Baha did mention my health so do not worry about me precious and good sisters and dear ones at home . . . Now is the time for spreading the cause, for the people are needy . . . God only knows how it will turn out, and we feel that God is with us. Please do not worry about me, Abdul-Baha will protect me, and we will again be united if not in this world then the other.'⁴⁵

Alma had about 760 German Marks to make it through the War (about 185 US dollars).⁴⁶ During the war it was not possible for her to get more money from home. From Leipzig, Mr and Mrs Kurt Döring offered their help and financial assistance. They wrote to Alma to welcome her to stay with them with the words, 'where 2 have to eat, then 3 will also have plenty'.⁴⁷

On 25 September, Alma wrote from Stuttgart to Albert Windust in Chicago:

> Everything is perfectly quiet here – all are busy taking care of the wounded soldiers. The arrangements here are splendid – all are well cared for. The Lazaretts (hospitals) are comfortably arranged and the wounded soldiers are well

remembered with flowers, cigars, chocolates and cakes. The prisoners receive the same care, yet a good many of them are mistrustful and believe they will be killed yet. What astonishes me the most is that so little hatred is shown by the Germans, though the German soldiers are almost always brought back in a terrible condition . . .[48]

The prayer meetings fell on the shoulders of the women as the men left for the battlefield. The regular meetings at the Frauen Club were held at the home of Margarethe in August and September. In Degerloch the regular meetings held by Rosa Schwarz were 'for ladies only' since her husband was also at the battlefield.[49] Alma wrote, 'There are so many Bahá'í soldiers at the battlefield, does it not seem strange?'[50]

The German Bahá'ís united to help the German soldiers. 'Everyone is anxious to do something for the soldiers who are in the front, they all say when they return that it is simply dreadful, many have lost their minds and I've heard from several doctors who have written to their families their hair has turned grey and they are young men . . .'[51] The Herrigels arranged gatherings where the friends would knit for the soldiers. Margarethe sent many bags of supplies to the field to unknown soldiers.[52]

Things became increasingly complicated. Letters were sometimes lost, and it was not easy to send money. Correspondence had to be in German for transparency in the case of surveillance.

By the end of 1914, there were 'always new faces at all the meetings'. Lydia Bauer opened a Sunday School where the children learned the Hidden Words.[53] There were so many opportunities to teach! Alma began to teach in Gmünd, in the Swabian Alps where Miss Paula Fry, Mrs and Mr Maier and their sons became believers. Maria Rupp, a nurse from Baden-Baden, came to receive the teachings.[54]

At the same time, people in Europe realized that the War would last much longer than they thought. Alma described the early days of the War:

My letters have arrived; how happy I was when I received Pauline's letters. I was surprised she sent $100. One was of the opinion that the war could not last long due to the modern guns, but now one thinks differently. It can extend long into the future; I have good coverage and a strong trust in God.[55]

36

CRISIS AND VICTORY DURING THE WAR

As early as January 1907, Mason Remey wrote a long letter to Mr Herman Faber explaining the Bahá'í teachings in detail.[1] Although Remey had various contacts in Munich, there were no sustained teaching efforts and no Bahá'ís in Munich until late 1914.

In 1914, Alma was determined to fulfil the Master's wishes and build up new communities all over Germany. This mission was her primary concern for the rest of her days in Germany. At that time a Bahá'í community was a group of believers who prayed and deepened together, shared the message with others and celebrated Bahá'í Holy Days together.

To fulfil her mission, Alma visited contacts who were living in remote communities. To build up communities, Alma first needed 'to get acquainted with the people', meaning to 'work her way through and win the confidence of the people first', which was 'of course, not done in a few days or weeks'. Alma remarked, 'It is a quite different matter after it [the community] is established, and visitors come, and the believers invite their friends to meet and hear their guests.'[2] After Alma felt a community was established, she could then move on to a new place.

House visits were even more challenging during the War. Alma lived on a tight budget of 100 Marks per month. Even when the government rationed food, Alma needed to bring food when visiting or inviting people.

Alma described teaching in Munich to Fanny:

I very seldom got to bed before 12 and have found quite a circle of friends, and that is for me the hardest work in a new place, how different people are, you can be assured that I am glad when I can teach, then I am in my element, but I have to create the circle first. After this is done, progress is naturally the result. That is why I cannot give you a glorious account of my work and must let the future speak for itself.³

Klara Krieger, Anna Köstlin's friend who was the daughter of Mayor Krieger from Aalen, had married Mr Böttger and moved to Munich. At the beginning of November 1914, Alma visited her in Munich. Klara introduced Alma to her new relatives and friends and the doors in Munich began to open. After spending Christmas in Stuttgart, Alma returned to Munich as promised on 10 January 1915.

The Böttgers hosted Alma in their home for seven months. Every day during that time, Alma visited friends and shared the teachings. Klara introduced Alma to many people including Princess Gisela and Prince Leopold of Bavaria.⁴ Alma met many very fine people in Munich who were attracted to the teachings, including several doctors, Baron v. Nottenrode and his wife the Baroness, a charming lady who liked Alma very much.⁵

Public meetings were organized in Munich to inform people about the Bahá'í Faith.⁶ By February 1915 a group had been formed, and regular meetings were being held at the home of Klara's aunt, Mrs Böttger. On 6 February, Alma wrote, 'How very thankful I am for the good start made here in Munich. We have nine who accepted the Truth and several others who very cordially invited me to come and visit them being interested in the Cause.'⁷ Alma wrote to Agnes Alexander in Tokyo, 'We are also making progress here.'⁸

Mr Domhuber, a 'strong anarchist-atheist' and an important local leader, also joined the meetings with his wife at the beginning of 1915 and began to open his heart to the teachings.⁹ In May, the largest Bahá'í meeting was held in Munich at the home of Domhubers, with new seekers.

Soon meetings were being held at the home of the Fäbring

family where the friends shared contacts, deepened their understanding of the teachings, and planned charitable work to support a local 'Lazaretto', a makeshift hospital in a Munich school building filled with hundreds of injured soldiers. Such Lazarettos were the interface between the battlefield and the German people. Typically, injured soldiers shared their stories while they received treatment, and when they had somewhat recovered, they were returned back to the battlefields. When the soldiers told of their experiences it was 'beyond words'. Alma spent many weeks visiting and caring for Emil Götz and his brother on behalf of their ill mother.[10] Emil suffered from bad head and face injuries caused by a grenade which had struck his trench, killing every one of his comrades, and burying him under the debris. Despite the terrible injuries, he and his brother were sent back into battle after some weeks.[11]

Siegfried Junker, a journalist who had heard about the Faith through Julia Stäbler, gave Alma contact information for several interested ladies in Munich.[12] They wrote Alma two letters of questions: 'What is meant by original sin? In what way has the woman equality with man? How can you prove the existence of God? What is the difference between the animal and the human body?' They were impressed with the answers they received, and a meeting was arranged.[13]

In June Alma wrote, 'It is hard work to attend different cafes to meet the different people to teach – Just had a visit from Miss Böttger (Klara Böttger's niece) who has accepted the teachings and is doing what she can to spread them among her friends.'[14]

The most important part of community building was receiving confirmation from 'Abdu'l-Bahá. As always, Alma sent petitions to the Master from the new believers and waited for His response. She sent many petitions to 'Abdu'l-Bahá from Munich,[15] and wrote home,

> If you have any chance to communicate with Abdul-Baha, please ask if I should remain here. We have had no news directly from Abdul-Baha since the war has broken out. We have sent many petitions from here. Last month I received

a card from Mirza Azizollah in which he says that Abdul-Baha is well. If you have any news, please let us know. I am rather anxious, for they no doubt are in very much worse condition than we have here in Germany and are cut off. What great hardships must there be amongst the natives.[16]

Throughout the War, the Master never forgot the German friends, but sometimes communication was not possible or delayed. On 3 August 1915 Azízu'lláh Bahádur wrote to Bertha Bahnmüller, 'you know dear sister the fact that He did not write an answer personally is due to the fact that Persian letters will not be forwarded. The friends must be patient and pray to God to settle these present troubles and then see that they shall be rained with Tablets from the Beloved of their hearts.'[17] In May 1915, He sent them the following Tablet:

To the believers of Germany
May their lives be happy!
He is God!

O Ye real friends!
   Although correspondence has come to a standstill yet do I continually think of you, asking for each and all the breath of the Holy Spirit.
   The divine Bestowals are infinite. They have had no beginning nor will they ever have an end. The doors of the kingdom are open and the voice of the Lord of the Kingdom reaches the ear of the heart.
   Heart-uplifting news are being received from the believers of Germany that praise be to God they are in the utmost firm and steadfastness and attracted to the Kingdom of God. It is My hope that the power of the Holy Spirit may transform that Empire into the delectable paradise and the effulgence of the Sun of Reality may illumine that region. May it advance in all the spiritual degrees, may the light of Guidance shine forth, may the Breeze of the Garden of God blow, may the cloud of mercy pour down and that

country & nation bloom forth in the upmost freshness and newness.

Convey the utmost longing to each and all of the friends of God.[18]

The German believers sent other letters to 'Abdu'l-Bahá to which he responded through Azízu'lláh Bahádur in late July 1915. He sent a message from 'Abdu'l-Bahá to the Bahá'ís of Germany through Alice Schwarz: 'O dear friends! Praise be to God, we are all well and safe under the shelter of divine patronage and protection.'[19] On 30 July 1915, Azízu'lláh Bahádur wrote to Alma,

> I translated all the enclosed letters immediately and offered them to our beloved Abdul-Baha. He became very happy thereby. He loves all of you, dear friends. He often speaks highly of the character of his German children. He says: 'They are pure, their nature is not stained by any disagreeable quality. They are readily confirmed by the hosts of the Kingdom. They are blessed in their activities in serving and helping the negligent and distressed. Their success in the service of the kingdom of God is sure.'
>
> Dear sister, he praises them so often that I do not know which time to write. I have only to congratulate all for their nobility of character which attracts so many blessings from him.
>
> Also, I pray that he may keep them always under his guarding staff, safe from the thieves of worldly desires, pride and negligence. I am sure he does this, and consequently, they will always strive and shine brilliantly among other friends upon the horizon of the Cause.[20]

When Bahádur was giving the Master the petitions from Munich, someone interrupted to give Him other papers. 'Abdu'l-Bahá looked at them and said, 'I do not care about these papers for they are about material things; I only care about these papers (holding the papers from Germany) because they indicate of the spiritual world concerning my Mission. They speak of the Children of the Kingdom and their life-giving activities.' Bahádur wrote to Alma, 'Then He poured upon you, dear sister, the showers of His divine kindness. He is much pleased with you and blessed you marvellously. You have to feel it in your cause of service and realize its expression vividly in your work.'[21]

On 17 July 1915, after almost seven months of service in Munich, Alma returned to Stuttgart. The friends in Munich regretted her departure and she promised to return. After she left, Alma received beautiful letters from friends in Munich, where a culture of teaching was now established. In October 1915, new believers from Munich also wrote to her.[22] The following Spring, Naw-Rúz was celebrated in Munich, even without Alma, demonstrating that Munich had become a mature and independent community. After receiving stones engraved with the Greatest Name from 'Abdu'l-Bahá, they had them set at once. Dr Junker wrote from Munich, 'I will devote my life for the promotion of the Cause of God.' They encouraged Alma to return.[23] In just seven short months, the Bahá'í community of Munich had been born.

Despite the War, probably because Turkey and Germany were fighting in alliance, in August 1915 a Tablet from the Master reached Alma, reassuring her that although 'material' communication had been cut off, 'spiritual' communication was continuous, and that he hoped her efforts would continue to be confirmed.[24]

Although Alma was very busy, at times she experienced acute homesickness. She seemed detached from time, and wrote home, 'You and Pauline dreaming of my returning, may mean that I am to remain here for a longer time . . . Who knows!'[25] And, 'I do not wish to get homesick so I try to stay busy.'[26] In February 1915 she wrote,

> I naturally wish sometimes that I were at home, for the conditions will only grow worse in Europe. But if Abdul-Baha does not send me I will not ask, for I will gladly sacrifice

my life for the cause. The words from Abdul-Baha when I came, 'But as to her stay, she must stay as long as possible.' How time passes and we are now in those terrible days and how wonderfully we have been saved and protected from the horrors of the war . . . One good thing I have enough clothing to last for several years, so even if the food goes up in price, I will be able to get along.[27]

Alma loved Germany and the Germans, but privately she never really felt that she belonged. She confided in Pauline, 'Strange but I am never taken for German no matter where I go.'[28] She described her position as follows:

I really love all the Germans, and this war brings all the different kingdoms together, and binds them strong together, into one solitary strong nation, as never before, and awakened the feeling of being proud to be a German . . . In reality, I have no home in Germany, and know that it is always to be so, just as it was with other Bahai teachers. When they have done all they could, then one must move on, for they wish to use what they have received and one's end is attained.[29]

Alma returned to Stuttgart in the summer of 1915. The Bahá'í meetings there were well attended, and wounded soldiers also participated. Rosa Schwarz held large meetings in Degerloch, and her husband became a believer and helped with the teaching work.[30] Many soldiers attended; 'they had never heard the Bible explained in that way', and they 'seemed so thankful'.[31] Mina Diegel started weekly meetings supported by Alice Schwarz, who gave weekly readings in Bad Mergentheim.[32]

Margarethe had been nervous all winter; she had had no vacation and was over-worked. She invited Alma to join her in Bad Frankenhausen am Kyffhäusen near Thuringen in the heart of Germany for recovery. Margarethe's father had been born in a village near Bad Frankenhausen. It is a very quiet place, not very populated, and yet more than 1,000 men from that little town were serving in the War. Margarethe and Alma spent their spare time sharing the message with the people there. A young lady, Mrs Kirchner, fully accepted the teachings and invited Alma to visit her in Berlin when the War ended. Mrs Kirchner's husband had been serving as an officer at the front since the beginning of the War and she had been visiting her parents when she met Alma.[33]

From Bad Frankenhausen, Alma went to Erfurt to visit Mrs Schoenfeld, an isolated believer whom Alma and Fanny had taught in Flüelin, Switzerland in 1913. From there, Alma visited the small communities in Gotha and Gera. Susan Pollock and Marie Plessner in Gotha invited more of their friends to meet Alma, including another woman who invited her to visit and teach her with her daughter in Berlin.[34]

In Gera, Alma was overjoyed to see the Greatest Name embroidered in gold and framed on the wall next to a framed picture of 'Abdu'l-Bahá when she entered the Dörings' home. Despite the very tough times, the friends in Gera had made donations to the US Temple Fund in December 1914.[35]

Towards the end of 1915, Alma wrote to Pauline,

> You see Abdul-Baha is my guide and protector, for I have no one to assist me, no one gives me names and addresses or invites me to a new place, I have to work the ground with much care and in time results are seen from the hard, strenuous work, pushing through the hard crushing earth the tender plants reach the sunlight and enfold their beauty. In Gera, through the efforts of Kurt Döring and his wife, there are several beautiful Bahá'ís, they are illumined, and so grateful for having received the Light of Truth. In Frankenhausen, Margarethe and I also met several beautiful spiritual souls ready for the message which they accepted fully, and the way opened for public lectures next summer.[36]

The crisis of the First World War combined with the teaching efforts of the German Bahá'ís sowed the seeds for the victory in the years ahead. 'Abdu'l-Bahá expressed His good pleasure at all the teaching in Germany at this time. On 10 January 1916, after reading a letter from Margarethe Döring, He is reported to have remarked,

> How sincere and dutiful to God they are! (German friends) In spite of all their worldly troubles and anxieties they do not neglect their spiritual and religious services. They have a very bright future. I have often said: That after the war their progress will be very rapid.[37]

In another letter to Alice Schwarz, Azízu'lláh Bahádur wrote that while he was with 'Abdu'l-Bahá on 27 June 1916, He said:

> The religion of God has now been proclaimed in Germany. If the divine seeds take root in the soil they will automatically spread and other roots appear and extend into the depths of the hearts.
>
> Now the Cause of the Almighty God has taken root in Germany and its roots are going to radiate like trees in full bloom. In the same manner that pernicious and destructive types of men have a contagious influence, so the spiritual and divine type exert some influence that is far reaching and permeating nature.
>
> It is well known, that once a blessed soul of nay [any] nation steps into the religion of God, it is capable of saving the whole community from the darkness of the world, from materialism and animalism. He brings them to divine qualities and frees them from indifference towards God, from prejudices which are found on ignorance, from animal instincts, and from attachment to the material world and the surrender of self to it – by attachment of the material world I do not mean social intercourse and economic relations upon which the progress of the world depends, but I mean the ascendancy of the lower life over the higher ideals of human society. Now, God be praised, shining and divine realities have penetrated into Germany.[38]

37

THE CRUCIBLE OF WAR AND THE REVELATION OF THE DIVINE PLAN

Despite the wars, 'Abdu'l-Bahá called the twentieth century the 'century of light'.[1] He said, 'for in this century of radiance Bahá'u'lláh has proclaimed the reality of the oneness of the world of humanity and announced that all nations, peoples and races are one'.[2]

'Abdu'l-Bahá knew that there was no escape for the believers who were trapped inside these warring countries. His correspondence to them during these dark days was always uplifting. For example, in a Tablet to the German Bahá'ís on 25 July 1915, He consoled them:

> God be praised! Strong love is produced between Germany and Islam. The Islamic world is in love with the Germanic world. The former loves exceedingly, the latter.
> What a good friendship is produced! We hope that this love and friendship will give rise to great results, that it will influence others (nations) also.[3]

Naturally, the War affected the German believers, and they were influenced by it. The situation was clearly described by Shoghi Effendi in 1933:

> We cannot segregate the human heart from the environment outside us and say that once one of these is reformed

everything will be improved. Man is organic with the world. His inner life molds the environment and is itself deeply affected by it. The one acts upon the other and every abiding change in the life of man is the result of these mutual reactions.[4]

Alma's euphoria for the Kaiser throughout the War is hard to understand from today's perspective. Ironically, perhaps it was part of her success. Shoghi Effendi would later write that pioneers who were working in the early stages of building Bahá'í national communities should be careful not to 'overlook the fundamental prerequisite for any successful teaching enterprise, which is to adapt the presentation of the fundamental principles of their Faith to the cultural and religious backgrounds, the ideologies, and the temperament of the diverse races and nations whom they are called upon to enlighten and attract'.[5]

Alma looked forward to the day when men would realize that they would find peace through diplomatic negotiations and not the battlefield, but she *could* understand that young men would want to give their lives for the fatherland, nonetheless.

In March of 1915, food rations were being assigned to control German food prices and provisions. The government arranged survival seminars instructing people how to avoid sickness and starvation. Precautions were being taken to prevent sickness from other countries entering Germany. For example, soldiers on the front were no longer allowed to send their laundry home.

Alma asked Pauline to keep in contact with Miss Gambler and Mr Daniel Jenkyn in England.[6] She remarked, 'America is also preparing for war, the world seems to be ablaze and no one knows when it will end.'[7] She wrote to Pauline,

> Oh, I do wish peace would come and still we know that it will come sooner or later and that very hard times are ahead of us. It will be terrible to have all communications between America broken off . . . blockade and battle against England is unavoidable, so as to put an end to it as soon as possible.

The Bahá'í house in Esslingen. The summer schools were held here for many years from the 1920s to after the Second World War; it is still a place of visitation

Esslingen, 1921. Back row, left to right: Mr Gfaller, Heinrich Schwab, Richard Theophil Imanuel Aeckerle (he became a well-known painter and painted the portrait of 'Abdu'l-Bahá over Alma's desk), Mr Bender. Front row, left to right: Mr Gillismong (?), Anna Köstlin, Luise Fingerle, Charles Mason Remey (?)

Stuttgart, 6 September 1914. Left to right: George Latimer, Max Bender, Charles Mason Remey. Max Bender, Mírzá Azízu'lláh Bahádur, Dr Habíbu'lláh Khudábakhsh, Gustav Eger, Alma Knobloch, Julia Stäbler, Hugo Bender, Margarethe Döring, Richard Kohler

Stuttgart, 6 September 1914, a commemoration at the grave of Sophie Stäbler, the mother of Julia and Elise Stäbler. Sophie Stäbler had passed away on 1 March 1912; her funeral was the first Bahá'í funeral in Germany. Left to right: George Latimer, Charles Mason Remey, Gustav Eger, Dr Habíbu'lláh Khudábakhsh, Richard Kohler, Julia Stäbler, Mírzá Azízu'lláh Bahádur, Max Bender, Hugo Bender, Margarethe Döring, Alma Knobloch

Left to right: Margarethe Döring, unidentifed, and Alma at Schlossgarten, Starnburger See, 23 May 1915

Alma in Munich, 1915, the "brain photograph" taken by Hildebrandt Schneevoigt who "likes to make her portraits reflect the brain"; Fanny, however, did not like it (see Chapter 14)

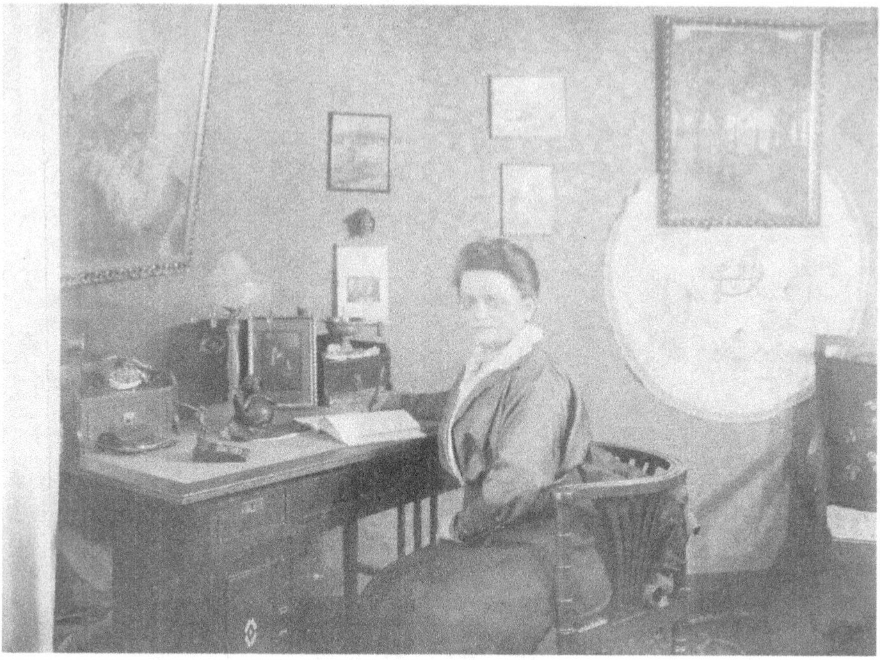

© USBNA

Alma sitting at her desk at 23 Neue Weinsteig, Stuttgart, 17 July 1917. The painting of 'Abdu'l-Bahá is by Richard Theophil Imanuel Aeckerle. The metal box on the left holds hair scarves from Bahíyyih Khánum and candles from the Shrines

Courtesy Judy Hannen Moe

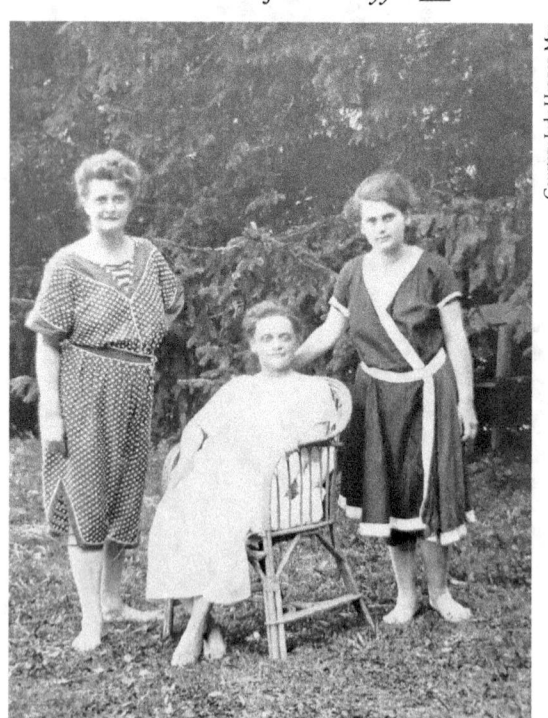

Margarethe Döring, Alma Knobloch and Paula Sarsky in Bad Worishofen, 30 July 1917

Margarethe and Alma in Bad Wörishofen, August 1917

Alma in Bad Frankenhausen, Thüringen, 1918

The Degerloch Bahá'í community, December 1919; Alma is seen behind the photograph of 'Abdu'l-Bahá; Franz Pollinger in front, left

Festival held to raise money for the Bahá'í Temple in Wilmette, despite the extreme deprivations imposed on the German Bahá'í community from the Treaty of Versailles at this time. Alma (circled) just over halfway back, on the left

God only knows how it will turn out. Every effort will be made by the Germans to protect their women and children from invasion and starvation.⁸

European Bahá'ís could not escape the dilemma: on the one hand to fight the War with conviction and on the other to teach the oneness of humanity. Alma met several German soldiers in the hospitals who told stories about living 'a stone's throw' away from the French soldiers in the trenches. They reported that the soldiers had become very friendly with each other; every morning they exchanged greetings. She wrote, 'each one knows that the other must follow the commands when they're given . . . But personally, we have no problem with each other.' Unfortunately, the governments did not wish for peace.⁹

The American Bahá'í community focused on peace. Ella Goodall and the Bahá'í friends in California invited Wilhelm Herrigel to attend a peace congress in 1915. He had to decline the invitation which was 'unthinkable due to the war'. Herrigel responded that 'Abdu'l-Bahá had written to the German Bahá'ís that 'Germany has a great future', that 'the entire German kingdom will be illumined with the light from the Kingdom of God', and that 'from Germany Light would illumine all of Europe'.¹⁰ This shows that at least some of the German friends interpreted the Master's words as confirmation that Germany would be victorious in the War.

Many German Bahá'ís were called to serve in the War, including Friedrich Schweizer, Max Staub, all three of the Staub sons (Alma's landlord and one of the first believers in Leipzig), Mr Zimmer (related to the Herrigels), Richard Glitz from Chemnitz, Mr König from Gera, Arthur Rössler (Alma's cousin), Professor Braun's two sons, both the Eckstein sons,¹¹ Consul Schwarz (although not on the front line), Gustav Eger, Richard Kohler, Max and Hugo Bender (from Esslingen; he later served on the National Spiritual Assembly of Germany). In fact, Alma wrote in 1916, 'Of the young men in Esslingen there is but one left, Mr. Kohler, all [the rest] are at the Front and all are well to the present time.'¹²

On 7 May 1915, the RMS *Lusitania* was sunk, and 128 Americans died. Public sentiment in the United States towards Germany was changing. Fighting a war and simultaneously maintaining safe seas for American passenger and merchant vessels was not possible. On 9 June 1915, William Jennings Bryan resigned as US Secretary of State. He had kept America on a path of neutrality. President Wilson appointed his intimate friend Colonel House to replace him. He had a different perspective, and the United States started to change its attitude towards the War.

The loss of neutrality was visible in the newspapers. These were expensive, but still available in Germany. Alma wrote, 'Martin wished for some English papers, and so I bought some New York Herald printed in Paris. You can't imagine how very distorted the accounts were. They were really laughable . . .'[13]

Nobody was free from the discussion about which side was right. For Alma, the changing sentiments of family and friends were difficult for her to take. In February 1916, she wrote home, 'It seems you are beginning to believe the outrageous lies (pardon the expression) the allies circulate . . . God grant that Abdul-Baha's words will be fulfilled, that "Germany will become wholly illuminated." The truth will come out at last . . . one thing they must admit, and that is that the Germans are the most conscientious and truthful nation in the world.'[14] Alma thanked George Latimer for his 'real friendly feeling' for the Germans and that he 'set straight the distorted reports that are circulated' in the United States.[15]

All the Bahá'ís were striving towards the same goal. Mason Remey wrote to Alma about a social discourse event in Portland. Over 200 people came together to discuss the ethics of compulsory military training. The Bahá'ís presented their concept that true and lasting peace could only be achieved through the establishment of 'the foundation of spiritual love amongst mankind'.[16] Klara Böttger translated and distributed Mr Remey's letter. They rejoiced about the 'splendid success'.[17] Alma thanked George Latimer for his donation in the name of the German friends to the Temple Fund, commenting that when the Bahá'ís focused on the world they lived in they saw the crisis and when they focused on the Bahá'í Faith, they beheld victory.[18]

On 10 January 1916, Azízu'lláh Bahádur wrote to Alma that he had presented letters from Alma and the other German believers to the Master, who

> read them deliberately. As he was reading them, I noticed on his Beloved face signs of happiness. When he finished dear sister Margarethe's letter, he turned to me and one of the friends who has newly come from home, saying, 'How sincere and beautiful to God they are! In spite of all the worldly trouble and anxiety, they do not neglect their spiritual and religious services. They have a very bright future. I have often said that after the war their progress will be very rapid.'[19]

At the beginning of 1916, Alma was again living with Mrs Staub in Leipzig. She attended Cousin Melanie's elaborate church wedding in Bautzen and gave them a framed picture of 'Abdu'l-Bahá.[20] She wrote to Fanny,

> It is the result of our sacrifices made for her [Melanie] during her visit [to Stuttgart] and ['Abdu'l-Bahá] told me to tell her that he loves her very much and to give her His love and greetings and it was as though they had met and He will pray on her behalf for blessings and bounties. These prayers have been most wonderfully answered. Who would've thought 23 years ago when I was here on my first visit that such changes would take place and I would be here attending her wedding and she would be here a beautiful Bahá'í![21]

Fanny and Pauline were having a difficult time. Fanny had badly injured her foot and Pauline was very sick. In February 1916 Alma asked the Master for permission to visit her family. She wrote home, 'I have again asked Mirza to ask our Beloved about a return visit as you put it and hope an answer may be received in a few months. Be assured I will look after you my unselfish whole-hearted sister and will make good for all the loving sacrifices made. I do not expect any thanks from the friends here or anyone else. Since we have the love and blessing of the Beloved and He is pleased with us and that is worth a world of riches. He is our friend and the best of all, he knows the sacrifices made.'[22] And again, 'Should I receive permission to return for a visit, I certainly will come, although there is so much danger at present and really no one to run the risk if not necessary. I received an answer to the letter in which I asked but Mirza Azizollah does not refer to it . . .'[23]

At the midpoint of the War, 'Abdu'l-Bahá began to reveal the Tablets of the Divine Plan, one of the Mighty Charters of the Bahá'í Faith. Commemorating this 100 years later, the Universal House of Justice wrote:

> Set forth in those fourteen Tablets, Shoghi Effendi explains, is 'the mightiest Plan ever generated through the creative power of the Most Great Name'. It is 'impelled by forces beyond our power to predict or appraise' and 'claims as the theatre for its operation territories spread over five continents and the islands of the seven seas'. Within it are held 'the seeds of the world's spiritual revival and ultimate redemption'.[24]

On the morning of 11 April 1916, in His room in Bahjí, 'Abdu'l-Bahá revealed the seventh Tablet of the Divine Plan, in which He mentions Alma Knobloch:

> Likewise, Miss Knobloch traveled alone to Germany. To what a great extent she became confirmed! Therefore, know ye of a certainty that whosoever arises in this day to diffuse the divine fragrances, the cohorts of the Kingdom of God shall confirm him, and the bestowals and the favors of the Blessed Perfection shall encircle him.
>
> O that I could travel, even though on foot and in the utmost poverty, to these regions, and, raising the call of 'Yá Bahá'u'l-Abhá' in cities, villages, mountains, deserts and

oceans, promote the Divine teachings! This, alas, I cannot do. How intensely I deplore it! Please God, ye may achieve it.[25]

Only three believers are mentioned in the Divine Plan: Alma, Agnes Alexander, and May Maxwell. The seventh Tablet was first read at the 'Unveiling of the Divine Plan for the Islands of the Sea', at the Bahá'í Congress held in New York City at the McAlpin Hotel, 26–30 April 1919. Having received the book *Unveiling the Divine Plan* in October 1919, Alma's first response was that it was meant as much for Fanny as it was for herself.[26]

In the summer of 1916, Alma visited her contacts in Berlin where 'the Cafes are filled, people are bright and one sees nothing of the war, only the prices are high'.[27] George Latimer considered making another teaching trip to Germany, but unfortunately had to postpone it. Alma wrote, 'We were all very much disappointed and sincerely hope that you will be able to come in the near future.'[28]

In July, Consul Schwarz erected a memorial stone at Bad Mergentheim to commemorate 'Abdu'l-Bahá's visit to that spot in 1913. After the dedication, Alma was a guest of the Schwarz family in Bad Mergentheim for 19 days.

Finally, on her birthday, 9 September, Alma received an answer to her request from Mírzá Bahádur: 'I asked permission for you to go to visit your sisters in America. He gave and granted permission. Nine years of labour, which has been crowned with success, having the assurance of the Beloved. How wonderful it is that this card comes this morning.'[29] But for some reason, although 'Abdu'l-Bahá had granted her permission, Alma was not able to leave. Perhaps she did not have the money or the necessary papers since she was now a German citizen; or perhaps the War just got in the way. Alma once again focused on teaching and consolidation; over the next year she visited friends in Munich, Bad Mergentheim, Bad Wörishofen, Ludwigshafen, Heidelberg, and Karlsruhe.[30] In November 1916, Alma and Margarethe visited Miss Rupp in

Freudenstadt. They celebrated Bahá'u'lláh's birthday in a large hall in Stuttgart which was 'filled to overflowing and all felt that the heavenly atmosphere was a symbol of the Dawn of a New Day'. The celebration was attended by special guests including Gustav Eger and Max Bender. Gustav, now a large strong man, was home on furlough. Max Bender did not look so well. His three brothers were also home.[31]

In November 1916, Fanny's work moved her to Springfield, Massachusetts, where she began to build a Bahá'í community with some of Pauline's contacts, including Mrs Olive Kretz, who also worked for the Viavi company. Olive became an important friend to the three Knobloch sisters.

It was at this time that a German U-boat sunk an Italian liner; 27 American passengers died. Germany apologized to the United States, but the diplomatic relationship became increasingly cold. Towards the end of 1916, Fanny noticed that checks to Alma were not being cashed and the family was worried.[32] Indeed, Alma could no longer receive the money Fanny and Joseph kept trying to send. Alma wrote to Pauline, 'How I wish I could be with you all, who knows. Perhaps next year, so God will. I will be with you all in prayers and thoughts and thank God that I am permitted to be able to serve in His Vineyard.'[33] On 18 December Germany lost the battle of Verdun; one million French and German soldiers had lost their lives.

On 3 February 1917, a German submarine sunk the London-chartered *Housatonic* cargo ship with provisions from the United States. Diplomatic relations between Germany and the United States were immediately cut. Nobody was killed because the German commander allowed the crew to depart on lifeboats before he sunk the ship.

In Leipzig, the Chief of the Police Department had investigated Alma's activities and concluded that her work was 'good and advised [her] to continue her work and to hold public meetings in a larger hall if needed'. Lack of money, and the need for security, brought Alma once more back to Stuttgart to stay with Margarethe. She wrote home, 'It was wise to come here for a time; I have more work than I can do . . . This is possible where one is better known at least for the present.' The reliable activities in Stuttgart attracted many people from all over who then 'carried the message out in all directions'.[34] Not having access to money from her family, Alma was now fully financially dependent on the Bahá'ís for her survival.

On 6 April 1917, the United States entered the War on the side of the Allies, despite the fact that many Americans wanted to stay neutral. On 14 May 1917 Alma sent a telegraph home informing her family that she was fine.[35] After this, correspondence with the United States was not possible until the War ended. The most difficult times had begun. To survive, Alma focused ever more on service. The more difficult the times became, the more opportunities for service arose. Alma now relied on the Bahá'í community for her survival; it was an opportunity for the community, itself under extreme privation, to sacrifice to help her.

The Knoblochs now found themselves on conflicting sides. Pauline's son, Carl, who as a child had lived with Alma in Degerloch in 1910, was now a young man and joined the US Navy. He was fortunate to get non-combatant service and spent most of his time in the Asiatic, but the burden of this War was great for all family members.

In June 1917 Alma visited the friends in Munich.[36] In July, 'Abdu'l-Bahá sent a moving Tablet to Margarethe Döring, expressing His pleasure that Alma was staying with her, and that her house had thus become a 'nest' for Alma, where 'divine birds gather in that place with a sweet melody', for Alma was 'loved at the Threshold of God'.[37] Margarethe responded by providing her support and care for Alma like a loving sister in these hard times.[38] Alma too received a Tablet from 'Abdu'l-Bahá which gave her focus, telling her not to imagine that she was forgotten or that He was not praying for her. On the contrary, He was continuing to ask for unlimited confirmations and blessings for her spiritual progress, so that through the Holy Spirit she would become the cause of life for others.[39]

The Master's love comforted the friends in these extremely hard times. In a Tablet to Mrs Zimmer, a relative of Wilhelm

Herrigel whose husband had fallen in 1914, 'Abdu'l-Bahá wrote in July 1917,

> Although thy dear husband drank the cup of martyrdom and has given his life on the Battlefield, nevertheless be not grieved nor sorrowful, for he has sacrificed his life for the nation, and his honor was the protection and sustaining of his fatherland.
> He was attracted to the universum of the Kingdom, and illumined through the Light of Guidance. Such souls hasten in reality from this world into the next one, and arise from this universum of dust to the Realm of God.
> The meeting which thou didst hold will at the end, bring forth great results and be the cause of spreading the Light.[40]

Alma continued to raise up communities: Karlsruhe, Heidelberg, Mannheim, Nuremberg. At the end of 1917, she spent nine days with friends in Ludwigshafen, and from there went to Mannheim and Heidelberg, where she shared the teachings with Mrs Pfisterer, her daughter Gertrude and her husband. Afterwards she visited Dr Trainer in Karlsruhe.[41]

On 24 December, Christmas Eve 1917, the British 41st wing Royal Flying Corps bombed Mannheim and Ludwigshafen. On 14 January 1918, the same unit dropped 2,752 pounds of bombs around Karlsruhe.[42] After the War, Alma wrote about these days, 'We have been so wonderfully protected, for the air bombs were very dangerous, although most interesting at first to watch them, there were several directly over our house, sometimes we only heard the shooting and firing and saw the smoke that was all, but usually they returned and dropped bombs some quite near us, but on the whole little damage was done.'[43]

In March 1918, Alma, Margarethe and Alma Übelhack went to Nuremberg and visited the Übelhack family, thereby opening Nuremberg to the Faith. They met Freda Übelhack and Dora Rapps (who had attended meetings in Stuttgart)[44] at the depot. They stayed at the Übelhack home where there was a large gathering. Mrs Brennecker also opened her home and invited her friends to hear about the Faith. On 19 April, another spiritual meeting was held at the Rapp home. Alma was invited to stay for a long time to build up a centre in Nuremberg.[45]

Also in April, Mrs Brennecker brought Alma to meet her sister Mrs Kälble in Esslingen. She was most happy to hear all about the Master and 'she could not hear enough about the teachings'. She invited Alma to return on Sunday afternoon, 'to come early and stay long'. She wanted Alma to share the teachings with her son and to help her pray for illumination.[46]

Margarethe invited Alma to join her to the Ostseebad Dahme in August 1918. Here they made friends with the other guests, who were deeply interested in the Faith.[47]

In September 1918, they visited Pastor Heydran in Blankenese, Hamburg. He had learned about the Faith through correspondence with Wilhelm Herrigel and had spread the teachings a great deal, although he had never met any of the Bahá'ís personally.[48] It was encouraging for the Bahá'ís to see Herrigel, Margarethe and Alma teaching and working together.

After Hamburg, Alma and Margarethe went to Gera. It was the first time Margarethe had visited her brother since his marriage, and Kurt was extremely happy to see his sister. Margarethe could only stay three days, but Alma stayed 19 days to help them teach the Faith. They introduced her to prominent families, including Dr Ulrich, Mrs Jahn and her daughter, Mrs and Miss Bruckledge, and Miss Vogel. They held a lovely celebration for the Birth of Bahá'u'lláh.[49]

These were dramatic times in the history of Germany. The 'Sailors' Revolt' at Wilhelmshaven at the end of October spread throughout Germany. On 9 November, the abdication of Kaiser Wilhelm was announced, followed by the capitulation of Germany. On 11 November 1918, the Armistice that ended World War I between the Allies and Germany finally went into effect, one day before the 101th anniversary of the birthday of Bahá'u'lláh.

It is estimated that about 13.25 million men served in the German military in World War I. Two million of them fell on the battlefields. The military was made up of about 85 per cent of the male population between the ages of 17 and 50.

The German Bahá'í community suffered as did the rest of the nation. The combined effects of the blockade and the German Revolution of 1918–1919 led to crucial food shortages, great suffering, and widespread death and disease. The believers tried to support each other as best they could. In Degerloch, Rosa Schwarz's family were suffering starvation, and had it not been for the generosity of Margarethe Döring they would not have survived.[50] Many Bahá'í soldiers were injured, including Willy Schmand, a young Bahá'í poet from Esslingen,[51] and both the Braun sons, one of whom had died in battle before the end of 1914,[52] as did Mr Zimmer.[53] Mr König, the young man who had left from Leipzig with a Bahá'í book over his heart, also fell in battle in 1916.[54] Max Staub was wounded in his shoulder and lung in Russia in June 1915 and sent to a Lazzaretto in Breslau.[55] Gustav Eger from Esslingen, who had accompanied Alma on her historic trip to Paris to visit the Master in 1913, became a prisoner of war until 1919. Alma wrote, 'the last are returning' in October 1919 – but not all did return.[56] Mr Aeckerle, who had painted the picture of 'Abdu'l-Bahá above Alma's desk,[57] and Heinrich Schwab, were prisoners of war until March of 1920.[58] Carl Diehlmann fell in battle at Verdun in 1916 and Conrad Roster died after suffering from lung trouble from the War.[59] Many other young men who had taken an interest in the Bahá'í Cause had fallen.[60] Many husbands, brothers and other family members who had had to serve in the War returned with a myriad of social, economic and psychological troubles. And yet, despite these losses, the community had grown – not only in numbers but also in locations. Already before the War, the German Bahá'í community had been the most widespread in Europe; how much more so afterwards! Heinrich Schwab later recalled:

> . . . during the years of separation in trouble, when one nation was fighting against the other, and the hatred was overflowing the world, the desire in our hearts, to communicate with the friends of the Cause has been greater

always. In these days, we were consoled only by the words of our beloved Abdul-Baha, which have been recorded: 'I have often said that after this war is over the progress of the German believers shall be great and rapid.' And now is the time, where this prophecy must be fulfilled.⁶¹

Alma wrote that Schwab and Aeckerle returned,

> ablaze with the enthusiasm of the teachings, they immediately started to work and are bringing the Esslingen Assembly to more activity. Mr. Schwab gives talks about the latest sciences, etc. Mr. Aeckerle gives the children instructions on drawing; he's quite an artist. They have a hall especially for this purpose and it is well attended. They also have a Bahá'í library just started.⁶²

Despite all the political chaos, the Deutsche Bahá'í Bund was founded in Stuttgart on 12 December 1918, to care for the administrative needs of the German Bahá'í community. The members were: Wilhelm Herrigel, Paul Gollmer, Samuel Häfner, Professor Waldschmidt, Emil Ruoff, Miss Theuerer, Miss Rebmann, Alma Knobloch, Julius Grünzweig, Annemarie Schweizer, and Anna Köstlin.⁶³ 'Abdu'l-Bahá turned to this important and united assembly to protect the German believers. It was an important step towards a national Bahá'í institution.⁶⁴

38

THE LOVE OF GOD THAT BUBBLES OVER

'Hearken the Fire of the Love of God that it bubbles over.'
Letter from Alma, 1920

On 9 November 1918, the abdication of Kaiser Wilhelm was announced to the crowds in Berlin. Germany was freed from the monarchy and a new era began with the Weimar Republic. Bahá'u'lláh had foretold that radical changes were coming to humanity.

For Alma, it was a great relief to be able to communicate with her family once more. For two years there had been no reliable communication with the United States; Alma had not received any letters since the beginning of 1917. On 19 November 1918, she wrote home from Leipzig:

> At last, I can write you in the hope that you will receive it, I have written very often during the past two years, by way of the Red Cross and Stockholm Sweden and hope that you received at least some of them. I was so glad to hear from Joseph, the only line since two years and oh how very thankful to hear that you are all well . . . I was really homesick during the last two years it was terrible not receive any news from you. So many inquired how they could send letters to America and hoped that I could send word for them. They little knew how very sad I was not to have heard from you myself.[1]

On 24 November 1918, she wrote to Fanny,

> God grant that in the coming year a lasting peace may be established and our little family again united. May God richly bless you for all you have done, for this beloved country . . . Abdul-Baha's words have been fulfilled . . . you will always be remembered here . . . No matter how dark and gloomy things look at present God will not forsake us and give us strength to rise and His glorious words will become realized . . . So many write and wish me to come and stay a long time and they long for the teachings. This, however, is different at present, for the want of food is felt everywhere. Nevertheless, during the past two years I have been showered with kindness and love from all sides. I received many invitations as never before and the greatest hospitality has been shown me, it was really touching in many instances. You'll be surprised to hear that I often visited Mannheim during the greatest danger of the conflicts. Great damage was done by throwing bombs, to life and property many women and children were killed. The people were very quiet. I was really amazed.[2]

Wilhelm II, King of Württemberg, abdicated on 30 November 1918. Revolutionaries had stormed the castle and the city of Stuttgart took over the Wilhelm Palais. Germany was in turmoil; communication was sporadic and sometimes impossible. Finally, in the Spring of 1919, communication was fully re-established, and Alma cabled home through the Red Cross: 'Am happy to receive your lines, to know that you are all well. I am very well also all the friends . . . all are active in loving service.'[3] Shoghi Effendi, then acting as secretary to 'Abdu'l-Bahá, reported:

> What strikes us most vividly is the good news of the welfare and safety of the friends of God. All throughout the years of war, civil as well as national, of loot and of riot and rebellion and of bloodshed, the friends have been continuously

engaged in service to the Cause of God. Their meetings have not been discontinued, their fervor has not decreased, and their energy has not relaxed.

This news from such a part of the world, together with the letters that have been received from Alma Knobloch and Consul Schwarz, have opened up all the closed channels of correspondence which the war had sealed with the Holy Land. The Beloved is in perfect health, strong and vigorous, happy and joyous and often does he wake up at midnight in order to peruse the contents that are being received from the East as well as the West . . .[4]

On 18 January 1919, the Conference of Versailles began and the treaty signed on 28 June ensured that the hard times for Germany would not end for a long time to come. Alma wrote, 'the suffering of the masses is beyond all descriptions . . . there is such a large number who are in want, 4 years is a long time . . .'[5] Around this time, Dr Arthur Brauns (later a Disciple of 'Abdu'l-Bahá) and his wife Marta accepted the Bahá'í Faith. A short time later Marta's father, Professor Dr Auguste Forel, also accepted Bahá'u'lláh.

Since the war began, there had been little contact with Richard Glitz, the young 19-year-old who had been sent to Strasbourg in August 1914. He had advanced in the military ranks.[6] On 16 February 1919, Richard Glitz sent Alma the following letter from Chemnitz:

> Please do not blame me for not writing so long since I've always been prevented from doing so. I'm grateful for the instructive hours you have spent with me and remember with pleasure all the details. Since then, I have lived through many strange times. If I had ever imagined living a God-pleasing life in the past, I was terribly often reminded during these times what it is that is missing. This struggling and wrestling in me, this ruthless conscience that brought everything before my soul and then this judging! I was often in a terrible state and I realized I was spared nothing. I

could not realize earlier that I had done much evil. I became increasingly aware that it would be all or nothing and I decided on the former. There was no other choice. Now this theory has become a successful practice; in other words, changing words into deeds, for which God may help me.[7]

In July 'Abdu'l-Bahá encouraged the friends in Paris,

> Some of the regions of Europe are extremely enthusiastic. Day by day more souls enter the Cause. You have heard of this certainly. Now, make an effort, and with all your might enkindle the fire of love of the Covenant, so that Paris may surpass the other regions; and if the Covenant is made to shine forth as it should, in a short time wonderful results will become apparent; for, in this day, the moving power throughout the whole world is the power of the Covenant: it is the artery pulsating in the body of the phenomenal . . .[8]

In the Fall of 1919, the Templer Germans from Haifa who had served in the German military were compelled to return to Germany. Many relocated to Bad Mergentheim and Stuttgart where to their surprise they met the Bahá'ís, saw the commemoration stone of 'Abdu'l-Bahá's visit in the park in Bad Mergentheim and learned of His teachings. One of the Templers, Dr Fallscheer, had been the physician to the Holy Family. She became the new tenant of the Schwarz family. At first, she said she was 'too well-grounded in her religion to accept something new', but as she got to know the friends, this changed.[9]

In October 1919, the Master sent Dr Habíb Moayyad, 'Azízu'lláh Bahádur and two other Persian Bahá'ís from the Holy Land to Germany. They were granted visas on account of coming as Bahá'í teachers. This greatly surprised everyone because no one had been allowed to enter Germany since the end of the War.

Alma was extremely homesick and inquired about a chance to visit home. Tears fell when she learned that only

German-Americans with American papers could leave Germany. But 'Abdu'l-Bahá's promise of the glorious future ahead for Germany gave her hope and sustained her through these difficult times.

She wrote home on 2 January 1920 complaining that her family was not responding to her letters. It turned out that she had been using the wrong stamps which were not valid for international post, so her family had not heard from her. She wrote, 'I am homesick, that is what is the matter with me.'[10]

Around this time Fanny spontaneously decided to teach the faith in South Africa. The time had come for her to make her own page in Bahá'í history. Fanny later described this event as follows:

> Whence comes the urge to carry the glad tidings twelve thousand miles from home? After weeks of helplessness due to a complete nervous collapse, suddenly an overwhelming desire to go to Johannesburg seized me. Friends tried to dissuade me. Members of the firm reasoned against it – offered me an ocean trip. Not the slightest temptation was this to me. Permission was asked in a cable to 'Abdu'l-Bahá: 'if according to divine wisdom will you authorize me to teach in South Africa?' Answer came: 'your plan highly advisable,' signed 'Abdu'l-Bahá.[11]

On 12 January Alma wrote home, 'I must first become accustomed to the thought that our little family instead of becoming united will become separated even more; God's ways are wonderful and will submit to all He sends and does . . . God willing that I can help our precious darling sister who has always been so self-sacrificing for others.'[12]

In late January of 1920, Alma often saw a strong, bright, beautiful light at night, even with her eyes closed, and believed it was a sign that the Faith was spreading.[13] On 23 January Pauline's husband Joseph was hit by an automobile while crossing 6th Street between Massachusetts Avenue and K Street in Washington DC.[14] He was taken to the Emergency Hospital and then sent home to recover.[15] It was on that same day that 'Abdu'l-Bahá wrote a Tablet to Pauline and Joseph granting His permission for Alma to return for some time to America.[16] Tragically, Joseph's injury proved fatal and he passed away unexpectedly on 27 January. The shock was great for Bahá'ís everywhere. Alma wrote:

> I have never been so homesick as now, and oh it may take some time before Germans can enter the U.S. I so long to have a talk with you all, can sympathize with dear Pauline, dear, dear sister, am longing to hear more, how I would love to comfort her in sad heartsick hours, it will take time for both Pauline and mother [Joseph's mother] to recover from this dreadful shock. I have been thinking of what Mrs. Lua Getsinger told us one day during her stay there, that she saw Joseph streaming with blood and surrounded with many people having died a Martyr's death.[17]

Alma felt close to Pauline in these times, especially since she had suffered a similar fate with her fiancé years before. She wrote to Pauline that it had taken her a long time to overcome the shock, although they had not yet been married.[18] Pauline had not only lost Joseph, but was also losing her sister Fanny, who left the United States for South Africa in July.[19] Service to the Faith always came first.

Although Alma wanted to teach in Leipzig, it had become very expensive and over-filled with German refugees from the East, so she was living with Margarethe in Stuttgart.

On 30 January, 'Abdu'l-Bahá wrote to her that all obstacles to her going to Leipzig had been removed, and 'Before going to America thou shouldst busy thyself with the service so that the love of God in Leipzig may effervesce with enthusiasm.'[20] This was now Alma's mission: to 'make the people in Leipzig bubble up with enthusiasm!'[21]

Hoping to fulfil the Master's orders, Alma planned a great teaching/consolidation trip to Leipzig. Margarethe had been sick with a bad respiratory infection for many months and

Alma had been caring for her. She was devastated over the news that Alma would be leaving and said, 'What will become of me when you go? I will go to pieces without you.'[22] So Alma took Margarethe with her and in May 1920 they left Stuttgart to visit Nuremberg and Karlsruhe for consolidation work on the way to Leipzig. The trip proved to be essential, because conditions had changed and the new believers in these areas still needed to learn much about their new Faith. Alma regretted that she would not be able to stay and help them build up their community, as her goal was Leipzig first, so Margarethe stayed behind and worked with the new believers.

In June Alma submitted the papers at the German embassy to enable her to return to America for a visit. Her family there processed papers verifying that they would cover Alma's expenses while she was in the United States.[23] Both sides pleaded that she had only become German in order to stay in Germany to teach the Bahá'í Faith.

Alma rented a room in Leipzig from Mrs Ammyrie, a relative of the famous General Blücher of the Battle of Waterloo, who invited Alma to share the Bahá'í Faith with her high-standing acquaintances.[24] In June 'Abdu'l-Bahá sent Grace and Harlan Ober from the Holy Land to support the teaching efforts in Germany on their return trip to Massachusetts. The combination was magic. There were public meetings, numerous talks and firesides. Leipzig was ablaze! Dr Vollrath publicly announced his new faith. Mason Remey joined them, and more large gatherings were organized.

The turning point for Alma took place at a talk given by Grace and Harlan, where the future Hand of the Cause Hermann Grossmann, then studying in Leipzig, first heard about the Bahá'í Faith along with Adam and Lina Benke, then fugitives from Crimea.[25] When 'Abdu'l-Bahá heard of this night he called Alma, 'little mother of many children bigger than herself'.[26] Hermann Grossmann visited Alma daily and prolonged his stay in Leipzig to learn all he could before returning home to Hamburg.[27] In 1931, the Benkes joined Marion Jack teaching in Bulgaria, where their ability to speak Russian was important.²⁸ Adam Benke died in Bulgaria the following year; Shoghi Effendi later wrote that he was the 'first European martyr for the Faith'.²⁹

In mid-July 1920, the day before the Obers left for the United States, Mason Remey arrived in Leipzig from Holland. He stayed in Leipzig for six busy days, which Alma had fully planned and organized for him. There were two advertised public meetings at the Theosophical Society and many rounds of personal visits with people of various types and stations in life, including a university professor and his wife, several working people, and sick people in both hospitals and in their homes. Remey was deeply touched by the undernourished, 15-year-old Rudolph Rohr from Leipzig who was on fire with the Faith. Rudolph's eyes filled with tears as he asked Remey to mention him to 'Abdu'l-Bahá when he saw Him in Palestine.³⁰

Alma moved in with the Markgraf family, new Bahá'ís whom she had taught. This remained her address until she returned to the United States. The Markgrafs became one of the strongholds of the Leipzig community. In 1946, Eva Gleichmann became a Bahá'í through them; she maintained her Faith through the Cold War and was the last remaining Bahá'í in Leipzig when the Berlin Wall finally fell in 1989. She passed away in 2003.³¹

After Leipzig, Alma and Remey visited Kurt Döring and his wife in Gera for three days. Kurt organized a series of gatherings, including a public meeting where 125 people came to hear about the Bahá'í teachings. After the talk, Alma asked Remey if the people were bubbling over. He replied, 'Why yes, they are sizzling!'³²

From there Alma travelled to Karlsruhe and Nuremberg. In Nuremberg a great feast was held, with over 300 people attending from the surrounding cities and towns.

At the end of August Alma and Remey visited Freiburg, a beautiful city in the Black Forest close to the Western Front; it had been used as a military garrison during the War and was one of the most bombed cities in Germany. Emma Helling, a Theosophical lecturer they had met earlier in the summer in Leipzig, had invited them to visit Freiburg and she arranged parlour talks and public meetings with the hope of opening a Bahá'í centre there. Over 600 people attended the public meeting where Alma and Remey gave a dynamic talk on 30 August. The room was overflowing, and they had to turn many interested people away. Freiburg was a Catholic city where the Church was opposed to the Faith. At the gathering, a Catholic priest told the large audience that he had been in the United States and had not heard of this religion while he was there. The discussion became quite lively and many lawyers and educated people participated in it. At some point the discussion turned, and those who had opposed the Faith were for it! People who were interested in forming a Bahá'í centre were invited to a smaller hall for planning purposes. This too was filled to overflowing and a study group was formed.[33] Alma stayed until September to help with the follow-up meetings and teaching work.[34]

From 1 to 4 October, Alma visited the Pfister family in Mannheim and Ludwigshafen. In Mannheim, the grand hall in which Alma and Mason Remey presented the Bahá'í teachings was filled with over 400 people. On 4 October they visited Heilbronn, where the teachings were presented by Herrigel and the Schwarzes in a hall filled with 50 people.

Finally, on 5 October, Alma was able to secure passage on the steamship *Nieuw Amsterdam* which would be departing on 10 December for New York from Amsterdam.[35] On 25 October she returned to Leipzig where she held nightly firesides, and daily teaching appointments were made to consolidate the believers. She had little time to organize things for her return home. At the beginning of November, she travelled to Berlin and secured her papers and travel documents with no trouble. While there she was able to meet Miss Gebhardt, a friend of Miss Edith Horn from Atlantic City. In November 1920, Alma sent Pauline a copy of a Tablet from 'Abdu'l-Bahá to Edith Horn revealed in August 1920, approving her visit to Germany and hoping that she would become a source to joy to the friends there and prove active in the establishment of the Covenant and Testament.[36]

So it was that Edith Horn would replace Alma and continue her illustrious service to the German Baháʼí community. Edith settled in Frankfurt, but had to flee in the Second World War when charges by the Gestapo were raised due to her visit to Haifa and her relationship to Shoghi Effendi. For six months she had to hide in a house in Colmar in Alsace, to avoid a case before the Special Court.[37]

On 14 November, Alma wrote her last letter home from Germany:

> There is so much work here . . . My time will not permit me to go to Nuremberg or Hamburg . . . but will leave it to others . . . Can you realize my happiness that I have at last reached my goal, that I am wished for in different cities and towns to give the blessed teachings? Everywhere the people are cheered through the glad Tidings and so many receive the message that I can hardly trace them . . .[38]

She later recalled:

> When the time came for leaving, the love and esteem of the believers made it difficult and they kindly reminded me that it was only for a visit . . . These dear souls brought flowers & all kinds of love tokens, depriving themselves of necessities of life, to show their appreciation . . . The friends at Stuttgart gave a large feast about 250 plus the believers were present coming from near towns . . . They filled the rooms with flowers. These flowers were sent to the different hospitals. They did not blame me, after fourteen years of strenuous labor to wish to visit my dear ones at home, but they made me promise to return in two years.[39]

On 9 April 1920 ʻAbduʼl-Bahá sent the following Tablet:

> . . . Therefore it is certain that the Teachings of the Most High, Baha o llah, will in that region and country spread to the utmost, and souls from Germany will be like unto

candles, enkindled and radiantly streaming beams into all directions. Therefore I am giving thee the Glad-Tidings that the favor is directed upon thee and the Rays of the Sun of Reality are the adornments of your hearts. There is no greater confirmation than this.[40]

For Alma, this was the crowning success of her mission, the confirmation of the illustrious future of the German Bahá'í community. She wrote to Fanny that now she (Fanny) might 'understand what Abdul-Baha means when He says that I should, 'Hearken the Fire of the Love of God that it bubbles over.'[41]

When the time came to leave, Alma was indeed sad. She knew that many financial challenges were ahead of her in the United States on her return. She wrote to Fanny that she had been given permission from 'Abdu'l-Bahá to return for a visit and this permission was under the condition that she return to Germany. In 1925, at age 66, Fanny expressed her feelings about this: 'you may tell those German Baha'is they can easily club together and so make it possible for you to return to them. It will certainly be beyond my means to have you take another journey shall we say, for some years to come! But, after one reaches their 61st birthday, one's earning capacity decreases and we may as well face the truth of our situation bravely.'[42]

On 9 December 1920, at the age of 57, Alma left Germany, sailing from Rotterdam to New York. Her paperwork lists her Uncle B. (Bruno) Rössler in Bautzen living at Stift Str. 7 to be notified in case of emergency, her citizenship as German, and her occupation that of a teacher.[43] In the words of 'Abdu'l-Bahá, 'Alma Knobloch raised the Banner of Guidance in Germany and was unusually confirmed'.[44] She left behind a thriving Bahá'í community.

39

IN AMERICA AGAIN

Fanny wrote, 'How often I try to visualize your homecoming! For years I have planned and wondered how it would be how changed you would find us. How your former friends would meet you. And now I am not there to enjoy any of these phases with you. I am deeply grateful to Abdu'l-Baha for your return at this time!'[1]

Alma arrived in Hoboken, New Jersey on 19 December 1920 and disembarked the following day. Hooper and Gertrude Harris, and Harlan Ober, met her. After lunch, Alma boarded a train to Washington DC, where she was received by Pauline and her family.

All were surprised how much they had all changed in the years of separation. Alma was shocked at how different Washington had become, the display of material wealth, food and fine stores. Everything in plenty – quite different from Germany. Both her nephews, Carl and Paul, who had been little boys when she left, were married now. Carl even had two sons of his own! The house on 23rd Street where she had lived with her mother had been emptied, the furniture stored, and the house rented. The community was filled with new faces. Alma felt like a stranger. The Feasts and meetings had a different spirit from those in Germany. She found it difficult to digest the heavy meals and after the many invitations she received became sick from the rich food.

Alma, Fanny and Pauline had one common goal in life and that was to teach the Faith. They shared and distributed all their financial resources, which came from sales and salaries at Viavi and rent from their properties in Washington DC. In February

1921, Alma visited Pauline's friend, spiritual child and Viavi colleague Mrs Olive Kretz in Springfield, Massachusetts. She also reconnected with Mrs and Mr Ensel, who had become believers in Esslingen years before.² Olive offered Alma a fixed salary to help support Fanny. The deal was that Alma could live with Olive and sell one Viavi treatment per week, for which a portion of the money generated could be sent to Fanny in South Africa. Alma wrote, 'How I will ever get in touch with people to sell Viavi I do not know, but we hope we can be successful so as to send dear Fanny money so she can stay longer where she is and God willing it will be brought about.'³ Pauline was hopeful that Alma would be successful, but in March Alma wrote to her, 'I have not been able to make any sales as yet, but I hope to, I have given all my thoughts to the teachings . . . I'm not going to worry, naturally I would like to attend a convention, but if I can't, I will have to submit, would also like to visit different assemblies . . .'⁴

Alma and Olive had more success collaborating on spreading the Bahá'í teachings than they did with selling Viavi treatments. They met a group of German women who invited Alma to hold meetings at their club hall. Afterwards, a study group was established at the Kretz home. Alma also taught German immigrants in West Springfield. Naw-Rúz was celebrated with 30 Bahá'ís and interested German-speaking friends in New Haven, Connecticut.

Alma was invited to speak at the United Church in Hamilton, Massachusetts. The church was filled, and her talk was well received. Interested people were visited and all were invited to attend the weekly meetings at Mrs Kretz's home. Alma became friends with Mrs Cramer, whose daughter Bessie had health problems which prevented her from finishing her studies to become a teacher. Alma and Mrs Cramer met to pray at dawn for the health of young Miss Cramer, who was shocked when she recovered, and asked her mother, 'What are you doing? I feel so much better.' She finished her studies with excellent marks and came to the meetings to express her thankfulness to all those present and said she would dedicate her life to the Cause. She found a position in Maui, Hawaii and trained as a Bahá'í teacher in the months before she left. Her home in Hawaii became a Bahá'í centre.⁵

In the Spring of 1921, Alma served as the delegate for Springfield, Massachusetts to the Thirteenth US National Convention, where she was honoured to share her European teaching experiences. In his report of the Convention, Louis Gregory described her as 'the little woman who went into Germany and captured the hearts'. In her talk, Alma quoted from one of the Tablets received from 'Abdu'l-Bahá: 'The blessing of God shall descend in torrents like the great waves of the ocean. Pure souls will arise to spread the teachings out of love for Baha'o'llah; throughout, that land and that country shall become illumined.'⁶

In August 1921, Alma received her last Tablet from 'Abdu'l-Bahá:

> O thou who heraldeth the Kingdom of God!
>
> Thy letter was received. The contents became the cause of spirituality. Praise be unto God, in every Assembly, the hearts were overflowing with the love of God, that the Convention of Chicago was in the utmost love and unity and the Convention of Washington was the cause of harmony and love between the White and Colored.
>
> Extend My respectful greetings to Mr. and Mrs. . . . I supplicate to the Divine Bounties and ask that they may become more attracted, become two lighted candles of the love of God and that the White and the Colored may, in their meetings fall in each other's arms. I also ask that Mr and Mrs . . . may hold luminous meetings in their house and through thy help teach the Colored.
>
> . . . I also hope that just as thou wert confirmed in Germany thou mayest also be confirmed in America.
>
> Praise be unto God, in Leipzig and Stuttgart, the friends of God are occupied in service and are assisted by the unlimited Bounties. Thy dear sister, in South Africa, served with all her power, and she was assisted and confirmed . . .⁷

Thus Alma returned to her service in the field of race unity with the confirmations of the Master. In Washington DC, she worked with Pauline and Mr Patzer to organize several very successful interracial meetings that attracted the enthusiasm of many young people and new seekers. Unfortunately, Mrs Allen (whose sister Susan Pollock Alma had taught in Gotha) and her husband protested against these meetings; they believed that interracial meetings would damage the reputation of the Bahá'ís in Washington. Although Agnes Parsons and the Board had decided to uphold the meetings, asking Mrs Allen not to attend them if she was opposed to them, Mrs Allen did not listen and continued to attend the meetings to protest. After much consultation, the meetings were discontinued. The community struggled to decide how to teach the Faith to white seekers who were not yet comfortable with the Bahá'í community if it held interracial meetings. In her last letter to the Master, Alma described the sad situation of the racial disunity in Washington DC.[8]

In September of 1921, Fanny returned from South Africa.[9] It had been fourteen years since the three sisters had been together.

In October, Alma returned to New York to help Gertrude and Hooper Harris with their weekly study classes at the Genealogical Hall. She was given a coloured study class to work with. Soon a lady opened her home, and another study class began. Afterwards, Alma spent three months in Springfield, Massachusetts where she helped Olive Kretz with the preparations for the second Race Amity Convention. This was organized with the blessings of the Master after the tremendous success of the first Race Amity Convention in Washington held from 19 to 21 May 1921. The second Convention was organized by Olive Kretz, Grace Decker and Roy Williams, and was held in Springfield from 5–6 December 1921, despite the shock and grief at the passing of 'Abdu'l-Bahá a few days earlier.[10] It was a tribute to the beloved Master, 'Abdu'l-Bahá, the founder of the Western Bahá'í community, He who gave His life for the Bahá'í Faith and the unification of the entire human race.

40
THE ASCENSION OF 'ABDU'L-BAHÁ

In His last Tablet to the American Bahá'ís 'Abdu'l-Bahá addressed a supplication to His Father, Bahá'u'lláh:

> O thou Baha'ullah! I have forsaken the world and its people, am heartbroken because of the unfaithful – and am weary. In the cage of this world I flutter like a frightened bird and long for the flight to Thy Kingdom.
> O thou Baha'ullah! Make me to drink the cup of sacrifice, and free me! Relieve me from these difficulties, hardships, afflictions and troubles! Thou art the Assister, the Helper, the Protector and the Supporter![1]

In late 1921, John and Louise Bosch from California visited Germany on their way to the Holy Land and gave talks in Göppingen, Esslingen, Heilbronn, Heidelberg, Ludwigshafen, Karlsruhe and Freiberg. They departed Germany for Haifa accompanied by Johanna Hauff.

Shortly after their arrival in Palestine, tragedy struck the entire Bahá'í community. On 28 November 1921, a cablegram was sent to the Bahá'ís of the United States:

> HIS HOLINESS ABDUL BAHA ASCENDED TO ABHA KINGDOM INFORM FRIENDS
> GREATEST HOLY LEAF[2]

The shock for the Bahá'ís of the world was incalculable. Bahíyyih

Khánum, Bahá'u'lláh's illustrious daughter, heroically put aside her own deep grief and arose to guide the community through this terrible time. On Tuesday, 29 November, ten thousand people from all walks of life gathered to pay their last respects as His blessed earthly remains were laid to rest in the unfinished Shrine of the Báb.

Grief-stricken, His noble grandson Shoghi Effendi was completely devastated by the unexpected news. Passport difficulties kept him from leaving England until 16 December, and he didn't arrive in the Holy Land until the 29th. On 3 January 1922, Shoghi Effendi learned that he had been appointed by 'Abdu'l-Bahá to be the Guardian of the Bahá'í Faith. Thus, he inherited the responsibility to guide and protect the Faith of Bahá'u'lláh. This was communicated to the friends in the United States in a cable from Bahíyyih Khánum on 16 January.

It must have deeply touched Alma that the last Tablet of the Master, written shortly before He passed, was to the Stuttgart Bahá'í community. Johanna Hauff, a young German believer whose family Alma had known well in Stuttgart, was privileged to be one of the seven Western believers present in Haifa when the Master took His last breath. She left this account:

> It had come so suddenly for all of them [the family], although the Master had spoken for months continually of his going – they had not understood, probably because they simply could not believe it. Now only do they begin to realize it.
>
> And he was so weary, so tired! He said it to us, he said it to everybody. Mrs. Bosch told me even on the first day: 'His work is done, completely done, everything has been said; every further day is a gift of grace.' We did not dare to ask questions, nor dare to deliver the letters, because we heard 400 letters were still lying there unanswered, but in his great love and kindness for Germany he wanted to have them nevertheless and his very last Tablet is going to Germany.[3]

'Abdu'l-Bahá dictated His last Tablet, but He was too weak to sign it. He said:

O ye beloved of the Lord! In this mortal world, nothing whatsoever endureth. The peoples of the earth dwell therein and spend a number of days uselessly, ultimately descending neath the dust, repairing to the home of eternal silence leaving behind them no achievement, no blessing, no result, no fruit. All the days of their life are thus brought to naught: whereas the children of the Kingdom sow seeds in the fertile soil of Truth that will eventually spring up and bring forth many a harvest and shall forever bestow upon mankind its increase and bountiful grace. They shall obtain eternal life, attain unto the imperishable bounty and shine even as radiant stars in the firmament of the Divine Kingdom. The Glory of Glories rest upon you.[4]

Unusually, the Knobloch sisters were probably together in Washington at this time, so no letters exist regarding how they received the terrible news or their reaction to it.

In February and March 1922, selected Bahá'ís were invited to Haifa to discuss future plans for the development of the Faith. On 7 February, Consul Albert Schwarz received a telegram from the Greatest Holy Leaf: 'Your presence, or Mrs. Schwarz or Herrigels end of February highly desirable.'[5] Consul Schwarz asked Herrigel if he would like to go, but Herrigel did not have the financial resources for the journey. Consul Schwarz was not well and needed to spend some time in recovery in a sanatorium. He considered sending Herrigel but decided to travel with his wife Alice alone instead.

The Schwarzes arrived on 10 March, after the other delegates had arrived and the discussions had started. When Herrigel learned that their purpose was to discuss the founding of the Universal House of Justice and the administrative future of the Bahá'í Faith, he was disappointed that the Schwarzes had not offered him financial support to send him. He felt that had the Consul sent him, he would have at least been on time to represent the German position.[6]

Shoghi Effendi was the only one who realized that the institutions needed to elect the Universal House of Justice did not yet exist! He had never considered that he would be the Guardian of the Faith. Devastated at the loss of his beloved Grandfather, Shoghi Effendi also felt shocked and unworthy of this position; he knew what it meant. But it was not a choice. Divine guidance was his and he immediately took the necessary steps leading the Bahá'í community into the Formative Age. He asked Consul Schwarz and Ethel Rosenberg from Britain to send verbal messages to the friends at home to form Local Spiritual Assemblies and to arrange for the election of a National Spiritual Assembly in each country.[7] In addition, on 5 March 1922 he sent a message to the United States instructing the believers to elect a Local Spiritual Assembly in 'every locality where the number of adult declared believers exceeds nine' and to make 'provision for the indirect election of a Body that shall represent the interests of all the friends and Assemblies throughout the American Continent.'[8]

Thus, the Heroic Age of the Bahá'í Faith came to a close and the Formative Age began. Alma and her sisters now placed their lives in the hands of the young Guardian, Shoghi Effendi. In a copy of what is probably the first letter Alma wrote to the Guardian on 15 May 1923, she pledges her support to 'His Holiness Shoghi Effendi, Oh thou who art our blessed Guardian, we thank God for this great Bounty and blessing which He has bestowed upon us through His great Love.' In this letter she shares news of all the teaching activities she was involved in, especially including many details of the race amity work. The Bahá'ís in Washington were still struggling with racially segregated activities. Alma had been working closely with Mr and Mrs Ashton, Black Bahá'ís who were 'very sore about the colord [sic] question' and believed that they were 'unjustly tested'. On a positive note, she shared information about the racially integrated meetings, classes and feasts which were being held at the home of Mrs Harper, and the growth that was coming from the regular Sunday afternoon classes which were held at the home of another Black couple, Mr and Mrs Keyes. She told the Guardian about Pastor Stevenson from Baltimore who 'turned over his service to' the Bahá'ís and afterwards 'arose and thanked

[them] most earnestly and begged [them] to come often, that [they] would always find open hearts and listening ears'. Alma deplored that a Bahá'í Centre could not be organized for both White and Black believers, hoping that God would 'grant this in the near future'. She also wrote that Bessie Cramer, whom Alma had taught the previous year, had now moved with her parents to Maui and that Mason Remey had asked Alma to go there to support their teaching efforts.

One last point was mentioned in her letter to the Guardian:

> Now dear Shoghi, I have a very important question to ask of Thee, that is important to me and my dear ones. Mrs. Nourse of this city, a member of the board, invited me to her home the first of the month to make the following proposition which was rather a surprise. Mrs. Nourse with the assistance of a wealthy lady friend, wish to pay for my return trip to Germany, to settle all my affairs here and go there to stay, find some work to earn my livelihood and let her know in a week or so. This has given me much to think about and my dear ones are rather taken aback at such a proposition, not having given any cause for such a proposal. Nothing gives me more joy and there is only pleasure in serving the Cause and I long to do according to Thy good pleasure what Thou mayest approve of... From Germany many letters are received wishing for my return soon especially the friends at Leipzig. It was the Beloved Master's wish that I teach in all the cities in that country and in Nice. It is my heart's desire to do His Will and also to try to serve according to thy good pleasure. Thou knowest the conditions there, and I will arise immediately to do whatever thou thinkest best (the uncertainty is making me ill).[9]

Shoghi Effendi's response to this letter has not been found. But although Alma was longing to return to her beloved friends in Germany, it was not to be.

41

THE GERMAN BAHÁ'Í COMMUNITY AFTER ALMA

On 5 March 1921, the German Bahá'ís elected the '5er-Commission' to oversee activities. It consisted of five 'people' whereby married couples were elected as one person. Members were Mr Golmer, Miss Schütz, Mr and Mrs Herrigel, Consul and Mrs Schwarz, and Mr and Mrs Waldschmidt. Later this was expanded to be the 'Council of 9', including Margarethe Döring, Mr Jaeger, Friedrich and Annemarie Schweizer and Elise Stäbler.¹ This group was intended to represent the national Bahá'í community, but its members were only from the Stuttgart area, making cooperation between it and the other German Bahá'í communities challenging. Emma Helling wrote to Alma that the harmony from 1920 was gone and were it not for her deep belief in the Bahá'í Faith and the loving guidance from 'Abdu'l-Bahá, she would have lost hope.² But things were about to change.

All the Bahá'ís in Germany gathered together from 16 to 18 September 1922 at the second German Bahá'í Congress to 'elect the National Spiritual Assembly of Germany according to the wishes of 'Abdu'l-Bahá, and for the purpose of electing the first National Spiritual Board, as requested by Shoghi Effendi'. The event was a source of unity for the entire community. Margarethe reported, 'It was as though the heaven of happiness had opened and this world had disappeared.'³

Bahá'í groups had been established with regular meetings

in many localities including Freiburg, Heilbronn, Leipzig, Karlsruhe, Mergentheim, Esslingen, Stuttgart, and Zuffenhausen.[4] The Stuttgart Bahá'ís began to relocate in order to consolidate the new communities which Alma had created. Mr Schwab moved to Mannheim and the Kohlers moved to Ludwigshafen.[5] In the Summer of 1921, Bahá'í teachers travelled to support the various communities including Leipzig,[6] Munich and Vienna. Alice Schwarz wrote to George Latimer, 'If you see Miss Knobloch, send her our heartfelt love and tell her that her work in Germany is carrying fruit.'[7]

Margarethe had hoped to join Alma in America,[8] but unfortunately, her health began to rapidly deteriorate.[9] She wrote to Alma that she could not come due to her poor health and her financial situation. In addition, she did not own a suitcase, did not have the necessary papers to be able to make such a journey, and was concerned that the Wohnungsamt (government property authorities) would confiscate her apartment if she were to abandon it.[10] By the end of the summer of 1921, Margarethe's health had drastically deteriorated: her kidneys, liver, and stomach were diseased, and she could not eat. She prayed for health or death – and wrote to Alma, 'Everything that is associated with our pride will be taken from us so that we take the path of humility. I pray to God that I will not become dependent on others unless it is good for the Cause.'[11] Lydia Bauer considered accompanying Margarethe, should she decide to travel to the United States, but she also lacked the financial resources for the trip.[12]

Despite her great physical pain, Margarethe tried to help others. Mr Braun provided a heated room for her and Lydia Bauer to use to make clothes for the many needy children. Margarethe held meetings in her home, always cheerful so that others would not see how sick she actually was. She had not been able to work since the end of the war, and Alma sent her money from what little she had. Through Wilhelm Herrigel, who now controlled the incoming donations from the international Bahá'í communities, some friends sent her rations. Some of these she never received, for example, sugar. Margarethe wrote, 'Who is there to trust if not the Bahá'ís?' She had now become immobile and had lost contact with the community.

In May 1923 Margarethe was hospitalized for a long period for which she was not able to pay the bills.[13] After her hospitalization, she had some good days and some bad days, but it became clear that she was reaching the end.[14] The doctors were amazed at her ability to keep up her good spirits despite the intense physical pain she suffered.[15] Old friends came to visit her up to the last fourteen days, when she developed a strong infection and fever. On 18 October 1923, after many years of intense suffering, Margarethe Döring took her last breath.[16] A beautiful funeral was arranged; Miss Stäbler sang and Mr Stäbler played the violin. Herrigel gave the speech at her grave and at the funeral reception.

Alice Schwarz received the sole right of disposition after Margarethe's death. She liquidated the property, paid Margarethe's hospital debt, and distributed her assets, not knowing that some of the property actually belonged to Alma and not Margarethe.[17]

Leipzig became a strong and supportive community. Young Rudi Rohr, the bright-eyed child who had begged Mason Remey to mention his name to the Master, finally left the hospital on crutches. Adam Benke was hospitalized for six weeks and also returned home on crutches with an expensive treatment bill. Failure to pay meant expulsion to Russia,[18] and Alma responded with a large financial contribution to the Leipzig friends to use as needed. The friends dispersed it amongst themselves based on need. All were thankful for the help given to Adam, who had taken on the organizational responsibilities for the Leipzig Bahá'í community. Leftover funds were made into the Alma Knobloch Fund and administered by three Bahá'ís.[19] Adam Benke and the Rohr family tried to start a business together.

Wilhelm Herrigel visited the friends in Leipzig and stayed with the Markgraf family, whose home became a 'Bahá'í home'.[20] Annemarie Schweizer also visited the Leipzig community, whose members missed Alma very much. Each one tried to help the others to get by financially in the difficult years.

42

THE SAD STORY OF WILHELM HERRIGEL

Wilhelm Herrigel had sold his business so as to be able to give his time fully to the Faith. With Alma in the United States, he initially felt free to pursue this ambition. Herrigel wrote to Mason Remey that in 1920 he started to travel and give lectures 'to all the places where the friends were trying to encourage Alma to return'.[1]

Already in December 1918, the Deutschen Bahá'í Bund (German Bahá'í Federation, forerunner of the German National Spiritual Assembly) had been formed[2] and on 22 February 1919 the 'Verlag des Deutschen Bahá'í-Bundes' (German Publishing Trust) was established,[3] with Herrigel as executive director.[4] The Treaty of Versailles left Germany in a terrible economic state and many of the believers were in dire straits. Herrigel was in charge of the publications, the distribution of donations, care packages and goods received from the United States[5] and the financial resources of the German Bahá'í community, and he had a strong influence over the use of the teaching funds. But there was some balance of control since Consul Albert Schwarz had contributed the bulk of the capital for the Deutschen Bahá'í Bund, owned the bank where the Bahá'í funds were held, and the bank account was in his name.[6] Herrigel could not privately access or control the fund. In 1922, he complained about this situation to John Bosch:

> I am sad that I feel the jealousy from Alexanderstrasse [Schwarz's address in Stuttgart]. Had it not been for the

donation from Mr Perron, they would have cancelled my [teaching] trip in the last moment, because they say that such talks have no value. Thank God I could see the value . . .[7]

Financial contributions for teaching activities in Germany came primarily from the American friends, many of whom had received hospitality over the years in the Herrigel home during their visits to Germany. Such friends included George Latimer and John Bosch. For example, Herrigel asked John Bosch if his Swiss sister-in-law could sell some of her jewellery to help cover the personal expenses of another German friend.[8] Bosch, in particular, sent large sums of money to help the Herrigels. In November 1922, the Bosches paid the Herrigels' mortgage and sent an additional sum for living expenses.[9] Generous contributions for the publication of Bahá'í literature in German and for teaching trips were made by Roy Wilhelm and Amelia Collins, and were distributed through Herrigel.[10]

When Shoghi Effendi called for the establishment of Local Spiritual Assemblies and the election of National Assemblies, much work was needed to consolidate the believers across Germany, which was by far the most widespread community in Europe. In the first part of 1922, Herrigel visited the friends in Berlin, Leipzig, Gera, Frankfurt am Main, Ludwigshafen, Karlsruhe, Freiberg, Munich, Nuremberg, Ulm, Geislingen, Göppingen, Esslingen, Zuffenhausen, Fellbach, Waiblingen, Freudenstadt, Tübingen, and many other places including in Austria.[11] Other German Bahá'ís also supported the teaching work and visited the friends in Leipzig, Vienna and Munich, Hamburg, Bremen, and Berlin.[12] Herrigel had a fine reputation and also gave lectures in Austria.[13]

Herrigel was responsible for the distribution of the German magazine *Sonne der Wahrheit* (Sun of Truth), the German equivalent of *Star of the West*. In addition, at least two-thirds of the Bahá'í literature listed in *Sonne der Wahrheit* was either written by or translated by Wilhelm Herrigel. In the March 1927 edition of the magazine, 15 of the 18 German book titles listed were either written by or translated by him.[14]

But as the Faith grew and the believers became more knowledgeable and steadfast, Herrigel's authority and influence were naturally diluted. By 1926 Herrigel was receiving personal financial aid from other believers in the United States, including Mrs Ruth White.[15] Ruth White was a wealthy American woman who would later cause many problems of Covenant-breaking. Herrigel's association with her had a bad influence on him, and increasingly he had trouble working with the other members of the National Assembly.

On 1 May 1926 Herrigel resigned from both the Stuttgart Local Spiritual Assembly and the National Spiritual Assembly. The last issue of *Sonne der Wahrheit* was published in March 1927. In late October, Herrigel was still receiving money from John Bosch, including money for a subscription to *Sonne der Wahrheit*. Herrigel thanked John and Louise Bosch for the money, this time on personal stationery and not the stationery of the Deutschen Bahá'í Bund,[16] but he did not inform them that he had resigned from any Bahá'í institution until 23 November 1927:

> I resigned from both the Stuttgart Assembly and National Assembly the first of May. It was not possible for me to participate; jealousy over my work in Germany spread profusely. Many of our dear friends could not understand this, but a general meeting of the friends convened by the National Assembly had taught the friends another lesson. Now they saw what kind of spirit was blowing in the National Assembly and the meeting ended in a general outrage against the National Assembly. The friends now saw that under these circumstances it was impossible for me to participate in these assemblies or to go on lecture tours. We still have our monthly meetings in the house. These were always attended by an average of 24 people, but on the Monday after this general meeting 39 came together with us and on the following Monday there were 45 friends who came to us, while the general meeting is now attended by little more than 20. This is a time of testing for us, but

we have to go through it patiently. Later we will see what it was good for. I have heard that this test of examination and purification is now going on all over the Bahá'í world and our beloved Master has also predicted it.[17]

The German Bahá'ís had hoped that Herrigel would resolve his issues and return to the community. There were mixed feelings amongst the friends in Stuttgart towards the situation. The election of the National Spiritual Assembly of Germany was not held in 1928, a matter that was especially disappointing for the Bahá'ís outside Stuttgart.[18] On 5 April 1929, Hermann Grossmann wrote to the National Spiritual Assembly on behalf of the Bahá'ís of Hamburg who were concerned that the election of 1929 would also be postponed. In his letter, he informed them that he had received a letter from Haifa in which he was made personally responsible to bring the matter before the friends and to help them to recognize the importance of supporting the national representatives who would be elected during Riḍván. Furthermore, he wrote that if the difficulties in Stuttgart made it impossible to hold the election at Riḍván, the Bahá'ís in Hamburg were prepared to do it and that they would do so if they did not receive a response within 14 days.[19]

Herrigel became a proponent of Ruth White, who challenged the authenticity of the Will and Testament of 'Abdu'l-Bahá, thereby challenging the authority of the Guardian. Mrs White reached out to many well-known Bahá'ís and Bahá'í institutions throughout America and Europe,[20] and Herrigel tried to use his connections to support her, particularly in Wiesbaden and Leipzig.[21] He, Mr Küstner, Mr Diebold and Mr Reichert translated Ruth White's book into German, printed 150 copies of it for distribution, and planned to visit communities throughout Germany to promote it.[22]

It was a difficult test for many. In 1930, Franz Pöllinger wrote to Alma from Vienna, that during his last visit to Stuttgart only a few Bahá'ís, including Edith Horn, were steadfast. He said that Edith Horn, Annemarie Schweizer and Anna Köstlin spent a lot of time repeatedly visiting the friends to help them to remain steadfast.²³ Outside Stuttgart, Herrigel's views were not so attractive. Adam Benke responded to the letters Herrigel sent to the Leipzig community with what Herrigel described as an 'unpleasant' letter. Herrigel believed that the friends in the community did not read his letters.²⁴

Herrigel was defeated. Consul Albert Schwarz from Stuttgart,²⁵ Adam Benke from Leipzig ²⁶ and Franz Pöllinger from Vienna responded to Herrigel's attack by uniting the believers to refute Ruth White's absurd claim and to avoid her on her trip to Germany. In Vienna the believers sent the 'Vienna Declaration of Trust' to the Guardian. Shoghi Effendi responded by sending Dr Youness Khan to Vienna to organize the first election of the Spiritual Assembly of Vienna. ²⁷

In October 1930, Ruth White presented her claim of forgery of the Will and Testament of 'Abdu'l-Bahá to the High Commissioner for Palestine and the Governor of Haifa. Shoghi Effendi fully cooperated with the expert examination, permitting them to have access to the original Testament and other documents. Consul Albert Schwarz, who passed away on 13 January 1931, did not live to see the triumphant end of this matter. On 10 July 1931, the expert examination from Egypt reported that the Will was authentic, and so Ruth White and Wilhelm Herrigel faded into oblivion.

The prophecy 'Abdu'l-Bahá had given to Alice Schwarz in 1913 was now fulfilled:

> Know ye this, that if any person is the least doubtful about the Covenant, he is immediately cut off, although he may be the greatest among men. The harmful results of such an event will appear in the future; consequently, give your utmost attention to this question . . .²⁸

In November 1919, while George Latimer was on pilgrimage, 'Abdu'l-Bahá described to him how the power of God had confirmed Alma:

Consider the power of God. Such a small woman! She is confirmed in service. She is greatly assisted. When a person compares her success with her physical body, a hundred people will not be so assisted as she – this woman is so short. That is why the confirmations of God are necessary.

We were at Acca when Kamel Pasha became Prime Minister. His brother became the Governor of Acca. In Turkey, the brother of the Prime Minister can do whatever he wishes. No one can object to him. One day he came with a carriage and we went out together. On the way, I noticed he had a hunting outfit and he had four or five large hunting dogs. A gazelle was sighted. These dogs chased after it.

One of the Bahais had a small dog. An Arab Bahai. He also had come. These five dogs of the Governor did not catch anything. This little dog caught a large gazelle. The Governor became ashamed. When the dogs returned, he began to beat them. He said: 'What can I do, the Bahais are assisted. These five large dogs of mine could catch nothing, but this little dog did.' He dismounted and took the little dog in his arms and kissed it. He told the owner of the dog that he would not give the dog back to him.

The idea is this, that Miss Knobloch has attracted the people. There is a large man, Mr. Herrigel, very large. She converted him.[29]

Wilhelm Herrigel's true ambitions at last overcame and revealed him. What a sorry end for someone who had so many opportunities and talents.

43
RETURN TO GERMANY?

Alma had written to the National Spiritual Assembly of Germany (the Counsel of 9) asking for their opinion on her return to Germany. In August 1923, Alice Schwarz responded:

> on behalf of the Spiritual Working Group [Geistigen Arbeitsgemeinschaft] in the presence of the National Assembly: You ask if it would be good for you to return to Germany... But from the perspective of the friends, this is not advisable today, since all those who can, flee Germany and the living conditions are becoming tougher every day. In addition, it is extraordinarily difficult to get a residence permit. Of course, Bahá'ís from all over the world have the choice, but foreigners have little influence as German Nationalism is rising since no nation raises its hand for Germany in this decisive crisis, although all are aware of the great injustice... I am afraid that the conditions are so precarious that Germany must help itself and the German Bahá'ís must do their part.[1]

Hermann Grossmann kept in close contact with Alma. He held a weekly meeting in Hamburg with 15 to 20 friends. In addition, he accompanied other groups in northern Germany; in Mecklenburg, Schwerin, and Rostock meetings were held and lectures were given. Travel and correspondence requirements were difficult not only for the friends in Hamburg. In July 1924 Hermann, who was serving as a member of the National Spiritual Assembly, wrote to Alma encouraging her to return to Germany:

> I come to you today with a request . . . Seeds have started to grow everywhere, and we are missing the hands to harvest them. I cordially ask you, please come for a while, maybe a year and if you can for longer and forever, join us and help us with our work here in the north, because in our small circle we will all very warmly welcome you . . . Please, come to us for the sake of the work being prepared and . . . stay now because it is too much for us! . . . the friends in southern Germany themselves did not have enough teaching support, we had no other help than yours.[2]

Alma responded on 9 August, and on 4 September Hermann wrote to Alma:

> With great happiness I received your kind letter . . . I strongly hope that it will be possible for you to settle your affairs and come to us, otherwise we will wait patiently the 1½ years until you can help us. How happy I will be when I can dedicate myself to work for the [Bahá'í] children . . . I have written to Shoghi Effendi and informed him that I have invited you come and help us in our work . . .
> Your thankful student Hermann Grossmann[3]

In November, another member of the National Spiritual Assembly, Annemarie Schweizer, wrote:

> My honorable Teacher! Doctor Grossmann and I met in June, we ask you to come to Germany. Now I learned from him that you will do this next year. I ask you to accept my home as your home during your stay in southern Germany. We look forward to seeing you again . . . Where you planted seeds, there is real life! God cannot bless you with anything but His confirmation for your service in His Holy Cause.[4]

Unfortunately, from 1924 to 1927 Alma lacked the financial resources to return to Germany. The resources the Knobloch sisters shared were needed to cover the teaching expenses of all three of them. Having supported Alma in Germany for so many years, Fanny had found her place of service in South Africa. During her first brief return to the United States in 1923,[5] she had encouraged Pauline to return to Africa with her and to help her spread the teachings. By the end of 1924, Alma had moved in with Pauline's son Carl in Milwaukee to help build up the community there, while Pauline considered joining Fanny in South Africa.[6]

In January 1925 Pauline decided to join Fanny, who was already back in South Africa. She organized her affairs and entrusted her rental properties in Washington to an agent who would forward two-thirds of the rent to the sisters in South Africa and keep the other third. During this time Alma stayed in Milwaukee.[7] On 26 February 1925 Pauline departed with the Eastern Glade Sailing Company for Cape Town,[8] where she and Fanny provided great services in South Africa and also opened Rhodesia, today Zimbabwe, to the Faith. On their return from Africa to the United States in the Fall of 1926, Fanny and Pauline passed through Germany to visit the friends in Stuttgart.[9]

On 9 March 1927 Hermann Grossmann wrote to Alma once more, 'We would be so happy if you would fulfil your intention and come to Hamburg, because we need your help to build things up. I believe you would be quite comfortable here.'[10] This was followed by a letter from Anna Grossmann on 28 May 1928: 'We would be very happy if you would come to Germany. We want to work hand in hand and make real progress.'[11] On 3 September 1928, Hermann wrote:

> We hope that you hold on to your plan to return to Germany, the work is constantly accumulating here and we desperately need loyal helpers who can work independently with us to find new ways to expand the old areas. I am sure that your presence, dear friend, would help us a lot, and I am sure that you will be very pleased with the spirit of understanding and cooperation that exists in our group and its external work.[12]

In addition to these letters of encouragement, Alma received other letters from Stuttgart explaining the fate of her furniture and other belongings.¹³ The problems regarding Wilhelm Herrigel were still ever present in the German Bahá'í community; there were mixed feelings about her return to Germany.

Since her arrival in the United States, Alma had served as a delegate to the National Convention almost every year. She was busy travel teaching and serving the National Teaching Committee in many places. In early 1929, she wrote to the Guardian asking for guidance regarding where she could best serve the Cause. She wrote:

> Beloved Shoghi Effendi, again and again such loving pleading letters have been received from believers in Germany, wishing me to come and strengthen them in the Cause. I would love to go and help them. With the same mail that brought the last letter, more entreating than the former, a letter was received that my Takoma Lot was bought and that gives me the means to go to Germany if it meets with your approval. It is my heart's desire to do your wish for it is your prayers and spiritual contact and guidance that gives life and progress. Will be very grateful to hear from you if it is according to your good pleasure. My dear sister Mrs Hannen has been ill so have served here and keeping busy and she is improving.¹⁴

With the sale of the Takoma property in Washington, the financial resources for a trip to Germany were at hand. The reply that came on 23 February 1929, however, did not encourage her to go; Shoghi Effendi told her that centres already established could 'take care of themselves', spreading the teachings through public meetings and lectures as well as by occasional visits from travelling teachers. What was needed now was to add to the number of centres by interesting new groups of people and creating new focal points.¹⁵

The German believers, however, did not give up hope that Alma would join them again. On 3 May 1929 Pauline Bothner from Stuttgart wrote to the National Spiritual Assembly of Germany:

> Our dear highly respected spiritual brother of the Holy Cause, Shoghi Effendi, has asked me to turn to the National Assembly with a great request. For years, my deepest wish has been to have Alma Knobloch return to Germany, but I did not have the living space to invite her. With the utmost effort I have now succeeded with God's help to achieve it. My apartment is furnished so that I can easily accommodate a dear Bahá'í sister. At the beginning of December 1st, I first wrote to Miss Alma Knobloch to hear if she is inclined to come. I immediately received her response that she is ready, stronger and healthier than before, and would quite gladly come back to Germany. She was very much looking forward to returning if her beloved brother Shoghi Effendi gave her his permission. I wrote to our beloved brother Shoghi Effendi right away, on April 8 and received his response in mid-April. Mr Schweizer from Zuffenhausen has kindly translated it for me. I was told to place this matter in the hands of the National Assembly, in which he has every confidence . . . I look forward to the decision of the Spiritual National Assembly . . .[16]

On 10 May 1929, Alice and Albert Schwarz, respectively the Secretary and Chairman of the National Assembly, sent a copy of Pauline Bothner's letter to the other members with four comments for consideration. First was the concern that the return of Alma Knobloch would be a direct 'slap in the face' for Mr Herrigel, with whom Alma had not had a harmonious relationship. Second, Miss Knobloch had lived outside of Germany for the past ten years and there was concern that her German language ability would not be strong enough to teach in Germany. Third, information from America indicated that Miss Knobloch had not performed any valuable service in America, so how could she serve in Germany? Fourth and finally, it was known that Miss Knobloch was without means and the Assembly did not advise Miss Bothner to take on the financial burden that this would involve. They wrote that there were many needy families in the German Bahá'í community and advised that Mrs Bothner should support them instead.[17]

Regarding the service Alma had rendered in the United States since her return, these comments were not justified, as one sees in the following letter she received on 27 June 1928 from May Maxwell, the Secretary of the National Teaching Committee:

> You cannot imagine the happiness your letter has brought me, because of what Shoghi Effendi wrote you of the effect of your work upon His heart. Nothing in life produces this happiness which the knowledge of his happiness brings. It is a strange feeling, different from other experience, and you must feel so happy and blessed to know that through your thorough and devoted services you have brought inexpressible happiness to His heart.
>
> There are those who believe that Shoghi Effendi sometimes writes by way of encouragement to His faithful servants, and this is true, but there is a certain way that He writes which is entirely different, a certain outburst of joyous enthusiasm, and when I reflect upon the six months I spent with him in Haifa, and saw the daily round of his overwhelming work, drudgery, strain and fatigue, I realize the sacred value of those messages of the good news which brought such joy to his heart and such rest to his soul.[18]

Alma wrote to Pauline Bothner on 28 May 1929, and sent her a copy of the Guardian's letter from 23 February 1929.[19] After all considerations, it was clear that Alma could not move back to Germany. On 20 June 1929, Pauline Bothner replied to Alma:

> The National Assembly of Germany is concerned about the fate of Germany, since one can never know how we will fare, whether inflation or the like will come upon us once again, and then one does not know whether one or

the other will be able to step in, should I ever lose my job, be left with no earnings.

Dear Sister Alma, I did not think that far. My thoughts were that whoever dives deep and performs even the slightest service in the holy cause will be under the very special protection of Bahá'u'lláh. Elijah was fed by ravens, so will the servants of 'Abdu'l-Bahá be provided for. It is certainly true, as the beloved brother in the Lord, Shoghi Effendi writes, one must consider everything carefully. He writes that I should surrender to that and accept it as the National Assembly determines. Thus, the National Assembly is not in favour of it, but only because of the predicament of Germany, so that you, dear sister, will not fall into distress if the situation here deteriorates. Many of the Bahá'ís have often asked me when Miss Knobloch will come, and they are therefore very sad about it. The will is there, but we are all poor already.

My dear, dear Bahá'í sister, we want to put the matter in God's hands. If it is His will, the difficulties will pass. I firmly believe in this. I cannot and will not change my mind. My home is always open to you. I long for you often, very often, dear sister. I would be very grateful if you would write to me about how you feel about the matter. I will write to you again soon.[20]

Clearly, the years 1925–1932 were turbulent for the German Bahá'ís. On 17 September 1931, these years are summarized in a letter written to a German believer on behalf of Shoghi Effendi:

> The German believers have undoubtedly experienced a very severe trial and their faith has been tested in an unprecedented way. Their staunchness, however, has been admirable and their sincerity deeply rooted. With the exception of a few they have proven that their conversion to the Faith had a solid foundation and that it withstood all the violent storms of recent years.[21]

The issue was finally put to rest on 21 January 1932 in a letter to Alma through Ruhi Afnan, Shoghi Effendi's secretary:

> ... The condition of the Cause at present in Germany, the many centres established there and the wonderfully sincere and promising persons that have embraced the Cause, should gladden your heart, you who are one of the early believers that introduced the Faith into that country.
>
> In your letter you asked the advice of Shoghi Effendi as to whether you could proceed to Germany and start again your teaching work. The Cause in Germany is now more or less firmly established. There are many centers, and many competent workers. They could easily take care of themselves. In fact, they are beginning to send out teachers to other neighbouring countries such as the Balkans and the Scandinavian Peninsular. Shoghi Effendi therefore believes that your services could be more profitably rendered in other countries where there are no Bahá'ís, or if there are, they do not seem so active. You should, he believes, consult the teaching committee or the National Spiritual Assembly and see where you could be of greatest use ...

Added in hand by the beloved Guardian, referring to a photograph of the three sisters, a postscript read: 'The lovely photograph you sent me will be placed in the Mansion of Bahá'u'lláh at Bahjí as a token and reminder of your distinguished service to His Cause.'²²

Consul Albert Schwarz passed away on 13 January 1931, aged 60. He was named a Disciple of 'Abdu'l-Bahá and his illustrious services to the Bahá'í community of Germany will never be forgotten. One year later, in 1932, Wilhelm Herrigel passed away.

Alma never returned to Germany. The German Bahá'í community will always remember her service, her perseverance, her steadfast dedication, her courage, her ability to teach in the German language, and most of all her eternal devotion and love for 'Abdu'l-Bahá. The German Bahá'í community emerged from these times as a strong independent national community that fully supported the Covenant and the Guardian.

44

SERVING THE GUARDIAN IN THE UNITED STATES

In 1925, Pauline's son Carl Hannen invited Alma to come and help with the teaching work in Milwaukee, Wisconsin. He and his wife Mineola offered to support Alma so that she could focus on teaching. Pauline wrote from Pretoria, 'The dear children, Carl and Mineola are serving the Cause most beautifully, even if they can or did no more than make it possible for you to go out in the work. Oh how grateful to God, I am, daily, that their home was so quickly and joyfully opened so that you might teach.'[1]

Alma organized activities and held talks in Racine, Milwaukee, Muskegon, Kenosha, and later in Grand Rapids, Michigan. In 1925 she served as a delegate to the National Convention held at Green Acre Bahá'í School, remaining afterwards to attend summer school. The news of the success of the summer school in awakening new capacities in the members of the community touched the heart of the Guardian. Dr John Esslemont wrote on behalf of Shoghi Effendi to those attending the school, that the Guardian sent his congratulations and thanks to all who had contributed to its success in any way, whether as speakers or audience. And Shoghi Effendi wrote in postscript:

> You are turning your thoughts to what is the most urgent, the most vital factor in the spread and the ultimate triumph of the Cause. What you will need is constancy, determination and unflagging devotion to your work and I pray from

the bottom of my heart that you may be granted strength to carry out the work you have so splendidly begun.[2]

Fanny and Pauline made historic contributions establishing Bahá'í communities in South Africa and Rhodesia (today, Zimbabwe). It is remarkable how much Fanny was able to spread the teachings since 1920. The seeds she spread on her first trip she supported through correspondence while back in the United States. When she returned on her second trip she worked hard to confirm more of her contacts and meet more of their friends. After Pauline reached South Africa, the two sisters dedicated their time to visiting these friends, deepening new believers and weaving their contacts into a community. These contacts consisted mostly of German and Dutch Europeans, and the social environment made teaching and community building especially difficult. Alternating crisis and victory were an inevitable part of such teaching work. Both Pauline and Fanny suffered with their health, and in August 1926 they returned from South Africa. They wrote to the Guardian from Amsterdam en route for the United States that health issues and lack of material means made their service impossible at that time; the Guardian was 'greatly saddened' by the news. He wrote, 'I trust you will recuperate for your future work in those regions.'[3]

On 13 September 1926, Alma completed the naturalization process and finally became a US citizen.[4] Around this time, Fanny joined Alma living with Carl's family in Milwaukee. The two sisters enjoyed teaching the Faith together; Fanny gave exciting talks, they held Friday meetings and visited many homes and friends.[5] In 1927, Alma was again elected delegate to the National Convention, which was held for the first time in Foundation Hall at the Temple. Pauline returned to work at Viavi to contribute to the support of Alma and Fanny.

Fanny's mind was with the friends in South Africa and she planned to return.[6] In the *Baha'i Newsletter* of September 1926 an article was posted explaining that the Guardian had instructed Fanny to 'leave her class with the Baha'i literature and that the students would confirm themselves'.[7] Fanny quickly wrote to Horace Holley, the editor: 'the reference made to the suggestions or instructions from Shoghi Effendi is a mistake – the first and only instructions received by me were after the return to America . . .',[8] namely 'I trust you will recuperate for your future work in those regions'. This comment weighed heavily on her mind; Fanny knew that if the community did not become steadfast it would not remain. She received a letter from Vernon Du Rose, a steadfast friend in Pretoria who wrote that the community there was experiencing challenges to stay united, and asking Fanny for help and guidance.[9] The sisters scraped together the rest of the money generated by the sale of the property in Washington to support Fanny, now sixty-eight years old, on her third and final return trip to South Africa from 3 July 1928 to 1930.[10]

Pauline hoped that Alma could also work for Viavi to support their expenses. Instead, a new field of service opened for Alma: Florida. Walter Bryant Guy and his wife, old friends from Washington, had moved to Saint Augustine, Florida where they hoped to build up a community. Alma was invited to come and help them, and Shoghi Effendi confirmed that it was important for Alma to go.[11] Upon hearing of this, Pauline secretly telegraphed May Maxwell, informing her that the family lacked the funds for Alma to serve. Pauline did not mention this to Alma because she did not want to arouse false hopes.

Saint Augustine, Florida

Alma, an experienced community builder, took on a new challenge to build up an interracial community in a state where such a thing did not exist. The field had been opened by Louis Gregory, who in 1927 was elected to the National Spiritual Assembly. Louis wrote to Alma:

> With people like Mrs. Kretz, the Atwaters and the Guys to consult with there is no limit to your activities among both races. Local conditions and needs are well known to them

and they can put you in touch with those who have been interested through the efforts of those who have preceded you. The financial help which comes to you is a personal provision from Mrs. May Maxwell in accordance with the wishes of our Guardian. She pays it through the National Treasurer. How long it will continue only the One who Knows All Things can tell . . . May you continue to 'Bubble up with enthusiasm' and set that region aflame with the joy of life.[12]

Alma formed a teaching duo with her old friend from Springfield, Olive Kretz, who was living in Miami and was suffering from malaria.[13] After Olive recovered, they travelled to Saint Augustine together. In March 1928 Alma wrote to her sisters:

> I know what it is to work here and there are so many who cannot go forth . . . The Sunday afternoon meetings will be turned into a study class, they wish to be able to talk and give the teachings . . . This is the hardest part of the work here, first it was dead and very difficult to start the meetings . . . the Colored people are slow about getting their meeting started. There are strict laws here and they cannot attend our meetings, would be put in jail. There are some movements against the Colored people called key men who are finding out who associates with the Colored people . . . it is difficult to describe the conditions here, very much worse than one imagines, the banks closing makes it worse and now a Building Association has closed down, people paying off for their homes have nothing but a piece of paper, this is the last breakdown.[14]

Alma looked to Louis Gregory for encouragement. He responded that he was 'puzzled by' her 'insistence upon suggestions from this servant'. He wrote, 'The people are there, with capacity and waiting for the glad tidings and you, an experienced teacher, are "Johnny on the spot!" I think you have read the divine plan for the southern states. I would follow that as much as possible.'[15] His response illustrates his unique talent in the art of accompaniment. He clearly empowered Alma to take the initiative and to find her inspiration in the writings of 'Abdu'l-Bahá.

Alma was in good company; there were more believers in Florida than in all the other southern states together,[16] including many dedicated and steadfast teachers. Many seeds had been sown, but the work was slow and strenuous.

In 1928, the Guys organized a Naw-Rúz celebration at the Florida Normal School and Industrial Institute in Saint Augustine. This was a school for 'Colored' youth that had been started by the Ladies Baptist Missionary Society in New York City. Initial contact came through one of Dr Guy's patients, who introduced him to the school principal, Nathan W. Collier, and assistant principal Miss Sarah A. Blocker.[17] Of the 40 people who attended, only nine were white.[18] Several teachers and faculty members said that they were touched by Alma's talk. Dr Guy praised it, and Alma wrote that it was 'the nicest compliment she had received in the US'.[19] Miss Wise invited Alma to speak at their Sunday afternoon church services and said, 'Well, I think I am a Bahá'í – and wish to be.' Mrs Guy introduced Alma and Olive to her friends, whom they invited to the Friday meeting. Alma was invited to speak at the Lutheran Sunday School and a Pastor from Jacksonville, Reverend Ford, gave the Guys contacts to arrange events there.[20]

Alma and Olive returned to Miami, at that time the 'most successful' community in Florida, which now had nine members and had made plans to form a Local Spiritual Assembly. The Atwaters and the Boyles had been serving in Miami years before 1919.[21] Meetings were held at Olive's office and the hotel of Mr Dorsey, a very wealthy Black man who was a banker and one of the trustees of the Normal School in Saint Augustine. After Alma's talk at the hotel, Mr Dorsey asked her to 'place his name on the list' and said that he 'wanted to do something for Shoghi Effendi'. He also said that he would send regular contributions to the National Spiritual Assembly. The Florida teaching team was excited: Mr Dorsey's 'coming out and wishing to be known as a Bahá'í' was very conducive to 'the spreading and establishment of the Cause in the South'. A plan was made to have Louis Gregory come and meet Mr Dorsey to form a 'Colored group' (legally impossible for whites), with regular Bahá'í meetings at his hotel. When Alma left the hotel, 'all had tears in their eyes'.[22]

Alma and Olive travelled back to Saint Augustine where they were invited to spend a day at the Florida Normal School. Before leaving the Guys' home that morning, Dr Guy told Alma he wished to open a Bahá'í study class there. Miss Blocker, one of the founders of the school nine years earlier, set up appointments for Alma to speak with two of the professors, one of whom was already a Bahá'í. Afterwards, Alma took a tour of the girls' building. After the tour, a devotional was held in the school chapel, where Miss Blocker reserved some time for Alma to speak. Before introducing her, she asked the students to repeat the name 'Bahá'u'lláh' several times. In this way the name of Bahá'u'lláh was familiar to everyone before Alma spoke. In closing, Miss Blocker openly declared her Faith and told all the students to 'study the teachings diligently'.

After lunch with Miss Blocker, Alma and Olive met with nine teachers who asked for a study class to be arranged at the school. Alma wrote, 'Their expression of gratitude . . . was worth one's life exertion and trials to receive such words of thanks and see the change in their faces.'[23] Both the principal, Mr Collier, and Miss Blocker accepted the Bahá'í Faith and remained members throughout their lives.[24] Alma attributed this success to the patient loving service of the Guys, who had spent many years accompanying them both. Olive and Alma then made a short visit to the Bahá'ís in Orlando, described later in this chapter.

In 1928, Alma represented the Bahá'ís of the Miami area at the National Convention in Chicago and shared stories of the Master's visit to Germany.[25] After the Convention, she returned to Milwaukee where kind letters had arrived from the friends whom she had taught in Florida. Alvina Jolly from Saint Augustine wrote, 'I'm going to keep your first letter to me among the things that I treasure most in life, for it helps me so much and was the inspiration to carry on beyond what I had considered my limit.'²⁶

On 7 May 1928, a letter on behalf of Shoghi Effendi reached Alma:

> Your admirable work in Miami, the possibility of establishing a Bahá'í Assembly there, and your co-operation with Dr and Mrs . . . at St Augustine, in spite of the many difficulties which you encounter and the formidable chasm that separates the coloured and the white, has been highly praiseworthy and has brought immense pleasure to the heart of Shoghi Effendi . . .

And Shoghi Effendi wrote in a postscript:

> My precious Bahá'í Sister:
> Your fragrant and inspiring letter has brought unspeakable joy to my heart. I will, I assure you, continue to pray for you from the very depths of my heart that you may be guided, cheered and strengthened by our Beloved's Spirit and be enabled to extend the scope of your activities and reinforce the foundation of His Cause in that southern state. You certainly occupy a warm place in my heart, and your recent endeavours and services have served to endear you to us all. Wishing you success, happiness and good health, Your affectionate and grateful brother.
> Shoghi.²⁷

After the Convention Alma returned to Milwaukee. Louis Gregory wrote to her in July:

> I hope that you will continue to keep in touch with [May Maxwell] and that you will return to the vast and inviting field of the south as soon as the way again opens. The warm weather is not the best time. Mrs. Maxwell is keenly interested in the work of that section and her committee has an

appropriation to sustain the general teaching work. It is not as large as it should be, but I am sure that with it she is not likely to forget you.[28]

Alma offered to return to Florida in September. The National Teaching Committee responded positively:

> ... whenever you have gathered a group ... arrange a series of public meetings or large group meetings, which Louis Gregory can address, thus extending the spirit of work and ever widening the circle ... Then Mrs. Ransom Kehler can follow Louis Gregory and develop the teaching, establish the souls and leave a circulating library in every center. This, briefly, is the plan of the National Teaching Committee ... This Committee only exists to serve such souls who ... are 'in the front ranks'. Therefore, please let us know in what way we can best further your plans ...[29]

The financial assistance from the Committee was quite a relief to Pauline, who was managing the sisters' money and could not find tenants for their rental property. She had saved only enough money to pay for Fanny's return to the United States, since Fanny's employment in South Africa was only secure for the first six months. Pauline sold her own home and moved to Cabin John, Maryland, in the Baltimore–Washington area. She continued searching for a buyer for their Washington DC properties,[30] some of which were sold at the end of 1928 and the beginning of 1929, leaving her free from having to manage these family properties. Her cottage in Cabin John would serve as the home base for the three sisters for the rest of their lives, and they took turns caring for it, depending on their situation. It served as a place for reflection as well as a home.

In February 1929 Pauline was diagnosed with diabetes, so Alma moved to Cabin John to help take care of her. The money generated from the sale of the Takoma properties had been set aside to cover the travel expenses should Alma return to Germany, to support Fanny in South Africa and cover the expenses for her return. So now, at age 65, Alma had to earn the money for her and Pauline's daily expenses. She found work as a housekeeper in the home of the 90-year-old Susie Haynes and Mr Lewis. She turned her job into a teaching opportunity, sharing the teachings with them until they both became strong believers. Their home became a centre for teaching where travelling teachers, including Mason Remey, came to give talks. Alma described these times:

> At these 5 o'clock teas we were able to give the message to many distinguished and influential people. At times, we invited the traveling Bahá'í teachers to give a talk, also we arrange for meetings at 8 PM in order that the attendance might be increased. In this manner, we reached many people through direct contact. Mrs. Grace Still, a distinguished, influential lady opened her home for Bahá'í meetings to which she invited her friends and the Bahá'í teachings were given in a direct manner. We had a number of glorious gatherings at her elegant home. Twice we had the opportunity of having Mr. Louis Gregory speak at her home and several times at the home of Miss Haynes. He was greatly appreciated by those present and we appreciated their interest and willingness to assist us in raising the standard of the oneness of humanity. Mr. and Mrs. Still also invited me for a weekend at their summer home at Point Lookout, MD. Inviting friends to come and hear the message to learn more of the teachings.[31]

The money Alma earned allowed her to buy a greatly needed new wardrobe. Fanny returned from South Africa by 1 October 1929, right before the stock market crash and the ensuing Great Depression.[32] Later that year, Alma and some of the Washington DC believers embroidered a special curtain which they sent to the Greatest Holy Leaf to be hung in the Holy Shrine of Bahá'u'lláh in Bahjí.[33]

Jacksonville, Florida

Fanny returned to Washington only briefly before heading off to Florida where she lived with Olive Kretz, teaching in Miami. Fanny's trip was funded by the National Teaching Committee which was running out of funds. On 20 March 1932, Mary Collison responded to a letter from Alma in which Alma had offered to support Orcella Rexford's teaching activities in Jacksonville at her own expense if the National Teaching Committee could pay her transportation costs. Mary responded:

> We were delighted to know that you could support yourself, but we thought that would mean your room and board while at a place and not a long expensive trip as it would be from Washington to Jacksonville. Unfortunately the N.T.C. is flat financially and it would be quite out of the question for us to pay your fare down and back. Your sister will be lucky if we have enough money left to get her home.[34]

On 30 March 1930 Alma received a second letter from the National Teaching Committee:

> Although we know from your past activities in Bahá'í teaching that your devotion and self-sacrifice for the Cause is without limit, we were nevertheless surprised as well as most grateful when we received your letter saying that you were prepared to go to Florida to assist Dr. Guy and his work in Jacksonville. Enclosed is a carbon copy of a letter to him and you will probably hear directly from him within a few days. Please let us know of the developments.[35]

The story is told that Alma left immediately for Jacksonville, without even packing all her clothes![36] Orcella Rexford's health classes had attracted 100 participants,[37] and Mrs Randall, one of her students, had an uncle who owned the Hotel Seminole in Jacksonville and offered to rent them a handsome hall at little cost. The first meeting at the hotel was a grand success and the hall was filled to capacity. Alma and Mrs Guy each gave an inspiring talk and fourteen people left their contact information.

Public meetings were held every Thursday evening. Some Bahá'ís were uncomfortable using the hotel, but it did attract many people since it was a neutral location. Alma wrote, 'It will take some time before we have a number who are really interested in the Bahá'í teachings so as to have a place of our own,'[38] and later, by the end of May, 'I had the opportunity to speak to 5 persons at one time and all were very much interested and all 5 attended the lecture last night at the hotel (front row). This is a more promising start than I have ever had, so of course I am happy.'[39]

Although the weekly lectures at the hotel were well attended, unity among the Bahá'í teachers was becoming a challenge. Each teacher had their own concept and method of teaching. Alma preferred a direct approach, and it was difficult for her to support Orcella's mixed approach with the teachings added to the health food lectures. Mrs H. Randall, on the other hand, could not attend all the Bahá'í meetings, since she was helping Orcella's colleague Dr Kloss with his lectures. She used the Bahá'í contact list from the public meetings to recruit additional support for them, but in mid-May Dr Kloss got into trouble with the Medical Association for practising medicine without a licence and in turn said unpleasant things about the Bahá'ís.[40]

Alma was also having difficulties working with the Guys, and Dr and Mrs Guy also had trouble working together, as each had a different approach.[41] Although the diversity seemed challenging, it was, in fact, constructive. Everyone's efforts began to bear fruit.

And in early June, Ruhi Afnan wrote to Alma on behalf of Shoghi Effendi, that the pioneer work that the three sisters were doing would surely bear rich fruits and fully reward their sacrifices. The Guardian added, by hand, that Alma's many services, past and present, were engraved on his heart, and that she should persevere and never feel discouraged.[42]

Mrs K. M. Clough had been making a great effort to study the writings and inviting her friends to attend the meetings;[43] Alma went through the Will and Testament of 'Abdu'l-Bahá with her and she fully accepted the Faith.[44] Another new contact, Mrs Wallace, invited Alma to teach a study class on Monday nights in her home and a small group celebrated the Master's birthday there.[45]

Kathryn Vernon, 'a beautiful intellectual lady',[46] attended one of the lectures at the Seminole Hotel. She became attracted to the Faith when Dr Guy told the audience, 'If you accept this revelation, I am not promising you health, wealth, and happiness, as most of the lecturers do, but you will have tests, you will have trials and persecutions, and possibly even martyrdom.' Kathryn recalled, 'Martyrdom did not sound at all inviting to me, but I could not forget his claim that the Promised One of God had come, known by the name of Bahá'u'lláh, the Glory of God . . . Two days later, I asked myself, "If it is the truth, why have I not heard it before?" Instantly I heard a small voice saying, "That is no reason, It IS the truth."' Although Kathryn's mother was initially opposed to the Faith, she became positively impressed and later also a believer.[47]

In all the commotion, Alma never forgot to write to Pauline, but she did forget to send her monthly teaching reports to the National Teaching Committee![48] By June they had moved the weekly public meetings to the Carling Hotel where the hall was free of charge. The meetings were advertised in the local paper and 16 to 30 people attended, and at the end of June, Dr Guy held a meeting in the Seminole Hotel where 35 people attended.[49]

On 15 July 1932, the Bahá'í world lost Bahíyyih Khánum, the Greatest Holy Leaf, the sister of 'Abdu'l-Bahá, leaving Shoghi Effendi alone. He was the last member of the Holy Family to lead the Bahá'í community. Alma and eighteen of the new friends sent a letter of condolence to the Guardian, including a description of all their activities to cheer him up. The group held a memorial service in honour of the Greatest Holy Leaf at the home of Dr and Mrs Wallace.[50] Shoghi Effendi replied that their message had imparted strength, joy and hope to his sorrow-laden heart, and that he was eager to hear of the progress of their activities.[51]

In July of 1932, the Guys headed north for vacation. Alma continued the weekly study classes; she was concerned that if she took a summer break the group would disperse.[52] In September Pauline visited Alma,[53] and at the end of the summer the Guys returned looking well rested after their summer vacation, but Alma, on the other hand, was exhausted from the hard work and heat in Florida.

The group began a study programme prepared by the National Teaching Committee which contained 35 lessons based on two works by 'Abdu'l-Bahá,[54] but tensions now arose in all directions. Dr Guy's public talks were no longer well attended. Alma noticed that at the public meetings each of the three of them tried 'to answer questions at the same time . . . one interfering with the other, and the people do not come back'. Alma decided to focus her energy on the Monday night study groups using the materials from the National Teaching Committee. This group was stable, reliable and growing, so Dr Guy wanted to combine his talks with the study group and make it a biweekly event.[55]

By December, attendance at the public meetings had improved and Mr Walter Bacon joined them from the north.[56] The first Bahá'í group in Jacksonville was formed on 29 January 1933 with Walter Bacon and the Guys (as 'Honorary Members' since they lived in Saint Augustine). Kathryn Vernon recalled, however, that by February the meetings were no longer attracting seekers and Kathryn's mother offered to hold the meetings in her home.[57]

In a letter to Pauline from Jacksonville, Alma describes her teaching strategy. While in Germany 'Abdu'l-Bahá had told her, 'when you go to a place where the Cause is not known, and you interest a number of people, they will make 10 Bahá'ís in a year, when they become attracted and confirmed.' In her report of 29 June 1932 to the National Teaching Committee she wrote:

> The idea is this – it takes much patience and a good understanding of the teachings, much love and tact to form a nucleus, which is necessary for a starting point, no matter how small the number. When perfect unity exists, it will attract the Divine Spirit and the fragrances of the Abha Kingdom will be diffused. This Divine Spirit attracts kindred spirits, very different in type and from different paths of life and through this spiritual power spirituality is attained and numbers are increased.[58]

Alma sent a report of her activities to the Guardian on 26 December 1932, and Shoghi Effendi responded on 22 January 1933, urging her to do all she possibly could to ensure that she could continue and extend her pioneering in the southern states – a work he greatly admired and for which, he wrote, he cherished the brightest hopes.

In January 1933, Alma narrowly escaped a fire in the apartment building she lived in. Another tenant, Mrs Hooper, was not as lucky: she lost her voice and her hands were severely burnt. In her letter to Pauline Alma wrote that she would tell her all about it and then continued by reporting about the splendid attendance at their teaching activities. Then she wrote, 'Last week I had no expenses and since the fire I am right across the street from the large grey corner house and with Mrs Thompson who found the room and does not wish me to pay rent . . .' Alma was thankful that Mrs Vernon invited her for meals.[59]

Alma felt that her services in Jacksonville were coming to an end. In addition, she was homesick – longing to be with Pauline and the family again. She returned home at the end of January 1933. On 16 March the National Teaching Committee wrote:

> The NTC would like to see you continue your work in the South . . . We know of no more difficult undertaking than to present the racial principles, for which the Bahá'í Cause stands, in a section where racial feeling is so strong . . .

The NTC would like to assist you to continue with this work. Unfortunately, we have no funds. All financial support is now concentrated in building the temple and it is no longer the policy of the National Spiritual Assembly to permanently maintain teachers in the field. If in the future special means should be provided for teaching work in the South, we will certainly call upon you . . .[60]

In August, Alma returned to Jacksonville briefly to meet the friends, and from there she and her friend Georgie Wiles travelled to Nashville, Tennessee, to share the Faith with Georgie's family.[61] In Nashville they had two (White) declarations and spent time with the Black friends of the Baháʼí community.[62] The work in Nashville was followed up by Louis Gregory who arrived on 1 March 1934 to serve as a pioneer.[63] He accompanied the little Nashville community of six Whites and one Black to build the first Local Spiritual Assembly of Nashville in 1935.[64]

Alma remained in Jacksonville at her own expense. In September the National Teaching Committee sent her five dollars to show their appreciation for her dedicated work and detailed reports.[65] On 23 October Hussein Rabbani sent a letter of appreciation to Alma for her work in Florida, and informed Alma on behalf of the Guardian:

> He would particularly urge you to fix your residence in the South, as your efforts are particularly needed in this part of the States . . . What is mostly needed is patience, perseverance and full concentration on the ways and means whereby to spread the teachings.

Shoghi Effendi added his personal words of encouragement:

> Dear and precious co-worker:
> I am deeply appreciative of the magnificent efforts you exert for the spread of our beloved Faith. The memory of your historic work heartens and cheers me in my stupendous

and arduous task. I will continue to pray for you from the depths of my heart. Rest assured and persevere.

    Your true brother,
      Shoghi[66]

At the end of 1933, Dr Guy had a terrible accident which almost cost him his life.[67] His skull was fractured, and he could not serve as actively as before.

Alma was now serving in the southern states at the request of the Guardian.[68] Although the National Teaching Committee rejoiced at the praise Alma received from the beloved Guardian and sent constant encouraging words, there were no funds available for travel teachers. With the completion of the dome of the temple in Wilmette in January of 1934, the National Teaching Committee launched a rigorous teaching project and invited Alma to arrange a teaching circuit for one month or six weeks to visit various Local Assemblies in the south. Alma gladly took up the challenge. On 9 February 1934 Hussein Rabbani wrote on behalf of the Guardian encouraging her to make frequent and intimate contacts between the believers and various Bahá'í centres and groups. Shoghi Effendi's postscript to this letter expressed his pleasure and gratitude for the 'splendid record' of her services, and said that Alma and her sisters were often in his thoughts and prayers.[69]

Alma shared her experiences with the Guardian as she carried out the mandate he had bestowed upon her. On 12 May 1934 Hussein Rabbani wrote to her on behalf of Shoghi Effendi:

> The difficulties which you have to overcome are, indeed, tremendous. But for a pioneer teacher like you such obstacles do not amount to much. Through perseverance, courage and faith the cause you are endeavoiring to promote will assuredly triumph. You need, therefore, have no doubt as to the effectiveness of your labours . . .'

And the Guardian's postscript read:

With the assurance of my abiding gratitude for the memorable services you are rendering, the magnificent example you have set, and the inspiring spirit which you so powerfully display in your manifold activities.
    Your true and grateful brother,
    Shoghi[70]

When the National Teaching Committee had encouraged Alma to continue her service in the south,[71] Alma responded, 'after 25 years of service in the Cause, I feel that I must ask the National Teaching Committee for financial assistance to go forth with this great task, for I would rather it came through that channel'.[72] On 26 November 1934, Leroy Ioas to wrote Alma:

> I have delayed responding . . . hoping the way might open for some financial help to be given you, so as to permit of continuing your teaching work in the south. However, the conditions of the national treasury are such, that it seems it may be some little time before funds can be diverted from the temple construction work. The fact of the matter is that at the present time we are behind some $10,000, on those expenses. The Guardian has instructed that the first collective task of the friends at this time, is the completion of the temple work . . . I hope the doors may open for you to continue your teaching work in the south.[73]

Efforts in Jacksonville were upheld, and in March 1935 Alma went to Jacksonville at the request of the Teaching Committee to help the friends there elect their first Local Spiritual Assembly.[74] On 21 March the Committee wrote to Alma:

> . . . the Teaching Committee would deeply appreciate if you could return to Jacksonville in the very near future so that it may be the better prepared for this very important step [election of the LSA of Jacksonville] . . . the Teaching Committee will arrange to provide whatever financial assistance may be necessary for you to make the trip to

Jacksonville. As usual, we reiterate that we have no budget, but in circumstances such as this one the N.S.A. is very glad to cooperate to the extent of small financial assistance.[75]

Orlando, Florida

The Bahá'í community of Orlando, Florida had been founded in April 1912, when William Ripley moved there with his wife Annie and his daughter Bessie (Elizabeth Wigfall). 'Abdu'l-Bahá had rented their vacated apartment during His stay in Washington DC in 1912.[76] Teaching was quite a challenge in Orlando, known then as the 'City of Churches': 'Mr. Ripley spent much of his time walking in the park, speaking with people about the Bahá'í Faith, and distributing pamphlets to those who were willing to listen.'[77]

As mentioned above, Alma, Olive Kretz and Dr Guy visited the friends in Orlando in 1928. Mr Lange gave some talks at the Spiritualist Church, but the visitors were unable to teach anyone. Although they had not found any seekers, the friends were happy to be visited.[78]

In November 1933, Alma and Georgie Wiles stayed in Orlando and held Wednesday afternoon meetings in their home. They visited the isolated believers in Pine Castle and connected the Ripleys with new seekers including the Bidwells and the Newtons.[79] There were three new seekers at the Ripley home on Alma's next visit the following month: Laura Craig, Carrie Peterson, and Doris Tornstrom,[80] three strong women who, after suffering through the Great Depression, studied the major religions of the world and became ardent believers.

The Bahá'ís had established a good reputation in Orlando. When a local missionary asked his audience if they had heard of the Bahá'í Cause, Mrs Peterson, a seeker at the time, raised her hand. The missionary told the audience that 'he had met 'Abdu'l-Bahá in Haifa and that his teachings were of great importance and to harken unto them'.[81]

Carrie Peterson's daughter was the assistant librarian in Sead, South Dakota, where in earlier years Phoebe Hearst had donated a number of Bahá'í books.⁸² In 1938, Mrs Peterson moved to Sead, and represented South Dakota at the National Convention.⁸³ Laura Craig wrote, 'I miss dear little mother Peterson, night after night we would come up to her door and hear her saying the Bahá'í prayers. When she would put her book down, we then would go in.'⁸⁴

In 1934, Alma organized a teacher training class in Orlando for eleven women and one man. Her concept was to rotate the job of chairperson at these meetings, but the friends asked her to do it because of her ability to keep them focused.⁸⁵ Alma felt that 'discussions about local and personal affairs knocked the conversation down'.⁸⁶ The community was progressing. Pine Castle held Nineteen Day Feasts and offered training classes. These classes became very popular and developed into the first 'intergroup meeting' in Orlando on 25–26 March, to which all the Bahá'ís in Florida were invited. Alma felt that even if few people attended, 'nevertheless it will be splendid to come together and discuss ways and means for a better and more effective work in the South'.⁸⁷ She set out to mobilize the other communities to attend.

There were many challenges for the Florida friends. It was challenging to coordinate the southern teaching initiatives with Bahá'ís from the north who travelled south in the winter months to support the local activities. Alma later reported to the Teaching Committee, 'They have lost some of their finest acting believers on account of not working unitedly.'⁸⁸ She explained to Pauline how she was helping the friends in Miami at that time:

> The conditions in Miami were so terrible when I went there, they were almost crazy over the losses. Telling them that the early Christians lost everything etc. does not go – you don't get anywhere – the conditions and climate have a great effect – everyone that comes down there has money looking for a good time. It took patience, love, quietness, happiness, smiling, smiling, and smiling. Talks that made them smile and forget their own troubles, it was my happiness that won

them back. To do that kind of work is much more strain on the nerves than to open new fields of labor.[89]

Alma realized that everyone longs for joy and happiness, and she prayed to be 'filled with the joy that will awaken happiness' in all those with whom she came in contact. 'What others do or don't do it is of little importance. Joy and happiness will win and help to overcome all obstacles.'[90]

On a very stormy night in February 1934, Alma and Dr and Mrs Guy visited the friends in Saint Augustine, where the Bahá'í Spiritual Assembly met at a Black home and had all Black officers. At that time, the Guys were the only White friends who attended those meetings. Although the Black believers were unhappy about that, they decided to continue the study course, to raise up Black teachers who could teach more Black people. In addition, they planned to connect the study classes with the classes in Orlando.[91] Although Dr Guy was still recovering from his accident, he and Alma visited the Normal School and had a wonderful time with Miss Blocker and Professor Collier. Afterwards they visited Jacksonville and attended Kathryn Vernon's first public talk. Kathryn's mother opened her home and the Vernon household became the cornerstone of the Jacksonville community.[92]

In March 1934, Bahá'ís from Sarasota, Miami, Lakewood, Jacksonville, and Saint Augustine attended the first Florida Intergroup Meeting in Orlando. They received a letter from Haifa calling for a better organized teaching campaign for the south.[93] A unanimous decision was made to continue the annual meetings and the next one was scheduled to be held in Saint Augustine.[94]

After attending the National Convention in Chicago in 1934, Alma visited the Seker family in Pittsburgh, a multiracial community with 'five white and four refined and well-educated Colored believers'.[95]

When Alma returned to Orlando in February 1935, the community asked her to start the regular meetings.[96]

Augusta, Georgia

The first believer in Augusta was Mrs Margaret Klebs, a friend of Sarah Farmer, the founder of Green Acre. Mrs Klebs was a voice teacher who taught in Augusta and shared the Bahá'í message with those she knew. Daisy Moore, the daughter of Mr and Mrs Jas. H. Jackson, was one of her students and both Daisy and her mother accepted the Bahá'í teachings. In response to the Divine Plan, Joseph Hannen had travelled to Augusta in 1917/1918 to support the teaching efforts of Mrs Klebs, followed by a visit from Mason Remey and John Bassett in March/April of 1919, when a large teaching meeting was held in the home of Mrs Jackson. The atmosphere was very spiritual and more than forty people bombarded Remey and Bassett with questions.[97] Although a group of believers was established, unfortunately most of these older believers had not maintained contact with the Faith.

Alma arrived in Augusta sometime in June 1935 to support the teaching efforts of Dr Marie Kershaw and her husband, the young Clayton Fletcher, Mrs Klebs, Esther Sego, Annie Ripley and her daughter Bessie Wigfall, and the Bidwells, whom Alma had taught in Orlando

In that summer of 1935, Clayton organized a youth group consisting of 60 youth; the youth gatherings were 'dancing parties'. With Alma's help the community also started children's classes with four children.[98]

In 1936, Alma served as a correspondent at the National Convention, where the south was well represented by Mrs Holt for Miami, Dr Guy for Saint Augustine, Mr Bacon for Jacksonville, Mr Bidwell for Augusta, and Georgie Wiles for Nashville.[99] At the National Convention the exciting telegram from the beloved Guardian about the upcoming Seven Year Plan was read:

CONVEY AMERICAN BELIEVERS ABIDING GRATITUDE EFFORTS UNITEDLY EXERTED TEACHING FIELD. INAUGURATED CAMPAIGN SHOULD BE VIGOROUSLY PURSUED SYSTEMATICALLY

EXTENDED. APPEAL ASSEMBLED DELEGATES POWER HISTORIC APPEAL VOICED BY 'ABDU'LBAHÁ TABLETS DIVINE PLAN. URGE EARNEST DELIBERATION WITH INCOMING NATIONAL ASSEMBLY ENSURE ITS COMPLETE FULFILLMENT. FIRST CENTURY BAHÁ'Í ERA DRAWING TO A CLOSE. HUMANITY ENTERING OUTER FRINGES MOST PERILOUS STAGE ITS EXISTENCE. OPPORTUNITIES PRESENT HOUR UNIMAGINABLY PRECIOUS. WOULD TO GOD EVERY STATE WITHIN AMERICAN REPUBLIC AND EVERY REPUBLIC IN AMERICAN CONTINENT MIGHT ERE TERMINATION THIS GLORIOUS CENTURY EMBRACE LIGHT FAITH BAHÁ'U'LLÁH AND ESTABLISH STRUCTURAL BASIS OF HIS WORLD ORDER.[100]

The beloved Guardian was leading the American Bahá'í community into the systematic execution of the Divine Plan. Alma wrote to her sisters,

> How thankful we can be to have been able to serve, and am grateful that our family name is mentioned in the Divine Plane [sic], which Shoghi Effendi has asked every believer to study and the assemblies to form study groups for that purpose. Shoghi Effendi is [sic] also taken great interest in the German believers, they too are mentioned in the Divine Plane [sic] to arise and teach.[101]

As the world of politics disintegrated, the Divine Plan of God was moving forward, leading humanity to the Most Great Peace. In 1919, 'Abdu'l-Bahá had written in a Tablet that was read by US President Woodrow Wilson: 'the establishment of Universal Peace will be realized fully through the Power of the Word of God.'[102]

In July, Shoghi Effendi called the American believers to rededicate themselves to fulfil the Divine Plan:

ENTREAT AMERICAN BELIEVERS PONDER AFRESH URGENCY REDEDICATE THEMSELVES TASK COMPLETE FULFILLMENT DIVINE PLAN. NATIONAL ASSEMBLY'S ENERGETIC LEADERSHIP

CAREFUL PLANNING INEFFECTUAL UNLESS SUPPLEMENTED BY VIGOROUS ACTION BY EVERY BELIEVER HOWEVER HUMBLE HOWEVER INEXPERIENCED. TIME IS SHORT. SANDS CHAOTIC DESPAIRING CIVILIZATION STEADILY RUNNING OUT. FOUNDED ON UNITY UNDERSTANDING SO SPLENDIDLY ACHIEVED, FUNCTIONING WITHIN FRAMEWORK ADMINISTRATIVE ORDER LABORIOUSLY ERECTED, INSPIRED VISION TEMPLE EDIFICE NOBLY REARED, GALVANIZED INTO ACTION REALIZATION RAPIDLY DETERIORATING WORLD SITUATION, AMERICAN BAHÁ'Í COMMUNITY SHOULD RISE AS NEVER BEFORE HEIGHT OPPORTUNITY NOW CONFRONTING IT. AUDACITY, RESOLUTION, SELF-ABNEGATION IMPERATIVELY DEMANDED. IMPATIENTLY PRAYERFULLY WAITING.[103]

45

CABIN JOHN, MARYLAND, AND A YEAR OF REFLECTION

After the National Convention in 1936, Alma visited Carl and his family in Wilmette. While there, she was invited to the home of Corinne True where she met the new believers in Evanston and Winnetka, among them this author's grandparents Dorothy and Harvey Redson, who had recently joined the Bahá'í Faith.[1]

In July, Alma returned to Cabin John, while Pauline and Fanny visited Carl's family. Pauline's health was declining. In September, Fanny wrote to Alma, 'Pauline is very sick, cannot hold her head up and cannot write. Pauline could get very quickly worse . . . and have again the sickness she experienced earlier.'[2] While Alma remained in Cabin John, her work in Augusta was covered by the much-loved Dr Zia Bagdadi, who helped the Augusta community build up nine new believers.[3] On 30 September 1936, Alma received a letter written on behalf of Shoghi Effendi, voicing his concern for Pauline, and the greatest reward of all, a postscript from Shoghi Effendi telling her that future generations would remember with pride and gratitude 'the share you have had in advancing the vital interest of the faith'.[4]

Shoghi Effendi had written to the American believers on 28 July 1936:

> I am eagerly awaiting the news of the progress of the activities initiated to promote the teaching work within, and beyond the confines of, the American continent. The

American believers, if they wish to carry out, in the spirit and the letter, the parting wishes of their beloved Master, must intensify their teaching work a thousandfold.[5]

Alma was determined to honour the Guardian's request for her to serve in the south. In view of the necessity at that time to stay in Maryland, she decided to do this in nearby Baltimore, which is located geographically below the Mason-Dixon Line, the line that divides the northern and southern states. When Pauline heard this, she wrote, 'Fanny hopes you will not waste your time in Baltimore, I say do as you feel moved to do. They do need new blood . . . all believers must make room for the new.'[6]

Soon Alma reported to the Guardian:

> The believers in Baltimore Md [Maryland], wish me to write and tell you that they have arisen afresh to assume their Bahai activities, and that they are thankful for the renewed courage. Have started a weekly study class for public speaking last month, and they are all enthusiastic about their talks, and already they have made progress.
>
> The youth group that has been sleeping for over a year will become active and hold their first meeting this week. Also, the Bahai reading rooms will be reopened, they are centrally located and pleasant. The sign at the window will be replaced by a larger more attractive one . . . These trips to Baltimore are from Friday to Sunday, giving me a chance to come in close touch with the believers . . . Although I was having a heavenly time at Wilmette, serving as a guide . . . I felt I must go South according to your wish and Cabin John Park is below the Dixy Line South . . . precious sister Pauline Hannen is still in Wilmette, gaining her strength and health slowly, but is happy to be so near the temple . . .[7]

The Guardian answered, in postscript,, that he was delighted to hear Alma's news and admired her perseverance, devotion and loyalty; he would pray on her behalf at the Shrines and would never forget her.[8]

Despite all her accomplishments in the United States, Alma regarded her service in Germany as her primary contribution to the Faith. It had been Alma and Fanny's joint response to the call of their beloved Master.

In the 1930s, the dramatic political developments in Germany were of grave concern to all. After Adolf Hitler was appointed Chancellor of Germany on 30 January 1933, he established a totalitarian regime in which all political parties were forbidden, except his own, the NSDAP (the National Socialist German Workers' Party, commonly known as the Nazi Party). In 1933, Germany was refused 'equality of status' by the League of Nations. Adolf Hitler responded on 14 October 1933 with the announcement that Germany would withdraw from the League of Nations on the basis that the Treaty of Versailles had been unjust, and that Germany had the right to build up its military forces. Concerned about this announcement, Adelbert Mühlschlegel, the Secretary of the National Spiritual Assembly of the Bahá'ís of Germany, wrote to Shoghi Effendi on 30 January 1934, asking for guidance for the German National Spiritual Assembly and the Bahá'ís of Germany.

On 11 February 1934, Shoghi Effendi's secretary replied on his behalf clarifying what the German Bahá'ís should do in light of the political circumstances. It is a fundamental and far-reaching explanation of the Bahá'í principle of obedience to government:

> The Bahá'í Cause being essentially a religious movement of a spiritual character stands above every political party or group, and thus cannot and should not act in contravention to the principles, laws, and doctrines of any government . . . It follows, therefore, that our German friends are under the sacred obligation to whole-heartedly obey the existing political regime, whatever be their personal views and criticism of its actual working.
>
> . . . whereas the friends should obey the government under which they live, even at the risk of sacrificing all their administrative affairs and interest, they should under

no circumstances suffer their inner religious beliefs and convictions to be violated and transgressed by any authority whatever. A distinction of a fundamental importance must, therefore, be made between *spiritual* and *administrative* matters. Whereas the former are sacred and inviolable, and hence cannot be subject to compromise, the latter are secondary and can consequently be given up . . . In matters of belief, however, no compromise whatever should be allowed, even though the outcome of it be death or expulsion.

. . . the Bahá'í philosophy of social and political organization cannot be fully reconciled with the political doctrines and conceptions that are current and much in vogue today. The wave of nationalism, so aggressive and contagious in its effects, which has swept not only over Europe but over a large part of mankind is, indeed, the very negation of the gospel of peace and of brotherhood proclaimed by Bahá'u'lláh . . . The world is drawing nearer and nearer to a universal catastrophe which will mark the end of a bankrupt and of a fundamentally defective civilization.[9]

Shoghi Effendi gave further strength to the German Bahá'í community a month later, stating, 'As 'Abdu'l-Bahá has so often remarked, Germany will one day be destined to lead all the nations and peoples of Europe spiritually, that from its very heart the Bahá'ís will spread all over the European continent, proclaiming with one voice the glad-tidings of this New Day.'[10]

In addition, Shoghi Effendi encouraged strong believers from other countries to visit and support the German Bahá'ís. That summer of 1936, thousands of participants attended the World Bahá'í Youth Symposium conferences, of which eighteen were held in America and eleven others in Germany, India, England, Hungary, Iraq and Iran. 'It is especially interesting', one report states, 'that five of the conferences were held in Germany (Heidelberg, Stuttgart, Esslingen, Göppingen, and Karlsruhe)'.[11] Bahá'ís from 12 countries travelled to visit the Bahá'í Summer School and Convention in Germany, including

Marion Jack and May Maxwell, whose daughter Mary was serving in Germany at that time. Mary Maxwell was teaching in Germany for one and a half years, until 1937 just before she married the Guardian, Shoghi Effendi. Alma wrote to her sisters that Mrs French of the US National Spiritual Assembly was asked by the Guardian to visit the German Summer School in Esslingen.¹²

In the Fall of 1936, Alma attended a talk given by Doris Lohse,¹³ who had been granted approval by the Guardian to attend this historic event. Doris told Alma that the Guardian had written to her that 'he fully approved of her visiting the Summer School at Esslingen, that she would learn much and that she would or could help the German believers and then give much advice to the American believers'. Doris described the beautiful and sacred atmosphere of the German Summer School and Convention; she was 'overwhelmed at the marvellous and deep talks that were given' and she was most impressed by the 'profound humility, earnestness and reverence all the German believers express in their attitude towards the Cause'. Alma wrote to her sisters, 'Mrs Maxwell and daughter was [sic] there also Miss Jack, will tell you sometime what happened to Mary Maxwell for the Germans insist upon order and have thereby obtained the recognition and good will of the government. They have suffered much and are aware of the troubles and tests ahead of them.' Furthermore, she explained, 'Dr. Hermann Grossmann received a letter from the Guardian telling him to come to Haifa and bring his wife and sister and no one else. When he told of his visit to Haifa Mrs Maxwell said – Oh I will also go – but he showed his letter <u>no one else</u>. They feel it is very significant concerning the present time and conditions.'¹⁴

But the inexorable march of Nazism was taking its toll. During the middle of the German Bahá'í Summer School in 1937, Heinrich Himmler outlawed the Bahá'í Faith and in June 1937 the Gestapo closed the doors of the 'Häusle', the Bahá'í Centre in Esslingen.¹⁵ Anna Köstlin sent a message to Doris Lohse with a friend who was travelling to the United States, that the conditions were very serious and the friends should not write to them; if they did, they must not mention the Faith, but it was best not to write at all!'[16]

In March 1938, the Faith was outlawed in Austria. Franz Pöllinger wrote to Martha Root, 'But there is some wisdom in that which we do not yet understand today, we are happy knowing you are in good health and always led by God's infallible guidance.'[17] The Bahá'ís in Germany were no longer allowed by law to meet in groups (more than two people) for the following eight years.[18]

Years later, Hartmut Grossmann told the Bahá'ís in Frankfurt that once, when his mother met with Annemarie Schweizer, she took him, as a young child, with her. That made them a 'group' of three and they were prosecuted for having broken the law. That meant that already as a child Hartmut Grossmann became a 'criminal'. Even after the War, his 'criminal' record prohibited him from being allowed to graduate from a university in Germany and therefore he studied abroad. In 2003, through legal efforts made from the German Embassy in Israel while he was serving on the Universal House of Justice, his record was finally cleared.[19]

Alfred Khurshed Schweizer, the first son of Friedrich and Annemarie Schweizer and the first Bahá'í baby born in Germany, was killed on 21 February 1942 on the Eastern Front; the Schweizers responded by putting all their efforts into copying and dispersing the Holy Writings. Among other Baha'is, Annemarie Schweizer was imprisoned for her Faith under the Gestapo.[20]

As early as 1930, Shoghi Effendi had attempted to protect the German Bahá'ís by encouraging them to integrate Max Greeven, an American Bahá'í working in Bremen, into their activities. Max, an American citizen, was soon elected to serve on the National Spiritual Assembly of the Bahá'ís of Germany. In the Fall of 1937 and the Summer of 1938, he formally requested both from within Germany as well as from Holland that all confiscated materials be returned to the Bahá'ís. He was assured they would be returned, but they never were.[21]

Alma would not live to see the end of the Second World War, or hear the heroic stories of her spiritual children, Hermann Grossmann, Annemarie Schweizer, Anna Köstlin, Franz Pöllinger, and her friends such as Marion Jack, who were caught in the unfolding troubles in Europe. Fortunately, Alma donated most of her photographs of the German believers to the US Archives.[22] They are highly valued, because in Germany most of the photographs did not survive the two World Wars.

The German Bahá'í community never forgot Alma. Many wrote to her during that eventful summer of 1936, including Elsa Marie Grossmann and Marion Jack from Leipzig,[23] Julia Stäbler,[24] Lydia Bauer, the Brauns, the Schweizers, and many others.[25] On one postcard they wrote: 'these are the seeds that you have sown in Germany'.[26]

Surprisingly, Mason Remey, not Alma, was now asked to write the history of the German Bahá'í community. This was a painful moment for Alma, who shared her disappointment in a postcard to her sisters, 'What would you think of someone writing your history in the Cause?' Pauline wrote to her in September, comforting her:

> My one thought was 'Alma is strong in her faith and this will not weaken her. It was arranged by those in charge, therefore as far as *you* are concerned: the Hand of God. Darling Alma, my physical sister, I suffered for your human side. Yet no one else could have written it better aside from you, than Mason, who holds you in highest respect . . . Humanly I believe he will do you justice. But whether or not, your station is established forever by indestructible Tablets from our Master and hundreds if not thousands have heard from His Blessed lips the marvellous praise on your behalf.[27]

Alma bounced back fast, writing to Fanny and Pauline a month later, 'I am very glad that Mason has about finished his history of Germany, he has been writing on it for several years, that is why he asked Pauline for our photographs . . . no doubt it will be very fine, Mason said he has kept every scrap of paper – good or bad – he has received that pertains to the Cause.'²⁸

Remey never completed his task. He left only a manuscript from 1915 entitled *Through Warring Countries*. Later, in 1943, when he was asked to write the obituary of Consul Schwarz for *The Bahá'í World*, he wrote to Jessie Revell, 'As for the sketch of Cunsul [sic] Schwarz activity in the Bahai Faith; Alma Knobloch should do this far better than I could. She taught in Stuttgart for six years or was it seven years? While I was only there at few and brief intervals . . . She will be able to tell you of those days and just what are services the Schwarz family did for the cause . . .'²⁹ Jessie Revell immediately asked Alma to provide a photo of Consul Schwarz for the article in *The Bahá'í World* about the nineteen Disciples of 'Abdu'l-Bahá.³⁰ Unfortunately, by that time Alma had had an accident which affected her vision,³¹ and instead of the picture of Consul Schwarz, a picture of Arthur Brauns is given with Consul Schwarz's name under it.³² No article is published with that illustration.

Alma was, however, invited to submit her story to Volume VII (1936–1938) of *The Bahá'í World*.³³ Her article 'The Call to Germany' remained until recently the only tribute to her great service in Europe.³⁴

As Alma continued to serve in Maryland, in 1937 she was the delegate to the National Convention for the Cabin John Assembly³⁵ and was appointed as one of the National Teachers.³⁶ In May 1937, Dr Zia Bagdadi, who had replaced Alma in Augusta, Georgia, while she was in Cabin John, passed away.³⁷ The Assembly of Augusta wrote twice to Alma requesting her to resume her post. This became possible in June, after Fanny returned to Cabin John.

46
IN THE SOUTH ONE LAST TIME

Alma used all the experiences of her life in her final round of service in the southern states. Now almost 74 years of age, she resumed her post in Augusta, Georgia, on 20 June 1937. Knowing that Pauline's condition was fragile, Alma wrote at the top of almost all her letters to her sisters, 'If you should *need me*, am *always ready* to come at *once*.'

A week after her return, Alma sent her first report to the Regional Teaching Committee on 26 June.[1] There was a regular well-attended public meeting at the Augusta Bahá'í Center, a small, centrally located house where Dr Bagdadi had lovingly planted bushes and flowers and had lived with his family.[2] There were regular Bahá'í activities held through the summer, including Esperanto classes, weekly public meetings and study classes,[3] and Dr Bidwell gave additional lectures.[4] The Augusta Bahá'ís published weekly programmes in two newspapers and had permission for radio time.[5] In the late 1930s the larger communities in Florida had similar events emphasizing Esperanto and youth activities.[6] Alma helped the Assembly organize teaching activities, one of which was to work with Clair Glover to continue the efforts of Esther Sego in raising up a cadre of teachers amongst the Black community.[7] Three cousins of Professor Collier of the St Augustine Normal School were involved in this effort.[8] In addition, Alma visited the nine friends that Dr Bagdadi had been teaching at their homes and invited them to activities. She also started a youth meeting with the son of one of these families.[9]

The Baháʼí house in Esslingen. The summer schools were held here for many years from the 1920s to after the Second World War; it is still a place of visitation

Esslingen, 1921. Back row, left to right: Mr Gfaller, Heinrich Schwab, Richard Theophil Imanuel Aeckerle (he became a well-known painter and painted the portrait of ʻAbdu'l-Bahá over Alma's desk), Mr Bender. Front row, left to right: Mr Gillismong (?), Anna Köstlin, Luise Fingerle, Charles Mason Remey (?)

Mary Maxwell and Jeanne Bolles with Maria Braun at the German Bahá'í Summer School in Esslingen, 1936

Jeanne with her cousin Mary (later Amatu'l-Bahá Rúḥíyyih Khánum), 1936

Alma reported to the Guardian, on 11 September 1937, that the Wednesday meetings had grown from six to twenty-four participants who studied the Faith through the summer.[10] On 15 October she received a letter telling her that the Guardian was praying for these friends, and a loving postscript.[11] Soon there were six new believers.[12]

Bristol, Florida

Edward Young was the first Bahá'í to settle in Bristol. He was an early Washington believer who had learned about the Faith through Pauline.[13] In the 1920s, he was giving lectures in which he linked the Bahá'í Faith to his personal occult beliefs. These talks were publicized in the *Washington Post* with a picture of him dressed in a priest-like costume.[14] When he had a difficult time keeping away from Covenant-breakers in contact with Dr Fareed,[15] Louis Gregory tried to help him and together they gave lectures regarding the succession of 'Abdu'l-Bahá.[16] Soon after this, Edward Young faded out of the community.

On 28 March 1933 Edward Young wrote to Shoghi Effendi of his deep belief in the Bahá'í Faith, and on 17 April 1933 he received an encouraging reply with a postscript: 'May the Almighty guide you and illumine your understanding and assist you to promote the interests of His invincible faith.'[17] In 1937, Edward wrote to the National Teaching Committee asking for support with some study circles he was organizing in Bristol.[18] The Committee could find no record of him and was uncertain if he was a Bahá'í. Edward explained that he had been affiliated with the friends in Washington, but the Washington DC community reported that there was no record that Mr Young had participated in obligatory study courses for new believers and that he was not a community member.[19] Apparently no one had had contact with him for over a decade.

On 4 November 1937, the National Teaching Committee sent Alma a $25 stipend for her to visit Edward Young in Bristol. She was to accomplish two tasks: first, to determine if Edward Young truly was an isolated believer; and second, to determine if there were other believers in Bristol whom he had taught and if so, to determine if they understood the Bahá'í Faith. In this way the Committee could decide what, if any, support would be sent to Bristol. Alma was asked to submit a report to Lucille Hoke of the Regional Teaching Committee for Florida and Alabama.[20]

Alma arrived in Bristol that same month, November 1937. At that time, Bristol was poor and underdeveloped, the houses did not have numbers, and everyone seemed to be related to one another.[21] Bristol provided no sewage, no water, and only a few houses had electric light.[22] That winter the water was frozen over and an inch thick, thereby destroying the water pump to the house she stayed in. The church lacked heating and was freezing cold,[23] as were the classrooms in the schools she visited that winter. Alma's room was heated by a fireplace with an open hearth that 'is pretty to look at and does keep one side that is turned to it good and warm, the other side when it gets its chance'.[24] While serving in Bristol six months later, Alma still suffered from the lack of water; even drinking water was limited and there was not enough water for a bath: 'I will enjoy a hot bath or cold bath – any kind of bath – this bowl washing does for a short time but it is very warm the last days.'[25] Alma's impression was that Bristol was 'about the least attractive place I have ever been in' and 'the smallest town I have ever visited', with about 1,000 widely dispersed inhabitants, a few little stores and a post office, and pigs and cows that, she was told, 'keep the streets clean'. In addition, they had a new school that served the surrounding area.[26]

Alma described Edward as a stout man who had come to Florida for health reasons, lived on little, and was unsuccessful in his business.[27] He had been mostly teaching the poor Black people of Bristol; a list he made on 22 November 1937 shows six believers with interested family members and eight other interested people.[28] On her first morning, Alma visited the local church where Edward had interested about fifteen people and one family, the Parkers, who had accepted the Faith. Alma and Edward visited the Parker family who suffered under extreme poverty. Mr Parker worked in a local lumber mill. Mrs Myrtle Parker had only one leg and so could not find work. They had four children; the little boys collected wood to earn for the family and their daughter, Marcella, sold peanuts after school.[29] They lived in a rented house that 'made one's heart break'.[30] It was the poorest house Alma had ever seen, with holes in the wall as big as a fist, inch-wide cracks in the floor and windows with no glass in them.[31]

Alma reported to the Regional Teaching Committee:

> The Colored believers are afraid for us to come to their home or meet them in a group, so we will meet them singly. Knowing the conditions in the South, I understand their fears. Especially in a small place it is dangerous for them to associate with the whites . . . the conditions are so sad and trying as it is throughout the South, perhaps more difficult in such a small place . . . Have not been able to meet them as yet, they are afraid to have a meeting at their home, so Mr Young will have them come to his office singly and give them more of the teachings, two are retired pastors . . . Taking it all in all Mr Young has certainly been serving the cause most sincerely and since there is no business enterprise here . . . Bristol seems too isolated for a promising center, unless Mr Young can stay here and keep on with the noble work he has started . . . I will remain here as long as possible, feeling that I can be of some benefit to the friends here.[32]

The harsh winter weather, the primitive infrastructure, and the poverty of the people made life in Bristol very challenging, but the teaching opportunities were abundant. Alma became friends with Virginia and Jack Harrell. Virginia was a teacher, and they were very interested in the Bahá'í Faith. They invited her for hunting and dinner. Unfortunately, the hunting was unsuccessful and they ate squirrels for dinner![33]

Alma reported to the Regional Teaching Committee the names of those who accepted the Faith and who were interested, including quite a few families and students in the high school, as well as the publicity she was given in a local paper, and the positive reception she received at Virginia Harrell's school. She added a postscript dated 5 December, 'Mr Young left on the 1st for Jacksonville on account of insufficient means to remain . . . Mr and Mrs Harrell are the most promising and both are deeply interested . . . they come to see me every day and are studying the Teachings.'[34]

Having completed her report, Alma travelled to Miami in December where she stayed with Lucille Hoke and joined in all the teaching activities with the friends there. Lucille sent Virginia Harrell a Christmas card and Virginia sent her a reply thanking her for the card and writing, '[Alma] gave us more than was possible to return. I have never met anyone who attracted me so much, I appreciate her talking to my pupils, she lifted them up. They enjoyed her greatly and beg for her to come back, which she did, but still they were not satisfied.'[35]

Hard times came to Bristol in January 1938, when the entire business sector of the town burned down, including all eight stores and the drugstore.[36] In February, the National Teaching Committee sent Alma back to Bristol for the purpose of starting a youth group with Virginia Harrell.[37] Dr Kershaw drove Alma there on 18 March to spare her the long trip by bus with several transfers.[38] Virginia gave them 'a hearty welcome' and some of the 'young folks' came in and asked Alma if she would talk to their history class.[39]

Alma and Virginia formed a good team. The students at Virginia's school were very fond of Alma and gave her the nicknames 'Snow White' and 'Snow Flake'.[40] Virginia got the consent of the principal for Alma to speak in three classes on one afternoon and Alma 'gave much of the Bahá'í teachings'. Virginia sat with some other teachers at the back of the class with 'their eyes wide open'. They were impressed with how Alma connected history to the 'facts going on in the world'.[41]

Fanny wrote, 'You, Alma, have every reason to look forward to your Bahá'í work, no matter where you are with joy a great big bubbling one of happiness for you have the assurance that

'Abdu'l-Bahá is your confidant and guide and that your services are confirmed. Souls will in the future generations wish they were in your place . . .'[42]

In the first months of 1938 Edward Young returned, but still had no income. Alma felt as though she was reliving her early days in Germany with Edwin Fisher. Edward, who had lost all his money six months earlier, had somehow managed to purchase 155 acres of wild land four miles outside Bristol.[43] Alma, who always lived on a very tight budget, wrote:

> My personal affairs never come into that of the Cause and I'm so thankful . . . It never bothers me what others do and how they do it. God grant us strength to the end so as to serve his cause . . . As for Mr. Young, Fanny he is a sick man and really in some ways worse than Dr. Fisher, it is a good thing that I had experiences which are most valuable especially now in this serious time. On my first trip here Mr. Young was continually telling me how little he had to eat and that the people are looking starvation in the face. He is doing the same thing now.[44]

Edward wrote to the National Teaching Committee, and to Shoghi Effendi, that he was building a great community park for the believers. His letters greatly exaggerated the status of his plans. The Guardian responded enthusiastically through his secretary, but his postscript was brief.[45] The necessary financial resources were utterly lacking for such a scheme, the property was in poor condition and had no access to water. Furthermore, Edward was deep in debt. He was trying to sell his little house.[46]

Alma focused on teaching. She started meetings at the home of Mr and Mrs Wil Larkins who lived in the Mystic Lake region of Bristol. By their third meeting in April, the group had grown to 18 adults and six children.[47]

Alma continued her efforts working with the youth at the school and encouraging them to think for themselves. Virginia's annual teaching contract was expiring and so far she was not placed on the list for renewal,[48] she would know for sure after the Bristol Commissioner elections and school Board Appointments.⁴⁹ She asked the Superintendent to invite Alma to talk to the students,⁵⁰ but she did not want to be directly involved in starting a youth group, due to the upcoming elections. The situation was very political. Virginia took Alma to hear the speech of a Congressman, after which they visited 'the new section of town for the Colored people' where improvements had been made in the homes and washing machines and refrigerators had been installed. This housing was for the Black elite who supported the local politicians. Alma wrote, 'There is no doubt that the Colored people here are under strict city controls, they have no trouble with them, and they do not wish any . . . They do not want any changes.'⁵¹

When visiting Alma, Virginia always pulled the blinds down for fear of upsetting anyone.⁵² The next time, Alma joined the students on a picnic at Rock Bluff instead of meeting in the school.

Alma continued to attend church in Bristol where she discussed the Faith with those she met there. She wrote, 'My services are having some results, the Pastors of the Methodist and Baptist churches have arisen to protest against the Bahai Religion – a false Prophet . . .'⁵³ Later she was invited to teach at the Methodist Sunday School.⁵⁴

Alma's unprejudiced behaviour attracted attention. She wrote:

> I know that my letters have been opened and my every move has been watched and taken note of. It reminded me of conditions in Persia. But I am an old veteran and not easily disturbed and what has been undertaken . . . what can the world do about it? . . . [I] always try to hold on, and do what the Guardian wishes, what others think about it can't matter very much. It is a beautiful experience to find the precious souls, no matter where they may be, it seems that our Lord guides his servants to find them.⁵⁵

She also wrote, 'The Guardian has told me what he wishes

me to do and [I] have been trying my best to do so. Teach in the South – have always felt being under guidance and that is something worthwhile.'[56]

Jack Harrell was transferred to work in Willacoochee, Georgia, a small town located about 20 miles from Augusta with a population of 1,200.[57] Virginia and Jack planned to move at the end of the school year. Virginia told Alma, 'I am certainly glad that you came to Bristol for I feel my life has been greatly enriched by your coming. You have given me a brighter outlook on life and have more or less revived me, so to speak . . . I feel that we are kindred souls, indeed you have no idea how much pleasure my knowing you has brought to me. I am reading *Some Answered Questions*.'[58]

The Harrells invited Alma to Willacoochee. Before they left, Alma and Virginia visited Mrs Parker. Mr Parker had lost his job at the mill. The only other job available was in bridge construction, but they had 'men from other places, most of them Southern, for that work'. They had 'a very delightful visit' despite the hard times the Parkers were facing.[59] Alma tried to say something uplifting and they promised to visit again.

The Harrells and Alma left Bristol on 24 May 1938, drove directly into an electrical storm and were stranded with a flat tyre. After a few days in Willacoochee, they went to Augusta for a busy few days. Dr Kershaw planned to include them in many exciting teaching events, with something new every night. Virginia stayed with Esther Sego, since laws prohibited Blacks and Whites from residing overnight together. The Bahá'í community held events every evening. They were invited to picnics, luncheons, dinners, and meetings at the homes of all the different believers, as well as at the Bahá'í Center. Alma wrote to her sisters, 'Virginia enjoyed her visit very much and had tears in her eyes when she left and has won the love of all of us.'[60]

Shortly afterwards, Alma and Virginia returned to Bristol to pick up Virginia's sister. Everyone was surprised to see them again so quickly. Surprisingly, they met Edward Young by chance at the Post Office. He was not looking well. He still did not have his membership card from the National Teaching Committee and he told Alma he was in contact with a Covenant-breaker who had been removed from the community by the Master after she had printed articles supporting Dr Fareed![61] At the end of June he wrote to Alma that he had been at 'Death's door' in pitiful shape with blood poisoning from a brass plate on his shoe and it had taken two days to get a doctor to visit him at his remote home.[62]

Alma then returned to Augusta shortly before travelling to Taylor, South Carolina to visit Dr and Mrs Bidwell at his sanatorium on 26 June 1938. Other Bahá'ís from Florida also came to visit the Bidwells[63] and spent their time getting to know Dr Bidwell's patients, but they could not teach them directly as it would interfere with his medical practice.[64] Alma encouraged Pauline to come for diabetes treatment. She felt that Dr Kershaw and/or Dr Bidwell could heal her and Dr Bidwell offered to adjust his price to what Pauline could pay.[65] Pauline did not travel south, however; she remained with Fanny, living with her son Carl and his family in Wilmette.

Alma returned to Cabin John in August to help manage the property and the tenants while Fanny helped care for Pauline in Wilmette. Alma attended study classes with Emogene Hoagg and continued teaching, held firesides, and planned activities with Carrie Fuhrman in Washington; her letters are filled with community news from the Washington area. Pauline's son Paul lived in the area and Alma spent time with his family. The *Bahá'í News* summarized the rest of Alma's travel teaching campaign for 1938: 'Miss Alma Knobloch recently spent several months in Bristol, Augusta, and Taylor, S.C. Beside many fireside groups, a direct presentation of the Faith was arranged for two hundred students of the Theological Class of Cook's College, given jointly by Miss Knobloch and Miss Clair Glover of Augusta.'[66] Alma sent a detailed report to Shoghi Effendi on 23 November, to which he replied on 4 January 1939, saying that the news of Pauline's serious illness, which had compelled Alma to interrupt her teaching work in the south, had grieved him deeply; he hoped she would be able to take up her work there again but advised her to make every effort to ensure

Pauline's comfort and welfare before doing so.[67]

The Knobloch sisters' financial situation was always precarious, but as we have seen, they lived very economically; in November 1938 Alma wrote from Cabin John to Fanny and Pauline, 'we have those lots to fall back on when needed. I have not cashed the checks you speak of; I have not used but very little . . . I have been able to earn a little by selling [dresses], the dresses look OK, but it takes me so long to do it . . . My love for you all is great – it is so great, then it is painful, that is real love they say.'[68]

But by March 1939 Alma was back in action in the south. Soon she received financial support from the National Teaching Committee.[69] She spent three days in Greenville with the Bidwells, where they introduced her to Dr Williamson and his family, who became very interested in the teachings and invited Alma to Spartanburg, South Carolina. From there she joined Dr Kershaw on many visits in Augusta and then headed off to Bristol.[70]

Edward Young had defaulted on his property loan and lost ownership. Unfortunately, some of the small group of seekers he had been teaching were financially involved with him. When they complained, he replied that 'Abdu'l-Bahá had said 'associate and cooperate' but do not 'affiliate'.[71] Edward tried to finance his property by selling smaller plots to others, and the Parker family had purchased one such lot.[72] When Edward's financial situation became critical and he defaulted on his payments and was forced to return the property to the seller, he also did not fulfil his obligations to the Parker family and could not refund their money to them. These poor friends responded by filing a warrant for his arrest for breaking Florida law, and they left the Faith. The crime he committed was a state offence and the penalty was imprisonment.

Mrs Parker had been the first believer in Bristol and this crisis threatened the good name of the Cause. Alma and Virginia set out to remedy the situation. The Sheriff told them they would need to bring both parties before the county judge to throw the case out.[73] Virginia arranged a visit with the Parkers and helped convince them to drop the case if they could have the ownership of the cottage. Shortly before the trial began, Alma bought the cottage for the Parker family and interceded for Edward Young with the judge and the County Clerk, and the case was withdrawn.[74] Edward promised to repay Alma for the cottage.[75]

A few months later Edward Young received a loan in Washington to buy equipment, including a van equipped for sleeping to give 'rolling lectures' including Bahá'í talks when he travelled.[76] He visited Alma's sisters in Cabin John – Pauline received him and stayed up with him until 10 p.m – Fanny was 'indisposed'![77] After that, Edward Young rolled himself out of Bahá'í history. About nineteen months later, the following announcement was published in a Washington DC newspaper: 'Morning Star Church of Christ: Rev E. H. Young will speak. Topic, "A New Revelation".'[78]

Before leaving Bristol, Alma and Virginia worked to clear the good name of the Faith, as many 'strange reports' had been circulated.[79] Virginia used her contacts to enable Alma to speak at the school once more with the permission of the school principal.[80] In addition, they visited their friends at Mystic Lake once more.[81] Alma and Virginia reunited with the students at Rock Bluff for further discussion, after which they were invited to more visits where they shared the teachings and the list of interested contacts grew. A talk entitled 'Return of Christ' was also given at a church overflowing with guests and filled with flowers, and a children's choir sang.[82]

Virginia and Jack Harrell had moved to Douglas, Georgia; Jack worked in forestry and they often moved to new places as his job demanded. In May 1939, Alma visited them for the last time in Douglas, where they had taken a small flat. It was a difficult time for them. Again, due to her white skin, Alma had to stay in a room in a house nearby. Jack picked her up in the mornings and returned her in the evenings. They introduced Alma to some of their friends who were helping them fix up their new home. Alma wrote, 'who knows if or when this place will be visited again . . . Virginia has gotten a great deal of the teachings and I love her like Margarethe [Döring].'

Virginia's pupils at her school asked her if she was a Bahá'í and she responded, 'Yes, I am a Bahá'í!' She told Alma, 'They all opened their eyes wide and looked at her and no sound not a word from any of them.' It made a deep impression and the children even spoke of it at home. After that, Virginia was not given her class again for the next term. 'It is politics', Alma wrote, 'and whatever comes, she will take it as for the best.'[83]

Alma returned to Augusta in early June, where Rabbi Joseph Leiser gave a talk at the public meeting entitled, 'The Religion of Making a Living'. After a long and confusing introduction, he spoke 'very bitterly about Hitler . . . very fiery and bitter'. Marie Kershaw was chairman and cut his talk short, saying there was another speaker: Esther Sego had prepared a Bahá'í talk on the subject. Afterwards, the Rabbi told Esther he really liked her talk. During the refreshments, Alma approached the Rabbi, who was hard of hearing. She lovingly and patiently overlooked his constant interruptions. At last, 'he dropped his head in his hands almost on his knees and wept' and Alma 'wiped away his tears'. She wrote, 'He was deeply impressed with what I had to say – the closing of which was no one is without fault – his people of whom he has been talking, as well as we, must make strenuous effort to embrace this truth that has come in this day. It is through the light that we will disperse the darkness. Two wrongs never make a right.'[84]

South Carolina

In March 1939, Alma had been shocked to read a report from the National Teaching Committee which included South Carolina on the list of states with less than one believer. She quickly sent the Committee a list of names and addresses of active believers in South Carolina. She sent a copy of this letter on 7 March to the Guardian with a very long list of the names of many of the friends in Florida, Georgia, Tennessee, and South Carolina and asked for prayers at the Shrines for them all.[85] The Guardian sent an encouraging response, saying that he was 'thrilled'.[86]

The Committee replied that they had checked their rosters

and found that none of the people Alma had listed qualified as believers in the state of South Carolina, since none of them were registered with the National Spiritual Assembly. The Committee enclosed registration cards for them all: white cards for those who were enrolling for the first time and yellow ones for community members who had moved away into isolated places.[87]

Alma wrote to the friends in South Carolina; the response was terrific. North Augusta, South Carolina, is located across the river from Augusta, Georgia. Although they are in two different states, the communities had provided support to each other since the earliest days in 1919. It was Mrs Jackson from North Augusta who had rented the house in Augusta, Georgia to Dr Bagdadi, which became the Bahá'í Center of Augusta. After the passing of Mrs Klebs, Mrs Jackson provided land and ensured she had a proper grave. Alma called these friends 'some of the last noble Southerners'. By April 1939, Clair Glover, Mrs Jackson, and her daughter Daisy Moore were determined to form the first Spiritual Assembly in South Carolina.[88]

The following month, the Bidwells settled as Bahá'í pioneers in South Carolina. When the National Teaching Committee offered them financial assistance, the Bidwells responded that they did not need it, 'but if they wish to help with teaching in the south to help Miss Knobloch who is sacrificing her personal heirlooms as to continue in her teaching activities.'[89] Alma wrote home that the Guardian had accepted the Bidwells' services as pioneers, and that Dr Bidwell 'has interested six already in Greenville and nearby, to form a group will be the next step and that is hard sometimes'.[90]

Dr Jerry Williamson, whom Alma had met at Dr Bidwell's sanatorium in Greenville (see above),[91] invited Alma to visit Spartanburg, South Carolina to visit the Williamsons and help build up a community. In June, Alma and Dr Marie Kershaw went to Spartanburg for the first time. The trip was successful, and they were invited to return. Alma did return in August 1939 to the beautiful 'Health Haven' where the Williamsons treated her to a few days of relaxing recuperation before introducing her to their friends, the Jones family, to share the message. Dr Williamson then invited her to stay to share the message with his patients.[92]

In June 1939, Mr Barton from North Augusta visited Alma in Augusta and invited her to spend a day at his home and at the home of Mrs Lillian Poole Golden on Summerhill Road to make the necessary preparations for the first regular Friday meeting of the North Augusta Bahá'í group.[93] Alma came to North Augusta to help invite people to this meeting and ten people attended. Three ladies became very interested in the faith, including Mrs Golden and Mrs Barton's sister Elizabeth Hutchinson.[94] Both had young children, and a few weeks later Mrs Hutchinson invited Alma to spend a day with her family, where Alma found herself in a room 'filled with children, all asking questions'. The happy children asked if Alma could spend a whole day with them and she agreed.[95] The members of the Regional Committee attended the public meeting in North Augusta and thirty people were present. Later Alma asked if they could change the name of their teaching meetings from 'fireside' to something else, since the temperatures in Northern Augusta were 105 Fahrenheit (almost 41 Celsius) that summer![96]

In July, Dr Kershaw invited several of her friends from North Augusta to visit Alma in Augusta to hear about the teachings. All expressed interest and were invited to the meetings at the Barton home.[97]

By August, Mr Barton had started a Bahá'í children's group with 16 children, mostly boys. He included outdoor sports with a half-hour Bahá'í study class. In addition, the Black friends began to plan a Bahá'í Teen Group.[98] On 1 May 1940, after Alma's return to Cabin John, Daisy Moore sent her the following joyous message:

> Dearest Miss Alma . . . I know you will be thrilled to hear South Carolina is now represented in the Bahá'í Cause. We now have an assembly in North Augusta. Thanks to your untiring efforts here last summer . . . I am sure you will be

interested in the names of the members, Morgen Barton and his wife, Mrs. Golden, Carlton Sample, George Frain, Sue Blackshear, Clair and her husband and myself...[99]

Many bounties came from this first Spiritual Assembly in South Carolina. Lillian Golden and her husband Jackson Herbert Golden hosted successful firesides in their Summerhill Road home for many years and were blessed to be present at the First World Congress in 1963. Their children Carolyne, Nell and Robert all became Bahá'ís. Their daughter Carolyne later served at the Bahá'í World Centre in several capacities, including as a guide at the Shrines and the Archives Building, while her husband John Patrick Fulmer served as the Coordinator of the Gardens Department.[100] Their youngest daughter Nell is the longest-serving volunteer at the Bahá'í World Centre. After decades of service as secretary to Amatu'l-Bahá Rúḥíyyih Khánum, Nell continues to serve in the Holy Land with exemplary dedication to the Universal House of Justice to this day. In 2014, the Bahá'í Faith was the second most popular religion after Christianity in South Carolina, a state which today boasts one of the largest Bahá'í populations in the United States.[101]

The *Bahá'í News* summarized Alma's work as follows:

> Miss Alma Knobloch has worked intensively in Georgia, at Augusta and Forest Hill; and in South Carolina, at Columbia, Spartanburg, Greenville, and North Augusta. She was especially successful with youth in several of these communities.[102]

It is encouraging to note that a 75-year-old woman was 'especially successful with youth!'

Alma's service in the southern states was her last great adventure.

47

THE LAST YEARS

For most of her life, Fanny had always been the stronger one, the family earner, the person everyone depended on. Getting old and learning to accept help from others was a great challenge for her. Regarding this new and uncomfortable situation, she had written to Alma in late 1937, "Abdu'l-Bahá wanted them to live free like birds – Well Alma we are getting close to that!'[1] Three weeks later she wrote:

> I think I wrote you of that short visit with Mrs. Greenleaf – who sensed my longing to pass on because of having outlived my usefulness and am an expense to Pauline, Carl and Mineola, it costs to feed one more, and hurts seeing the youngsters in need – Mrs. Greenleaf had come to the place where she too felt she had outlived her day – wrote to the Guardian – who replied: Every remaining hour of those who were near to 'Abdu'l-Bahá are of value to this world – that brought back to memory our wonder why the Guardian considered the passing of the Greatest Holy Leaf as a calamity – no I do not <u>understand</u> but I <u>know</u> it is so.[2]

Pauline had suffered from cancer in 1929 and her health remained delicate from that point onwards. In 1938, she and Fanny stayed with Carl's family near Wilmette while she again received medical treatment. Alma hoped to help care for her sisters when they returned to Cabin John. She wrote, 'Pauline, I do wish you to be perfectly plain spoken about my coming to Cabin John when you return and [I will] do the cooking and take care of the dirt for the time. I have done it before and can do it now. All these lovely invitations hold good for later on.'³

Although Pauline and Fanny were planning to return to Washington in July 1938,⁴ things took a turn for the worse. Pauline suffered from partial paralysis and could not speak. The family asked Alma to return to the cottage so that if Pauline passed away, she could be buried next to Joseph at Prospect Hill in Washington DC.⁵ Fanny warned Alma, 'you mention what matters these little things – which brings to mind that you and I should be fully aware that the cottage and practically all it contains are Pauline's property – not ours'. Pauline was worried about the prospect of homelessness for her sisters when she would be gone.⁶ But in September 1938 Alma received a letter from Pauline herself saying that she was much better and encouraging her sister to continue her services:

> Dearest and dearly beloved Alma:
> Another and seemingly confirmed year has passed and unquestionably a very blessed year in which you have been enabled to serve your Lord. May you be granted the privilege of being one of those who will be carried through the terrible days of God, and be among those to be the servants of Baha'u'llah when the New World Order is to be established. The Guardian gives very great importance to those souls who come through triumphantly.
> Oh Alma if <u>any one</u> has that courage, <u>you have</u>. God's Will be done, and we are content. You have always been a wonderful, spiritual power in my estimation. I thank God, from the bottom of my heart that I was born into such a family of spiritual dynamos, all of them and to be chosen by such a powerful servant of Abdul Baha as Joseph.
> Alma, I do pray for you that you may reach the very highest attainment possible for humans.⁷

Sometime between Alma's 1938 southern tour and her return in March 1939, she paid a five week visit to Pauline before returning to Cabin John. The Guardian sent a letter saying that he was very happy to hear that Alma had been able to spend

Alma serving as a guide at the Bahá'í House of Worship in Wilmette, about 1938

Fanny and Alma Knobloch, the last years (date unknown)

Courtesy Judy Hannen Moe

First Spiritual Assembly of the Bahá'ís of Cabin John, Maryland. Left to right: Mr Herman, Mrs Camphare, Mrs Lewis, Paul Hannen, Pauline Hannen, Alma Knobloch, Mrs Herman, Mrs Patzer, Mr Patzer

Courtesy Judy Hannen Moe

The house in Cabin John, Maryland, where Alma passed away

*The three Knobloch sisters.
Left to right: Alma, Pauline, Fanny.
This is the picture Shoghi Effendi hung at Bahjí*

so much time with Pauline.⁸ Alma was thus enabled to stay at her post in the south, returning to Cabin John only briefly from time to time until her final return in mid-August 1939. But on 4 October 1939 at 9:30 a.m., Pauline Hannen passed away, leaving behind her children, grandchildren and sisters. Pauline was the spiritual mother of her own mother Amalie, her husband Joseph, and both of her sisters, whose lives would have had no meaning had it not been for Pauline's perseverance, spiritual awareness, and receptivity in 1902.

Alma wrote to Pauline's son Carl, 'Pauline's passing is like a dream, feel as though she will return from a trip and must have everything ready for her. Pauline's things are just where they were – I feel as though on a visit still live out of my satchels, have one drawer – this is a strange world . . .'⁹

On 14 October, Alma shared the sad news with the Guardian, who expressed his profound sympathy and sadness:

> My heart overflows with deep and loving sympathy in the severe loss you have suffered. The Cause your sister served so lovingly suffers too by her passing, but her reward in the World Beyond is immense and undoubted. The memory of her past services will never perish. The spirit that so powerfully impelled her to serve so long and so devotedly will continue to inspire those who will labour after her to follow her example and to extend the work she so zealously performed. I will specially and fervently pray for her departed soul.
> Your true and grateful brother,
> Shoghi[10]

Alma was not able to accept the Newtons' kind invitation to help the Orlando Bahá'í community in the winter of 1939. She and Fanny were left grief-stricken and alone to care for each other. The National Teaching Committee wrote:

> You have been through some very difficult weeks and we marveled that you have had the physical strength to sustain

you. I surely have no doubt that Bahá'u'lláh does assist us in all our trials and sorrows. Members of the NTC are greatly interested in your report of the work which is going forward in your own locality as well as in Augusta and the other cities which you have visited since last spring. Particularly encouraging is the good news that Mrs. Harrell in Bristol still continues to attract young people. We, too, hope that you can return there sometime and renew the many fine contacts that you made . . . All of us join in and sending you and your beloved sister our loving greetings and our best wishes that the year of 1940 may not be filled with the difficulties that seem to have visited you in too great numbers last year. We earnestly pray that both of you will soon be able to return to your active teaching services in the south.[11]

Before her passing, Pauline had reflected, 'What a blessing that I saved so many letters, no one saved mine. So, it was to be! If the Guardian wishes I will live in Fanny's account, and she mentioned me two or three times as her sister Pauline.'[12] Indeed, this book could not have been written without the letters Pauline saved!

In early 1940, the Washington DC Spiritual Assembly was suffering from disunity between the old and new believers. The community discussed their concerns at the Nineteen Day Feast, where a special visitor, May Maxwell, met the community on her last trip to Washington. Alma described this event:

> Mrs. Maxwell's last visit to Washington was unique and outstanding and undoubtedly will bring results of untold consequences . . . There was a very strange intense feeling at the hall, stillness as before a storm . . . As for me, tears would come – could not keep them back and there seems no reason, when the chairman asked for the prayer for the Guardian Mrs. Wood arose and said it, and tears rolling down her cheeks like myself. They did not offer a chair to Mrs. Maxwell, she leaned on the piano it was a strain and she naturally felt it . . .[13]

Alma silently prayed the Greatest Name throughout the meeting: 'Our beloved Mrs. Maxwell must have also felt it, for in the midst of her brilliant address she suddenly stopped and said oh there is Alma Knobloch and waited a few moments before continuing . . .'[14] May's loving and pure support brought a new life to the friends in their time of transition. Alma wrote that it was 'a marvellous experience, the tenseness had been overcome . . . All believers present responded to her appeal, and her inspiring account of her last visit to Haifa, her impressions and teachings received from the Beloved Guardian, fearless and direct explanations were given.'[15]

That very same day May called Alma and said, 'Alma, you ought to be the happiest woman on earth!' She asked whether Alma had reported about her work in the south to Shoghi Effendi? Alma responded regretfully that she had not because 'it had been the most trying Winter'. May replied that 'she expected to return to Washington a little later and then we would see a great deal of each other'.[16] This was not to be, for on 1 March 1940 May Maxwell laid down her earthly life in Buenos Aires as a Martyr of the Cause.[17]

Once more, Alma sent her condolences to the Guardian, as she had done at the passing of the Greatest Holy Leaf; she included a long report of the wonderful successes from the southern states to cheer his spirit. His response came on 15 October 1940, assuring her of his deepest appreciation for her exemplary service and of the spirit which so powerfully animated her.

In the Spring of 1942 Alma attended her last National Convention and afterwards joined Dorothy Baker for a visit to Lima, Ohio.[18] That June, Pauline's youngest son Paul began flight training after joining the US forces now that the United States had entered the Second World War.[19] In her notes, Alma recalled meeting another Bahá'í soldier in 1942:

> It was a great pleasure to meet John [Eichenauer] and his brother Marshall when they returned [from pioneering in El Salvador] 1 December 1942, to enter the merchant Marines. They gave a splendid outline of their work under

happy, joyful enthusiasm . . . carried one back to years of full activities. They wished to visit Cabin John, but time did not permit. With a hearty embrace and goodbye to this useful pioneer. We wish them Godspeed blessings and Bahá'í love, protection and guidance . . .[20]

While crossing the Atlantic, heading into the battlefields of the Second World War, John Eichenauer read a copy of *The Bahá'í World* and discovered the details of the German Bahá'í community. He prayed to God and promised that if he lived, he would work to re-establish communication between the German Bahá'í community and the Guardian. On a dark night he was able to get a military vehicle and drive into Stuttgart alone. Although there was a curfew he met a man on the street and asked him, 'Do you know any of the Bahá'ís in Stuttgart?' The man was afraid, since he should not be out after curfew and John Eichenauer was in uniform. He answered 'yes', and took him to the home of the Eger Family on Gollen Strasse. The Bahá'ís had been under surveillance for so long that when Mrs Eger saw the soldier ringing her doorbell she was quite afraid. She fearfully answered the door and said, 'Hallo', and John Eichenauer answered her with 'Allah'u'Abha!' Tears of joy filled their eyes. What an exciting evening that was![21] With fellow soldiers Bruce Davison and Henry Jarvis, John Eichenauer later

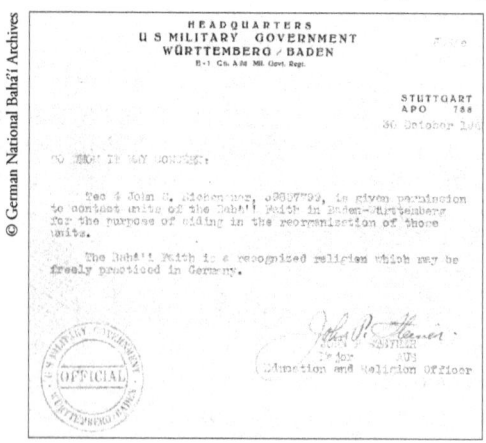

Permission for John Eichenauer to re-establish the Bahá'í Faith in Germany after the Second World War

contributed to re-establishing the legal rights of the Bahá'ís of Germany in the post-war period.[22]

In December 1942, Alma wrote to the National Teaching Committee offering her services in response to the Guardian's appeal for Bahá'í pioneers in the Seven Year Plan. The surprised Committee responded,

> The basis on which settlers are now moving into these areas is that of securing employment so that they can become self-supporting and permanent residence. This is relatively easy for a young person, particularly one who has an office or business experience, but some of our older friends are finding it a bit more difficult to make the change. We are wondering just what you have in mind. With your sister Fanny so depending upon you we wonder whether you would be able to leave her; since you are both doing so much teaching now perhaps you may decide that your best place of service for the time being is right in Cabin John . . . We are also wondering whether your moving from Cabin John would affect the status of the local spiritual assembly there. It was our understanding some time ago that your membership was very small and of course it would not be advisable to move away from there and allow Cabin John to become a disbanded assembly, and therefore another task of the 7 Year Plan! Will you write us again and let us know what plans you have . . .[23]

Despite the loss of Pauline and the weakness of Fanny's physical health, Alma was offering her services once again! Perhaps she was unaware that her remarkable life of service was closing or perhaps she wanted to be laid to rest in the deep south. A few weeks later, on 7 February 1943, Alma gave her last public talk, entitled 'The Dynamic Power of the Light that Arises in the East and Shines in the West' at the Bahá'í Hall in Washington DC.[24]

On 30 March she wrote to the National Teaching Committee from Cabin John that she and Fanny had accepted an invitation to visit Mrs Kiser, a new believer in Verona, Virginia, and that they 'would also like to visit some of our dear believers who have kindly invited me for a short time when it can be arranged at Dr. and Mrs. Bidwell Greenville, NC, Mrs. V. Harrell, Douglas, GA – Miami – and Florida City, Florida.'[25] And she followed it up with another letter, to which the Committee responded that it 'was greatly impressed with your letter of April 4 containing your offer to help with the teaching work in Greenville'; however:

> We're not quite sure whether it is your intention to settle there permanently. If you are thinking about this we hope you will seriously consider what effects your moving will have upon the continuance of your present Bahá'í assembly. Obviously, we do not want to add any more disbanded assemblies to our list during the seven-year plan. If you can move, however, without endangering the existence of Cabin John assembly, then we would certainly approve your settlement in Greenville.[26]

From 9 to 21 April 1943, Alma and Fanny took their last travel teaching trip to Vernon and Staunton, Virginia where they shared the teachings with a large number of friends and relatives of Mrs David Kiser's family and gave a number of talks on the Bahá'í Faith at private homes, including a talk to eighteen youth who were interested in the teachings.[27]

The sisters continued to serve on the Cabin John Assembly, where the community was still growing, albeit slowly. The friends worked to establish a course for children and youth in the area. The work on the Assembly remained a difficult challenge because of various differences which had accumulated amongst the members over many years, and Fanny wanted to resign from the Assembly. The sisters wrote to the Guardian, who responded through his secretary on 10 December 1943 that he felt it would be better if Fanny did not resign unless her health made it imperative for her to do so. He commented that conditions of inharmony often arose because of the immaturity of the believers, but the cure was not to leave the work, but rather, through prayer and insisting that the teachings be followed, to try to clear up any unhealthy conditions. Further, if the Bahá'ís were not able to demonstrate an atmosphere of love and patience in their communities, they could scarcely expect others to want to join them.²⁸

Two weeks later, at the age of 79, Alma suffered a heart attack during the night of 23 December 1943, and passed into the Abhá Kingdom.²⁹

* * * * *

Alma Knobloch's contribution to the Bahá'í Faith is astounding, especially considering that she was already 40 years old when she accepted the Faith. Her outstanding achievements were often overlooked by many of her contemporaries. Her 'In Memoriam' in *The Bahá'í World*, written by Rosa Schwarz, recounted her services in Germany but not those in the United States. It did, however, honour her memory, saying that it 'will ever linger in the hearts of the German believers; and their children and children's children will remember her unselfish service in the Faith of Bahá'u'lláh'.³⁰ *The Bahá'í World* accidentally published a photograph of Pauline instead of Alma with Alma's obituary.³¹

After Alma's passing, Fanny was left to carry on. On 21 May 1945 the Guardian's secretary wrote to Fanny:

> The many devoted, historic services rendered by the Knobloch sisters are never forgotten by him, and he is pleased to see that, in spite of your years, you are able to move about and inspire and help the younger generation of believers. Indeed this is of the greatest importance – that such old, tried and tested, and staunch believers as your dear self, should imbue the newer and younger ones with that faith and love which are the very essence of the Cause.
>
> You may rest assured he will pray for all those whom you love . . . He will also pray for you in the Holy Shrines, that the Beloved may assist you to serve His Faith till the last moment of your life.

And in postscript, from Shoghi Effendi directly:

> May the Beloved bless, protect and sustain you, at all times and under all conditions, reward you abundantly for the many services you have rendered His Faith, during so many years, and for the superb and exemplary spirit you have so strikingly displayed in your constant efforts for its promotion and consolidation.
> Your true and grateful brother,
> Shoghi[32]

Fanny was the first child born to Amalie and Karl August Knobloch, and the last to pass away. The last years of her life were spent in a nursing home near Carl and Mineola's home in Glenview, Illinois, not far from the House of Worship. Her only wish at that point was to join her beloved family in the Abhá Kingdom – a wish that was granted in 1949. Amalie Knobloch rests at Prospect Hill Cemetery in Washington DC surrounded by her saintly children: Fanny, Alma, Pauline and Joseph. The Tablet of Visitation revealed for Amalie has made this grave a special point of prayer for all Bahá'ís.

Alma's services will be forever remembered in the history of the Bahá'í Faith in the United States, Canada, Germany, Switzerland, Austria, and the Czech Republic. Her spiritual station is preserved throughout eternity in her many Tablets from 'Abdu'l-Bahá and letters from the beloved Guardian. Most of all, her name will be remembered in the seventh Tablet of the Divine Plan:

> Likewise, Miss Knobloch travelled alone to Germany. To what a great extent she became confirmed! Therefore, know ye of a certainty that whosoever arises in this day to diffuse the divine fragrances, the cohorts of the Kingdom of God shall confirm him, and the bestowals and the favors of the Blessed Perfection shall encircle him.[33]

BIBLIOGRAPHY

Books and articles

'Abdu'l-Bahá. 'Letter from Abdu'l Baha to the First Universal Races Congress', in *Papers on the Interracial Problems Communicated to the First Universal Races Congress, Held at the University of London, July 26–29, 1911*. London: King & Son, 1911; Boston, The World's Peace Foundation, 1911; RP Forgotten Books, 2012.

— *The Promulgation of Universal Peace: Talks Delivered by 'Abdu'l-Baha During His Visit to the United States and Canada in 1912* (1922, 1925). Comp. H. MacNutt. Wilmette, IL: Bahá'í Publishing Trust, 2nd ed. 1982.

— *Selections from the Writings of 'Abdu'l-Bahá*. Comp. Research Department of the Universal House of Justice. Haifa: Bahá'í World Centre, 1978.

— *Tablets of 'Abdu'l-Bahá* (etext in the Ocean search engine; originally published as *Tablets of Abdul-Baha Abbas*. 3 vols. Chicago: Bahá'í Publishing Society, 1909–1916). Wilmette, IL: National Spiritual Assembly of the Bahá'ís of the United States, 1980.

— *Tablets of the Divine Plan*. Wilmette, IL: Bahá'í Publishing Trust, rev. ed. 1977.

Adamson, Hugh; Hainsworth, Philip. *Historical Dictionary of the Bahá'í Faith*. Lanham, MD: Scarecrow Press, 1998.

Afroukhteh, Youness. *Memories of Nine Years in 'Akká*. Trans. Riaz Masrour. Oxford: George Ronald, 2003.

Badiei, Amir (comp.). *Stories Told by 'Abdu'l-Bahá*. Oxford: George Ronald, 2017.

Bahá'í Prayers: A Selection of Prayers Revealed by Bahá'u'lláh, The Báb, and 'Abdu'l-Bahá. Wilmette, IL: Bahá'í Publishing Trust, rev. ed. 1991.

The Bahá'í World: An International Record. Vol. I (*Bahá'í Yearbook*, 1926), vol. II (1926–1928), vol. III (1928–1930), vol. V (1932–1934); vol. VII (1936–1938), vol. IX (1940–1944), RP Wilmette, IL: Bahá'í Publishing Trust, 1980–81.

Bahá'u'lláh. *The Kitáb-i-Aqdas: The Most Holy Book.* Haifa: Bahá'í World Centre, 1992.

— *Tablets of Bahá'u'lláh Revealed after the Kitáb-i-Aqdas.* Comp. Research Department of the Universal House of Justice. Haifa: Bahá'í World Centre, 1978.

Balyuzi, H. M. *'Abdu'l-Bahá: The Centre of the Covenant of Bahá'u'lláh.* Oxford: George Ronald, 1971.

Bidwell, R. L. *Currency Conversion Tables: A Hundred Years of Change.* London: Rex Collings, 1970. https://marcuse.faculty.history.ucsb.edu/projects/currency.htm.

Blackbourn, David. *History of Germany 1780–1918.* Oxford: Blackwell Classic Histories of Europe, 2nd ed. 2003.

Buck, Christopher. 'Alain Locke: Faith and Philosophy', in *Studies in the Bábí and Bahá'í Religions*, vol. 18. Los Angeles: Kalimát Press, 2005.

— 'The Bahá'í "Pupil of the Eye" Metaphor – What Does It Mean?', online article, 28 September 2016, at bahaiteachings.org/bahai-pupil-eye-metaphor.

Burke, Sarah. 'Without Due Process: Lynching in North Carolina 1880–1900', online article at https://uncw.edu/csurf/Explorations/documents/withoutdueprocess.pdf.

Cameron, Glenn; Momen, Wendi. *A Basic Bahá'í Chronology.* Oxford: George Ronald, 1996.

Cobb, Stanwood. *Ayesha of the Bosphorus: A Romance of Constantinople.* Boston: Murray and Emery Company, 1915. Introductory comments by Bei Dawei, 2014, at https://Bahá'í-library.com/cobb_ayesha_bosphorus.

Cumbler, John T. A. *Social History of Economic Decline: Business, Politics and Work in Trenton.* New Brunswick and London: Rutgers University Press, 1989.

Ettlich, Guido. *Konsul Albert Schwarz: Banker, Bürger und Bahá'í in Stuttgart und Bad Mergentheim.* Berlin: Die Erzälverlag, 2018.

Finch, Ida A.; Knobloch, Fanny; Knobloch, Alma. *Flowers Culled from the Rose Garden of Acca.* Privately printed, 1908.

Gail, Marzieh. *Arches of the Years.* Oxford: George Ronald, 1991.

— *Summon Up Remembrance*. Oxford: George Ronald, 1987.

Gourdin, J. Raymond; Greene, Marvin V. (eds). *Voices from the Past: 104th Infantry Regiment, USCT Colored Civil War Soldiers from South Carolina*. Heritage Books, 2007.

Grundy, Julia M. *Ten Days in the Light of 'Akká* (1907). RP Wilmette, IL: Bahá'í Publishing Trust, 1979.

Hannen Moe, Judy. *A Flame with Devotion: The Hannen and Knobloch Families and the Early Days of the Bahá'í Faith in America*. Wilmette, IL: Bahá'í Publishing Trust, 2019.

— *Fanny Knobloch: An Adventuresome Spirit*. Manuscript in progress.

Jasion, Jan Teofil. *Never Be Afraid to Dare: The Story of General Jack*. Oxford: George Ronald, 2001.

Knobloch, Alma S. 'The Call to Germany' in *The Bahá'í World*, vol. VII (1936–1938), pp. 732–45.

Knobloch, Fanny; Kirkpatrick, Bertha. 'South African Mission', in *World Order Magazine*, November 1946.

Koven, Seth; Michel, Sonya. 'Womanly Duties: Maternalist Politics and the Origins of Welfare States in France, Germany, Great Britain, and the United States, 1880–1920', in *The American Historical Review*, vol. 95, no. 4, 1990, pp. 1076–1108. www.jstor.org/stable/2163479.

Kuhn, Phillip. *Psychoanalysis in Britain, 1893–1913: Histories and Historiography*. Lexington Books, 2017.

Langness, David. 'Man, Organic with the World', online article, 26 April 2014, at bahaiteachings.org.

Latimer, George. *The Lesser and the Most Great Peace*. Wilmette, IL: Bahá'í Publishing Trust, 1944. https://bahai.works/The_Lesser_and_the_Most_Great_Peace/Text.

— *The Light of the World*. Haifa, Palestine, November 16–27, 1919.

Liedtke, Harry. *The German Bahá'í Community under National Socialism: A Historical Perspective with Notes and Postscript*. Kelowna, BC: Okanagan Publishers, 1999.

Lights of Guidance: A Bahá'í Reference File. Comp. H. Hornby. New Delhi: Bahá'í Publishing Trust, 5th ed. 1997.

Mayo, Lynette. 'A History of the Greater Orlando Bahá'í Center', Rollins College Affiliate Project.

McNamara, Brendan. *The Reception of 'Abdu'l-Bahá in Britain: East comes West*. Leiden: Brill, 2020.

Metelmann, Velda. *Lua Getsinger: Herald of the Covenant*. Oxford: George Ronald, 1997.

Morrison, Gayle, *To Move the World: Louis G. Gregory and the Advancement of Racial Unity in America*. Wilmette, IL: Bahá'í Publishing Trust, 1982.

National Spiritual Assembly of the Bahá'ís of Germany. *Der Bahá'í-Glaube in Deutschland: Ein Ruckblick*.

Pfaff-Grossmann, Susanne. *Hermann Grossmann, Hand of the Cause of God: A Life for the Faith*. Oxford: George Ronald, 2009.

Redman, Earl. *Visiting 'Abdu'l-Bahá*. 2 vols. Oxford: George Ronald, 2019, 2020.

Remey, C. M. 'A Report to Abdul Baha of the Bahai Activities in the States of North Carolina, South Carolina, Georgia and Florida March – April 1919'. University of California/archive.org.

— *Through Warring Countries*. US National Bahá'í Archives, Manuscript. https://bahai-library.com/remey_through_warring_countries.

Research Department of the Universal House of Justice. *Social and Economic Development*, a compilation (2000). https://www.bahai-library.com/compilation_social_economic_development.

Reymann Banken, Richard. *Geschichte der Stadt Bautzen Bearbeitet*. Druck und Verlag von Gebr, Müller 1902.

Rhodes, Jane. *Mary Ann Shadd Cary: The Black Press and Protest in the Nineteenth Century*. Bloomington: Indiana University Press, 1998.

Schwarz, Alice. ((Schwarz-Solivo). 'Report to the Friends in the East and West', in *Sonne der Wahrheit*, Jahrgang 3, Heft 4 (June 1923).

— *Zeiten die mein Herz Berührten* (Times that Touched My Heart). Hofheim-Langenhain: Bahá'í Verlag, 2013.

Seifert, Siegfried. *Der Dom Sankt Petri zu Bautzen*. Berlin: Union Verlag, new ed. 1980.

Shoghi Effendi. *Bahá'í Administration: Selected Messages 1922–1932*. Wilmette: Bahá'í Publishing Trust, 1980.

— *Citadel of Faith: Messages to America, 1947–1957*. Wilmette, IL: Bahá'í Publishing Trust, 1965.

— *The Light of Divine Guidance*: *The Messages from the Guardian of the Bahá'í Faith to the Bahá'ís of Germany and Austria*. 2 vols. Hofheim-Langenhain: Bahá'í-Verlag, 1982, 1985.

— *Messages to the Bahá'í World, 1950–1957*. Wilmette, IL: Bahá'í Publishing Trust, 2nd ed. 1971.

— *This Decisive Hour: Messages from Shoghi Effendi to the North American Bahá'ís, 1932–1946*. Wilmette, IL.: Bahá'í Publishing Trust, 1992, 2003.

— *Unfolding Destiny: The Messages from the Guardian of the Bahá'í Faith to the Bahá'í Community of the British Isles*. London: Bahá'í Publishing Trust, 1981.

—; Lady Blomfield. *The Passing of Abdu'l-Bahá*. Originally published Haifa: Rosenfeld Brothers, 1922, later abridged for *World Order*, vol. 6, no. 1 (Fall 1971), pp. 6–18.

Smith, Clifford P. 'Early History of Christian Science in Germany', in *The Christian Science Journal*, September 1934. https://journal.christianscience.com/shared/view/1m6x5fr3egs.

Smith, Jeffrey R. 'The Monarchy versus the Nation: The "Festive Year" 1913 in Wilhelmine Germany', in *German Studies Review*, vol. 23, no. 2, 2000, pp. 257–274. www.jstor.org/stable/1432674.

Smith, Peter, *Bahá'ís in the West*. Studies in the Bábí and Bahá'í Religions, vol. 14. Los Angeles: Kalimát Press, 2003.

Steeples, Douglas; Whitten, David O. *Democracy in Desperation: The Depression of 1893*. Westport, CT: Greenwood Press, 1998.

Steinlein, Volker (comp.). *Geschichtliches über die Christliche Wissenschaft in Stuttgart*. Stuttgart: Erste Kirche Christi, Wissenschaftler, n.d.

Stockman, Robert H. 'The American Bahá'í Identity, 1894 – 1921', in *Bahá'í Studies Bulletin*, vol. 6, no. 4 / vol. 7, nos. 1–2.

— *The Bahá'í Faith in America: Early Expansion 1900–1912*. Vol. 2. Oxford: George Ronald, 1995.

— 'The Bahá'í Faith in England and Germany', in *World Order*, vol. 27, no. 3. http://Bahá'í-library.com/pdf/s/stockman_england_germany_1900-1913.pdf.

— *Thornton Chase: First American Bahá'í*. Wilmette, IL: Bahá'í Publishing Trust, 2002.

Taherzadeh, Adib. *The Covenant of Bahá'u'lláh*. Oxford: George Ronald, 1992.

Tilley, Helen. 'Racial Science, Geopolitics, and Empires: Paradoxes of Power', in *Isis*, vol. 105 (2014), no. 4, pp. 773–781. https://www.journals.uchicago.edu/doi/pdf/10.1086/679424.

Universal House of Justice, *Century of Light*. Haifa: Bahá'í World Centre, 2001.

— Letter from the Universal House of Justice to the Bahá'ís of the World acting under the Mandate of 'Abdu'l-Bahá, 26 March 2016. https://www.bahai.org/library/authoritative-texts/the-universal-house-of-justice/messages/20160326_001/1#749196100.

van den Hoonaard, Will C. *The Origins of the Bahá'í Community of Canada, 1898–1948*. Waterloo, Ontario: Wilfrid Laurier University Press, 1996.

Verhey, Jeffrey. *The Spirit of 1914: Militarism, Myth and Mobilization in Germany*. Cambridge: Cambridge University Press, 2000.

Vernon, Kathryn. *Bahá'u'lláh's Garden: History of the Bahá'í Faith in Jacksonville 1919–1969*. https://bahai-library.com/pdf/v/vernon_bahaullahs_garden.pdf

Watson, Alexander. *Enduring the Great War: Combat, Morale and Collapse in the German and British Armies, 1914–1918*. Cambridge University Press, 2008.

— 'Recruitment: Conscripts and Volunteers during World War One', 29 January 2014. The British Library. https://www.bl.uk/world-war-one/articles/recruitment-conscripts-and-volunteers.

Weatherly, Ulysses G. 'The First Universal Races Congress', in *American Journal of Sociology*, vol. 17, no. 3 (November 1911), pp. 315–328. https://www.jstor.org/stable/2763167.

Williams, George K. *Biplanes and Bombsights: British Bombing in World War I*. Air University Press, Maxwell Air Force Base, Alabama May 1999. https://media.defense.gov/2017/Mar/31/2001725261/-1/-1/0/B_0068_WILLIAMS_BIPLANES_BOMBSIGHTS.PDF.

Wilson, Reid. 'The Second-Largest Religion in Each State', in *The Washington Post*, 4 June 2014.

Zander, Wolfgang. *Die Mormonen im Südwesten Deutschlands auf d. Spuren ihres Lebens und ihrer Geschichte* Stuttgart: Pfahl, 1986.

Zarqání, Mírzá Maḥmúd. *Chronik der Reisen 'Abdu'l-Bahá in Europe*. Hofheim-Langenhain: Bahá'í Verlag, 2014.

— *Maḥmúd's Diary: The Diary of Mírzá Maḥmud-i-Zarqání Chronicling 'Abdu'l-Bahá's Journey to America*. Trans. Mohi Sobhani with the assistance of Shirley Macias. Oxford: George Ronald, 1998.

Archival collections

Annual Report of the Commissioner of Patents for the Year 1879, Thursday 1 January 1880. Publication Serial Set Vol. No. 1916 Report H. Exec. 33; patent No. 215.940, U.S. Patent and Trademark Office Patents, 1790–1909. GenealogyBank.com.

Baltimore Passenger Lists, 1820–1948 and 1954–1957, National Archives and Records Administration (NARA), Washington DC.

Bürgerliches Gesetzbuch (1. Fassung-Reichsgesetzblatt 1896, S. 195, Nr. 21, ausgegeben am 24. 08. 1896, in Kraft seit 01. 01. 1900), 18 August 1896.

Chronicling America: Historic American Newspapers. Library of Congress. http://chroniclingamerica.loc.gov.

District of Columbia Deaths and Burials, 1840–1964. https://familysearch.org/pal:/MM9.1.1/F7RT-138.

FamilySearch.org. The Church of Jesus Christ of Latter-day Saints Church Websites.

German National Baháʼí Archives: various collections.

'History of St. Paul's Evangelical Lutheran Church, Wilmington, North Carolina, 1858–1958'. https://archive.org/stream/historyofstpaulsoohess/historyofstpaulsoohess_djvu.txt.

Immigrant Ships Transcribers Guild. https://immigrantships.net/v6/1800v6/germania18680321_02.html.

National Archives and Records Administration (NARA), Washington DC: Soundex Index to Naturalization Petitions for the United States District and Circuit Courts, Northern District of Illinois and Immigration and Naturalization Service District 9, 1840–1950 (M1285); Microfilm Serial: M1285; Microfilm Roll: 103.

Records of the US Customs Service, RG36, Series T844, Roll: 24. http://search/ancestry.com/content/viewerpf.aspx?h=457252&db=bpl&id=mdt844_24-0424&sp=0.

Staatsarchive Hamburg, vol. 373-7 I, VIII A 1, Band 272, p. 4269. Microfilm no. K_1834. www. ancestry.de.

USBNA (United States Baháʼí National Archives). Wilmette, Illinois. Various collections.

US Census, 1880.

US City Directories 1821–1898. http://search.ancestry.com/content/viewerpf.aspx?h=1032570572&db=USDirectories&id=15952200&sp=0.

Washington DC Bahá'í Archives, Hannen-Knobloch Collection.

Washington DC Directories. Genealogy.com.

Wilmette Institute Library. http://wilmetteinstitute.org/library.

Newspapers and periodicals

Asheville Citizen Times (1897).

Bahá'í Nachrichten

Baha'i Newsletter. https://bahai.works/Baha%27i_News_Letter/.

Bahá'í Studies Review

The Brooklyn Daily Eagle. Newspapers.com.

The Church Times

The Daily Review. Wilmington, North Carolina. http://chroniclingamerica.loc.gov.

Der Deutsche Correspondent. http://chroniclingamerica.loc.gov.

Evening Star. http://chroniclingamerica.loc.gov.

Oregonian. Portland, OR. GenealogyBank.com.

Philadelphia Inquirer. GenealogyBank.com.

The San Francisco Call. http://chroniclingamerica.loc.gov.

The Sun. New York, 1833–1916.

New York Herald

Sonne der Wahrheit: Organ des Deutschen Bahá'í-Bundes

Star of the West: The Bahai Magazine. Periodical, 25 vols. 1910–1935. Vols. 1–14 RP Oxford: George Ronald, 1978.

St. Catherines Standard. Ontario, Canada. St. Catherines Public Library Online Resources.

Trenton Evening Times. Trenton, NJ. Various issues, 1884–1903. GenealogyBank.com.

Trenton State Gazette. GenealogyBank.com.

The Washington Post

The Washington Times. https://chroniclingamerica.loc.gov.

Aalen 161, 174, 177, 190, 236, 242, 267

NOTES AND REFERENCES

Introduction
1. 'Abdu'l-Bahá, *Tablets of the Divine Plan*, p. 41.

1 The Knobloch Family
1. Blackbourn, *History of Germany 1780–1918*, p. 49.
2. Reymann Banken, *Geschichte der Stadt Bautzen Bearbeitet von Richard Reymann Banken*, p. 917 – 2002A20515.
3. Smith, *Bahá'ís in the West*, p. 88.
4. Washington DC Bahá'í Archives, Hannen-Knobloch Collection, Box 3: Alma's memoirs.
5. Seifert, *Der Dom Sankt Petri zu Bautzen*, p. 8.
6. Blackbourn, *History of Germany 1780–1918*, p. 146.
7. ibid. p. 147.
8. Staatsarchiv Hamburg, *Hamburger Passagierlisten*, Mikrofilmnummer: K_1712 373-7 I, VIII A 1 Band 021 A.
9. Immigrant Ships Transcribers Guild, passenger nos. 333, 334 and 335. National Archives and Records Administration, Film M237, Reel 292, List 201.
10. *Evening Star*, 24 June 1878.
11. US Census, 1880, Obituary of Amalie Knobloch.
12. *Annual Report of the Commissioner of Patents for the Year 1879*, Thursday 1 January 1880; U.S. Patent and Trademark Office Patents, 1790–1909, patent No. 215.940.
13. 'Success of a Wilmington Enterprise', in *The Daily Review*, 7 December 1887.
14. 'A Home Enterprise', ibid. 30 August 1887.
15. Burke, 'Without Due Process: Lynching in North Carolina 1880–1900'.
16. Washington DC Bahá'í Archives, Hannen-Knobloch Collection, Box 8: Pauline Hannen memoirs.
17. 'History of St. Paul's Evangelical Lutheran Church, Wilmington, North Carolina, 1858–1958'.
18. ibid.
19. 'Concert for Church Expenses an Enjoyable Evening of Music in St. Mathew's Lutheran Church', in *The Brooklyn Daily Eagle*, 13 December 1889, see also *The Daily Review*, 18 September 1889, p. 1.
20. US City Directories 1821–1898: Knoblochs at 31 Massachusetts Avenue.
21. *Der Deutsche Correspondent*, 26 July 1893; *Evening Star*, 29 July 1893, p. 2.

22. *Evening Star*, 21 October 1893, p. 7.
23. *Washington Post*, Thursday 9 November 1893, p. 5.
24. District of Columbia Deaths and Burials, 1840–1964: Paul Gerhart Martin Knobloch, 03 Mar. 1894.
25. *Evening Star*, 21 June 1902, p. 3; ibid. 28 June 1902.
26. In the 1900 Federal Census Fanny Knobloch is listed on 8 June 1900 as living at 86 Green Street, Cumberland, Maryland, Allegheny County, as a boarder at the home of Family Elizabeth and Helen Paisely. Her job is listed as Rep Aqts. Pate. Medicine. The Cumberland County City Directory, 1901, lists Fannie A. Knobloch as a manager of Eastern Viavi Co. and her address as bds. 86 Green.

2 Discovery of the Bahá'í Faith

1. Hannen Moe, *Fanny Knobloch: An Adventuresome Spirit*, Manuscript page, 65–6 in progress.
2. USBNA, Ahmad Sohrab Collection: Letter from Pauline Hannen, May 1909.
3. Hannen Moe, *A Flame with Devotion: The Hannen and Knobloch Families and the Early Days of the Bahá'í Faith in America*, p. 20.
4. ibid.
5. Gail, *Summon Up Remembrance*, pp. 180–81.
6. Hannen Moe, *A Flame with Devotion*, p. 20.
7. *Evening Star*, Monday 24 June 1901, p. 7; Baltimore Passenger Lists, 1820–1948 and 1954–1957, National Archives and Records Administration (NARA); Records of the US Customs Service, RG36, Series T844, Roll 24; *Der Deutsche Correspondent*, 20 June 1901 and 7 February 1902.
8. Washington DC Bahá'í Archives, Hannen-Knobloch Collection, Box 2: Alma's memoirs. These general memoirs are written on loose sheets of paper; one set of these is written chronologically by year. All of them are handwritten.
9. ibid.: Alma's chronological memoirs.
10. ibid.: Alma's memoirs.
11. ibid.: Alma's chronological memoirs.
12. ibid.; also USBNA, Hannen-Knobloch Collection: Letter from Pauline Hannen, May 1909.
13. Washington DC Bahá'í Archives, Hannen-Knobloch Collection, Box 2: Alma's memoirs.
14. ibid.: Alma's chronological memoirs.
15. ibid.
16. 'Abdu'l-Bahá, *Tablets of Abdul-Baha Abbas*, vol. II, pp. 243–4. Also in Washington DC Bahá'í Archives, Hannen-Knobloch Collection, Box 1. Translated by Ahmad Sohrab, 26 December 1903, Washington DC, and sent 'Through his honor Mirza Esphahani to the Maid-Servant of God, Alma S. Knobloch, Washington, D. C.'

3 Mírzá Abu'l-Faḍl

1. *The Washington Times*, 24 June 1902, p. 3.
2. ibid. 28 February 1904.
3. Gail, *Summon Up Remembrance*, pp. 180–81.
4. USBNA, Ahmad Sohrab Collection: Letter from Pauline Hannen to Ahmad Sohrab, May 1909.
5. Washington DC Baháʼí Archives, Hannen-Knobloch Collection, Box 2: Alma's memoirs.
6. ibid.
7. ibid.
8. ibid.
9. *Oregonian*, 9 March 1906, p. 5, and 11 March 1906, p. 27.
10. See https://bahaipedia.org/Hyde_Dunn.
11. *The Baháʼí World*, vol. V (1932–1934), pp. 180–85.
12. Washington DC Baháʼí Archives, Hannen-Knobloch Collection, Box 2: Alma's memoirs.
13. ibid.
14. USBNA, Ahmad Sohrab Collection: Letter from Pauline Hannen to Ahmad Sohrab, May 1909.
15. Washington DC Baháʼí Archives, Hannen-Knobloch Collection, Box 2: Alma's memoirs.
16. ibid.
17. ibid.

4 The Church

1. Stockman, 'The American Baháʼí Identity, 1894–1921'.
2. *Evening Star*. 16 July 1904.
3. *Evening Star*, 22 October 1904.
4. Is. 9:6–7.
5. Washington DC Baháʼí Archives, Hannen-Knobloch Collection, Box 2: Alma's memoirs.
6. ibid.
7. Luke 17: 20–30.
8. Washington DC Baháʼí Archives, Hannen-Knobloch Collection, Box 2: Alma's memoirs.
9. ibid.
10. ibid.
11. ibid.
12. ibid.
13. ibid.
14. ibid.
15. USBNA, Ahmad Sohrab Collection: Letter from Alma to Mírzá Abu'l-Faḍl, 28 November 1904.
16. Tablet from ʻAbdu'l-Bahá to Amalie Knobloch, translated by Hussein Rouhy, quoted in Hannen Moe, *A Flame with Devotion: The Hannen*

and *Knobloch Families and the Early Days of the Bahá'í Faith in America*, pp. 52–3.

5 Bringing the Black Community into the Faith

1. USBNA, Ahmad Sohrab Collection: Letter from Pauline Hannen, May 1909. See also Buck, 'Alain Locke: Faith and Philosophy', p. 38.
2. Washington DC Bahá'í Archives, Hannen-Knobloch Collection, Box 2: Alma's memoirs.
3. Buck, 'Alain Locke: Faith and Philosophy', p. 33.
4. Stockman, *The Bahá'í Faith in America*, vol. 2, p. 225.
5. ibid.
6. Washington DC Directories, at Genealogy.com.
7. Washington DC Bahá'í Archives, Hannen-Knobloch Collection, Box 3: Alma's notebooks.
8. Tablet from 'Abdu'l-Bahá to Pocahontas Pope, in Buck, 'Alain Locke: Faith and Philosophy', p. 41. This Tablet is also found in USBNA, Carl Hannen Family Collection. See also https://bahaichronicles.org/pocahontas-pope/, where 'Abdu'l-Bahá's Tablet to Pocahontas Pope is given as follows:

   > Render thanks to the Lord that among that race thou art the first believer, arisen to guide others. It is my hope that through the bounties and favours of the Abha Beauty thy countenance may be illumined, thy disposition pleasing, and thy fragrance diffused, that thine eyes may be seeing, thine ears attentive, thy tongue eloquent, thy heart filled with supreme glad-tidings, and thy soul refreshed by divine fragrances, so that thou mayest arise among that race and occupy thyself with the edification of the people, and become filled with light. Although the pupil of the eye is black, it is the source of light. Thou shalt likewise be. The disposition should be bright, not the appearance. Therefore, with supreme confidence and certitude, say: 'O God! Make me a radiant light, a shining lamp, and a brilliant star, so that I may illumine the hearts with an effulgent ray from Thy Kingdom of Abha.'

9. Washington DC Bahá'í Archives, Hannen-Knobloch Collection, Box 3: Alma's notebooks.
10. Washington DC Bahá'í Archives, Hannen-Knobloch Collection: Tablet from 'Abdu'l-Bahá to Charles Mason Remey, 12 December 1906, sent through Hooper Harris. Also in USBNA, Louis Gregory Collection and Hannen-Knobloch Collection. Published in Buck, 'The Bahá'í "Pupil of the Eye" Metaphor – What Does It Mean?'.

6 A Missed Pilgrimage

1. USBNA, Ahmad Sohrab Collection: Letter from Alma to Mírzá Abu'l-Faḍl, 28 November 1904.
2. USBNA, Hannen Knobloch Collection: Letter from Mírzá Abu'l-Faḍl to Alma S. Knobloch, 22 November 1904.
3. Gail, *Summon Up Remembrance*, p. 148.

4. USBNA, Ahmad Sohrab Collection: Letter from Alma to Mírzá Abu'l-Faḍl, 28 November 1904.
5. Balyuzi, *'Abdu'l-Bahá*, pp. 112–14.
6. Taherzadeh, *The Covenant of Bahá'u'lláh*, p. 232.
7. Grundy, *Ten Days in the Light of Acca*, pp. 81–6.
8. Redman, *Visiting 'Abdu'l-Bahá*, vol. 1, p. 117.
9. Quoted ibid.
10. *Evening Star*, 20 June 1904.
11. Washington DC Bahá'í Archives, Hannen-Knobloch Collection, Box 4: Tablet from 'Abdu'l-Bahá to Mme d'Ange d'Astre, 9 August 1903.
12. ibid. Box 2: Alma's chronological memoirs.
13. ibid.
14. ibid. Box 3: Letter to Alma from Joseph Hannen, 3 October 1906.
15. http://gw.geneanet.org/gdevienne09?lang=nl&p=georgina&marie&n=baze.

7 Homefront Pioneering in New York State

1. Washington DC Bahá'í Archives, Hannen-Knobloch Collection, Box 1: Supplication sent to 'Abdu'l-Bahá by the believers who were gathered at Camp Mineola in the Summer of 1905 and the Tablet He sent in response; Hannen-Knobloch Collection, Box 6: Leone St. Clair Barnitz declaration card.
2. ibid. Hannen-Knobloch Collection, Box 7: Letter from Alma to Pauline written circa 1908.
3. ibid. Box 2: Alma's experiences with 'Abdu'l-Bahá.
4. USBNA, Ahmad Sohrab Collection: Letter from Henrietta Mills in Buffalo to Ahmad Sohrab, 14 May 1907.
5. Washington DC Bahá'í Archives, Hannen-Knobloch Collection, Box 2: Alma's memoirs.
6. See https://centenary.bahai.us/news/abdul-baha-will-come-buffalo-anyway-june.
7. Washington DC Bahá'í Archives, Hannen-Knobloch Collection, Box 2: Alma's experiences with 'Abdu'l-Bahá.
8. USBNA, House of Spirituality Chicago: Letter from Henrietta Mills in Buffalo to the House of Spirituality, 17 October 1905.
9. ibid.: Letter from the House of Spirituality to Henrietta Mills, 6 November 1905.
10. Washington DC Bahá'í Archives, Hannen-Knobloch Collection, Box 2: Alma's experiences with 'Abdu'l-Bahá.
11. Tablet from 'Abdu'l-Bahá to Alma Knobloch, in *Tablets of Abdul-Baha Abbas*, vol. II, p. 244. Also in Washington DC Bahá'í Archives, Hannen-Knobloch Collection, Box 3: 'Translated by Mirza Ahmad Espahani Washington D.C.'
12. Tablet from 'Abdu'l-Bahá to Mason Remey, in *Tablets of Abdul-Baha Abbas*, vol. II, pp. 467–8. Also in USBNA, Charles Mason Remey Collection, 14 November 1906.

13. Washington DC Bahá'í Archives, Hannen-Knobloch Collection, Box 2: Alma's memoirs.
14. Tablet from 'Abdu'l-Bahá to Alma Knobloch, 12 December 1906, in *Tablets of Abdul-Baha Abbas*, vol. II, p. 245. Also in USBNA, Fanny Lesch Collection.
15. van den Hoonaard, *The Origins of the Bahá'í Community of Canada, 1898–1948*, p. 35.
16. Washington DC Bahá'í Archives, Hannen-Knobloch Collection, Box 3: Letter from Alma in Buffalo to 'Beloved Ones at Home', 6 August 1906.
17. Tablet from 'Abdu'l-Bahá to Amelia Shadd Williamson, in *Tablets of Abdul-Baha Abbas*, vol. III, p. 554. Also in Washington DC Bahá'í Archives, Hannen-Knobloch Collection, Box 1, translated by Mirza Esphahani, 9 December 1906.
18. See https://coloredconventions.org/black-mobility/delegates/mary-ann-shadd-cary/.
19. See Stockman, *Thornton Chase: First American Bahá'í*.
20. See Gourdin and Greene, *Voices from the Past 104th Infantry Regiment, USCT Colored Civil War Soldiers from South Carolina*. See also National Park Service Civil War Soldier's database at https://www.nps.gov/civilwar/search-soldiers-detail.htm?soldierId=097C08A3-DC7A-DF11-BF36-B8AC6F5D926A.
21. Rhodes, *Mary Ann Shadd Cary: The Black Press and Protest in the Nineteenth Century*, p. 46.
22. *St. Catherines Standard*, 6 October 1906.
23. van den Hoonaard, *The Origins of the Bahá'í Community of Canada, 1898–1948*, p. 61.
24. Washington DC Bahá'í Archives, Hannen-Knobloch Collection, Box 2: Letter from Alma in Buffalo to 'Beloved Ones at Home', 6 August 1906.
25. ibid.
26. Tablet to the Spiritual Assembly of Buffalo, in *Tablets of Abdul-Baha Abbas*, vol. III, pp. 554–5. Also in USBNA, Thornton Chase Collection. Translated 7 September 1906.
27. Washington DC Bahá'í Archives, Hannen-Knobloch Collection, Box 2: Alma to 'Beloved ones at Home', 6 August 1906.
28. ibid. Box 5: Newspaper article with no date showing a talk Alma gave in Buffalo.
29. USBNA, Hannen Knobloch Collection: Letter from Pauline to Alma, 29 August 1906.
30. Washington DC Bahá'í Archives, Hannen-Knobloch Collection, Box 5: Letter from Charles Mason Remey to Alma Knobloch, 7 September 1906.
31. See http://bahaihistoricalfacts.blogspot.com/2015/07/1900-board-of-counsel-of-bahai-assembly.html.
32. Washington DC Bahá'í Archives, Hannen-Knobloch Collection, Box

5: Letter from Charles Mason Remey to Alma Knobloch, 28 September 1906.
33. ibid.: Letter from Charles Mason Remey to Alma Knobloch, 6 October 1906.
34. USBNA, Hannen Knobloch Collection, Box 16: Letter from Ralph Osborne in Syracuse to Alma Knobloch, 2 October 1906.
35. ibid.
36. ibid.
37. ibid.: Letter from Ralph Osborne in Syracuse to Alma Knobloch, 9 October 1906.
38. ibid.: Letter from Ralph Osborne in Syracuse to Alma Knobloch 10 September 1906.
39. 'Insane', in *The Sun*, 13 October 1906, p. 8, image 8.
40. Washington DC Bahá'í Archives, Hannen-Knobloch Collection, 33, Box 5: Letter from Charles Mason Remey to Alma Knobloch in Buffalo, 6 October 1906.
41. ibid. 20 October 1906.
42. Tablet to the Spiritual Assembly of Buffalo, in *Tablets of Abdul-Baha Abbas*, vol. III, p. 555. Also in USBNA, Thornton Chase Collection, Box 8.
43. USBNA, Hannen Knobloch Collection, Box 17: Letter from Henrietta Mills in Buffalo to Alma Knobloch, 6 November 1906.
44. ibid.: Letter from Henrietta Mills to Alma Knobloch, 7 November 1906, postmark 8 November 1906.
45. Washington DC Bahá'í Archives, Hannen-Knobloch Collection, Box 1: Tablet from 'Abdu'l-Bahá to Amalia Knobloch. Translated by Mírzá Ahmad Esphahani 4 p.m., 9 December 1906.
46. Tablet from 'Abdu'l-Bahá to Alma Knobloch, in *Tablets of Abdul-Baha Abbas*, vol. II, pp. 245-6. Also in USBNA, Fanny Lesch Collection, 1906.
47. Tablet from 'Abdu'l-Bahá to Henrietta Mills, in *Tablets of Abdul-Baha Abbas*, vol. III, pp. 556-7. Also in USBNA, Fanny Lesch Collection, 1906.
48. USBNA, Hannen Knobloch Collection, Box 17, 24 February 1907.
49. Washington DC Bahá'í Archives, Hannen-Knobloch Collection, Box 1: Tablet from 'Abdu'l-Bahá to Alma Knobloch, translated on 16 February 1907.
50. USBNA, Ahmad Sohrab Collection, Box 6: Letter from Henrietta Mills in Buffalo to Ahmad Sohrab, 12 March 1907.
51. ibid. Box 1: Tablet from 'Abdu'l-Bahá to Ahmad Sohrab, 3 March 1907.
52. ibid. Box 6: Letter from Henrietta Mills in Buffalo to Ahmad Sohrab, 13 March 1907.
53. ibid. Box 1: Letter from Henrietta Mills in Buffalo to Ahmad Sohrab, 1 May 1907.
54. Washington DC Bahá'í Archives, Hannen-Knobloch Collection, Box 2: Alma's memoirs.

8 Dr Edwin Fisher

1. Washington DC Baháʼí Archives, Hannen-Knobloch Collection, Box 7: Letter from Alma in Stuttgart to 'Dearly beloved Pauline and Joseph', 31 December 1909: 'Regarding Dr Fisher, he said he came here to Stuttgart the later part of April 1905.'
2. Cumbler, *Social History of Economic Decline; Business, Politics and Work in Trenton*, p. 2.
3. 'First Gas Was Tried then Chloroform: Murdered Mrs Kniffin's Little Boy Lennie Prattles of the "Burglaries" and Throws a Flood of Light on the Crime', in *New York Herald*, Monday 6 January 1890, p. 3.
4. ibid.
5. 'City Notes', in *Trenton Evening Times*, Thursday, 29 May 1884.
6. *Trenton Evening Times*, Sunday, 4 March 1888, p. 5; see also http://en.wikipedia.org/wiki/Pennsylvania_College_of_Dental_Surgery.
7. FamilySearch: New Jersey, Marriages, 1678–1985, K. Edwin Fisher and Josephine Dickinson, 11 August 1887; citing reference p. 81 In 01, FHL microfilm 495706.
8. 'To Give a Clinic in Germany', in *Trenton Evening Times*, Friday, 6 July 1888, p. 3.
9. 'Steamer Werra, July 15, 1888', in *New York Herald*, Wednesday, 8 May 1889, p. 7.
10. 'Sport in the Saddle: Ladies and Gentlemen Who Find Pleasure in Horseback Exercise', in *Trenton Evening Times*, Sunday, 29 November 1891, p. 3.
11. 'Jottings from New Jersey', in *Philadelphia Inquirer*, Sunday, 23 April 1893, p. 13.
12. FamilySearch: New Jersey, Births and Christenings, 1660–1980, Edwin Fisher in entry for Fisher, 17 May 1889; citing reference v32 p 319, FHL microfilm 494214.
13. FamilySearch: New Jersey, Births and Christenings, 1720–1988, Fisher, 1892; citing reference V37-345-12, FHL microfilm 589793.
14. Cumbler, *Social History of Economic Decline: Business, Politics and Work in Trenton*, p. 2.
15. ibid.
16. See, for example, Steeples and Whitten, *Democracy in Desperation: The Depression of 1893*.
17. 'A Thief at the Y.M.C.A.: Frank Gaston Arrested for Stealing Valuables', in *Trenton Evening Times*, Wednesday, 6 March 1895, p. 5.
18. Ancestry.com: New Jersey, State Census, 1895 Record.
19. 'Dr Fisher's Sad Condition: The Well-Known Young Dentist Suddenly Bereft of His Reason while Seeking Health', in *Trenton Evening Times*, Sunday, 30 June 1895, p. 1.
20. *Trenton State Gazette*, vol. XLV, issue 1 (Saturday, 1 January 1898), p. 10.
21. *Trenton Evening Times*, Monday, 4 January 1897, p. 2.
22. 'People We Meet', in *Trenton Evening Times*, Sunday, 14 March 1897, p. 4.

23. *Asheville Citizen Times*, 27 November 1897, p. 4.
24. 'Dr Fisher Ends Visit', in *Trenton Evening Times*, Wednesday, 26 August 1903, p. 6.
25. Stockman, 'The Bahá'í Faith in England and Germany', in *World Order*, vol. 27, no. 3, p. 35.
26. Stockman, *The Bahá'í Faith in America*, vol. 2, 242–3.
27. Gail, *Summon Up Remembrance*, p. 171.
28. Wilmette Institute Library, letter from T. Chase to Mrs Mariam Haney, Chicago, 8 November 1904, at http://wilmetteinstitute.org/library/ch.1903-04.html; letter from T. Chase to I. Brittingham, copy 81, Chicago, 14 September 1902, at http://wilmetteinstitute.org/library/ch.1897-1902.html.
29. USBNA, Ahmad Sohrab Collection: Letter from Edwin Fisher in New York, 434 Fifth Avenue, to Ahmad Sohrab ('Dear Brother in the Truth'), 19 September 1903.
30. ibid.: Letter from Edwin Fisher in New York, 434 Fifth Avenue, to Ahmad Sohrab ('Dear Brother'), 23 September 1903.
31. Bahá'u'lláh, *Tablets of Bahá'u'lláh Revealed after the Kitáb-i-Aqdas*, p. 26.
32. See https://bahai-library.com/stockman_chase_notes#1905.
33. ibid.
34. USBNA, Ahmad Sohrab Collection: Letter from Edwin Fisher to Ahmad Sohrab ('Dear Brother'), 5 June 1904.

9 Edwin Fisher Raises the Call in Germany

1. Zander, *Die Mormonen im Südwesten Deutschlands auf d. Spuren ihres Lebens und ihrer Geschichte*.
2. Stockman, 'The Bahá'í Faith in England and Germany', in *World Order*, vol. 27, no. 3, p. 35.
3. '100-Jahre Bahá'í Religionen in Deutschland', in *Bahá'í Nachrichten*, 4/162, 1 September 2005.
4. Adamson and Hainsworth, *Historical Dictionary of the Bahá'í Faith*.
5. Stockman. 'The Bahá'í Faith in England and Germany', p. 35.
6. USBNA, Bosch Collection: Memories of Wilhelm Herrigel.
7. Washington DC Bahá'í Archives, Hannen-Knobloch Collection, Box 5: Alma's memoirs of Edwin Fisher.
8. USBNA, Tablet from 'Abdu'l-Bahá to Edwin Fisher, 16 June 1907. Part of this Tablet, about eating meat, is published in *Lights of Guidance*, no. 1006, p. 296, as 'to an individual, translated from the Persian'.
9. USBNA, Ahmad Sohrab Collection: Letter from Edwin Fisher to Ahmad Sohrab, 8 July 1907.

10 Alma's Call to Germany

1. Alma S. Knobloch, 'The Call to Germany' in *The Bahá'í World*, vol. VII (1936–1938), p. 732.
2. Tablet from 'Abdu'l-Bahá to Ahmad Sohrab, in USBNA, Ahmad Sohrab Collection, Box 1: revealed 10 May 1907 and translated 6

June 1907. Also in the German National Bahá'í Archives, Hermann Grossmann Files B 10 D 1907–1921 A1.
3. Washington DC Bahá'í Archive, Hannen-Knobloch Collection, Box 5: Letter from Fanny to Alma, no date, probably May or June 1907.
4. Bahá'u'lláh, *The Kitáb-i-Aqdas*, para. 58, p. 40. 2.
5. Washington DC Bahá'í Archives, Hannen Knobloch Collection, Box 7: Letter from Pauline to 'Dearest and most wonderfully best Sister in the Greatest Cause!', no date, probably May or June 1907.
6. USBNA, Hannen Knobloch Collection.
7. Alma S. Knobloch, 'The Call to Germany', in *The Bahá'í World*, vol. VII, p. 732.
8. ibid. A slightly different translation of this Tablet appears in USBNA, Fanny Lesch Papers, giving the date of the Tablet as 7 October 1907. Also in the Washington DC Bahá'í Archives, Hannen-Knobloch Collection, Box 1; and German National Bahá'í Archives, Hermann Grossmann Files B 06 E 1907 A1.
9. Washington DC Bahá'í Archives, Hannen-Knobloch Collection, Box 2: Alma's memoirs.

11 Unusual Confirmations

1. 'Abdu'l-Bahá, Tablet to the Bahá'ís of the United States and Canada, in *Tablets of the Divine Plan*, p. 41.
2. Washington DC Bahá'í Archives, Hannen-Knobloch Collection, Box 5: Notebook of Alma Knobloch. She wrote the story in her notebook many times and labelled the versions X and XX and 5X.
3. ibid. Box 7: 'Alma's experiences with Abdu'l-Bahá'.
4. ibid. Box 1: Letter from Alma on board the *Dampfer Main* to 'Beloved ones at home',17 July 1907.
5. ibid.
6. ibid. Box 5: Notebooks of Alma Knobloch.
7. ibid. Box 1: Letter from Alma on board the *Dampfer Main* to 'Beloved ones at home',17 July 1907.
8. ibid. Box 3: Letter from Alma in Stuttgart to 'my own dear sister Fanny', 29 August 1907.
9. ibid.
10. ibid.
11. USBNA, Hannen Knobloch Collection: Letter from Geo F. Bredemeier to Alma, 20 July 1922.
12. Alma S. Knobloch, 'The Call to Germany', in *The Bahá'í World*, vol. VII, p. 733.
13. USBNA, Thornton Chase Collection: Letter from Thornton Chase to William Herrigel at Hölderlein St. 35, Stuttgart, 5 May 1910.
14. Alma S. Knobloch, 'The Call to Germany', in *The Bahá'í World*, vol. VII, p. 734.
15. USBNA, Ahmad Sohrab Collection: Letter from Edwin Fisher in Stuttgart to Ahmad Sohrab, 8 July 1907.

16. Washington DC Bahá'í Archives, Hannen-Knobloch Collection, Box 7: Letter from Alma in Stuttgart to 'dearly Beloved Ones at Home!', 25 May 1908
17. ibid. Box 3: Letter from Alma in Stuttgart to 'My Own Dear Sister Fanny', 12 September 1907.
18. ibid.
19. ibid. Box 3: Letter from Alma in Stuttgart to 'My Own Dear Sister Fanny', 29 August 1907.
20. ibid. Box 1: Letter from Alma in Stuttgart to 'Dearly Beloved Ones at Home', 28 November 1907.
21. ibid.
22. ibid. Box 2: Alma's memoirs.
23. ibid. Box 3: Letter from Alma Letter from Alma in Stuttgart to 'My own dear sister Fanny, 12 September 1907..
24. Jasion, *Never be Afraid to Dare: The Story of General Jack*, p. 216.
25. Washington DC Bahá'í Archives, Hannen-Knobloch Collection, Box 7: Letter from Alma to 'Dearest Pauline', 1 August 1913. (No location for Alma given.)
26. ibid. Box 1: 'XIII Memories', Notebook of Alma Knobloch.
27. ibid. Box 2: Alma's memoirs.
28. ibid. Box 3: Letter from Alma in Stuttgart to 'My Beloved Sister Fanny', 5 October 1907.
29. ibid. Box 7: Letter from Alma to 'My own dear sister Fanny', 12 September 1907.
30. ibid. Box 1: 'XIII Memoires', Notebook of Alma Knobloch; Box 1: Letter from Alma in Stuttgart, Olga Str. 102, to 'Most dearly beloved ones', 3 November 1907.
31. ibid. Box 5: Letter from Alma in Stuttgart to 'My own dear sister Fanny', 16 October 1907.
32. ibid. Box 1: Letter from Alma in Stuttgart, Olgastr 102, to 'Dearly Beloved ones', 3 November 1907.
33. ibid.
34. ibid.
35. ibid.: Letter from Alma to 'Dearly Beloved Ones at Home', 28 November 1907.
36. ibid.: 'XIII Memoires', Notebook of Alma Knobloch.
37. ibid. Box 7: Letter from Alma to 'My dearest sister Pauline', 13 November 1907.
38. ibid. Box 1: Letter from Alma in Stuttgart, Olgastr 102, to 'Dearly Beloved Ones', 3 November 1907.
39. ibid. Box 1: Letter from Alma in Stuttgart to 'Beloved Mama and Fanny', 9 December 1907.
40. See https://history.blog.gov.uk/2017/08/31/anglo-russian-entente-1907/.

12 Rapid Expansion in Stuttgart

1. Steinlein, *Geschichtliches über die Christliche Wissenschaft in Stuttgart*, pp. 1–2.
2. ibid. See also Smith, 'Early History of Christian Science in Germany', in *The Christian Science Journal*, September 1934, at http://de.wikipedia.org/wiki/Christian_Science.
3. See http://www.christian-science-stuttgart.de/hp/Geschichte.html.
4. USBNA, Bosch Collection, Box 3: Letter from Wilhelm Herrigel to John Bosch, 29 January 1910.
5. Washington DC Baháʼí Archives, Hannen-Knobloch Collection, Box 1: Letter from Alma in Stuttgart to Ahmad Sohrab, 19 February 1908.
6. ibid.: Letter from Alma in Stuttgart to 'My own dear sister Fanny', 16 October 1907.
7. USBNA, Bosch Collection, Box 3: Letter from Wilhelm Herrigel to John Bosch, 29 January 1910.
8. Washington DC Baháʼí Archives, Hannen-Knobloch Collection, Box 2: Alma's memoirs; Box 1: 'XIII Memoires', Notebook of Alma Knobloch, 4 April 1908. Papers, Box 2: Notebook of Alma Knobloch, 4 April 1908.
9. ibid. Box 1: Letter from Alma in Stuttgart to 'My own dear sister Fanny', 16 October 1907.
10. ibid.: Letter from Alma to 'Dearly Beloved ones at home', 4 January 1908.
11. USBNA, Bosch Collection, Box 3: Letter from Wilhelm Herrigel to John Bosch, 29 January 1910.
12. ibid. Charles Mason Remey Collection: Letter from Wilhelm Herrigel to C. M. Remey, 7 July 1926.
13. ibid.
14. Alma was under the impression that Sydney Sprague was English (he was American).
15. Washington DC Baháʼí Archives, Hannen-Knobloch Collection, Box 1: Letter from Alma in Stuttgart to Ahmad Sohrab, 19 February 1908.
16. USBNA, Bosch Collection: Letter from Wilhelm Herrigel to John Bosch, 29 January 1910.
17. ibid. Charles Mason Remey Collection: Letter from Wilhelm Herrigel to C. M. Remey, 7 July 1926.
18. Washington DC Baháʼí Archives, Hannen-Knobloch Collection, Box 4: Letter from Alma in Stuttgart to Ahmad Sohrab, 19 February 1908.
19. ibid. Box 2: Alma's memoirs.
20. See http://www.christian-science-stuttgart.de/hp/Geschichte.html.
21. Washington DC Baháʼí Archives, Hannen-Knobloch Collection, Box 2: Alma's memoirs, 4 April 1908.
22. See Zander, *Die Mormonen im Südwesten Deutschlands auf d. Spuren ihres Lebens und ihrer Geschichte*.

13 Bahá'í Identity, Community Building and Consolidation

1. Washington DC Bahá'í Archives, Hannen-Knobloch Collection, Box 1: Tablet from 'Abdu'l-Bahá to Fanny Knobloch, 10 April 1907, translated by Mírzá Ahmad Esphahani 23 May 1907.
2. ibid. Box 1: Letter from Alma in Stuttgart to 'Beloved sister Fanny', 4 April 1908.
3. ibid. Box 7: Letter from Alma in Stuttgart to 'Dearly beloved sister Pauline', 3 June 1908.
4. ibid. Box 3: Letter from Alma in Stuttgart to 'My own precious sister Fanny', 5 March 1908.
5. ibid. Box 1: Letter from Alma in Stuttgart to 'My beloved sister Fanny', 4 April 1908.
6. ibid.
7. ibid.
8. ibid.
9. ibid.
10. ibid. Box 7: Letter from Alma in Stuttgart to 'My own precious Sister Pauline', 13 June 1908.
11. ibid. Box 1: Letter from Alma in Stuttgart to 'My beloved sister Fanny', 4 April 1908.
12. ibid.
13. ibid. Box 7: Letter from Alma in Stuttgart to 'My precious sister Pauline', from Stuttgart, 14 February 1910.
14. ibid. Box 1: Letter from Alma in Stuttgart to 'Dearly beloved ones', 2 June 1908.
15. ibid.: Letter from Alma in Stuttgart to 'Dearly beloved ones at home', 18 July 1908.
16. ibid. Box 7: Letter from Alma in Stuttgart to 'My own precious sister Pauline', 13 June 1908.
17. ibid. Box 1: Letter from Alma in Leipzig to 'Most beloved ones', 14 October 1908.
18. ibid.: Letter from Alma in Stuttgart to 'Dearly beloved ones at home', 2 June 1908.
19. ibid. Letter from Alma, 'Allaho Abha! My own precious sister', 1908 (no date).
20. Shoghi Effendi, *Messages to the Bahá'í World, 1950–1957*, p. 157.
21. Washington DC Bahá'í Archives, Hannen-Knobloch Collection, Box 1: Letter from Alma in Stuttgart to 'Dearly beloved ones at home', 18 July 1908.
22. ibid.: Letter from Alma in Stuttgart to 'Dearly beloved ones at home', 2 October 1908.

14 Alma and Edwin Fisher

1. Washington DC Bahá'í Archives, Hannen-Knobloch Collection, Box 1: Letter from Alma in Stuttgart, Olgastr 102, to 'Most dearly beloved ones', 3 November 1907.

2. ibid.: Letter from Alma in Stuttgart to 'My own dear sister Fanny', 16 October 1907.
3. ibid.: Letter from Alma in Stuttgart, Olgastr 102, to 'Most dearly beloved ones', 3 November 1907.
4. ibid.: Letter from Alma in Stuttgart to 'My own dear sister Fanny" undated, 1907.
5. ibid. Box 7: Letter from Alma in Stuttgart to 'My own precious sister Pauline', 14 February 1910. In this later letter to Pauline, Alma explains the story about the medium and the beginning of the disunity.
6. ibid. Box 1: Letter from Alma in Stuttgart, Olgastr 102, to 'Most dearly beloved ones', 3 November 1907.
7. ibid. Box 7: Letter from Alma in Stuttgart to 'Beloved sister Pauline', 13 June 1908.
8. ibid.: Letter from Alma in Stuttgart to 'Dearly beloved sister Pauline', 3 June 1908.
9. ibid. Box 3: Letter from Alma in Munich to 'My own precious Fanny', 9 April 1915.
10. ibid.: Letter from Alma in Gera to 'My beloved sister Pauline', 5 October 1915.
11. ibid.: Letter from Alma in Leipzig Sehl to 'My precious sister Fanny' 3 November 1915.
12. ibid. Box 1: Letter from Alma in Stuttgart to 'Dearly beloved ones', 2 June 1908.
13. ibid.: Letter from Alma in Stuttgart to 'Dearly beloved ones at home', 18 July 1908.
14. ibid.: Letter from Alma in Stuttgart to 'Dearly beloved ones at home', 24 August 1908.

15 Invitation to the Holy Land, and the Passing of Amalie Knobloch

1. Washington DC Bahá'í Archives, Hannen-Knobloch Collection, Box 1: Letter from Alma in Stuttgart to 'Dearly beloved ones at home', 24 August 1908.
2. ibid.
3. ibid.: Letter from Alma in Stuttgart to 'My own dear sister Fanny', 15 June 1908.
4. ibid.: Letter from Alma in Stuttgart to 'Meine Liebe Gute Mama', 29 July 1908.
5. ibid.: Letter from Alma in Stuttgart to 'Dearly beloved ones at home', 24 August 1908.
6. ibid. Box 2: Alma's memoirs.
7. ibid. Box 1: Tablet from 'Abdu'l-Bahá 'to the Maidservants of the Merciful, Mrs. Hannen and Miss Fanny Knobloch', 9 June 1908.
8. ibid.: Letter from Alma in Stuttgart to 'Dearly Beloved Ones at Home', 2 October 1908.
9. ibid.: Letter from Alma in Leipzig to 'Most Beloved Ones', 14 October 1908.

10. ibid.
11. ibid.: Letter from Alma in Stuttgart to 'Dearly Beloved Ones at Home', 2 October 1908.
12. USBNA, Hannen Knobloch Collection: Letter from Pauline Hannen to 'My precious Sister Alma'; quoted in Hannen Moe, *A Flame with Devotion*, p. 104.
13. ibid. p. 105.
14. Washington DC Bahá'í Archives, Hannen-Knobloch Collection, Box 3: Letter from Fanny in Miami to 'Dearest Alma', 7 September 1932.
15. 'Abdu'l-Bahá, quoted in Finch, Knobloch and Knobloch, *Flowers Culled from the Rose Garden of Acca*, p. 16.
16. Hannen Moe, *A Flame with Devotion*, pp. 107–8.
17. Tablet from 'Abdu'l-Bahá for Amalie Knobloch, quoted in Finch, Knobloch and Knobloch, *Flowers Culled from the Rose Garden of Acca*, pp. 39–40.

16 Pilgrimage

1. Washington DC Bahá'í Archives, Hannen-Knobloch Collection, Box 1: Letter from Alma in Leipzig to 'Most Beloved Ones', 14 October 1908.
2. ibid: two handwritten copies of Tablet to Alma Knobloch, translated by Ahmad Sohrab 7 October, with a note to the effect that the letter from Ahmad was dated 9 October 1908.
3. ibid. Box 1: Letter from Alma, at Hotel Continental in Naples, Italy, to 'Dearly Beloved Ones' 23 October 1908.
4. See https://www.bahai.org/documents/essays/yazdi-ali-m/memories-abdul-baha.
5. Washington DC Bahá'í Archives, Hannen-Knobloch Collection, Box 5: 'Memoires', Notebook of Alma Knobloch.
6. ibid.
7. ibid. Box 2: Alma Knobloch, Notes at Acca,
8. See Stockman, *The Bahá'í Faith in America*, pp. 68, 109, 111, 116, 174–5.
9. Washington DC Bahá'í Archives, Hannen-Knobloch Collection, Box 5: 'Memoires', Notebook of Alma Knobloch.
10. ibid.
11. Finch, Knobloch and Knobloch, *Flowers Culled from the Rose Garden of Acca*, p. 2.
12. Reported words of 'Abdu'l-Bahá, ibid.
13. Reported words of 'Abdu'l-Bahá, ibid. p. 17.
14. ibid. p. 21.
15. Washington DC Bahá'í Archives, Hannen-Knobloch Collection, Box 5: 'Memoires', Notebook of Alma Knobloch.
16. ibid.
17. ibid.

18. ibid.
19. ibid.
20. ibid.
21. Washington DC Bahá'í Archives, Hannen-Knobloch Collection, Box 7: Letter from Alma to Pauline, 30 November 1909.
22. ibid. Box 2: Alma Knobloch, Notes at Acca.

17 Distractions

1. 'Abdu'l-Bahá, *Selections from the Writings of 'Abdu'l-Bahá*, no. 217, p. 270.
2. See Kuhn, *Psychoanalysis in Britain, 1893–1913: Histories and Historiography*.
3. Jasion, *Never Be Afraid to Dare*, pp. 37– 8.
4. Washington DC Bahá'í Archives, Hannen Knobloch Collection, Box 1: Letter from Alma at Hotel Continental, Naples, Italy to 'Dearly beloved ones', 23 October 1908.
5. ibid.: Letter from Alma in Leipzig to 'Most beloved ones', 14 October 1908.
6. ibid.: Tablet from 'Abdu'l-Bahá to the believers in Stuttgart, 12 November 1908.
7. ibid.: Letter from Alma in Degerloch, Stuttgart to 'Beloved ones at home', 10 January 1909.
8. ibid.: Letter from Alma in Degerloch, Stuttgart to 'Dearly beloved ones!', 31 December 1908.
9. Bahá'í International Community, *Century of Light*, p. 11.
10. Washington DC Bahá'í Archives, Hannen Knobloch Collection, Box 1: Letter from Alma in Degerloch, Stuttgart to 'Beloved ones at home', 10 January 1909.
11. 'Abdu'l-Bahá, *Selections from the Writings of 'Abdu'l-Bahá*, no. 45, p. 88.
12. USBNA, microfilm: Tablet from 'Abdu'l-Bahá to Alma Knobloch, translated 14 December 1908 by Mírzá Ahmad Esphahani, Washington DC. A different translation of this Tablet is in the Washington DC Bahá'í Archives.

18 Germany 'As Long as Possible'

1. Alma S. Knobloch, 'The Call to Germany', in *The Bahá'í World*, vol. VII, p. 732.
2. Washington DC Bahá'í Archives, Hannen-Knobloch Collection, Box 7: Letter from Alma in Stuttgart to 'Dearly Beloved Sister Pauline', 3 June 1908.
3. ibid. Box 3: Letter from Alma in Stuttgart to 'My Own Precious Sister Fanny', 5 March 1908.
4. ibid. Letter from Alma in Stuttgart to 'My Own Dear Sister Fanny', 15 June 1908.
5. ibid. Box 5: 'Memoires', Notebook of Alma Knobloch. Also quoted in Finch, Knobloch and Knobloch, *Flowers Culled from the Rose Garden of Acca*, p. 2.

NOTES AND REFERENCES

6. Washington DC Bahá'í Archives, Hannen-Knobloch Collection, Box 1: Letter from Alma in Degerloch, Stuttgart to 'Dearly Beloved Ones', 30 December 1908.
7. ibid. Box 7: letter from Alma in Degerloch to 'My Beloved Pauline', 15 May 1909.
8. ibid. Box 3: letter from Alma in Stuttgart to 'Dearly Beloved Sister Fanny', 3 January 1910.
9. ibid.: Letter from Alma in Stuttgart to 'My own precious sister Fanny', 25 January 1911.
10. ibid. Box 7: Letter from Alma in Stuttgart to 'My Dearest Sister', 3 January 1912.
11. ibid. Box 3: Alma in Leipzig to 'my Precious Sister Fanny', 23 April 1912.
12. ibid. Box 1: Letter from Alma in Degerloch, Stuttgart to 'Dearly Beloved Ones', 31 December 1908.
13. ibid.: Letter from Alma in Degerloch to 'My Own Dear Sister Fanny', 26 May 1909.
14. ibid.: Letter from Alma in Stuttgart to 'My Own Dear Sisters', 31 May 1909.
15. ibid. Box 3: Letter from Alma in Stuttgart to 'My own Dear Sister Fanny', 7 August 1909; also Box 7: Letter from Alma in Stuttgart to 'My Own Dear Beloved Sister Pauline', 11 August 1909.
16. ibid. Box 7: Letter from Alma in Stuttgart to 'My Own Dear Beloved Sister Pauline' 11 August 1909.
17. ibid. Box 3: Letter from Alma in Stuttgart to 'My Own Dear Sister Fanny', 14 August 1909.
18. ibid.: Letter from Alma in Stuttgart to My Own Dear Sister Fanny 12 September 1909.
19. ibid. Box 6: Letter from Alma in Stuttgart to 'My Dear brother Joseph', 12 August 1909.
20. ibid. Box 3: Letter from Alma in Stuttgart to 'My Own Dear Sister Fanny', 12 September 1909.

19 Beyond Stuttgart

1. Washington DC Bahá'í Archives, Hannen-Knobloch Collection, Box 4: Letter from Alma in Stuttgart to Ahmad Sohrab, 19 February 1908.
2. ibid. Box 7: Letter from Alma in Stuttgart to 'Dearly beloved sister Pauline', 3 June 1908.
3. ibid.: Letter from Alma in Stuttgart to 'My own precious sister Pauline', 13 June 1908.
4. *Sonne der Wahrheit*, Heft 9 (November 1924), p. 138.
5. Washington DC Bahá'í Archives, Hannen-Knobloch Collection, Box 1: Letter from Alma in Stuttgart to 'Dearest Sister', 25 February 1908.
6. *Sonne der Wahrheit*, Heft 9 (November 1924), p. 138. 8.
7. Washington DC Bahá'í Archives, Hannen-Knobloch Collection, Box

7: Letter from Alma in Stuttgart to 'My Own Precious Pauline', 30 March 1910; and Box 5: Alma's memoirs.
8. ibid. Box 7: Letter from Alma to 'My darling sister Pauline', 2 December 1910.
9. ibid. Box 1: Letter from Alma to 'Dearly beloved ones', 20 December 1909.
10. ibid. Box 7: Letter from Alma in Stuttgart to 'My own dear sister Pauline', 27 September 1909.
11. ibid. Box 3: Letter from Alma in Stuttgart to 'My Dear Beloved Sister' [Fanny], 4 December 1909.
12. ibid. Box 7: Letter from Alma in Stuttgart to 'Dearly Beloved Pauline and Joseph', 31 December 1909.
13. ibid.: Letter from Alma in Stuttgart to' My own dear beloved sister [Pauline] and brother [Joseph]!', 12 December 1910; and Box 3: Letter from Alma in Stuttgart to 'Dearly beloved sister Fanny', 3 January 1910.
14. ibid. Box 7: Letter from Alma in Stuttgart to 'My own precious sister Pauline', 14 February 1910.
15. ibid. Box 8: Letter from Alma in Stuttgart to 'My dearly beloved sister Fanny', 27 February 1910.
16. ibid.
17. ibid.
18. USBNA, microfilm; also in Washington DC Bahá'í Archives, Hannen-Knobloch Collection, Box 1: 'sent through Mr. Dreyfus in Paris to AK'.
19. *Star of the West*, vol. II, no. 17 (19 January 1912), p. 7.

20 The Stuttgart Board of Counsel

1. USBNA, microfilm.
2. USBNA, Hannen Knobloch Collection: Letter from Munírih Khánum from Mount Carmel to Alma, 27 February 1909.
3. Washington DC Bahá'í Archives, Hannen-Knobloch Collection, Box 3: Letter from Alma to 'My own precious sister Fanny', 13 March 1909.
4. ibid. Box 5: 'Alma's Memories of Dr Fischer'.
5. ibid. Box 3: Letter from Alma to 'My own precious sister Fanny', 27 April 1909.
6. ibid.
7. ibid. Box 1: handwritten duplicate with notes
8. ibid.: Letter from Alma in Degerloch to 'My own dear sisters and Joseph', 18 April 1909.
9. ibid.
10. ibid. Box 7: Letter from Alma to 'My own precious sister Pauline', February 1910.
11. ibid.
12. ibid.: Letter from Alma to 'My dear beloved sister Pauline', 2 August 1910.
13. ibid. Box 1: Letter from Alma to 'My precious Sisters', 12 May 1909.
14. ibid.: Letter from Alma to 'My own dear Sister Fanny', 28 June 1909.

NOTES AND REFERENCES

15. ibid. Box 1: Tablet from 'Abdu'l-Bahá to Margarethe Döring, translated 6 May 1909 by Ahmad Sohrab; handwritten pdf scanned in file 'AB tab hk collection'.
16. USBNA, microfilm: Tablet from 'Abdu'l-Bahá to Alma Knobloch, 10 June 1909.
17. Washington DC Bahá'í Archives, Hannen-Knobloch Collection, Box 1: Tablet from 'Abdu'l-Bahá to Wilhelm and Marie Herrigel, 3 July 1909.
18. ibid. Box 3: Letter from Alma to 'My own dear Fanny', 7 August 1909; also Box 7: Letter from Alma to 'My own dear beloved sister Pauline', 11 August 1909.
19. ibid.: Letter from Alma to 'My own dear Pauline', 12 September 1909.
20. ibid.: Letter from Alma to 'My own dear Pauline', 27 September 1909.
21. ibid.
22. ibid. Box 1: Tablet from 'Abdu'l-Bahá to Alma Knobloch, translated by Dr A. Fareed, 12 August 1909; also in USBNA, microfilm.

21 The Role of Women in the Community

1. Koven and Michel, 'Womanly Duties: Maternalist Politics and the Origins of Welfare States in France, Germany, Great Britain, and the United States, 1880–1920', in *The American Historical Review*, vol. 95, no. 4, pp. 1076–1108.
2. ibid. p. 1076.
3. ibid. p. 1078.
4. See https://www.marxists.org/archive/kollonta/1907/is-conferences.htm.
5. Washington DC Bahá'í Archives, Hannen-Knobloch Collection, Box 1: Letter from Alma in Stuttgart to 'My own dear sister Fanny', 16 October 1907.
6. ibid. Box 7: Letter from Alma in Stuttgart to 'My own dear sister Pauline', 2 August 1909.
7. ibid. Box 1: Letter from Alma in Stuttgart to 'Dearly beloved ones at home', 24 August 1908.
8. ibid.: Letter from Alma in Degerloch,to 'My own dear sister Fanny', 26 May 1909.
9. ibid. Box 6: Letter from Alma in Stuttgart to 'My dear brother Joseph', 12 August 1909.
10. ibid. Box 3: Letter from Alma in Stuttgart to 'My dear beloved Sister', 4 December 1909.
11. ibid. Box 7: Letter from Alma in Stuttgart to 'Dearly beloved Pauline and Joseph', 31 December 1909.
12. ibid.: Letter from Alma to 'My precious sister Pauline', 3 November 1912.

22 Two Dreams, Two Meetings

1. Washington DC Bahá'í Archives, Hannen-Knobloch Collection, Box 7: Letter from Alma in Stuttgart to 'Dearly beloved Pauline and Joseph', 31 December 1909.

2. ibid.: Letter from Alma in Stuttgart to 'My own precious sister Pauline', 14 February 1910.
3. ibid. Box 1: Tablet from Abdu'l-Bahá to Mr and Mrs Ruoff, translated by Ahmad Sohrab, 18 November 1909.
4. ibid. Box 7: Letter from Alma in Stuttgart to 'My own precious sister Pauline' 14 February 1910.
5. ibid.
6. ibid.
7. ibid.
8. ibid.
9. ibid. Box 3: Letter from Alma in Stuttgart to 'My Precious Sister Fanny', 12 January 1911.
10. Washington DC Bahá'í Archives, Hannen-Knobloch Collection, Box 7: Letter from Alma in Stuttgart to 'My own precious sister Pauline', 14 February 1910.
11. ibid.: Letter from Alma in Stuttgart to 'My Own Precious Pauline', 30 March 1910.
12. See Cobb, *Ayesha of the Bosphorus: A Romance of Constantinople*.
13. USBNA, Hannen Knobloch Collection.
14. Washington DC Bahá'í Archives, Hannen-Knobloch Collection, Box 7: Letter from Alma in Stuttgart to 'Dearly Beloved Sister Pauline', 14 March 1910.
15. USBNA, Hannen Knobloch Collection: Letters from Moneer Zaine in Haifa to Alma, 21 February 1910.
16. ibid.
17. ibid.
18. Washington DC Bahá'í Archives, Hannen-Knobloch Collection Box 3: Letter from Alma in Stuttgart to 'Dearly Beloved Sister Fanny', 27 February 1910.
19. ibid.: Letter from Alma in Stuttgart to 'Most dearly beloved sister Fanny', 27 March 1910.
20. ibid. Box 7: Letter from Alma in Stuttgart to 'My Own Precious Pauline', 30 March 1910.
21. USBNA, microfilm: Tablet from 'Abdu'l-Bahá to Alma Knobloch, 'Sent through Mr. H. Dreyfus in Paris', March 1910.
22. USBNA, microfilm: Tablet from 'Abdu'l-Bahá to Alma Knobloch, 2 April 2010, through Hippolyte Dreyfus. Also in Washington DC Bahá'í Archives, Hannen-Knobloch Collection, Box 6: Copy in German language typed
23. Washington DC Bahá'í Archives, Hannen-Knobloch Collection, Box 1: Tablet from 'Abdu'l-Bahá to Fanny Knobloch, 'Tablet Through Ahmad Sohrab and the Maidservant of God Lua', 5 May 1910.
24. ibid. Box 7: Letter from Alma in Stuttgart to 'My Darling Sister Pauline', 21 May 1910.
25. ibid.: Letter from Alma in Stuttgart to Pauline, enclosed with Alma's 21 May 1910 letter but undated.

26. ibid.: Letter from Alma in Stuttgart to 'My Own Precious sister Pauline', 26 May 1910.
27. ibid. Box 1: Partial letter, undated, but after July 1910.
28. ibid.: Letter from Alma in Stuttgart to 'My dearly beloved sister Pauline', 5 November 1910.
29. ibid.

23 Steadfastly Building Community

1. USBNA, Hannen Knobloch Collection: Letter from Alma to 'Dearly Beloved Sister Fanny', 5 December 1910; Washington DC Baháʼí Archives, Hannen-Knobloch Collection, Box 7: Letter from Alma in Stuttgart to 'My darling sister Pauline', 2 December 1910.
2. Washington DC Baháʼí Archives, Hannen-Knobloch Collection, Box 7: Letter from Alma (no location) to 'My Precious Sister Pauline', 22 September 1910.
3. Tablet from ʻAbdu'l-Bahá 'through Monsieur Dreyfus to the friends and maid-servants of God, Stuttgart, Germany', in *Bahai News (Star of the West)*, vol. 1, no. 13 (4 November 1910), p. 14.
4. ibid.
5. Washington DC Baháʼí Archives, Hannen-Knobloch Collection, Box 6: Letter from Alma in Stuttgart to 'My Dear Beloved Brother Joseph', 14 July 1910.
6. ibid. Box 1: Partial letter probably from July 1910 (no location)
7. ibid. Box 7: Letter from Alma in Stuttgart to 'Dearly beloved sister Pauline', 18 July 1910.
8. ibid.
9. ibid. Box 7: Alma's memoirs.
10. ibid. Box 6: Letter from Alma in Stuttgart to 'My dear beloved brother Joseph', 14 July 1910.
11. ibid. Box 8: Letter from Alma to 'Dearly beloved sister Fanny', 10 August 1910.
12. ibid. Box 3: Letter from Alma in Stuttgart to 'Dearly Beloved Sister Fanny', 9 July 1910.
13. ibid. Box 7: Letter from Alma to 'My Own Dear Sister Pauline'; Box 5: 'Alma's Chronological Memories'.
14. *Bahai News (Star of the West)*, vol. 1, no. 13 (4 November 1910), p. 15.
15. Washington DC Baháʼí Archives, Hannen-Knobloch Collection, Box 7: Letter from Alma in Stuttgart to 'My own dear sister Pauline', 29 January 1911.
16. ibid.: Letter from Alma in Stuttgart to 'Dearest Sister Pauline', 8 February 1911.
17. USBNA, Hannen Knobloch Collection: Letter from Alma to 'My own dear sister Fanny', 28 December 1910.
18. Washington DC Baháʼí Archives, Hannen-Knobloch Collection, Box 7: Letter from Alma in Stuttgart to 'My darling sister Pauline', 2 December 1910.

19. USBNA, John Bosch Collection: Letter from Anna Köstlin to 'My dear friend and Bahai brother', 17 December 1911.
20. Washington DC Baháí Archives, Hannen-Knobloch Collection, Box 7: Letter from Alma in Stuttgart to' My own dear sister Pauline', 29 January 1911.
21. ibid.: Letter from Alma in Stuttgart to 'Dearest Sister Pauline', 8 February 1911; see also USBNA, Hannen Knobloch Collection, Alma to 'My own dear sister Fanny', 28 December 1910.
22. Washington DC Baháí Archives, Hannen-Knobloch Collection, Box 7: Letter from Alma in Stuttgart to 'My own dear sister Pauline', 29 January 1911.
23. ibid.
24. ibid. Box 7: Letter from Alma in Stuttgart to 'My dear beloved sister Pauline', 2 August 1910.
25. ibid.: Letter from Alma in Stuttgart to 'My darling sister Pauline', 2 December 1910.
26. ibid.: Letter from Alma in Stuttgart to 'My dear beloved sister Pauline', 2 August 1910.
27. ibid.: Letter from Alma in Leipzig to 'My dear beloved sister Pauline', 17 August 1910.
28. ibid: Box 8: Letter from Alma to 'Dearly beloved sister Fanny', 5 December 1910.
29. Washington DC Baháí Archives, Hannen-Knobloch Collection, Box 7: Letter from Alma (no location) to 'My precious sister Pauline', 22 September 1910.

24 Tablets to the German Believers

1. Washington DC Baháí Archives, Hannen-Knobloch Collection, Box 3: Letter from Alma in Stuttgart to 'My own precious sister Fanny', 6 February 1911.
2. ibid. Box 1. Also in German National Baháí Archives, Hermann Grossmann Files B 1920 EE.
3. ibid. Box 1. Also in German National Baháí Archives, Hermann Grossmann Files B19 E 1911 A1: Tablet from 'Abdu'l-Bahá, 'To the Friends of God and Maid-servants of the Merciful in Stuttgart', 1 March 1911; various copies, handwritten and typed.
4. ibid.
5. USBNA, microfilm. Also in Washington DC Baháí Archives, Hannen-Knobloch Collection, Box 1; German National Baháí Archives, Hermann Grossmann Files B 1920 E E.
6. Washington DC Baháí Archives, Hannen-Knobloch Collection, Box 1. Also in German National Baháí Archives, Hermann Grossmann Files B 25 D 1911 to 1921: Tablet from 'Abdu'l-Bahá to Mr and Mrs Herrigel, 'Translated by Mírzá Y. Dawud, March 1st 1911, London', with German translation.
7. Washington DC Baháí Archives, Hannen-Knobloch Collection, Box

NOTES AND REFERENCES

7: Letter from Alma in Stuttgart to 'My precious sister Pauline' 26 May 1911.
8. Washington DC Bahá'í Archives, Hannen-Knobloch Collection, Box 3: Letter from Alma in Stuttgart to 'Dearly Beloved Sister Fanny', 11 March 1911.
9. ibid.: Letter from Alma to 'My Precious Sister Fanny', 11 March 1911.
10. ibid.: Letter from Alma to 'Dearly Beloved Sister Fanny', 11 March 1911.
11. ibid.
12. Washington DC Bahá'í Archives, Hannen-Knobloch Collection, Box 6: Letter from Alma in Stuttgart to 'My dear brother Joseph', 29 March 1911.
13. ibid. Box 3: Letter from Alma in Stuttgart to 'Dearly Beloved Sister Fanny', 11 March 1911; ibid. Box 6: Letter from Alma to 'My dear brother Joseph', 29 March 1911.
14. ibid. Box 3: Letter from Alma in Stuttgart to 'Dearly beloved sister Fanny' 25 April 1911.
15. *Star of the West*, vol. II, no. 17 (19 January 1912), pp. 6-7; also in USBNA, Hannen Knobloch Collection; quoted in Morrison, *To Move The World*, p. 47.
16. Washington DC Bahá'í Archives, Hannen-Knobloch Collection, Box 7: Letter from Alma in Stuttgart to 'My Precious Sister Pauline', 26 May 1911.
17. ibid.
18. ibid.
19. ibid.
20. ibid.
21. ibid.
22. ibid.
23. ibid.: Letter from Alma in Stuttgart to 'My beloved sister Pauline', 27 May 1911.
24. ibid.
25. ibid.: Letter from Alma in Stuttgart to 'My precious sister Pauline', 21 June 1911.
26. ibid.: Letter from Alma in Stuttgart to 'My precious sister Pauline', 17 July 1911.
27. ibid. Box 3: Letter from Alma in Stuttgart to 'Dearly Beloved Sister Fanny', 25 April 1911.
28. ibid.
29. ibid. Box 7: Letter from Alma in Stuttgart to 'My beloved sister Pauline', 27 May 1911.
30. ibid.: Letter from Alma in Stuttgart to 'My precious sister Pauline', 17 July 1911.
31. ibid. Box 1: Letter from Alma in Stuttgart to 'Dearly beloved ones at home', 5 December 1911.
32. *Star of the West*, vol. II, no. 17 (19 January 1912), p. 6.

33. Washington DC Bahá'í Archives, Hannen-Knobloch Collection, Box 7: Letter from Alma in Stuttgart to 'My dear precious sister Pauline', 10 August 1911.
34. Schwarz, *Zeiten die mein Herz Berührten* (Times that Touched my Heart), pp. 18-20.
35. Washington DC Bahá'í Archives, Hannen-Knobloch Collection, Box 1: Letter from Alma in Stuttgart to 'My precious sisters Fanny and Pauline', 23 August 1911.
36. ibid. Box 3: Letter from Alma in Stuttgart to 'My precious sister Fanny', 25 August 1911.

25 The German Bahá'ís Meet 'Abdu'l-Bahá in London and Paris

1. Weatherly, 'The First Universal Races Congress', in *American Journal of Sociology*, vol. 17, no. 3 (November 1911), pp. 315-28.
2. 'Letter from Abdu'l Baha to the First Universal Races Congress', in *Papers on the Interracial Problems Communicated to the First Universal Races Congress Held at the University of London, July 26-29, 1911*.
3. Tilley, 'Racial Science, Geopolitics, and Empires: Paradoxes of Power', in *Isis*, vol. 105 (2014), no. 4, pp. 773-781.
4. *'Abdu'l-Bahá in London*, p. 59.
5. Washington DC Bahá'í Archives, Hannen-Knobloch Collection, Box 2: Alma's memoirs.
6. ibid.
7. ibid.
8. ibid.
9. McNamara, *The Reception of 'Abdu'l-Bahá in Britain*, pp. 138-9.
10. Washington DC Bahá'í Archives, Hannen-Knobloch Collection, Box 2: Alma's memoirs.
11. *The Christian Commonwealth*, 20 September 1911, cited in *Star of the West*, vol. 2, no. 12 (16 October 1911), and in Balyuzi, *Abdu'l-Bahá*, pp. 146-8, and McNamara, *The Reception of 'Abdu'l-Bahá in Britain*, pp. 138-9.
12. *The Church Times*, 24 May 1912, p. 732.
13. McNamara, *The Reception of 'Abdu'l-Bahá in Britain*, p. 142.
14. USBNA, Hannen Knobloch Collection: Letter from Alma in Cabin John to 'My precious sisters', 29 August 1938.
15. McNamara, *The Reception of 'Abdu'l-Bahá in Britain*, p. 142.
16. Washington DC Bahá'í Archives, Hannen-Knobloch Collection, Box 1: Letter from Alma in Stuttgart to 'My precious Sisters!', 30 October 1911.
17. ibid.
18. ibid. Box 7: Letter from Alma in Stuttgart to' My dear beloved Pauline and Joseph', 16 December 1911.
19. USBNA, Charles Mason Remey Collection: Letter from Wilhelm Herrigel to C. M. Remey, 7 July 1926.
20. Washington DC Bahá'í Archives, Hannen-Knobloch Collection, Box 2: Alma's memoirs.

21. ibid. Box 3: Letter from Alma in Stuttgart to 'Dearest Mother (probably Joseph Hannen's mother), 6 October 1911.
22. ibid.
23. ibid.
24. ibid. Box 7: Letter from Alma in Stuttgart to 'My precious sister Pauline', 17 October 1911.
25. *Star of the West*, vol. II, no. 17 (19 January 1912), p. 8.
26. Washington DC Bahá'í Archives, Hannen-Knobloch Collection, Box 3: partial letter from Alma in Stuttgart to 'My precious sister Fanny', 12 October 1911.
27. ibid. Box 7: Letter from Alma in Stuttgart to 'My Precious sister Pauline', 17 October 1911.
28. ibid.
29. *Star of the West*, vol. II, no. 17 (19 January 1912), p. 8.
30. Washington DC Bahá'í Archives, Hannen-Knobloch Collection, Box 1: Letter from Alma to 'My precious Sisters', 30 October 1911.
31. ibid.
32. ibid.
33. German National Bahá'í Archives, Hermann Grossmann Files B23 E D 1911 1912.
34. USBNA, microfilm of original Hannen Knobloch files: Tablet from 'Abdu'l-Bahá to Alma Knobloch, sent through Yuhanna Dawud, 27 November 1911. An alternative translation by Ahmad Sohrab, made on 5 December, is found in one of Alma's notebooks in the Washington DC Bahá'í Archives, Hannen-Knobloch Collection:

> O thou maid servant of God!
> Your letter was received. Thou hast written that the friends are gathered in One Assembly and with the utmost love you are engaged in the mentioning of God.
> The unity and harmony amongst the believers and the maid servants of the Merciful will become the cause of the promotion of the Kingdom of God and will attract the confirmation of the Holy Spirit. It is my hope that all the believers in Stuttgart may attain to this Grace. This is the utmost hope of the people of the Kingdom.
> If there is no unity, the foundation of the cause of God will be shaken.
> I hope that ye may all become as one soul and one heart and that ye may entertain but one thought.
> I am very pleased with the believers in Stuttgart and have the utmost love for them.
> Upon thee be Baha El Abha!
> (signed) Abdul Baha Abbas
> Translated by Ahmad Dec. 5, 1911.

35. Washington DC Bahá'í Archives, Hannen-Knobloch Collection, Box

7: Letter from Alma in Stuttgart to 'My precious sister Pauline', 27 March 1913.

26 Lady Blomfield and the Stuttgart Bahá'í Community

1. Washington DC Bahá'í Archives, Collection 33, Hannen-Knobloch Papers, Box 14: '5 December 1911 Stuttgart'.
2. United Kingdom National Bahá'í Archives: 'Blomfield, An Account of the Visit to Stuttgart', p. 3. Courtesy of Robert Weinberg.
3. ibid.
4. *Star of the West*, vol. II, no. 17 (19 January 1912), p. 8.
5. United Kingdom National Bahá'í Archives: 'Blomfield, An Account of the Visit to Stuttgart', p. 11; also Washington DC Bahá'í Archives, Hannen-Knobloch Collection, Box 3: Letter from Alma in Stuttgart to 'dearly beloved ones at home!', 5 December 1911 Stuttgart'; and Box 7: Letter from Alma to 'Dearly Beloved Pauline and Joseph', 16 December 1911.
6. Washington DC Bahá'í Archives, Hannen-Knobloch Collection, Box 3: Letter from Alma in Stuttgart to 'Dearly beloved ones at home!', 5 December 1911.
7. ibid.: Letter from Alma to 'My Precious Sisters', 24 May 1912.
8. United Kingdom National Bahá'í Archives: 'Blomfield, An Account of the Visit to Stuttgart', pp. 16-17.
9. ibid. pp. 19 and 21.
10. ibid. p. 23.
11. Washington DC Bahá'í Archives, Hannen-Knobloch Collection, Box 3: Letter from Alma in Stuttgart to 'My dearly beloved Fanny!', 30 Dec 1911.
12. ibid. Box 7: Letter from Alma in Stuttgart to 'My dear beloved Pauline', 16 December 1911; ibid.: Letter from Alma in Stuttgart to 'My darling sister', 3 January 1912; also Box 3: Letter from Alma in Stuttgart to 'My precious sister Fanny', 8 January 1912.
13. United Kingdom National Bahá'í Archives: 'Blomfield, An Account of the Visit to Stuttgart', p. 4.
14. ibid. p. 5-6.
15. In November 1908 Reverend O. M. Fisher was giving talks in New York on the Seven Valleys (see *The Bahai Bulletin*, October-November 1908, in a section under New York. http://www.h-net.org/~bahai/docs/vol7/NYCB.pdf). He continued these talks in England in 1910 (see Weinberg, *Ethel Jenner Rosenberg*).
16. *Star of the West*, vol. II, no. 17 (19 January 1912), pp. 6-8.
17. ibid. p. 7.
18. Washington DC Bahá'í Archives, Hannen-Knobloch Collection, Box 1: Tablet from 'Abdu'l-Bahá to Alma Knobloch, received 19 January 1912.
19. ibid. Box 7: Letter from Alma in Stuttgart to 'My darling sister Pauline', 22 January 1912.

20. ibid.: Letter from Alma in Stuttgart to 'My precious sister Pauline!', 9 February 1912.
21. ibid.: Letter from Alma in Stuttgart to 'My precious sister Pauline!', 17 February 1912.
22. ibid.: Letter from Alma in Stuttgart to 'My precious sister Pauline!', 9 February 1912.
23. ibid.: Letter from Alma in Stuttgart to 'My precious sister Pauline!', 17 February 1912.
24. ibid.: Letter from Alma in Stuttgart to 'My precious sister Pauline!', 24 February 1912.
25. ibid.
26. ibid. Box 3: Tablet from 'Abdu'l-Bahá 'to the Assembly at Stuttgart', typed copy in English included with a letter from Alma to 'My Precious Sister Fanny', 27 February 1912; the German translation was printed in *Brief und Botschaften, Organ des Deutschen Bahai Bundes*, 1 Jahrgang, Heft No. 1 (9 November 1921), p. 141.
27. Washington DC Bahá'í Archives, Hannen-Knobloch Collection, Box 7: Letter from Alma in Stuttgart to 'My precious sister Pauline!', 24 February 1912.
28. ibid. Box 3: Letter from Alma to 'My Precious Sister Fanny', 27 February 1912.
29. ibid. Box 7: Letter from Alma in Stuttgart to 'My precious sister Pauline!', 2 March 1912.
30. ibid. Box 3: Two letters from Alma in Stuttgart to 'My Precious Sister Fanny', 5 March 1912 and 1 April 1912.
31. ibid. Box 3: Letter from Alma in Stuttgart to 'My darling sister Fanny', 13 March 1912.
32. ibid.: Letter from Alma in Stuttgart to 'My Precious Sister Fanny', 5 March 1912.
33. ibid. Box 7: Letter from Alma in Stuttgart to 'My Precious sister Pauline', 2 March 1912.
34. ibid.: Letter from Alma in Stuttgart to 'My precious sister Pauline', 25 March 1912.
35. ibid. Box 3: Letter from Alma in Stuttgart to 'My darling sister Fanny', 13 March 1912.
36. USBNA, Bosch Collection: Letter from Anna Köstlin to Louise Bosch, 18 March 1912.
37. Washington DC Bahá'í Archives, Hannen-Knobloch Collection, Box 3: Letter from Alma in Leipzig to 'my Precious Sister Fanny', 23 April 1912.
38. ibid. Box 7: Letter from Alma in Stuttgart to 'My precious sister Pauline', 9 February 1912.
39. ibid. Box 1: Letter from Alma in Stuttgart to 'My dear Brother and sisters', 19 March 1912.
40. German National Bahá'í Archives, Hermann Grossmann Files B23 E D 1911 1912: Tablet from 'Abdu'l-Bahá to Alma Knobloch, translated by Mírzá Yuhanna Dawud, London 23 March 1912.

41. USBNA, A. Windust Collection.
42. USBNA, microfilm: Tablet from 'Abdu'l-Bahá to 'the friends of God and the maidservants of the Merciful', Stuttgart, Germany, translated by Ahmad Sohrab, 7 August 1912, Dublin, New Hampshire.
43. Washington DC Bahá'í Archives, Hannen-Knobloch Collection, Box 7: Letter from Alma in Leipzig to 'My precious sister Pauline', 29 May 1912.
44. ibid. Box 2: part of a letter home – first page missing.
45. German National Bahá'í Archives, Hermann Grossmann Files B 1920 E E.
46. Weinberg, *Lady Blomfield: Her Life and Times*, p. 103.
47. Washington DC Bahá'í Archives, Hannen-Knobloch Collection, Box 7: Letter from Alma in Stuttgart to 'My precious sister Pauline', 25 March 1912.
48. ibid.
49. ibid.
50. ibid. Box 3: Letter from Alma in Leipzig to 'my precious sister Fanny', 23 April 1912.

27 Leipzig at Last

1. Washington DC Bahá'í Archives, Hannen-Knobloch Collection, Box 1: Letter from Alma in Leipzig to 'My precious sisters!', 17 April 1912.
2. ibid.
3. ibid.: Letter from Alma in Stuttgart to 'My Dear brother and sisters', 19 March 1912.
4. ibid. Box 1: Letter from Alma in Leipzig to 'My precious sisters', 17 April 1912.
5. ibid. Box 3: Letter from Alma to 'my Precious Sister Fanny', 23 April 1912.
6. ibid. Box 1: Letter from Alma in Leipzig to 'My Precious Sisters', 17 April 1912.
7. USBNA, microfilm. Also in Washington DC Bahá'í Archives, Hannen-Knobloch Collection, Box 6: Tablet from 'Abdu'l-Bahá to Alma Knobloch, 8 August 1912.
8. Washington DC Bahá'í Archives, Hannen-Knobloch Collection, Box 3: Letter from Alma in Leipzig to 'My precious sister Fanny', 23 April 1912.
9. ibid.
10. ibid.: Letter from Alma to 'My precious sister Fanny' 19 June 1912.
11. ibid.: Letter from Alma to 'My precious sister Fanny', 2 May 1912.
12. ibid.: Letter from Alma to 'My precious sisters', 24 May 1912.
13. ibid. Box 1: Letter from Alma to 'My Precious Sisters', 7 July 1912.
14. ibid. Box 7: Letter from Alma in Leipzig to 'My precious Sister Pauline', 29 May 1912.
15. ibid. Box 3: Letter from Alma in Leipzig to 'My precious sister Fanny' 19 June 1912.
16. ibid.

17. Washington DC Baháʼí Archives, Hannen-Knobloch Collection, Box 7: Letter from Alma to 'Dearest Pauline', 1 August 1913.
18. USBNA, John Bosch Collection, Box 3: Letter from Wilhelm Herrigel to John Bosch, 7 June 1912.
19. *Baháʼí News*, no. 250 (July 1974), p. 12; USBNA, John Bosch Collection
20. Washington DC Baháʼí Archives, Hannen-Knobloch Collection, Box 1: Letter from Alma in Leipzig to 'My precious sisters', 7 July 1912.

28 Summer of 1912

1. Washington DC Baháʼí Archives, Hannen-Knobloch Collection, Box 1: Letter from Alma in Stuttgart to 'My Precious Sisters', 25 July 1912.
2. ibid. Box 1: Letter from Alma in Leipzig to 'My precious sister Fanny', 19 June 1912.
3. ibid.
4. ibid.: Letter from Alma in Stuttgart to 'My Precious Sisters', 25 July 1912.
5. ibid.
6. ibid.: Letter from Alma in Stuttgart to 'My dear beloved ones at home', 29 August 1912.)
7. ibid. Box 7: Letter from Alma in Stuttgart to 'My precious sister Pauline and brother Joseph', 11 September 1912.
8. *Star of the West*, vol. 3, no. 11 (27 September 1912), p. 4.
9. ibid. vol. 5, no. 13, p. 202.
10. USBNA, Hannen Knobloch Collection, Tablet 9 August 1912; also Washington DC Baháʼí Archives, Hannen-Knobloch Collection, Box 3: Tablet of ʻAbduʼl-Bahá to Mr Schweizer, translated by Ahmad Sohrab in Dublin, New Hampshire, 9 August 1912; see also Knobloch, 'The Call to Germany', pp. 742-3.
11. *Star of the West*, vol. 5, no. 13, p. 202.
12. USBNA, Thornton Chase Collection, Box 1: Letter from Wilhelm Herrigel to Thornton Chase, 15 September 1912.
13. Washington DC Baháʼí Archives, Hannen-Knobloch Collection, Box 7: Letter from Alma in Stuttgart to Pauline, 11 September 1912; USBNA, Thornton Chase Collection, Box 1: Letter from Wilhelm Herrigel to Thornton Chase, 15 September 1912.
14. USBNA, Thornton Chase Collection, Box 1: Letter from Wilhelm Herrigel to Thornton Chase, 15 September 1912.
15. Washington DC Baháʼí Archives, Hannen-Knobloch Collection, Box 7: Letter from Alma in Stuttgart to Pauline, 11 September 1912.
16. USBNA, Thornton Chase Collection, Box 1: Letter from Wilhelm Herrigel to Thornton Chase, 15 September 1912.
17. Washington DC Baháʼí Archives, Hannen-Knobloch Collection, Box 7: Letter from Alma in Leipzig to 'My precious sister Pauline', 3 November 1912.
18. ibid. Box 1: Letter from Alma to 'My Precious Sisters', 11 December 1912.

19. ibid.
20. Washington DC Bahá'í Archives, Hannen-Knobloch Collection, Box 7: Letter from Alma in Stuttgart to 'My Precious sister Pauline', 19 September 1912.
21. Stockman, 'The Bahá'í Faith in England and Germany', p. 38.

29 Alma's Family in Leipzig

1. Washington DC Bahá'í Archives, Hannen-Knobloch Collection, Box 7: Letter from Alma in Leipzig to 'My precious sister Pauline', 3 November 1912.
2. ibid. Box 1: Letter from Alma in Leipzig to 'My own precious Sisters', 30 December 1912.
3. ibid.: Letter from Alma in Leipzig to 'My precious sisters', 11 December 1912.
4. ibid.: Letter from Alma in Leipzig to 'My own precious Sisters', 30 December 1912.
5. ibid.: Letter from Alma in Leipzig to 'My precious sisters', 11 December 1912.
6. ibid.: Letter from Alma in Leipzig to 'My own precious Sisters', 30 December 1912.
7. ibid.: Letter from Alma in Leipzig to 'My Precious Good Sister Fanny', 9 January 1913.
8. ibid.
9. ibid. Box 3: Letter from Alma in Leipzig Sehl to 'My own precious darling sister Fanny', 23 February 1916.
10. ibid. Box 1: Letter from Alma in Leipzig to 'My own precious sisters', 30 December 1912.
11. ibid.
12. ibid.
13. ibid. Box 5: Letter from Alma in Stuttgart to 'My precious beloved sister Fanny', 8 February 1913.

30 Petitions to the Master

1. USBNA, microfilm; details of the Tablet sent through Alma are mentioned in USBNA, Hannen Knobloch Collection: Letter from Alma to 'Dearly Beloved Ones at home', 19 February 1913. The Tablet sent through Wilhelm Herrigel is in the Washington DC Bahá'í Archives, Hannen-Knobloch Collection, Box 6: Tablets of 'Abdu'l-Bahá.
2. Washington DC Bahá'í Archives, Hannen-Knobloch Collection, Box 1: Letter from Alma in Stuttgart to 'Dearly beloved ones at home', 19 February 1913.
3. ibid. Box 2: Alma's memoirs.
4. ibid.
5. ibid.
6. ibid.
7. ibid.: Letter from Alma in Stuttgart to 'Dearly Beloved Ones at home',

19 February 1913. Also in the German National Bahá'í Archives, Anna Köstlin Collection.
8. ibid.
9. ibid. Box 5: Letter from Alma in Stuttgart to 'My Precious Sister Fanny', 5 March 1913.
10. ibid.
11. USBNA, Louis Gregory Collection: Letter from Wilhelm Herrigel to Louis Gregory, 25 June 1913.
12. USBNA, Charles Mason Remey Collection: Letter from Wilhelm Herrigel to Charles Mason Remey, 7 July 1926 (in German, my translation).
13. ibid.
14. ibid.
15. ibid.
16. Washington DC Bahá'í Archives, Hannen-Knobloch Collection, Box 5: Letter from Alma in Stuttgart to 'My Precious Sister Fanny', 5 March 1913.
17. ibid. Box 7: Letter from Alma in Stuttgart to 'Beloved Pauline and Joseph', 26 March 1913.
18. ibid.: Letter from Alma in Stuttgart to 'My own precious sister Pauline' 27 March 1913.
19. Balyuzi, *'Abdu'l-Bahá*, p. 379.

31 'Abdu'l-Bahá in Germany

1. Shoghi Effendi, Message to the Intercontinental Conference, Stockholm, Sweden, July 1953, in Shoghi Effendi, *Messages to the Bahá'í World, 1950–1957*, p. 157.
2. Balyuzi, *'Abdu'l-Bahá*, p. 379.
3. 'Prophet Blesses Morgan', in *The New York Times*, 19 November 1912, p. 1; 'Prophet Blesses Morgan', in *Hawaiian Gazette*, 6 December 1912; 'Persian Highbrow Dubs Morgan "Some Philanthropist"', in *Buffalo New York News*, 19 November 1912.
4. USBNA, Ahmad Sohrab Collection: Letter from Ahmad Sohrab from the Hotel Marquardt, Stuttgart to 'Dear Harriet', 1 April 1913.
5. McNamara, *The Reception of 'Abdu'l-Bahá in Britain: East comes West*, p. 128.
6. Gail, *Arches of the Years*, p. 78.
7. Metelmann, *Lua Getsinger: Herald of the Covenant*, p. 151.
8. Zarqání, *Maḥmúd's Diary*, pp. 264–5.
9. *Star of the West*, vol. IV, no. 9 (20 August 1913), pp. 155–8.
10. USBNA, Ahmad Sohrab Collection: Letter from Ahmad Sohrab from the Hotel Marquardt, Stuttgart to 'Dear Harriet', 1 April 1913.
11. Washington DC Bahá'í Archives, Hannen-Knobloch Collection, Box 1: Letter from Alma in Stuttgart to 'My precious sisters', 3 April 1913.
12. USBNA, Ahmad Sohrab Collection: Letter from Ahmad Sohrab from the Hotel Marquardt, Stuttgart to 'Dear Harriet', 2 April 1913.

13. ibid.: Letter from Ahmad Sohrab from the Hotel Marquardt, Stuttgart to 'Dear Harriet', 5 April 1913; also Washington DC Baháʼí Archives, Hannen-Knobloch Collection: Box 1: Letter from Alma to 'My precious sisters Fanny and Pauline', 23 April 1913; also in Balyuzi, ʼAbduʼl-Bahá, p. 379.
14. USBNA, Ahmad Sohrab Collection: Letter from Ahmad Sohrab from the Hotel Marquardt, Stuttgart. to 'Dear Harriet', 2 April 1913.
15. Washington DC Baháʼí Archives, Hannen-Knobloch Collection: Box 1: Letter from Alma to 'My precious sisters', 3 April 1913.
16. ibid.
17. USBNA, Ahmad Sohrab Collection: Letter from Ahmad Sohrab from the Hotel Marquardt, Stuttgart to 'Dear Harriet', 2 April 1913.
18. ibid.
19. USBNA, Charles Mason Remey Collection: Letter from Wilhelm Herrigel to C. M. Remey, 7 July 1926.
20. USBNA, Ahmad Sohrab Collection: Letter from Ahmad Sohrab from the Hotel Marquardt, Stuttgart to 'Dear Harriet', 2 April 1913.
21. ibid.
22. Schwarz-Solivo, 'Report to the Friends in the East and West', in *Sonne der Wahrheit*, Jahrgang 3, Heft 4 (June 1923), p. 60.
23. Schwarz, *Zeiten, die mein Herz berührten* (Times that touched my heart), p. 55.
24. ibid. pp. 87–8.
25. Washington DC Baháʼí Archives, Hannen-Knobloch Collection, Box 7: Alma's memories of Consul Schwarz.
26. Schwarz-Solivo, 'Report to the Friends in the East and West', in *Sonne der Wahrheit*, Jahrgang 3, Heft 2 (April 1923), p. 29–30.
27. ibid. Heft 3 (April 1923), p. 44.
28. ibid.
29. Schwarz, *Zeiten, die mein Herz berührten*, p. 33.
30. Washington DC Baháʼí Archives, Hannen-Knobloch Collection, Box: 1: Alma's notes for the papers in England, 5 May 1913.
31. Schwarz-Solivo, 'Report to the Friends in the East and West', in *Sonne der Wahrheit*, Jahrgang 3, Heft 4 (June 1923), p. 58.
32. ibid. Heft 5, p. 73.
33. USBNA, Ahmad Sohrab Collection: Letter from Ahmad Sohrab from the Hotel Marquardt, Stuttgart to 'Dear Harriet', 4 April 1913; *Star of the West*, vol. IV, no. 9 (20 August 1913), pp. 155–8.
34. Schwarz-Solivo, 'Report to the Friends in the East and West', in *Sonne der Wahrheit*, Jahrgang 3, Heft 6 (August 1923), p. 91.
35. USBNA, Ahmad Sohrab Collection: Letter from Ahmad Sohrab from the Hotel Marquardt, Stuttgart to 'Dear Harriet', 4 April 1913; *Star of the West*, vol. IV, no. 9 (20 August 1913), pp. 155–8.
36. USBNA, Ahmad Sohrab Collection: Letter from Ahmad Sohrab from the Hotel Marquardt, Stuttgart to 'Dear Harriet', 5 April 1913, pp. 5–7.
37. Schwarz-Solivo, 'Report to the Friends in the East and West', in *Sonne*

der Wahrheit, Jahrgang 3, Heft 7 (September 1923), p. 107.
38. 'In Memoriam', in *The Bahá'í World*, vol. XVII (1976–1979) p. 473–4.
39. USBNA, Ahmad Sohrab Collection: Letter from Ahmad Sohrab from the Hotel Marquardt, Stuttgart to 'Dear Harriet', 5 April 1913; *Star of the West*, vol. IV, no. 9 (20 August 1913), pp. 155–8; Schwarz-Solivo, 'Report to the Friends in the East and West', in *Sonne der Wahrheit*, Jahrgang 3, Heft 8 (October 1923), pp. 121–2.
40. USBNA, Ahmad Sohrab Collection: Letter from Ahmad Sohrab from the Hotel Marquardt, Stuttgart to 'Dear Harriet', 6 April 1913.
41. Washington DC Bahá'í Archives, Hannen-Knobloch Collection, Box 7: Letter from Alma in Stuttgart to Pauline, 27 March 1913.
42. USBNA, Ahmad Sohrab Collection: Letter from Ahmad Sohrab from the Hotel Marquardt, Stuttgart to 'Dear Harriet', 5 April 1913.
43. ibid.
44. ibid.: Letter from Ahmad Sohrab from the Hotel Marquardt, Stuttgart to 'Dear Harriet', 6 April 1913.
45. Schwarz-Solivo, 'Report to the Friends in the East and West', in *Sonne der Wahrheit*, Jahrgang 3, Heft 9 (November 1923), p. 139.
46. *Star of the West*, vol. IV, no. 20 (August 1913), pp. 155–8.
47. Schwarz, *Zeiten, die mein Herz berührten*, p. 88.
48. Schwarz-Solivo, 'Report to the Friends in the East and West', in *Sonne der Wahrheit*, Jahrgang 3, Heft 11 (January 1924), p. 172.
49. Schwarz, *Zeiten, die mein Herz berührten*, p. 88; *Star of the West*, vol. IV, no. 9 (20 August 1913), pp. 155–8.
50. Schwarz, *Zeiten, die mein Herz berührten*, p. 92.
51. ibid. pp. 259–60.
52. Washington DC Bahá'í Archives, Hannen-Knobloch Collection, Box: Letter from Alma in Stuttgart to 'My Precious Sisters!', 10 April 1913.
53. ibid.
54. ibid.
55. ibid.
56. USBNA, Ahmad Sohrab Collection: Letter from Ahmad Sohrab from the Hotel Marquardt, Stuttgart to 'Dear Harriet', 8 April 1913, pp. 11–14.
57. *Star of the West*, vol. IV, no. 9 (20 August 1913), pp. 155–8.
58. USBNA, Ahmad Sohrab Collection: Letter from Ahmad Sohrab from the Hotel Marquardt, Stuttgart to 'Dear Harriet', 8 April 1913.
59. USBNA, Charles Mason Remey Collection: Letter from Wilhelm Herrigel to C. M. Remey, 7 July 1926.
60. USBNA, Ahmad Sohrab Collection: Letter from Ahmad Sohrab to 'Dear Harriet', 20 April 1913.
61. ibid.: Letter from Ahmad Sohrab to 'Dear Harriet', 23 and 24 April 1913.
62. Zarqání, *Chronik der Reisen Abdu'l-Bahás in Europa*, p. 230.
63. USBNA, Ahmad Sohrab Collection: Letter from Ahmad Sohrab from the Hotel Marquardt, Stuttgart to 'Dear Harriet', 26 April 1913.

64. ibid.: Letter from Ahmad Sohrab to 'Dear Harriet', 24 April 1913.
65. *Star of the West*, vol. IV, no. 9 (20 August 1913), pp. 155–8.
66. USBNA, Ahmad Sohrab Collection: Letter from Ahmad Sohrab to 'Dear Harriet', 24 April 1913.
67. Schwarz, *Zeiten, die mein Herz berührten*, p. 134.
68. Washington DC Bahá'í Archives, Hannen-Knobloch Collection, Box 1: Notebook of Alma Knobloch.
69. USBNA, Ahmad Sohrab Collection: Letter from Ahmad Sohrab to 'Dear Harriet', 25 April 1913.
70. ibid.
71. Zarqani, *Chronik der Reisen Abdu'l-Bahás in Europa*, pp. 231–2; German National Bahá'í Archives, Hermann Grossmann Collection, Box J 09 D A1: 'Errinerung besuch Abdu'l-Bahá', original newspaper article.
72. USBNA, Charles Mason Remey Collection: Letter from Wilhelm Herrigel to C. M. Remey, 7 July 1926. For the talk 'Abdu'l-Bahá wished to be read, see 'Abdu'l-Bahá, *The Promulgation of Universal Peace*, pp. 361–70.
73. Schwarz-Solivo, 'Report to the Friends in the East and West', in *Sonne der Wahrheit*, Jahrgang 4, Heft 6 (August 1924), p. 91.
74. USBNA, Ahmad Sohrab Collection: Letter from Ahmad Sohrab to 'Dear Harriet', 25 April 1913.
75. Washington DC Bahá'í Archives, Hannen-Knobloch Collection, Box 7: Letter from Alma in Stuttgart to 'My precious sister Pauline', 28 April 1913.
76. Schwarz-Solivo, 'Report to the Friends in the East and West', in *Sonne der Wahrheit*, Jahrgang 4, Heft 6 (August 1924), p. 91.
77. USBNA, Ahmad Sohrab Collection: Letter from Ahmad Sohrab to 'Dear Harriet', 25 April 1913.
78. Schwarz-Solivo, 'Report to the Friends in the East and West', in *Sonne der Wahrheit*, Jahrgang 4, Heft 6 (August 1924), p. 92.
79. Washington DC Bahá'í Archives, Hannen-Knobloch Collection, Box 7: Letter from Alma in Stuttgart to 'My precious sister Pauline', 28 April 1913; USBNA, Charles Mason Remey Collection: Letter from Wilhelm Herrigel to C. M. Remey, 7 July 1926.
80. Washington DC Bahá'í Archives, Hannen-Knobloch Collection, Box 7: Letter from Alma in Stuttgart to 'My precious sister Pauline', 28 April 1913.
81. Schwarz-Solivo, 'Report to the Friends in the East and West', in *Sonne der Wahrheit*, Jahrgang 4, Heft 6 (August 1924), p. 93.
82. USBNA, Ahmad Sohrab Collection: Letter from Ahmad Sohrab from the Hotel Marquardt, Stuttgart to 'Dear Harriet', 26 April 1913.
83. Schwarz-Solivo, 'Report to the Friends in the East and West', in *Sonne der Wahrheit*, Jahrgang 4, Heft 7 (September 1924), pp. 107–8.
84. USBNA, Ahmad Sohrab Collection: Letter from Ahmad Sohrab from the Hotel Marquardt, Stuttgart to 'Dear Harriet', 26 April 1913.

85. ibid.
86. Schwarz-Solivo, 'Report to the Friends in the East and West', in *Sonne der Wahrheit*, Jahrgang 4, Heft 8 (October 1924), p. 123.
87. USBNA, Ahmad Sohrab Collection: Letter from Ahmad Sohrab from the Hotel Marquardt, Stuttgart to 'Dear Harriet', 27 April 1913.
88. Schwarz-Solivo, 'Report to the Friends in the East and West', in *Sonne der Wahrheit*, Jahrgang 4, Heft 8 (October 1924), p. 123.
89. USBNA, Ahmad Sohrab Collection: Letter from Ahmad Sohrab from the Hotel Marquardt, Stuttgart to 'Dear Harriet', 27 April 1913.
90. Washington DC Bahá'í Archives, Hannen-Knobloch Collection, Box 7: Letter from Alma in Stuttgart to 'My precious sister Pauline', 28 April 1913.
91. USBNA, Ahmad Sohrab Collection: Letter from Ahmad Sohrab from the Hotel Marquardt, Stuttgart to 'Dear Harriet', 27 April 1913.
92. ibid.: Letter from Ahmad Sohrab from the Hotel Marquardt, Stuttgart to 'Dear Harriet', 28 April 1913.
93. ibid.: Letter from Ahmad Sohrab from the Hotel Marquardt, Stuttgart to 'Dear Harriet', 29 April 1913.
94. Washington DC Bahá'í Archives, Hannen-Knobloch Collection, Box 7: Letter from Alma in Stuttgart to 'My precious sister Pauline', 28 April 1913.
95. *Bahá'í Education*, p. 73. Original in German in Washington DC Bahá'í Archives, Hannen-Knobloch Collection, Box 10: Notes of Mrs Schweizer, 'Words of 'Abdu'l-Bahá' Hotel Marquardt Room 141.
96. USBNA, Ahmad Sohrab Collection: Letter from Ahmad Sohrab from the Hotel Marquardt, Stuttgart to 'Dear Harriet', 29 April 1913.
97. ibid.
98. ibid.: Letter from Ahmad Sohrab from the Hotel Marquardt, Stuttgart to 'Dear Harriet', 30 April 1913.
99. Schwarz-Solivo, 'Report to the Friends in the East and West', in *Sonne der Wahrheit*, Jahrgang 4, Heft 12 (February 1924), pp. 196–7.
100. USBNA, Ahmad Sohrab Collection: Letter from Ahmad Sohrab to 'Dear Harriet', 27 April 1913, pp. 13–14.
101. Washington DC Bahá'í Archives, Hannen-Knobloch Collection, Box 7: Letter from Alma in Stuttgart to 'My precious sister Pauline', 3 May 1913.
102. ibid.: Letter from Alma in Leipzig to 'My precious darling Pauline', 26 January 1914.
103. ibid.

32 Fanny's Illness and Recovery with Alma and 'Abdu'l-Bahá

1. Washington DC Bahá'í Archives, Hannen-Knobloch Collection, Box 7: Letter from Alma in Stuttgart to 'My Precious Sisters!', 10 April 1913.
2. ibid.: Letter from Alma in Stuttgart to 'My precious sister Pauline', 3 May 1913.

3. ibid.: Letter from Alma in Stuttgart to 'My precious sister Pauline', 28 April 1913.
4. ibid.: Letter from Alma in Stuttgart to 'My precious sister Pauline!', 19 May 1913; see also Hannen Moe, *Fanny Knobloch: An Adventuresome Spirit*, manuscript in progress, pp. 65– 6.
5. Hannen Moe, *Fanny Knobloch, An Adventuresome Spirit*, manuscript in progress, pp. 65– 6.
6. Washington DC Bahá'í Archives, Hannen-Knobloch Collection, Box 5: Fanny's pilgrim notes.
7. Schwarz, *Zeiten, die mein Herz berührten*, p. 234.
8. Washington DC Bahá'í Archives, Hannen-Knobloch Collection, Box 7: Letter from Alma in Flüelin, Switzerland to 'My dear precious sister Pauline', June 1913.
9. ibid.: Letter from Alma to 'Dearest precious Pauline', Fanny also writes, 'Dearest little sister!'; no location given, 3 July 1913.
10. ibid.: Letter from Alma from Stuttgart to 'My precious sister Pauline', 23 June 1913.
11. ibid.: Letter from Alma from Leipzig to 'My dear beloved sister Pauline!', 29 August 1913.

33 The Stuttgart Bahá'í Community 'Abdu'l-Bahá Created

1. *Star of the West*, vol. IV, no. 9 (20 August 1913), p. 158.
2. ibid.
3. Washington DC Bahá'í Archives, Hannen-Knobloch Collection, Box 7: Letter from Alma in Leipzig to 'My dear beloved sister Pauline', 29 August 1913.
4. ibid.: Letter from Alma in Flüelin, Switzerland to 'My dear precious sister Pauline!', June 1913.
5. ibid.: Letter from Alma to Fanny, 25 July 1913
6. ibid. Box 1: Letter from Alma in Leipzig to 'Beloved ones at home', 9 September 1913.
7. ibid. Box 7: Letter from Alma in Leipzig to 'My dear beloved sister Pauline' 29 August 1913.
8. ibid. Box 5: Letter from Alma in Leipzig to 'My precious good sister Fanny!', 5 November 1913.
9. ibid.
10. ibid. Box 1: Letter from Alma in Leipzig to 'Beloved ones at home', 9 September 1913
11. ibid.
12. ibid.
13. ibid.: Letter from Alma in Leipzig to 'Dearly beloved ones at home!', 9 September 1913.
14. *Star of the West*, vol. V, no. 13 (4 November 1914), p. 202.

34 The 'American Girl' Teaches Throughout Germany

1. Washington DC Bahá'í Archives, Hannen-Knobloch Collection, Box 7: Letter from Alma to 'Dearest Pauline', no location given, 1 August 1913.
2. USBNA, Agnes Parsons Collection: Tablet from 'Abdu'l-Bahá to Alma Knobloch, translated by Ahmad Sohrab in Paris, 6 May 1913.
3. USBNA, microfilm: Tablet from 'Abdu'l-Bahá to Fanny Knobloch from Ramleh, Egypt, translated by Ahmad Sohrab, 13 August 1913.
4. Washington DC Bahá'í Archives, Hannen-Knobloch Collection, Box 7: Letter from Alma in Leipzig to 'My dear sister Pauline and brother Joseph', 6 October 1913.
5. ibid.: Letter from Alma in Leipzig to 'My own precious sister Fanny', 2 October 1913.
6. ibid.: Letter from Alma in Leipzig to 'My dear sister Pauline and brother Joseph,' 6 October 1913.
7. ibid. Box 6: Tablet from 'Abdu'l-Bahá to Alma Knobloch from Ramleh, Egypt, translated by Ahmad Sohrab, 13 August 1913. Also in the German National Bahá'í Archives, Hermann Grossmann files B 36 E 1913.
8. Washington DC Bahá'í Archives, Hannen-Knobloch Collection, Box 7: Letter from Alma in Leipzig to 'My dear sister Pauline and brother Joseph', 6 October 1913.
9. ibid. Box 5: Letter from Alma in Leipzig to 'My precious good sister Fanny', 3 February 1914.
10. ibid. Box 7: Letter from Alma to 'My beloved sister Pauline', 25 November 1913.
11. ibid.: Letter from Alma in Leipzig to 'My beloved precious sister Pauline', 29 December 1913.
12. ibid.: Letter from Alma in Leipzig to 'My own precious good sister Fanny' 31 August 1913.
13. ibid.: Letter from Alma in Leipzig to 'My own precious darling sister Fanny', 23 February 1916.
14. ibid.: Letter from Alma to 'My precious beloved sister Fanny', 20 October 1913
15. ibid.: Letter from Alma in Leipzig to 'My own precious sister Fanny', 11 October 1913.
16. ibid.
17. USBNA, Agnes Parsons Collection: 'Albert Lutz and his sister, Mrs Blättner and her family, Mrs Fritz Scholz, Helmut and Irmgoth, Mr Arthur Rössler, Miss Marie Telle, His Honor Mr R. Munzing, the maidservant of God Mrs Wally Fisher, the maidservant of God Mrs Clara Pfutzner, Miss Clara and Mathilde Pax'.
18. USBNA, microfilm: Tablet from 'Abdu'l-Bahá, 23 September 1913, translated by Ahmad Sohrab. Also in Washington DC Bahá'í Archives, Hannen-Knobloch Collection, Box 1.
19. Washington DC Bahá'í Archives, Hannen-Knobloch Collection, Box 5: Letter from Alma in Leipzig to 'My own precious sister Fanny', 11 October 1913.

20. ibid.: Letter from Alma in Leipzig to 'My precious beloved sister Fanny,' 20 October 1913.
21. ibid.: Letter from Alma in Leipzig to 'My own precious sister Fanny', 11 October 1913.
22. ibid.: Letter from Alma in Leipzig to 'My Darling precious sister Fanny', 7 December 1913.
23. ibid.: Alma in Leipzig to 'My precious good sister Fanny!' 5 November 1913.
24. ibid. Box 7: Letter from Alma in Leipzig to 'My beloved sister Pauline, 25 November 1913.
25. ibid.: Letter from Alma in Leipzig to 'My precious sister Pauline!', 4 November 1913.
26. ibid. Box 1: Letter from Alma in Leipzig to 'Precious Beloved ones at home', 12 December 1913.
27. ibid.
28. German National Bahá'í Archives, Hermann Grossmann files B37 E 1914.
29. Washington DC Bahá'í Archives, Hannen-Knobloch Collection, Box 7: Letter from Alma in Leipzig to 'My darling sister Pauline', 16 May 1914.
30. ibid. Box 5: Letter from Alma in Leipzig to 'My precious sister Fanny', 29 June 1914.
31. ibid.: Letter from Alma in Leipzig to 'My own precious good sister Fanny', 5 June 1914.
32. ibid. Box 7: Letter from Alma in Leipzig to 'My precious sister Pauline', 9 June 1914.
33. ibid. Box 5: Letter from Alma in Leipzig to 'My precious sister Fanny', 29 June 1914.
34. ibid. Box 7: Letter from Alma in Leipzig to 'My dear beloved sister Pauline', 29 August 1913.
35. ibid.: Alma to 'Dearly beloved ones at Home!',18 December 1913.
36. USBNA, Carl Hannen Collection: Tablet from 'Abdu'l-Bahá from Ramleh, Egypt, 'revealed for the friends in Gotha', translated by Ahmad Sohrab, Ramleh, Egypt, 23 September 1913. The believers addressed were Miss Anna Eichler, Miss Winnie Coulters, Mrs Anna Grimm, Mrs Opez, Mrs Holzhausen, Miss Susan Pollock, Miss Frida Kiel, Miss Eva Schwarz, Mr Hans Plessner, Miss Marie Plessner.
37. Washington DC Bahá'í Archives, Hannen-Knobloch Collection, Box 5: Letter from Alma in Leipzig to 'My own precious sister Fanny', 5 October 1913.
38. ibid.: Letter from Alma in Leipzig to 'My precious good sister Fanny', 31 August 1913.
39. ibid. Box 1: Letter from Richard Glitz in Chemnitz to 'Sehr geehrte Miss Knobloch!', 6 September 1913.
40. ibid.: Tablet from 'Abdu'l-Bahá to Richard Glitz, translated by Ahmad Sohrab, Ramleh, Egypt. 23 September 1913.

41. ibid. Box 5: Letter from Alma in Leipzig to 'My Precious Sister Fanny', 19 June 1914.
42. ibid.: Letter from Alma in Leipzig to 'My precious sister Fanny', 2 May 1914.
43. ibid.: Letter from Alma in Leipzig to 'My Precious Sister Fanny', 19 June 1914.
44. ibid. Box 1: Notebook of Alma Knobloch.
45. USBNA, microfilm: Tablet from 'Abdu'l-Bahá to Alma Knobloch, translated by Ahmad Sohrab, 21 April 1914.
46. Staatsarchiv Hamburg, vol. 373–7 I, VIII A 1, Band 272, p. 4269. Microfilm Number K1834.
47. Washington DC Bahá'í Archives, Hannen-Knobloch Collection, Box 5: Letter from Alma in Leipzig to 'My Precious Sister Fanny' 19 June 1914.
48. *The San Francisco Call*, 14 October 1912. https://chroniclingamerica.loc.gov/lccn/sn85066387/1912-10-14/ed-1/seq-1/.
49. USBNA, microfilm: Tablet from 'Abdu'l-Bahá, translated 13 July 1914. Also in Washington DC Bahá'í Archives, Hannen-Knobloch Collection, Box 1.
50. Washington DC Bahá'í Archives, Hannen-Knobloch Collection, Box 7: Letter from Alma in Stuttgart to 'My own precious sister Pauline', 14 February 1910.
51. ibid.: Letter from Alma in Stuttgart to 'My own precious Pauline', 30 March 1910.
52. See Cobb, *Ayesha of the Bosphorus: A Romance of Constantinople*.
53. Washington DC Bahá'í Archives, Hannen-Knobloch Collection, Box 5: Letter from Alma in Stuttgart to 'My own precious sister Fanny!', September 1914.
54. ibid.: Letter from Alma in Leipzig to 'My precious sister Fanny', 26 November 1912.
55. ibid.: Letter from Alma in Leipzig to 'My precious good sister Fanny', 11 May 1914.
56. Jeffrey R. Smith, 'The Monarchy versus the Nation: The "Festive Year" 1913 in Wilhelmine Germany', in *German Studies Review*, vol. 23 (2000), no. 2, pp. 257–74.
57. Washington DC Bahá'í Archives, Hannen-Knobloch Collection, Box 5: Letter from Alma in Leipzig to 'My precious beloved sister Fanny', 20 October 1913.
58. *Star of the West*, vol. V, no. 12 (16 October 1914), pp. 179–80.
59. ibid. no. 11 (27 September 1914), pp. 163–5.

35 The War to End All Wars

1. Remey, *Through Warring Countries*, p. 20.
2. ibid. pp. 2–23.
3. ibid. p. 23.
4. Washington DC Bahá'í Archives, Hannen-Knobloch Collection, Box

7: Letter from Alma in Leipzig to 'My darling sister Pauline', 16 May 1914.
5. ibid. Box 5: Letter from Alma in Leipzig to 'My own precious good sister Fanny', 24 May 1914.
6. ibid. Box 7: Letter from Alma in Leipzig to 'My precious sister Pauline', 9 June 1914.
7. ibid. Box 5: Letter from Alma in Leipzig to 'My Precious Sister Fanny', 19 June 1914.
8. ibid.: Letter from Alma in Leipzig to 'My precious sister Fanny', 29 June 1914.
9. ibid. Box 7: Letter from Alma in Leipzig to 'Beloved sister Pauline', 30 July 1914.
10. ibid. Box 1: Letter from Alma in Stuttgart to 'My Precious Ones at home!', 14 September 1914.
11. Remey, *Through Warring Countries*, p. 43.
12. ibid.
13. ibid.
14. USBNA, Hannen Knobloch Collection: Letter from Alma in Leipzig to 'My dear brother Joseph' (Joseph Hannen), 22 July 1916.
15. Remey, *Through Warring Countries*, pp. 46–51.
16. ibid. p. 57; see Matt. 22:21.
17. ibid.
18. Washington DC Bahá'í Archives, Hannen-Knobloch Collection, Box 7: Letter from Alma in Stuttgart to 'meine Liebe Schwester Pauline', 23 August 1914 (in German, my translation).
19. ibid.: Tablet from 'Abdu'l-Bahá to Mr Eckstein, 12 August 1913; also Box 1: 'Excerpts from Mirza Ahmad Sohrab's Diary', nine typed loose pages dated 16 August 1913 to 2 September 1913.
20. ibid. Box 5: Letter from Alma to 'meine Liebe Schwester Fanny', 6 September 1914 (in German, my translation).
21. ibid.: Letter from Alma to Fanny, 28 September 1914 (in German, my translation).
22. *Star of the West*, vol. 5, no. 12 (16 October 1914), pp. 185–6.
23. Washington DC Bahá'í Archives, Collection 33, Hannen-Knobloch Papers, Box 5: Letter from Alma to 'My own precious sister Fanny', September 1914 (no day given).
24. ibid.: Letter from Alma to 'meine Liebe Schwester Fanny', 6 September 1914 (in German, my translation).
25. ibid. Box 1: Letter from Alma in Stuttgart to 'dear ones at home!', 5 December 1914.
26. ibid. Box 7: Letter from Alma in Stuttgart to 'meine liebe gute Schwester Pauline', 25 September 1914 (in German, my translation).
27. ibid. Box 5: Letter from Alma to 'meine Liebe Schwester Fanny', 6 September 1914 (in German, my translation).
28. ibid Box 1: Letter from Alma in Stuttgart to 'dear ones at home!', 5 December 1914.

29. ibid. Box 5: Letter from Alma in Stuttgart to 'My own precious sister Fanny', September 1914 (no day given).
30. ibid.: Letter from Alma in Stuttgart to 'Meine liebe gute Schwester Fanny', 28 September 1914 (in German, my translation).
31. Watson, 'Recruitment: Conscripts and Volunteers during World War One', 29 January 2014.
32. Washington DC Bahá'í Archives, Hannen-Knobloch Collection (box no. unknown): Notes of a partially deteriorated letter from Alma, 11 September.
33. ibid.
34. ibid. Box 5: Letter from Alma in Stuttgart to 'My liebe gute Schwester Fanny', 28 September 1914 (in German, my translation).
35. ibid.: Letter from Alma in Stuttgart to 'Meine inigst geliebte Fanny', 29 August 1914 (in German, my translation).
36. ibid. Box 7: Letter from Alma in Stuttgart to 'meine liebe gute Schwester Pauline', 25 September 1914.
37. ibid.: Letter from Alma in Munich to 'Precious Sister Fanny', 11 January 1915.
38. ibid.: Letter from Alma in Stuttgart to 'My own precious sister Pauline', 11 September 1914.
39. USBNA, photograph courtesy of Duane Troxel.
40. Washington DC Bahá'í Archives, Hannen-Knobloch Collection, Box 1: Letter from Alma in Stuttgart to 'My Precious ones at home!', 14 September 1914.
41. *Star of the West*, vol. 5, no. 13 (4 November 1914), p. 202. 'Original translated into German by Alma S. Knobloch, Stuttgart, Germany; retranslated into English by Mr, and Mrs, Chas. Ioas, Chicago.'
42. *Evening Star* (Washington DC), Sunday, 20 September 20, 1914, p. 71.
43. Washington DC Bahá'í Archives, Hannen-Knobloch Collection, Box 7: Letter from Alma in Leipzig to 'Beloved sister Pauline', 30 July 1914.
44. ibid. (box no. unknown): Notes of a partially deteriorated letter from Alma, 11 September.
45. ibid. Box 5: Letter from Alma in Stuttgart to 'Precious sister Fanny!', 16 September 1914.
46. Bidwell, *Currency Conversion Tables: A Hundred Years of Change*, pp. 22–4.
47. Washington DC Bahá'í Archives, Hannen-Knobloch Collection, Box 1: Letter from Alma in Stuttgart to 'My Precious ones at home!', 14 September 1914.
48. *Star of the West*, vol. 5, no. 13 (4 November 1914), p. 199. 'Original in German; translated into English by Mr. and Mrs. Chas. Ioas, Chicago.'
49. Washington DC Bahá'í Archives, Collection 33, Hannen-Knobloch Collection, Box 1: Letter from Alma in Stuttgart to 'My Precious ones at home!', 14 September 1914.
50. ibid. Box 5; Letter from Alma to 'My own precious sister Fanny', September 1914.

51. ibid. Box 3: Letter from Alma to 'My precious good sister Fanny', 26 October 1914.
52. ibid.
53. ibid. Box 1: Letter from Alma to 'dear ones at home!', 5 December 1914.
54. ibid. Box 7: Letter from Alma to 'My precious sister Pauline', from Munich, 11 January 1915.
55. ibid. Box 5: Letter from Alma in Stuttgart to 'Meine liebe gute Schwester Fanny!', 28 September 1914 (in German, my translation).

36 Crisis and Victory during the War

1. Washington DC Bahá'í Archives, Charles Mason Remey Collection: Letter from Mason Remey to Herman Faber in Munich: 'My dear Spiritual Brother!', 27 January 1907.
2. ibid. Hannen-Knobloch Collection, Box 3: Letter from Alma in Munich to 'My own precious sister Fanny', 9 April 1915.
3. ibid.: Letter from Alma in Munich to 'My precious sister Fanny', 6 May 1915.
4. ibid. Box 1: Letter from Alma in Stuttgart to 'My precious sisters and dear ones at home', 5 December 1914.
5. ibid.: Letter from Alma in Bad Frankenhausen an Kyffhäusen to 'My precious ones at home', 5 September 1915.
6. ibid. Box 3: Letter from Alma in Munich to 'My precious sister Fanny', 11 January 1915.
7. ibid. Box 7: Letter from Alma in Munich to 'My precious sister Pauline', 6 February 1915.
8. USBNA, Hannen Knobloch Collection: Letter from Alma to Agnes Alexander in Tokyo, 6 February 1915.
9. Washington DC Bahá'í Archives, Hannen-Knobloch Collection, Box 3: Letter from Alma in Munich to 'My own precious sister Fanny', 19 January 1915.
10. ibid. Box 7: Letter from Alma in Munich to 'My precious sister Pauline', 6 February 1915.
11. ibid. Box 3: Letter from Alma in Munich to 'My precious sisters Fanny and Pauline', 9 March 1915.
12. ibid. Box 1: Letter from Alma in Munich to 'My precious Sisters', 4 May 1915.
13. ibid.
14. ibid. Box 3: Letter from Alma in Munich to 'My precious sister Fanny', 26 June 1915.
15. ibid. Box 1: Letter from Alma in Bad Frankenhausen an Kyffhäusen to 'My precious ones at home', 5 September 1915.
16. ibid. Box 1: Letter from Alma in Munich to 'My precious Sisters', 4 May 1915.
17. German National Bahá'í Archives, G 147 No 12 or 17 from A. Bahador to Bertha Bopp (Bertha Bahnmüller became Bertha Bopp after her marriage), 3 August 1915.

18. USBNA: Tablet from 'Abdu'l-Bahá to the German believers, 9 May 1915. Translated by Ahmad Sohrab in Haifa, Syria.
19. 'Messages from Abdul-Baha to Bahais in Germany', in *Star of the West*, vol. 6, no. 13 (4 November 1915), p. 101.
20. ibid.
21. Washington DC Bahá'í Archives, Hannen-Knobloch Collection, Box 3: Quoted in a letter from Alma to 'my own precious sister Fanny', 19 June 1915; also Box 7: Letter from Alma in Munich to 'My precious sister Pauline', 28 June 1915.
22. ibid. Box 3: Letter from Alma in Gera to 'My Precious sister Fanny', 5 October 1915.
23. ibid. Box 3: Letter from Alma in Leipzig Sehl to 'My own precious sister Fanny', 3 April 1916.
24. ibid. Box 6: Tablet from 'Abdu'l-Bahá to Alma Knobloch, 10 August 1915, translated by A. Bahadur, Beirut.
25. ibid. Box 1: Letter from Alma in Munich to 'My dear Nephew Nategh' (Carl), 5 June 1915.
26. ibid. Box 3: Letter from Alma in Leipzig Sehl to 'My precious sister Fanny', 23 January 1916.
27. ibid. Box 7: Letter from Alma in Munich to 'My precious sister Pauline', 6 February 1915.
28. ibid. Box 3: Letters from Alma in Gera to 'My Precious sister Fanny', 5 October 1915, and to 'My beloved sister Pauline', 5 October 1915.
29. ibid.: Letter from Alma in Munich to 'My precious sister Fanny', 6 May 1915.
30. ibid.: Letter from Alma in Munich to 'My darling sister Fanny', 23 August 1915.
31. ibid.: Letter from Alma in Bad Frankenhausen an Kyffhäusen to 'My darling sister Fanny', 23 August 1915.
32. ibid. Box 7: Letter from Alma in Leipzig to 'My beloved sister Pauline', 3 November 1915.
33. ibid. Box 3: Letter from Alma in Bad Frankenhausen an Kyffhäusen to 'My darling sister Fanny', 23 August 1915.
34. ibid. Box 1: Letter from Alma in Leipzig to 'My dear beloved Ones at Home', 23 November 1915.
35. USBNA, Latimer Collection, Box 3: Letter from Alma in Leipzig Sehl to 'Dear Bahai brother!', 13 March 1916.
36. Washington DC Bahá'í Archives, Hannen-Knobloch Collection, Box 7: Letter from Alma in Leipzig to 'My beloved sister Pauline', 3 November 1915.
37. ibid. Box 1: 'Extracts from a letter written by Mirza Azizollah to Frau Schwarz', 23 December 1916.
38. ibid.: 'Extracts from a letter written by Mirza Azizollah to Frau Schwarz', 30 June 1916.

37 The Crucible of War and the Revelation of the Divine Plan

1. 'Abdu'l-Bahá, *The Promulgation of Universal Peace*, p. 74.
2. ibid. pp. 283–4.
3. 'Messages from Abdul-Baha to Bahais in Germany', in *Star of the West*, vol. 6, no. 13 (4 November 1915), pp. 101–02.
4. Letter on behalf of Shoghi Effendi to an individual, 17 February 1933, in Research Department of the Universal House of Justice, *Social and Economic Development*, p. 4; also quoted in Langness, 'Man, Organic with the World', online article, 26 April 2014.
5. Shoghi Effendi, *Citadel of Faith*, p. 25.
6. Washington DC Bahá'í Archives, Hannen-Knobloch Collection, Box 8: Letter from Alma in Munich to 'My precious sister Pauline', 6 February 1915; Daniel Jenkyn, of St. Ives, Cornwall, England, was 'the Secretary of the Bahai Assembly of London and the first Bahai teacher to visit the Netherlands' (Remey, *Through Warring Countries*, p. 41).
7. Washington DC Bahá'í Archives, Hannen-Knobloch Collection, Box 3: Letter from Alma in Munich to 'My precious sisters Fanny and Pauline', 9 March 1915.
8. ibid. Box 7: Letter from Alma in Munich to 'My precious sister Pauline', 6 February 1915.
9. ibid. Box 3: Letter from Alma in Munich to 'My own precious sister Fanny', 19 January 1915.
10. USBNA, Ella Cooper Collection: Letter from Wilhelm Herrigel to 'Liebe Bahai Schwester und Bruder', 26 January 1915.
11. Washington DC Bahá'í Archives, Hannen-Knobloch Collection, Box 1: Ahmad Sohrab's Diary.
12. USBNA, Hannen Knobloch Collection: Letter from Alma in Leipzig Sehl to 'My dear brother Joseph', 22 July 1916.
13. Washington DC Bahá'í Archives, Hannen-Knobloch Collection, Box 3: Letter from Alma in Leipzig Sehl to 'My Own precious sister Fanny', 3 February 1916.
14. ibid.: Letter from Alma in Leipzig Sehl to 'My Own precious and beloved sister Fanny', 18 February 1916.
15. USBNA, Latimer Collection: Letter from Alma in Leipzig Sehl to 'Dear Brother', 13 March 1916.
16. Washington DC Bahá'í Archives, Hannen-Knobloch Collection, Box 1: Letter from Mason Remey to Alma, 9 November 1915.
17. USBNA, Latimer Collection: Letter from Alma in Leipzig Sehl to George Latimer, 3 February 1916.
18. ibid.: Letter from Alma in Leipzig Sehl to 'Dear Brother Latimer', 13 March 1916.
19. USBNA, Hannen Knobloch Collection: Letter from Azíz'u'lláh Bahádur to Alma, 10 January 1916.
20. Washington DC Bahá'í Archives, Hannen-Knobloch Collection, Box 3: Letter from Alma in Leipzig Sehl to Fanny, 23 January 1916,
21. ibid.

22. ibid.: Letter from Alma in Leipzig Sehl to 'My Own precious sister Fanny', 3 February 1916.
23. ibid.: Letter from Alma in Leipzig Sehl to 'My own precious beloved sister Fanny', 18 February 1916.
24. Letter from the Universal House of Justice to the Bahá'ís of the World acting under the Mandate of 'Abdu'l-Bahá, 26 March 2016.
25. 'Abdu'l-Bahá, *Tablets of the Divine Plan*, p. 39.
26. Washington DC Bahá'í Archives, Hannen-Knobloch Collection, Box 3: Letter from Alma in Stuttgart to 'My own precious sister Fanny', 20 October 1919.
27. ibid. Box 7: Letter from Alma in Berlin Friedenau to 'My precious sister Pauline', 29 July 1916.
28. USBNA, Latimer Collection: Letter from Alma to George Latimer, 23 November 1916.
29 Washington DC Bahá'í Archives, Hannen-Knobloch Collection, Box 1: Letter from Alma to 'My precious sisters', 9 September 1916.
30. ibid. Box 7: Letter from Alma in Stuttgart to 'My beloved sister' (the rest of letter is in German, my translation), 31 December 1917.
31 USBNA, Latimer Collection: Letter from Alma to George Latimer, 23 November 1916.
32. Washington DC Bahá'í Archives, Hannen-Knobloch Collection, Box 6: Letter from Fanny to Joseph, November 1916.
33. ibid. Box 7: Letter from Alma in Stuttgart to 'My beloved sister Pauline!', 24 November 1916.
34. ibid. Box 3: Letter from Alma in Stuttgart to 'My precious sister Fanny', 29 March 1917.
35. USBNA, Hannen Knobloch Collection: Telegram from Alma through Geneva to 1252 8th Street, Washington DC, (14) 24 May 1919.
36. ibid.: Letter from Alma in Munich to 'Liebe Mrs Hötzel' (the letter is in German, my translation), 6 June 1917.
37. ibid.: Tablet from 'Abdu'l-Bahá to Margarethe Döring, translated by A. Bahadur, 27 July 1917. Also in the German National Bahá'í Archives, Hermann Grossmann Files B 11 D 1908–1920.
38. German National Bahá'í Archives, Hermann Grossmann Files B 11 D 1908–1920.
39. Washington DC Bahá'í Archives, Hannen-Knobloch Collection, Box 1: Tablet from 'Abdu'l-Bahá to Alma Knobloch, 25 July 1917.
40. ibid.: Tablet from 'Abdu'l-Bahá to Mrs Zimmer, translated by A. Bahadur, 13 July 1917.
41. ibid. Box 3: Postcard from Alma in Ludwigshafen dated 9 December 1917, with letter from Alma in Stuttgart to 'My dear good sisters', 4 December 1917.
42. See Williams, *Biplanes and Bombsights: British Bombing in World War 1*.
43. Washington DC Bahá'í Archives, Hannen-Knobloch Collection, Box 3: Letter from Alma in Stuttgart to 'My own precious good sister Fanny', 6 October 1919.

44. ibid.: Letter from Alma in Nuremberg to 'My beloved sister Fanny', 11 April 1918.
45. USBNA, Hannen Knobloch Collection: small note by Alma in a notebook, 30 March 1918.
46. Washington DC Baháʼí Archives, Hannen-Knobloch Collection, Box 3: Letter from Alma in Nuremberg to 'My beloved sister Fanny', 11 April 1918.
47. USBNA, Hannen Knobloch Collection: small postcards written on by Alma from Ostsee Bad Dahme, August 1918.
48. ibid.
49. Washington DC Baháʼí Archives, Hannen-Knobloch Collection, Box 3: Letter from Alma in Leipzig Sehl to 'My precious dear sister Fanny', 24 November 1918.
50. ibid. Box 1: Letter from Alma in Stuttgart to 'Precious Sisters', 2 January 1920.
51. ibid. Box 7: A poem for Alma from Willy Schmand.
52. ibid. Box 3: Letter from Alma in Munich to 'Precious Sister Fanny', 11 January 1915.
53. USBNA, Latimer Collection: Letter from Alma in Stuttgart to 'Dear Bahai Brother' (Mr George Latimer) 7 October 1919.
54. ibid.
55. Washington DC Baháʼí Archives, Hannen-Knobloch Collection, Box 3: Letter from Alma in Bad Frankenhausen to 'My darling sister Fanny', 23 August 1915.
56. ibid.: Letter from Alma in Stuttgart to 'My own precious sister Fanny', 6 October 1919.
57. ibid.: Letter from Alma in Leipzig Sehl to 'My own precious sisters Fanny and Pauline', 5 May 1920.
58. ibid. Box 1: Letter from Alma to 'Precious sisters', 16 March 1920.
59. USBNA, Latimer Collection: Letter from Alma to George Latimer, 7 October 1919.
60. Washington DC Baháʼí Archives, Hannen-Knobloch Collection, Box 3: Letter from Alma in Munich to 'Precious sisters Fanny and Pauline!', 9 March 1915.
61. USBNA, Latimer Collection: Letter from Heinrich Schwab to George Latimer, 29 January 1921.
62. Washington DC Baháʼí Archives, Hannen-Knobloch Collection, Box 3: Letter from Alma in Stuttgart to 'My own precious sisters Fanny and Pauline', 5 May 1920.
63. Ettlich, *Konsul Albert Schwarz: Banker, Bürger und Baháʼí in Stuttgart und Bad Mergentheim*, p. 165.
64. *Star of the West*, vol. 11, no. 13 (4 November 1920), p. 231.

38 The Love of God that Bubbles Over

1. Washington DC Bahá'í Archives, Hannen-Knobloch Collection, Box 3: Letter from Alma in Leipzig to 'My precious beloved sister Fanny', 19 November 1918.
2. ibid.: Letter from Alma in Leipzig Sehl to 'My precious dear sister Fanny', 24 November 1918.
3. USBNA, Hannen Knobloch Collection: Telegram From Alma through Geneva to 1252 8th Street, Washington DC, (14) 24 May 1919.
4. Letter from Shoghi Effendi to Dr Zia M. Bagdadi in Chicago, 25 April 1919, in *Star of the West*, vol. 10, no. 6 (24 June 1919), pp. 104–05.
5. USBNA, Latimer Collection: Letter from Alma in Stuttgart to 'My Dear Spiritual Brother!', 25 March 1919.
6. ibid. Hannen Knobloch Collection, Letter from Alma in Stuttgart to 'Dear Brother' (Joseph), 13 March 1916.
7. ibid.: Letter from Richard Glitz to Alma, February 1919.
8. 'Abdu'l-Bahá, 'Tablet to the Paris Assembly', 23 July 1919, in *Star of the West*, vol. 10, no. 12 (16 October 1919), p. 226.
9. USBNA, Latimer Collection: Letter from Alma in Stuttgart to George Latimer, 7 October 1919,
10. Washington DC Bahá'í Archives, Hannen-Knobloch Collection, Box 1: Letter from Alma in Stuttgart to 'beloved ones at home!', 2 January 1920.
11. Fanny Knobloch and Bertha Kirkpatrick, 'South African Mission', in *World Order Magazine*, November 1946.
12. Washington DC Bahá'í Archives, Hannen-Knobloch Collection, Box 1: Letter from Alma in Stuttgart to 'Precious sisters', 12 January 1920.
13. ibid.: Letter from Alma in Stuttgart to 'My precious Sisters!', 16 April 1920.
14. USBNA, Hannen Knobloch Collection: Letter from A. Bahádor to Alma, 1 March 1920.
15. *Evening Star*, 28 January 1920, p. 11.
16. Washington DC Bahá'í Archives, Hannen-Knobloch Collection, Box 6: 'Tablets from 'Abdu'l-Bahá', 23 January 1920, typed document.
17. ibid. Box 1: Letter from Alma in Stuttgart to 'My precious darling sister', 26 February 1920.
18. ibid. Box 7: Letter from Alma in Stuttgart to 'My Precious sister Pauline', 3 March 1920.
19. Hannen Moe, *A Flame with Devotion*, p. 313.
20. *Star of the West*, vol. 11, no. 13 (4 November 1920), p. 231. In the many copies of this Tablet in the Washington DC Bahá'í Archives, the word ''effervesce' given in *Star of the West* is translated as 'bubble up' or 'bubble over'. This is clearly the usage Alma retained.
21. Washington DC Bahá'í Archives, Hannen-Knobloch Collection, Box 1: Letter from Alma to 'My Precious sisters', 24 July 1920; also USBNA, Hannen Knobloch Collection: Letter from Alma in Leipzig Sehl to 'My dear precious sisters', 6 June 1920.

22. Washington DC Bahá'í Archives, Hannen-Knobloch Collection, Box 7: Letter from Alma in Stuttgart to 'My precious sister Pauline', 3 March 1920.
23. ibid. Box 1: Letter from Alma in Leipzig Sehl to 'My Precious Dear Sisters', 23 June 1920.
24. USBNA, Hannen Knobloch Collection: Letter from Alma in Leipzig Sehl to 'My own dear precious sister Fanny', 2 June 1920.
25. 'Hermann Grossmann (1899–1969): Ein Leben im Dienst der neuen Offenbarung' in *Bahá'í Briefe*, no. 38 (October 1969), p. 1038 (in German, my translation).
26. USBNA, Hannen Knobloch Collection: Letter from A. Bahádur to Alma, 18 August 1920.
27. Washington DC Bahá'í Archives, Hannen-Knobloch Collection, Box 7: Letter from Alma to 'My precious dear Pauline', 29 July 1920.
28. 'George Adam Benke', in *The Bahá'í World*, vol. V (1932–1934) p. 416.
29. Letter on behalf of Shoghi Effendi to the National Spiritual Assembly of the Bahá'ís of Germany and Austria, 21 June 1956, in Shoghi Effendi, *The Light of Divine Guidance*, vol. 2, p. 263.
30. USBNA, Charles Mason Remey Collection: 'Charles Mason Remey Report on Germany to the Master from his temporary address in Esslingen Württemberg, December 1920'.
31. 'In Memoriam: Eva Gleichmann', in *Bahá'í Nachrichten*. July 2003, p. 8.
32. Washington DC Bahá'í Archives, Hannen-Knobloch Collection, Box 1: Letter from Alma in Leipzig Sehl to 'My Precious Sisters', 24 July 1920.
33. ibid. Box 2: Alma's memoirs.
34. ibid. Box 7: Letter from Alma in Freiburg to 'My own precious sister Pauline', 2 September 1920.
35. ibid.: Letter from Alma in Stuttgart to 'My Precious Sister Pauline', 5 October 1920.
36. ibid.: Letter from Alma in Leipzig Sehl to 'My own precious sister Pauline', 2 November 1920; a copy of 'Abdu'l-Bahá's Tablet to Edith Horn, 15 August 1920, is in the letter.
37. Pfaff-Grossmann, *Hermann Grossmann: Hand of the Cause of God*, p. 67.
38. Washington DC Bahá'í Archives, Hannen-Knobloch Collection, Box 7: Letter from Alma in Leipzig Sehl to 'My dear good sister Pauline', 14 November 1920.
39. ibid. Box 2: Alma's memoirs.
40. Knobloch, 'The Call to Germany', in *The Bahá'í World*, vol. VII (1936–1938), p. 745.
41. USBNA, Hannen Knobloch Collection: Letter from Alma to 'My dear precious sisters', 6 June 1920.
42. Washington DC Bahá'í Archives, Hannen-Knobloch Collection, Box 3: Letter from Fanny in South Africa to Alma, 5 March 1925.

43. Information from Ancestry.com.
44. 'Abdu'l-Bahá, Tablet to Fanny Knobloch, in *Star of the West*, vol. 11, no. 13 (4 November 1920), p. 231.

39 In America Again

1. USBNA, Hannen Knobloch Collection: Letter from Fanny to Alma: 'Welcome, Welcome, Home, Alma dear', 26 November 1920. Although the location is not given, other letters from Fanny written in November 1920 indicate that she was in Cape Town, South Africa.
2. ibid. Agnes Parsons Collection: Letter from Alma Knobloch in Springfield to Mrs R. S. Parsons, 26 February 1921.
3. Washington DC Bahá'í Archives, Hannen-Knobloch Collection, Box 5: Letter from Alma in Springfield to 'My precious good sister Pauline', 22 February 1921.
4. ibid.: Letter from Alma in Springfield to 'My precious good sister Pauline', 26 March 1921.
5. ibid.: Letter from Alma in Springfield to 'my precious dear sister Pauline', 4 April 1921.
6. *Star of the West*, vol. 12, no. 4 (17 May 1921), pp. 72–3.
7. Washington DC Bahá'í Archives, Hannen-Knobloch Collection, Box 1: Tablet from 'Abdu'l-Bahá to Alma Knobloch, 3 August 1921, translated by Ruhi Afnan, Haifa, Palestine. Also in USBNA, microfilm.
8. ibid. Box 6: Letter from Alma Knobloch to 'Abdu'l-Bahá, 14 October 1921, carbon copy of letter.
9. *The Washington Times*, 10 September 1921, Final Home Edition, p. 4, image 4.
10. Louis Gregory, in *The Bahá'í World*, vol. VII (1936–1938), p. 656.

40 The Ascension of 'Abdu'l-Bahá

1. *Star of the West*, vol. 13, no. 1 (21 March 1922), p. 22.
2. ibid. vol. 12, no. 15 (12 December 1921), p. 245.
3. ibid. no. 19 (2 March 1922), p. 299.
4. ibid. vol. 13, no. 9, pp. 236–7; Shoghi Effendi and Lady Blomfield, *The Passing of 'Abdu'l-Bahá*.
5. USBNA, Latimer Collection, Box 6: Letter from Wilhelm Herrigel to George Latimer, 3 March 1922 (in German, my translation)
6. ibid.
7. Cameron and Momen, *A Basic Bahá'í Chronology*, p. 219.
8. Shoghi Effendi, *Bahá'í Administration*, p. 20.
9. Washington DC Bahá'í Archives, Hannen-Knobloch Collection, Box 1: Handwritten copy of a letter from Alma in Washington DC to Shoghi Effendi, 15 May 1923.

41 The German Bahá'í Community after Alma

1. USBNA, Hannen Knobloch Collection: Letter from Elise Stäbler in Stuttgart to Alma, 4 August 1921 (in German, my translation); election

results from 15 March 1921 were also in this file.
2. ibid.: Letter from Emma Helling to Alma, 29 April 1921 (Original in old German alphabet, Gunther Haug / Lutz Unkrig translation to German, my translation to English).
3. *Star of the West*, vol. 13, no. 10 (January 1923), p. 279.
4. USBNA, A. Windust Collection: Letter from Annemarie Schweizer to Albert Windust, 25 May 1921.
5. ibid. Latimer Collection: Letter from Annemarie Schweizer to George Latimer, 29 Sept 1921.
6. ibid. Hannen Knobloch Collection, Box 19: Letter from Robert Rör to Alma, 23 February 1921 (in German, my translation).
7. ibid. Latimer Collection: Letter from Alice Schwarz to George Latimer.
8. Washington DC Bahá'í Archives, Hannen-Knobloch Collection: Letter from Rosa Schwarz to Alma, 9 May 1921 (in German, my translation).
9. USBNA, Hannen Knobloch Collection: Letter from Alice Schwarz to Alma, July 1921 (in German, my translation).
10. ibid.: Letter from Margarethe Döring to Alma, care of Mrs Fritz, Springfield Mass., 23 July 1921 (original in old German alphabet, Gunther Haug / Lutz Unkrig translation to German, my translation to English).
11. ibid.: Letter from Margarethe Döring to Alma, 4 August 1921 (original in old German alphabet, Gunther Haug / Lutz Unkrig translation to German, my translation to English).
12. ibid.: Letter from Lydia Bauer to Alma, 8 August 1921 (in German, my translation).
13. ibid.: Letter from Margarethe Döring to Alma, no date but probably 1923 (original in old German alphabet, Gunther Haug / Lutz Unkrig translation to German, my translation to English).
14. ibid.: Letter from Lydia Bauer to Alma, 18 May 1924 (in German, my translation).
15. ibid.: Letter from Lydia Bauer to Alma, 13 November 1923 (in German, my translation).
16. ibid: Letter from Lydia Bauer an Alma, 23 October 1923 (in German, my translation).
17. ibid.: Letter from Rose Schwarz in Degerloch to Alma, 11 July 1924; and from Lydia Bauer to Alma, 15 May 1927 (in German, my translation).
18. ibid.: Letter to Alma from Leipzig (original in old German alphabet, Gunther Haug / Lutz Unkrig translation to Germany, my translation to English).
19. ibid.
20. ibid.: Letter from Adam Benke to Alma, 18 January 1924 (in German, my translation).

42 The Sad Story of Wilhelm Herrigel

1. USBNA, Charles Mason Remey Collection: Letter from Wilhelm Herrigel to C. M. Remey, 7 July 1926.
2. Ettlich, *Konsul Albert Schwarz: Banker, Bürger und Bahá'í*, p. 204.
3. USBNA, John Bosch Collection: Letter from Wilhelm Herrigel to John and Louise Bosch, 23 July 1919 (in German, my translation).
4. Ettlich, *Konsul Albert Schwarz: Banker, Bürger und Bahá'í*, p. 204.
5. USBNA, Mary Lesch Collection: Letter from Wilhelm Herrigel, 1 April 1920 (in German, my translation).
6. Ettlich, *Konsul Albert Schwarz: Banker, Bürger und Bahá'í*, p. 204.
7. USBNA, John Bosch Collection: Letter from Wilhelm Herrigel to John Bosch, 14 November 1922 (in German, my translation)
8. ibid.: Letter from Wilhelm Herrigel to John and Louise Bosch, 9 January 1923 (in German, my translation).
9. ibid.: Letter from Wilhelm Herrigel to John and Louise Bosch, 14 November 1922 (in German, my translation).
10. ibid.: Latimer Collection: Letters from Wilhelm Herrigel to George Latimer, 13 May and 17 October 1921 (in German, my translation).
11. ibid.: Letter from Wilhelm Herrigel to George Latimer, 30 September 1922; Hannen Knobloch Collection, Box 19 m-192 5: Letters from Franz Pöllinger to Alma, 3 April 1925 and September 1925 (in German, my translation).
12. ibid.: John Bosch Collection: Letter from Annemarie Schweizer to Family Bosch, 22 June 1922.
13. ibid.: Hannen Knobloch Collection: Letter from Franz Pöllinger to Alma, 3 April 1925.
14. *Sonne der Wahrheit* (March 1927), p. 16.
15. USBNA, Charles Mason Remey Collection: Letter from Wilhelm Herrigel to C. M. Remey, 7 July 1926.
16. ibid. Bosch Collection: Letter from Wilhelm Herrigel to John Bosch, 18 October 1927 (in German, my translation).
17. ibid.: Letter from Wilhelm Herrigel to John Bosch, 23 November 1927 (in German, my translation).
18. German National Bahá'í Archives, Annemarie Schweizer Collection, G-16 no. 11: Letter from Hermann Grossmann to the National Spiritual Assembly of Germany, 5 April 1929 (in German).
19. ibid.
20. USBNA, Agnes Parsons Collection: Letter from Ruth White to Agnes Parsons, 14 July 1927; Letter from Ruth White to the National Spiritual Assembly of the Bahá'ís of the United States and Canada, 3 December 1927; Letter from Ruth White to the National Spiritual Assembly of the Bahá'ís of the United States and Canada, 26 February 1928; Theodor Loeppert Collection: Letter from Wilhelm Herrigel to Theodor Loeppert, 21 March 1930 (in German, my translation).

21. ibid. Theodor Loeppert Collection: Letter from Wilhelm Herrigel to Theodor Loeppert, 11 April 1930 (in German, my translation).
22. German National Bahá'í Archives, Annemarie Schweizer Collection, G-16 no. 11: Letter from Der Geistige Nationalrat der Deutschen Baha'i (National Spiritual Assembly of the Bahá'ís of Germany) to the 'Mitglieder des Geistigen Nationalrats' (Members of the National Spiritual Assembly of the Bahá'ís of Germany), 21 February 1930.
23. USBNA, Hannen Knobloch Collection, Box 19: Letter from Franz Pöllinger in Vienna to Alma Knobloch, 23 April 1930 (in German).
24. ibid.
25. USBNA, Bosch Collection, Box 6: Letter from Alice Schwarz to Louise Bosch, 19 April 1932.
26. ibid. Theodor Loeppert Collection, Box 1: Letter from Wilhelm Herrigel to Theodor Loeppert, 11 April 1930.
27. ibid. Hannen Knobloch Collection: Letter from Franz Pöllinger to Alma, 23 April 1930, including the Vienna Declaration of Trust: to 'Geliebte Freund in Al-Abha' (Our loving friend in El Abha) from Bahá'í Gemeinde Vienna, 18 April 1930 (in German, my translation).
28. German National Bahá'í Archives, Alice Schwarz Collection: Tablet from 'Abdu'l-Bahá to Alice Schwarz, 4 July 1913.
29. Latimer, *Light of the World*, p. 44; see also Badiei, *Stories Told by 'Abdul-Baha*.

43 Return to Germany?

1. USBNA, Hannen Knobloch Collection: Letter from Alice Schwarz to Alma, 4 August 1923 (in German, my translation).
2. ibid.: Letter from Hermann Grossmann to Alma, 4 July 1924 (in German, my translation).
3. ibid.: Letter from Hermann Grossmann to Alma, 4 September 1924 (in German, my translation).
4. ibid.: Letter from Annemarie Schweizer to Alma, 2 November 1924 (in German, my translation).
5. Hannen Moe, *A Flame with Devotion*, p. 313.
6. Washington DC Bahá'í Archives, Hannen-Knobloch Collection, Box 3: Letter from Pauline to 'dearest Alma', 20 December 1924,
7. ibid.: Letter from Pauline to 'dearest Alma', dated 11 February 1924, but in fact 1925; Pauline wrote the wrong year.
8. ibid.
9. USBNA, Hannen Knobloch Collection: Bahá'í Arbeitsgemeinschaft, Esslingen, 16 October 1926 (German newsletter for the Month of Elm [Ilm], my translation).
10. ibid.: Letter from Hermann Grossmann to Alma, 9 March 1927 (in German, my translation).
11. ibid.: Postcard from Anna (Annel) Grossmann to Alma, 28 May 1928 (in German, my translation).
12. ibid.: Letter from Hermann Grossmann to Alma, 3 September 1928 (in German, my translation).

13. ibid.: Letter from Lydia Bauer to Alma, 15 May 1927 (in German, my translation).
14. Washington DC Bahá'í Archives, Hannen-Knobloch Collection, Box 3: Letter from Alma to Shoghi Effendi, 1 February 1929.
15. ibid.: Letter on behalf of Shoghi Effendi to Alma Knobloch, 23 February 1929.
16. German National Bahá'í Archives, Schweizer Collection: Letter from Pauline Bothner to the National Spiritual Assembly of the Bahá'ís of Germany, May 1929 (in German, my translation).
17. ibid. Uli Gollmer Collection: Letter from the Deutscher Baha'i Bund der Nationalrat (National Spiritual Assembly of the Bahá'ís of Germany) to 'Liebe Baha'i Freunde!' (Dear Baha'i friends), 10 May 1929 (in German, my translation).
18. USBNA, Hannen Knobloch Collection: Letter from May Maxwell to Alma on behalf of the US National Teaching Committee, 27 June 1928.
19. ibid.: Handwritten copy of Alma's Letter to Pauline Bothner, 28 May 1929 (written in old German alphabet, translated to normal German by Gerda and Gunther Haug).
20. ibid.: Letter from Pauline Bothner to Alma, 20 June 1929 (original in old German alphabet, translation into normal German by Gunther Haug; my translation into English).
21. Shoghi Effendi, *The Light of Divine Guidance*, vol. 2, p. 20.
22. Washington DC Bahá'í Archives, Hannen-Knobloch Collection, Box 1: Letter from Shoghi Effendi to Alma Knobloch, 21 January 1932. Published with the kind permission of the Bahá'í World Centre.

44 Serving the Guardian in the United States

1. Washington DC Bahá'í Archives, Hannen-Knobloch Collection, Box 8: Letter from Pauline to 'Dearest Alma', 19 July 1925.
2. ibid.: Letter from John Esslemont on behalf of Shoghi Effendi to the 'Members of the Summer School at Green Acre through Mr Albert Vail' 21 October 1925.
3. USBNA, microfilm: Postscript in the letter from Shoghi Effendi to 'My dearly beloved, most precious co-workers', 12 September 1926.
4. National Archives and Records Administration, Soundex Index to Naturalization Petitions for the United States District and Circuit Courts, Northern District of Illinois and Immigration and Naturalization Service District 9, 1840–1950 (M1285).
5. Washington DC Bahá'í Archives, Hannen-Knobloch Collection, Box 5: Letter from Alma in Milwaukee to 'My precious good sister Pauline', 22 November 1926.
6. USBNA, Hannen Knobloch Collection: Letter from Pauline to 'Dearest Alma', 9 September 1927.
7. *Baha'i Newsletter*, no. 13 (September 1926), p. 8.
8. USBNA, Hannen Knobloch Collection: Letter from Fanny to Mr

Horace Holley in New York, 21 November 1926.
9. ibid.: Letter from Vernon Du Rose in Pretoria to 'My Dear Mrs Hannen and Miss Knoblock', 7 January 1928.
10. Washington DC Bahá'í Archives, Hannen-Knobloch Collection, Box 3: Letter from Alma to 'precious sisters', 4 March 1928; ibid. Box 5: Letter from Alma to Pauline from Kenosha, 25 June 1928; ibid.: Letter from Pauline to Alma, 7 July 1928.
11. ibid. Box 3: Letter from Alma to 'precious sisters', 4 March 1928.
12. ibid.: Letter from Louis Gregory to 'Miss Alma Knobloch my dear Baha'i sister', 1 February 1928.
13. ibid.: Letter from Alma in Miami to 'my precious good Sisters' 2 April 1928.
14. ibid.: Letter from Alma in Miami to 'My precious good sisters', March 1928.
15. ibid.: Letter from Louis Gregory to Alma, 22 March 1928.
16. ibid.: Letter from Alma in Miami to 'My precious good sisters', March 1928.
17. Vernon, *Bahá'u'lláh's Garden: History of the Bahá'í Faith in Jacksonville 1919–1969*.
18. Washington DC Bahá'í Archives, Hannen-Knobloch Collection, Box 3: Letter from Alma in Miami to 'My precious good sisters', March 1928.
19. ibid.: Letter from Alma in Miami to 'My precious good sisters', 2 April 1928.
20. ibid., and letter from Alma in St Augustine to 'My precious sisters', 24–28 March 1928.
21. Remey, 'A Report to Abdul Baha of the Bahai Activities in the States of North Carolina, South Carolina, Georgia and Florida, March–April 1919', p. 15.
22. ibid.
23. Washington DC Bahá'í Archives, Hannen-Knobloch Collection, Box 3: Letter from Alma in Miami to 'my precious good Sisters', 2 April 1928.
24. Vernon, *Bahá'u'lláh's Garden: History of the Bahá'í Faith in Jacksonville 1919–1969*.
25. Washington DC Bahá'í Archives, Hannen-Knobloch Collection, Box 3: Letter from Alma in Chicago to 'My precious sisters', 29 April 1928.
26. ibid.: Letter from Alvina Jolly in Saint Augustine to Alma, 5 May 1928.
27. ibid. Box 1: Letter from Shoghi Effendi to Alma, 27 May 1928. Published with the kind permission of the Bahá'í World Centre.
28. ibid. Box 3: Letter from Louis Gregory to 'Miss Alma Knobloch my dear Bahá'i sister', 7 July 1928.
29. ibid.: Letter from May Maxwell on behalf of the National Teaching Committee to Alma, 27 June 1928.
30. ibid.: Letter from Pauline in Washington DC to 'Dearest Alma', 11 July 1928.

31. ibid.: Letter from Alma to Ruth Randall Brown, 29 June 1929.
32. USBNA, Hannen Knobloch Collection: Letter from Fanny Knobloch to 'Dear Bahai Sister', 1 October 1929, indicating she had returned by this time.
33. Washington DC Bahá'í Archives, Hannen-Knobloch Collection, Box 5: Letter from Soheil Afnan to Mason Remey, 30 December 1929; Letter from Mason Remey to Bahíyyih K͟hánum, sent through Dr Guy, 16 August 1929.
34. ibid. Box 3: Letter from Mary Collison to Alma Knobloch, 20 March 1932.
35. ibid.: Letter from Mary Collison to Alma Knobloch, 30 March 1932.
36. Vernon, *Bahá'u'lláh's Garden: History of the Bahá'í Faith in Jacksonville 1919–1969*.
37. ibid.
38. Washington DC Bahá'í Archives, Hannen-Knobloch Collection, Box 5: Letter from Alma in Jacksonville to 'Dearest Pauline', 3 May 1932.
39. ibid: Letter from Alma in Jacksonville to 'My precious Pauline', 30 May 1932.
40. ibid.
41. ibid.
42. ibid. Box 1: Letter on behalf of Shoghi Effendi to Alma, 1 June 1930:
43. ibid. Box 5: Letter from Alma in Jacksonville to 'My precious sister Pauline', 12 April 1932.
44. ibid.: Letter from Alma to Ruth Randall Brown, 29 June 1932.
45. ibid.: Letter from Alma in Jacksonville to 'My precious Pauline', 30 May 1932.
46. ibid.: Letter from Alma in Jacksonville to 'Precious Pauline', 8 July 1932.
47. Vernon, *Bahá'u'lláh's Garden: History of the Bahá'í Faith in Jacksonville 1919–1969*.
48. Washington DC Bahá'í Archives, Hannen-Knobloch Collection, Box 5: Letter from Ruth Randall Brown to Alma, on behalf of the National Teaching Committee, 15 June 1932.
49. ibid.: Letter from Alma in Jacksonville to 'Precious Pauline', 24 June 1932.
50. ibid.: Letter from Alma to Ruth Randall Brown, 14 August 1932.
51. ibid.: Letter from Shoghi Effendi to the Bahá'ís of Jacksonville c/o Alma Knobloch, 10 September 1932.
52. Vernon, *Bahá'u'lláh's Garden: History of the Bahá'í Faith in Jacksonville 1919–1969*; Washington DC Bahá'í Archives, Hannen-Knobloch Collection, Box 5: Letter from Alma in Jacksonville to 'precious Pauline', 8 July 1932.
53. Washington DC Bahá'í Archives, Hannen-Knobloch Collection, Box 5: Letter from Alma in Jacksonville to 'My precious sister Pauline', 16 September 1932.
54. ibid. Box 3: Alma to 'Beloved Co-workers in His Great Cause' (the Regional Teaching Committee), 17 October 1932.

55. ibid. Box 5: Letter from Alma in Jacksonville to 'My precious Pauline', 6 November 1932.
56. ibid.: Letter from Alma in Jacksonville to 'My precious ones at home', 29 December 1932.
57. Vernon, *Bahá'u'lláh's Garden: History of the Bahá'í Faith in Jacksonville 1919–1969*.
58. Washington DC Bahá'í Archives, Hannen-Knobloch Collection, Box 5: Alma's Report to Mrs Randall Brown of the National Teaching Committee, 29 June 1932.
59. ibid.: Letter from Alma in Jacksonville to 'Precious Pauline', 24 January 1933.
60. ibid. Box 3: Letter from Bishop Brown to Alma, on behalf of the National Teaching Committee, 16 March 1933.
61. ibid. Box 5: Letter from Alma in Nashville to "My precious Pauline', 22 September 1933.
62. ibid.: Letter from Alma in Nashville to "Precious Pauline', 31 September 1933.
63. ibid.: Letter from Alma in Orlando to 'My precious sister', 29 February 1934.
64. Morrison, *To Move the World*, p. 243.
65. Washington DC Bahá'í Archives, Hannen-Knobloch Collection, Box 3: Letter from Ruth Randall Brown to Alma, on behalf of the National Teaching Committee, 18 September 1933.
66. ibid. Box 1: Letter from Hussein Rabbani on behalf of Shoghi Effendi with postscript from Shoghi Effendi to Alma, 23 October 1933. Published with the kind permission of the Bahá'í World Centre.
67. ibid.: Letter from Mason Remey to Alma, 22 December 1933.
68. *Bahá'í News*, no. 85 (July 1934).
69. Washington DC Bahá'í Archives, Hannen-Knobloch Collection, Box 1: Letter to Alma from Hussein Rabbani with postscript from Shoghi Effendi, 9 February 1934.
70. ibid.: Letter to Alma from Hussein Rabbani with postscript from Shoghi Effendi, 12 May 1934. Published with the kind permission of the Bahá'í World Centre.
71. ibid. Box 3: Letters from Leroy Ioas, Chairman of the National Teaching Committee, to Alma, 15 January and 4 February 1934.
72. ibid.: Letter from Alma to Leroy Ioas, from Nashville, 13 May 1934.
73. ibid.: Letter to Alma from Leroy Ioas on behalf of the National Teaching Committee, 26 November 1934.
74. ibid.: Letter to Alma from the National Teaching Committee, 14 February 1935.
75. ibid.: Letter to Alma from the National Teaching Committee, 21 March 1935.
76. Zarqání, *Maḥmúd's Diary*, p. 85.
77. Mayo,'A History of the Greater Orlando Bahá'í Center', p. 1.
78. Washington DC Bahá'í Archives, Hannen-Knobloch Collection, Box

3: Letter from Alma in Miami to 'My precious good sisters', 2 April 1928.
79. ibid. Box 5: Letter from Alma in Orlando to 'Precious Pauline', 3 November 1933.
80. ibid.: Letter from Alma in Orlando to 'My Precious Pauline', 8 December 1933.
81. ibid.: Letter from Alma to Pauline, 9 February 1935.
82. ibid. Box 3: Letter from Alma to Leroy Ioas, from Nashville, 13 May 1934.
83. USBNA, Hannen Knobloch Collection: Letter from Alma in Bristol to 'Precious sisters', 28 April 1938.
84. ibid.: Letter from Laura Craig to 'Our Dear Miss Alma', 30 September 1937.
85. Washington DC Bahá'í Archives, Hannen-Knobloch Collection, Box 5: Letter from Alma in Orlando to Pauline, 17 January 1934.
86. ibid.: Letter from Alma in Orlando to 'Precious Pauline', 28 January 1934.
87. ibid.: Letter from Alma in Orlando to 'My Precious Sister', 29 February 1934.
88. ibid. Box 3: Letter from Alma to Leroy Ioas, from Nashville, 13 May 1934.
89. ibid. Box 5: Letter from Alma to 'My Precious Good Sister', 25 May, no year.
90. ibid.
91. ibid.: Letter from Alma to 'Precious Pauline', 20 February 1934.
92. ibid.
93. ibid.: Letter from Alma in Orlando to 'Precious Pauline', 26 March 1934.
94. ibid. Box 3: Letter from Alma to Leroy Ioas, 13 May 1934.
95. ibid. Box 5: Letter from Alma in Pittsburgh to Pauline, 30 June 1934.
96. ibid.: Letter from Alma in Orlando to 'My precious Pauline', 9 February 1935.
97. ibid.: Letter from Alma in Augusta to 'My precious Pauline', 4 July 1935; see also Remey, 'A Report to Abdul Baha' of the Bahai Activities in the States of North Carolina, South Carolina, Georgia and Florida March–April 1919', Preface and p. 10.
98. ibid.
99. ibid. Box 3: Letter from Alma to 'Precious Pauline and Fanny' 30 May 1936.
100. Shoghi Effendi, *This Decisive Hour*, no. 20.
101. USBNA, Hannen Knobloch Collection: Letter from Alma in Wilmette to 'My Precious Sister', 5 June 1936.
102. Tablet from 'Abdu'l-Bahá to David Buchanan, January 1919, sent to President Woodrow Wilson at his headquarters in Versailles. A reply was received, confirming that Wilson read this letter. Wilson and Buchanan were friends and had graduated from Princeton together. In Latimer, *The Lesser and the Most Great Peace*, pp. 15–16.
103. Shoghi Effendi, *This Decisive Hour*, no. 23.

45 Cabin John, Maryland, and a Year of Reflection

1. Washington DC Baháʼí Archives, Hannen-Knobloch Collection, Box 3: Letter from Alma in Wilmette to 'Precious Fanny and Pauline', 24 April 1936.
2. ibid. Box 5: Letter from Fanny to Alma, 4 September 1936.
3. ibid. Box 3: Letter from Alma to Horace Holley, secretary of the US National Spiritual Assembly, 24 June 1937.
4. ibid. Box 1: Letter on behalf of Shoghi Effendi with postscript to Alma, 20 September 1936.
5. Shoghi Effendi, *This Decisive Hour*, p. 12.
6. ibid. Box 8: Letter from Pauline in Wilmette to 'Dearest Alma', 6 October 1936.
7. ibid. Box 3: Handwritten copy of a letter from Alma to 'Beloved Shoghi Effendi Guardian of the Cause of God', 21 October 1936.
8. ibid. Box 1: Letter on behalf of Shoghi Effendi to Alma with postscript, 10 November 1936.
9. Letter on behalf of Shoghi Effendi to the National Spiritual Assembly of the Baháʼís of Germany (secretary Adelbert Mühlschlegel), 11 February 1934, in Shoghi Effendi, *The Light of Divine Guidance*, vol. 1, pp. 53–6.
10. Letter written on behalf of Shoghi Effendi, 15 March 1934, comp. Research Department of the Universal House of Justice, in *Baha'i Studies Review*, vol. 4, no. 1. Published with the kind permission of the Baháʼí World Centre.
11. *The Baháʼí World*, vol. VII (1936–1938), p. 462.
12. USBNA, Hannen Knobloch Collection: Letter from Alma in Wilmette to 'My Precious Sisters', 5 June 1936.
13. ibid.: Letter from Alma in Cabin John to 'My Precious Ones', 1 November 1936; German National Baháʼí Archives, Anna Köstlin Collection: Anna Köstlin's speech at the commemoration for Annemarie Schweizer-Warncke, February 1970, p. 10.
14. USBNA, Hannen Knobloch Collection: Letter from Alma in Cabin John to 'My Precious Ones',1 November 1936
15. German National Baháʼí Archives, Anna Köstlin Collection: Anna Köstlin's speech at the commemoration for Annemarie Schweizer-Warncke, February 1970, p. 10.
16. USBNA, Pauline Knobloch Collection: Letter from Pauline to 'Dearest Alma', 5 July 1937.
17. ibid. Martha Root Collection, Box 3.
18. German National Baháʼí Archives, Anna Köstlin Collection: Anna Köstlin's speech at the commemoration for Annemarie Schweizer-Warncke, February 1970, p. 10.
19. From a recording made of a talk in German in the Baháʼí Centre in Frankfurt by Hartmut Grossmann (minute 39:26).
20. German National Baháʼí Archives, Anna Köstlin Collection: Anna Köstlin's speech at the commemoration for Annemarie Schweizer-Warncke, February 1970, p. 10.

21. Pfaff-Grossmann, *Hermann Grossmann, Hand of the Cause of God: A Life for the Faith*, pp. 56–7.
22. Washington DC Bahá'í Archives, Hannen-Knobloch Collection, Box 3: Receipt to Alma Knobloch for the package of 72 small and 10 large photographs of German believers, 14 May 1939.
23. USBNA, Hannen Knobloch Collection: Postcard from Marion Jack, Doris Lohse, Else Grossmann, and others in Leipzig to Alma.
24. ibid.: Letter from J. Stäbler to Alma, 28 December 1936.
25. ibid.: Assorted postcards, 1936, from 'Various friends in Germany'.
26. ibid.: Postcard signed by many Bahá'ís in Germany, 28 December 1936.
27. ibid.: Letter from Pauline to Alma, 'Private Heart to Heart', 26 September 1936.
28. ibid.: Letter from Alma in to 'My Precious Fanny and Pauline', 22 October 1936.
29. Washington DC Bahá'í Archives, Hannen-Knobloch Collection, Box 3: Letter from Mason Remey to Jessie Revell, 23 June 1943.
30. ibid.: Letter from Jessie Revell to Alma, 25 June 1943.
31. ibid.: Letter from Alma to Annamarie Honnold, Chairman of the Regional Committee, 19 November 1943.
32. *The Bahá'í World*, vol. IV (1930–1932), pp. 118–19.
33. USBNA, Hannen Knobloch Collection: Letter from Pauline to Alma, 6 October 1936; Letter from Nellie French to Alma, 21 October 1936.
34. See *The Bahá'í World*, vol. VII (1936–1938), pp. 732–45.
35. *Bahá'í News*, no. 108 (June 1937), p. 5.
36. Washington DC Bahá'í Archives, Hannen-Knobloch Collection, Box 3: Newsletter containing National Teachers List, 1937.
37. *The Bahá'í World*, vol. VII (1936–1938), p. 535.

46 In the South One Last Time

1. Washington DC Bahá'í Archives, Hannen-Knobloch Collection, Box 3: Letter from Alma in Augusta to 'My Dear Co Worker in His Cause', 26 June 1937.
2. USBNA, Hannen Knobloch Collection: Letter from Alma in Augusta to 'Precious Sisters', 19 August 1937.
3. Washington DC Bahá'í Archives, Hannen-Knobloch Collection, Box 3: Letter from Alma in Augusta to 'My Dear Co Worker in His Cause', 26 June 1937.
4. USBNA, Hannen Knobloch Collection: Letter from Alma in North Augusta to 'My Precious sisters', 6 November 1937.
5. *Bahá'í News*, no. 115 (April 1938), p. 19.
6. USBNA, Hannen Knobloch Collection: Letter from Alma in Miami to 'Precious beloved Ones!', 15 February 1938.
7. ibid.: Letter from Alma in Augusta to 'Precious Sisters', 14 October 1937.

8. ibid.: Letter from Alma in North Augusta to 'My Precious sisters', 6 November 1937.
9. ibid.
10. Washington DC Bahá'í Archives, Hannen-Knobloch Collection, Box 1: Handwritten copy of letter from Alma to Shoghi Effendi 11 September 1937.
11. USBNA, Hannen Knobloch Collection: Handwritten copy of letter to Alma from Shoghi Effendi 15 October 1937.
12. ibid.: Letter from Alma in Augusta to 'Precious Sisters', 14 October 1937.
13. ibid.: Letter from Alma to her sisters, 28 April 1938.
14. Washington DC Bahá'í Archives, Edward Young Collection, Box 1: Article in *The Washington Post*, February 1922.
15. ibid.: Carbon copy of a letter sent to Convention in Chicago by Edward H. Young of Washington DC explaining all the Covenant-breakers he had contact with in detail, 10 April 1922.
16. ibid.: Event Calendar of the Washington Secular League where Edward Young gives a talk on the Succession of 'Abdu'l-Bahá, 24 December 1922.
17. ibid: Letter written on behalf of Shoghi Effendi to Edward Young, 17 April 1933.
18. ibid. Hannen-Knobloch Collection, Box 3: Letter from Charlotte Linfoot, secretary of the National Teaching Committee, to Alma, 4 November 1937.
19. ibid.: Handwritten copy of letter from Alma to 'Beloved co-workers in His Cause' (Regional Teaching Committee), 26 November 1937.
20. ibid.: Letter from Charlotte Linfoot, Bahá'í Teaching Committee under the supervision of the NSA of the United States and Canada, to Alma, 4 November 1937; this letter was probably a formality because Alma had already written wrote from Bristol on the same day, 4 November 1937.
21. USBNA, Hannen Knobloch Collection: Letter from Alma in Bristol to 'Precious Sisters', 4 November 1937.
22. ibid.: Letter from Alma in Bristol to 'Precious Sisters', 19 March 1938.
23. ibid.: Letter from Alma in Bristol to 'My Precious Sisters', 21 November 1937.
24. ibid.: Letter from Alma in Bristol to 'My Precious Sisters', 11 December 1937.
25. ibid.: Letter from Alma in Bristol to 'Precious Ones', 21 May 1938.
26. ibid.
27. ibid.: Letter from Alma in Bristol to 'My Precious Sisters', 21 November 1937.
28. ibid.: List of believers and interested contacts in Bristol, Florida, 22 November 1937.
29. ibid.: Letter from Alma in Bristol to 'Precious Sisters', 4 November 1937.
30. Washington DC Bahá'í Archives, Hannen-Knobloch Collection,

Box 3: Handwritten copy of Alma's Report to the Regional Teaching Committee (Dear Co-Workers), 27 November 1937.
31. USBNA, Hannen Knobloch Collection: Letter from Alma in Bristol to 'My Precious Sisters', 21 November 1937.
32. Washington DC Bahá'í Archives, Hannen-Knobloch Collection, Box 3: Handwritten copy of Alma's Report to the Regional Teaching Committee (Dear Co-Workers), 27 November 1937, with postscript dated 5 December 1937.
33. USBNA, Hannen Knobloch Collection: Letter from Alma in Bristol to 'Precious Sisters', 4 November 1937.
34 Washington DC Bahá'í Archives, Hannen-Knobloch Collection, Box 3: Handwritten copy of Alma's Report to the Regional Teaching Committee (Dear Co-Workers), 27 November 1937, with postscript dated 5 December 1937.
35. USBNA, Hannen Knobloch Collection: Copy of letter from Virginia Harrell to Lucille Hoke, 29 December 1937 included in a letter from Alma in Miami to 'Precious Ones', 3 January 1938.
36. ibid.: Letter from Alma in Miami to 'My Precious Ones', 20 January 1938.
37. ibid.: Letter from Alma in Miami to 'Precious beloved Ones!', 15 February 1938.
38. ibid.: Letter from Alma in Miami to 'Beloved precious Ones', 2 March 1938; also, Letter from Alma in Bristol, Florida to 'Dearly beloved Ones!', 19 March 1938.
39. ibid.: Letter from Alma in Bristol, Florida to 'Dearly beloved Ones!', 19 March 1938.
40. Washington DC Bahá'í Archives, Hannen-Knobloch Collection, Box 3: Letter from Alma in Bristol, Florida to Lucille Hoke of the Regional Teaching Committee, 16 April 1938.
41. ibid.
42. USBNA, Hannen Knobloch Collection: Letter from Fanny to Alma, 24 March 1938.
43. ibid.: Letter from Alma in Bristol, Florida to 'My Precious Sisters', 31 March 1938.
44. ibid.
45. ibid.: Letter on behalf of Shoghi Effendi to Edward Young, 8 April 1938.
46. ibid.: Letter from Alma in Miami to 'Beloved precious Ones', 2 March 1938.
47. Washington DC Bahá'í Archives, Hannen-Knobloch Collection, Box 3: Letter from Alma to Lucille Hoke, 16 April 1938.
48. USBNA, Hannen Knobloch Collection: Letter from Alma in Miami to 'Beloved precious Ones', 2 March 1938.
49. Washington DC Bahá'í Archives, Hannen-Knobloch Collection, Box 3: Letter from Alma to Lucille Hoke, 16 April 1938.
50. USBNA, Hannen Knobloch Collection, Letter from Alma to 'My precious Ones', 5 April 1938.

51 Washington DC Bahá'í Archives, Hannen-Knobloch Collection, Box 3: Letter from Alma in Bristol, Florida to Lucille Hoke, 16 April 1938.
52. ibid.
53. USBNA, Hannen Knobloch Collection: Letter from Alma to 'My precious Ones', 5 April 1938.
54. Washington DC Bahá'í Archives, Hannen-Knobloch Collection, Box 3: Letter from Alma in Bristol, Florida to Lucille Hoke. 16 April 1938.
55. USBNA, Hannen Knobloch Collection: Letter from Alma in Bristol, Florida to 'Precious Ones', 21 May 1938.
56. ibid.: Letter from Alma in Bristol, Florida to 'Precious Sisters', 10 May 1938.
57. ibid.: Letter from Alma in Bristol, Florida to 'Precious Ones', 21 May 1938.
58. ibid.: Letter from Alma in Bristol, Florida to 'Precious Sisters', 10 May 1938.
59. ibid.: Letter from Alma in Augusta, to 'Precious ones', 5 June 1938.
60. ibid.
61. ibid.
62. ibid.: Letter from Edward Young to 'Dear Bahá'í Co-Worker' (Alma; 'the time of your leaving'), 26 June 1938.
63. ibid.: Letter from Alma at Dr Bidwell's Sanatorium in Taylor, South Carolina to 'Beloved Ones', 28 June 1938.
64. ibid.: Letter from Alma at Dr Bidwell's Sanatorium in Taylor, South Carolina to 'Beloved Ones!', 1 July 1938.
65. ibid.: Letter from Alma in Cabin John to 'Precious Ones!', 16 August 1938.
66. *Bahá'í News*, no. 120 (November 1938), p. 4.
67. Washington DC Bahá'í Archives, Hannen-Knobloch Collection, Box 1: Handwritten copy of a letter from the Beloved Guardian to Alma, 4 January 1939.
68. USBNA, Hannen Knobloch Collection: Letter from Alma in Cabin John to 'Dearly beloved Sisters!', 22 November 1938.
69. ibid.: Letter from the National Teaching Committee to 'Alma Knoblock c/o Virginia Harrell, Bristol FL', signed Charlotte Linfoot, 4 April 1939.
70. Washington DC Bahá'í Archives, Hannen-Knobloch Collection, Box 5: Letter from Alma in Augusta to 'Precious Sister and Carl, Mineola, and the Dear Children', 17 March 1939.
71. USBNA, Hannen Knobloch Collection: Letter from Edward Young to Alma, 2 October 1938.
72. Washington DC Bahá'í Archives, Hannen-Knobloch Collection, Box 3: Handwritten copy of a letter from Alma to 'Beloved Guardian of the Cause', 24 April 1940.
73. ibid.: Letter from Alma to 'Precious beloved Ones', 30 April 1939.
74. ibid.: Handwritten copy of a letter from Alma to 'Beloved Guardian of the Cause', 24 April 1940.

75. ibid.: Letter from Alma to 'Precious beloved Ones', 30 April 1939.
76. USBNA, Hannen Knobloch Collection: Letter from Edward Young to Alma, 3 June 1939.
77. ibid.
78. Washington DC Bahá'í Archives, Edward Young Collection, Box 1: Small newspaper clipping from Morning Star Church of Christ, 1213 8th St N.W.
79. ibid. Hannen-Knobloch Collection, Box 3: Letter from Alma to Precious beloved Ones, 30 April 1939.
80. ibid.: Handwritten copy of a letter from Alma to 'Beloved Guardian of the Cause', 24 April 1940.
81. ibid.: Letter from Alma in Bristol, Florida to 'Precious beloved Ones', 30 April 1939.
82. ibid.
83. ibid.: Letter from Alma in Augusta to 'Precious sisters', 6 June 1939.
84. ibid.
85. ibid.: Letter from Alma in Cabin John to 'Mr Ioas', National Teaching Committee, 7 March 1939.
86. ibid. Box 1: Letter with postscript from Shoghi Effendi to Alma Knobloch, 31 March 1939.
87. ibid: Letter from the National Teaching Committee to Alma, 19 March 1939.
88. ibid. Box 3: Letter from Alma in Bristol to 'Precious beloved Ones', 30 April 1939.
89. ibid.
90. ibid.
91. ibid.: Letter from Alma in Augusta to 'Precious Sisters', 17 March 1939.
92. USBNA, Hannen Knobloch Collection: Letter from Alma in Greenville to 'Precious sisters', 16 August 1939.
93. ibid: Letter from Alma to 'Precious sisters', 6 June 1939.
94. ibid.
95. ibid.: letter from Alma in Augusta to 'Precious Sisters', 26 June 1939.
96. ibid.
97. ibid.: Letter from Alma in Augusta to 'Beloved Sisters', 20 July 1939.
98. ibid.: Letter from Alma in Augusta to 'Precious sisters,' 2 August 1939.
99. ibid.: Letter from Daisy Moore to Alma, 1 May 1940.
100. Email from Nell Golden to the author, 5 February 2022.
101. Wilson, 'The Second-Largest Religion in Each State', in *The Washington Post*, 4 June 2014.
102. *Bahá'í News*, no. 133 (February 1940), p. 7.

47 The Last Years

1. Washington DC Bahá'í Archives, Hannen-Knobloch Collection, Box 5: Letter from Fanny to Alma, 10 December 1937.

2. ibid.: Letter from Fanny in Wilmette to 'Dearest Alma', 30 December 1937.
3. USBNA, Hannen Knobloch Collection: Letter from Alma from Bristol to 'precious sisters', 20 May 1938.
4. Washington DC Bahá'í Archives, Hannen-Knobloch Collection, Box 3: Letter from Fanny in Wilmette to 'Alma dearest', 1 July 1938.
5. ibid.: Letter from Fanny in Wilmette to 'Alma dearest', 9 July 1938.
6. ibid.: Letter from Fanny in Wilmette to 'Alma dearest', 10 July 1938.
7. USBNA, Hannen Knobloch Collection: Letter from Pauline to Alma, 2 September 1938, quoted in Hannen Moe, *Fanny Knobloch, An Adventuresome Spirit*, manuscript, Ch. 31.
8. Washington DC Bahá'í Archives, Hannen-Knobloch Collection, Box 1: Letter on behalf of Shoghi Effendi to Alma, 31 March 1939.
9. ibid.: Letter from Alma (no location), to 'Beloved ones', 5 November 1939.
10. ibid.: Letter on behalf of Shoghi Effendi to Alma, 5 November 1939. Published with the kind permission of the Bahá'í World Centre.
11. ibid.: Letter from the National Teaching Committee to Alma, 10 January 1940.
12. ibid.: Letter from Pauline to Alma, 6 October 1936.
13. USBNA, Carl Hannen Collection: Letter from Alma to 'Beloved ones', 18 March 1940.
14. ibid.
15. ibid.
16. ibid.
17. Nakhjavani, *The Maxwells of Montreal*, vol. 2, pp. 357–67.
18. Washington DC Bahá'í Archives, Hannen-Knobloch Collection, Box 6: Letter from Alma in Wilmette to Mrs Heman, 5 May 1942.
19. ibid. Box 3: Letter from Paul Hannen at Navaly Training Base, Coronado, California, to Alma in Cabin John, 12 June 1942.
20. ibid.: Notes of Alma Knobloch.
21. Story first told to the author by John Eichenauer in 2007. Confirmed in 2013 on a visit to Stuttgart by Mrs Eger's great-granddaughter.
22. National Spiritual Assembly of the Bahá'ís in Germany, *Der Bahá'í-Glaube in Deutschland: Ein Ruckblick* (1908), p. 46.
23. Washington DC Bahá'í Archives, Hannen-Knobloch Collection, Box 3: Letter from the National Teaching Committee to Alma, 11 December 1942.
24. ibid.: Program of the Washington Bahá'í Assembly at Bahá'í Hall, January and February 1943.
25. ibid.: Letter from Alma to Charlotte Linfoot, secretary of the National Teaching Committee, 30 March 1943.
26. ibid.: Letter from the National Teaching Committee to Alma, 25 April 1943.
27. ibid.: Handwritten copy of a letter from Alma Knobloch to Annamarie Honnold of the Regional Teaching Committee, 12 May 1943.

28. USBNA, Hannen Knobloch Collection: Letter on behalf of Shoghi Effendi to the Knobloch sisters, 10 December 1942, handwritten copy.
29. *The Washington Post*, 26 December 1943, Obituary, p. 9 B; Vernon, *Bahá'u'lláh's Garden: History of the Bahá'í Faith in Jacksonville 1919–1969*.
30. *The Bahá'í World*, vol. IX (1940–1944), pp. 641–3.
31. 'The Bahá'í World Vol. IX: A correction', in *Bahá'í News*, no. 180 (February 1946), p. 3.
32. USBNA, microfilm: Letter from Shoghi Effendi to 'Miss Fanny A. Knobloch', 21 May 1945. Published with the kind permission of the Bahá'í World Centre.
33. 'Abdu'l-Bahá, *Tablets of the Divine Plan*, p. 39.

INDEX

Aalen 161, 174, 177, 190, 236, 242, 267
'Abdu'l-Bahá 13, 14-15, 17, 30-31, 57-8, 61, 63-6, 67, 73, 75, 83, 88-9, 95-6, 102-9, 110, 111, 115-16, 130, 134, 141-3, 147, 151, 158, 172, 176, 185, 191-2, 206-7, 236, 238-9, 242, 250, 252-5, 273-4, 275, 287, 292, 294, 342, 365, 371
 and Alma Knobloch *see* Knobloch, Alma
 Centre of the Covenant 2, 84, 114, 116, 119, 161, 210, 237, 247
 Disciples of 55, 211, 290, 324, 355
 passing of 2, 302, 303-5
 'petitions' to 83, 89-90, 101, 112, 114, 117, 128, 150, 201-04, 242, 268-71
 Tablets from 25-6, 54, 83-4, 101, 142-3, 146, 155-7, 160, 161, 181, 246, 346
  of the Divine Plan vii, 1, 67, 68, 280-81, 329, 346, 380
  to communities and individuals *see* individual entries
 talks by 1, 106-7, 164-6, 169, 192, 193, 199, 200, 208-9, 211-16, 220-21, 222-9, 251, 274
 visits to
  Austria 219-20
  Britain 163-8, 175-6, 196, 220, 257
  France 162, 168-70, 175, 198-205, 232-3
  Germany 136, 188, 195, 201-04, 207-19, 221-31, 258, 281, 291
  Hungary 219-20, 222, 257
  United States 35, 188, 199, 207, 251, 342
 Will and Testament 314, 315, 336, 337
 Writings 84, 141, 329, 337
Abu'l-Faḍl, Mírzá 1, 12-15, 17-20, 21-2, 25, 30-33, 54-6, 109, 110, 115, 119, 144
Aeckerle, Mr 190, 286-7
Afnan, Ruhi 324, 335
Agnew, Mary 43
Air Bath, Degerloch 73-4, 75, 82, 128-9, 137
'Akká 15, 30, 31-2, 42, 60, 88-90, 95, 97, 101-3, 107, 111, 142, 158, 160, 165, 206, 259
 Governor of 104, 316
Alabama 358
Alexander, Agnes 252-3, 267, 281
Alexandria, Egypt 101-2, 109, 133
Alhambra, Spain 215
'Alí-Akbar, Mírzá 235

455

Allen, Ásíyih 215
Alma Knobloch Fund 310
Alsace, Alsace-Lorraine 199, 217
Altdorf, Switzerland 233
Amatu'l-Bahá Rúḥíyyih Khánum 370 *see also* Maxwell, Mary
America, Americans 6, 17, 18, 37, 51, 60, 78, 79-80, 86, 92-3, 108, 113, 123, 166, 187-8, 191, 192, 194, 199, 239, 244, 249, 251, 252, 255, 257, 276, 278, 292, 301, 353
   Bahá'í community *see* Bahá'í community: United States (America) and Canada
   African-Americans 1, 3, 7-8, 9, 12, 27-9, 33, 37-41, 158, 302, 332, 306-7, 329, 339, 344, 356, 358, 362, 363, 369
American Missionary Association 41
Ammyrie, Mrs 294
Amsterdam 296, 326
Arabian(s) 199, 215, 225
Arabic language 223
Asadu'lláh, Mírzá 103, 107-8, 164, 172, 174-5, 205, 206, 248
Asheville, NC 53
Ashton, Mr and Mrs 306
Atlantic City 296
Atwater family 327, 329
Augusta, GA 345, 348, 355, 356, 363-5, 367-70, 374
   Bahá'í Center 356, 368
   Spiritual Assembly 348, 355
Australia 19, 36-7
   Bahá'í community 19
Austria 2, 6, 76, 77, 89, 126, 152, 190, 222, 257, 259, 312, 353, 380
   Bahá'í community 89, 126, 206, 312, 353
Austria-Hungary 4, 220, 222, 253
Austro-Prussian War 6
Avenue de Camöens, Paris 168

Báb, the 108
   Birthday of 117, 161
   Declaration of 110, 130, 184, 192
   Shrine of 130, 304
Bacon, Walter 337, 345
Baden-Baden 264
Bad Frankenhausen 272-3
Bad Homburg v.d. Höhe 73, 75, 78, 93
Bad Mergentheim 217-18, 272, 281, 291, 309
Bad Wörishofen 281
Badí'u'lláh, Mírzá 31
Bagdadi, Zia 348, 355, 356, 368
Baghdad 223
Bahádur, 'Azízu'lláh 254-5, 262, 269-70, 271, 274, 279, 280, 281, 291
Bahá'í Administrative Order 128, 221, 347
Bahá'í community 266
   Austria 2, 76, 89, 126, 152, 206, 312, 353
   Britain 163-8, 169, 176, 276, 306, 351
   'Abdu'l-Bahá's visits *see* 'Abdu'l-Bahá
   Czech Republic 2, 126, 190, 195-6, 380
   Europe 80, 168
   France 33, 80, 168-9, 199, 236, 252
   'Abdu'l-Bahá's visits *see* 'Abdu'l-Bahá; *see also* Paris
   Germany 2, 50, 74, 80, 84, 89, 129, 172, 194, 206, 211, 236-7, 286, 287, 297, 298, 308, 312, 320, 322, 324, 350, 351, 354, 376
   'Abdu'l-Bahá's visit *see* 'Abdu'l-Bahá
   5er-Commission 308
   Bahá'í Center (Häusle), Esslingen 352

Bahá'í Congress 308
Council of 9 308
Deutsche Bahá'í Bund
  (German National Federation) 287, 311, 313
messages and Tablets from
  'Abdu'l-Bahá 89, 112-14,
  117-18, 155-7, 172-4,
  175, 191-2, 198, 269-70,
  275, 277, 304-5, 308,
  351 *see also* entries for
  individuals and places
National Archives 159
National Convention 351-2
National Spiritual Assembly
  88, 215, 218, 277, 308,
  311, 313-14, 317-18, 321,
  350, 353
Summer School 351-2
Verlag (Publishing Trust) 311
see also individual entries for
  cities, towns and villages
Holland 196, 252
Hungary 251
United States (America) and
  Canada 17, 20, 21, 33, 46,
  48, 55, 58, 62, 63, 149, 182,
  188, 207, 228, 277, 303, 306,
  312, 314, 321, 245-7, 348-9,
  351, 352
  'Abdu'l-Bahá's visit *see*
    'Abdu'l-Bahá
  African-Americans 1, 3, 27-9,
    33, 40, 158, 302, 306-7,
    329, 339, 344, 356, 358,
    369, 392
  National Conventions 300,
    301, 320, 325, 326, 330-
    31, 343, 344, 345, 355,
    375
  National Spiritual Assembly
    324, 327, 329, 339, 352,
    368
  National Teaching
Committee 2, 320, 322,
  332, 334, 336-41, 357,
  360, 361, 363, 365, 367-8,
  373, 377
Regional Teaching Committee (Florida and Alabama)
  356, 358-9
Summer school 34, 325
Tablets from 'Abdu'l-Bahá
  303 *see also* individuals
  and cities
see also individual entries for
  towns and cities
Bahá'í International Community 116
Bahá'í News (American) 364, 370
Baha'i Newsletter 326
Bahá'í Proofs, The 55
Bahá'í scripture ix, 83, 85
Bahá'í World, The 19, 355, 376, 379
Bahá'í World Centre 370
Bahá'u'lláh 1, 28, 38, 98, 102, 105,
  107, 170, 192, 199, 206, 207,
  209, 212, 216, 221, 222, 223,
  224, 226, 233, 241, 303, 304,
  323, 330, 346, 372, 374, 379
  belief, faith in 26, 89, 115, 125,
    230, 290
  Birthday of 282, 285
  Covenant of 84
  message, teachings, Writings 2, 28,
    32, 40, 58, 64, 83-4, 117, 125,
    127, 136, 141, 145-6, 153, 160,
    216, 225, 228, 275, 288, 351
  Promised One 21, 115, 336
  Revelation of 83, 128, 211
  Shrine of 108, 333
Bahíyyih Khánum, Greatest Holy
  Leaf 19, 104, 108, 303-4, 305,
  333, 336, 371, 375
Bahjí 280
  Mansion 324
  Shrine of Bahá'u'lláh 108, 333
Bahnmüller, Bertha (later Bopp)
  215, 269

Baker, Dorothy 375
Balkan Commission 199
Balkan States 213, 324
Baltimore, MD 19-20, 22, 68-9, 306, 332, 349
Báqiroff, Aḥmad 205, 206
Barney, Alice 18
Barney, Laura Clifford (Dreyfus-Barney) 13, 19, 30, 58, 96, 116, 198, 200
Barnitz Leone St. Clair 14, 34, 48
Barton, Morgen, Mr and Mrs 369, 370
Basel, Switzerland 75
Bassett, John 345
Battle *see also* World War
  of Jena 4
  of Leipzig 187, 249
  of the Nations 4, 249
  of Verdun 282, 286
  of Waterloo 294
Bauer, Lydia 236, 245, 264, 309, 354
Bautzen 5-6, 88, 96-7, 101, 123, 190, 195, 246, 255, 279, 298
Bavaria 4, 267
Bebenhausen 229, 258
Beethoven, Ninth Symphony 212
Beg, Mr 190
Beiswanger, Mrs 123-4
Belgium, Belgian 257, 259
Bender, Hugo 137, 158, 186, 261, 277
Bender, Max 87, 137, 158, 186, 190, 261, 277, 282
Benke, Adam 2, 294-5, 310, 315
Benke, Lina 294
Bern, Switzerland 211, 236
Berlin viii, 5, 161, 253, 262, 273, 281, 288, 296, 312
Berlin Wall 295
Betzold, Miss 118
Bible 2, 5, 7, 12, 14, 16, 18, 19, 21-5, 2, 28, 69, 70-71, 78, 83, 105, 110, 160, 242, 254, 272
Bidwell, Dr and Mrs 342, 345, 356, 364, 365, 368, 378
Bismarck 6, 258
Blackshear, Sue 370
Blankenese, Hamburg 285
Blaricum, Holland 196
Blättner, Mrs, and family 425
Blocker, Sarah A. 329-30, 344
Blomfield, Lady 164-5, 168, 172-81, 185, 188, 193
Blücher, General 294
Böblitz 5
Bohemia 126
Böhm 196
Bombay 199
Bopp, Anneliese 216
Bopp family 215-16
Bosch, John 152, 188, 303, 311-13
  Tablet from 'Abdu'l-Bahá 188
Bosch, Louise 182, 303-4, 312-13
Bothner, Pauline 320-22
Böttger, Eugenie 242, 243, 249
Böttger, Klara (Krieger) 161, 267-88, 278
Böttger, Mr, Mrs and Miss 267-8
Bowman, Miss 74
Boyle family 329
Braun, Professor 81, 85, 112, 118, 132, 140-42, 152, 158, 172, 175, 181, 261, 277, 286, 309
Brauns, Arthur and Marta 290, 354, 355
Bredemeier, George 70
Bredemeier, Hannah 70
Bredemeier, Herman 70
Bremen 8, 51, 68, 70, 232, 312, 353
Brennecker, Mrs 285
Bristol, FL 357-66, 374
Britain 77, 135, 306 *see also* England
Brooklyn, NY 44, 176
Bruckledge, Mrs and Miss 285

Bryan, William Jennings 278
Buchanan, David 445
Bucherhof, Lorsch 137
Budapest 217, 219-23
Buddhists 225
Buenos Aires 375
Buffalo, NY 34-7, 42-9, 63, 65-6, 97
  Spiritual Assembly 34, 42-3
  Tablets from 'Abdu'l-Bahá 94-5
Buffalo News, The 36
Bulgaria 75, 294-5
Burbank, Luther 188
  Tablet from 'Abdu'l-Bahá 188
Burckhardt, Frau Med. Rat von 61, 81, 85
Bürger Museum, Stuttgart 81, 85, 172, 173, 179, 193, 201, 213, 222-4, 235
Burk, Laura 27
Burns, Rev. Anthony 38

Cabin John, MD vii-viii, 332, 348-9, 355, 364-6, 369, 371-3, 376-8
  Spiritual Assembly 355, 377-8
Cadwalader-Dickinson, Lambert and Elmira 51
Cairo, Egypt 31, 96, 109
California 180, 247, 248, 277, 303
Camp Mineola 34
Canada, Canadians 1, 37, 41, 42, 95, 199, 380
  African-Americans 1, 37, 39, 40-41
Canada West (Ontario) 37, 40-41
Cannstadt 78
Cape Town 319, 437
Carling Hotel, Jacksonville 336
Carlsbad 233
Cary, Mary Ann Shadd 40-41
Cedric, S.S. 207
century of light 224, 275
Chase, Thornton 40, 58, 156, 193

Chemnitz 242, 245, 255, 277, 290
Chicago 35, 43, 50, 74, 103, 261, 263, 301, 330, 344
  House of Spirituality 35, 103
  Spiritual Assembly 35
  University 103
China 256
Christian Commonwealth, The 165, 166
Christianity, Christians 17, 21-6, 69, 83, 102, 103, 165-6, 183, 225, 258, 343, 370
Christian denominations
  Baptist 38, 329, 362
  Catholic 5, 44, 126, 195-6, 220, 296
  Christian Science 53, 54, 57-8, 60, 72, 80-82, 83, 85-6, 88, 115, 128-9, 131, 144, 173
  Congregational 18
  Lutheran 1, 7, 8, 14, 19-20, 21-6, 86, 329
  Methodist 362
  Protestant 5
  see also Mormonism
Christian Endeavor (*also* Congress) 21-2
Church Times, The 166
Cleveland Tariff 52
Clough, Mrs K.M. 336
Cold War 295
Collier, Nathan W. 329, 330, 344, 356
Collins, Amelia 312
Collison, Mary 334
Colmar 297
Colonial Beach, Virginia 34
Columbia, SC 370
Communist Manifesto 5
Concordia Church 1, 7, 14, 19-20, 21-6, 29, 69
  Elders 23-4
  Sunday School 7, 22, 23-4
Constance, Lake 74, 76, 233

Coulters, Winnie 426
Covenant 13, 41, 84, 96, 114-15, 128, 140, 148, 152, 161, 183, 210, 235, 237, 250, 256, 262, 291, 296, 315, 324
Covenant-breakers 31, 108, 247, 313, 315, 357, 364
Craig, Laura 342-3
Cramer, Bessie 300, 307
Cramer, Mrs 300
Crimea 294
Cropper, *see* Thornburgh-Cropper
Cuba 51
Cumberland, Maryland 9, 390
Czech Republic 2, 126, 190, 196, 380

Daily Mail 207
D'Astre, Georgiana d'Ange 14, 18, 30, 32, 74
D'Astre, Mr 33
D'Astre, Odette 32-3
Dawud, Yuhanna 156, 161, 170
Davison, Bruce 376
Declaration of the Báb 110, 146, 184, 192
Degerloch 73, 87, 137, 144, 150-51, 158, 161, 191, 236, 259, 264, 272, 283, 286 *see also* Air Bath
De Lagnels, Josephine 232
dentistry 51-3, 55-9, 91
Depression, Great 333, 342
Diebold, Eugene 228, 314
Diegel, Mina 74, 75, 76, 137, 186, 208, 272
Diehlmann, Carl 286
Disciples of 'Abdu'l-Bahá 55, 211, 290, 324, 355
Domhuber, Mr and Mrs 267
Döring, Hetwig 246
Döring, Kurt, and Mrs 125, 187-8, 195, 242, 246, 249, 260, 263, 273, 295

Döring, Margarethe 61, 71, 72, 73, 74-6, 78-9, 85, 87, 91, 93, 96, 101, 112, 118, 125, 126, 128-9, 131-2, 136, 137, 150, 153, 157, 168-9, 175, 177, 178, 181, 184, 186-9, 190, 192, 193, 196, 200, 208, 217, 236, 258, 259, 260, 261, 264, 272-4, 279, 281-6, 293-4, 308, 309-10, 366
Tablets and message from 'Abdu'l-Bahá 131-2, 158, 177, 283
Dorsey, Mr 329-30
Douglas, GA 366, 378
Dresden 72, 343
Dreyfus, Hippolyte 79-81, 96, 159, 161, 164, 165, 169, 200
Dreyfus-Barney, Laura *see* Barney
Dublin, NH 191, 193
Dunn, Hyde 19
Du Rose, Vernon 327
Dutch 197, 326

Earle, Mrs 172-3, 175, 180-81
Eckert, Hans 78
Eckstein, Adolf 78-81, 85-6, 95, 101, 106, 112, 118, 125, 128, 130-31, 144, 168-9, 170, 172, 174-5, 180, 185, 208, 215, 244, 255, 261
Eckstein, Agatha 81, 85-6, 112, 131, 144, 168-9, 170, 172, 180, 181-2, 185, 215, 229, 244, 255
Eckstein, Otto 86, 255, 277
Eger, Gustav and family 137, 158, 177, 182, 186, 190-91, 198, 261, 277, 282, 286, 376
message from 'Abdu'l-Bahá 177
Eger, Mrs 87, 137, 193, 376, 452
Egypt 15, 17, 31, 102, 143, 153-4, 158, 199, 207, 236, 315
Eichenauer, John 375-6, 452
Eichenauer, Marshall 375
Eichler, Anna 426

INDEX

Elijah (prophet) 323
El Salvador 375
Engels, Friedrich 5
England, English 80, 111, 163, 166, 169, 172, 176, 199, 226, 244, 248, 255, 257, 259, 276, 304, 351, 400, 414
English language viii, 6, 27, 54, 55, 58, 72, 78, 79, 80-81, 83-4, 85, 87, 103, 155, 165, 173, 185, 187, 208, 215, 217, 219, 220, 227, 242, 278
Eningen 193
Ensel, Mr and Mrs 300
Enzlin, N. George 196
Esperanto 193, 196, 199, 219, 356
Esslemont, Dr John 325
Esslingen 87-8, 137, 144, 147, 152, 156, 157, 158, 171, 174, 177, 182, 183, 189, 190, 193, 201, 204, 208, 213, 219, 221, 230, 235-6, 250, 266, 277, 285, 286-7, 300, 303, 309, 312, 351-2
  Häusle (Bahá'í Center) 352
  Home of the Good Templers 235-6
  Spiritual Assembly 183, 236, 287, 312
Europe, European(s) 2, 4-5, 18-19, 32-3, 36-7, 52, 75, 76, 84, 116, 122, 142, 154, 156, 162, 168, 174, 185, 194, 197, 220, 232, 247, 249-51, 252, 256-7, 261, 264, 271, 277, 286, 291, 295, 301, 312, 314, 326, 351, 354, 355
European dress 206
European House of Worship 215
European Union 212
Evanston, Ill. 348
Evening Star (Washington) 6, 262

Faber, Herman 230, 266

Fäbring family 267-8
Fallscheer, Dr 291
Farahangiz Khanum 142
Fareed, Amin 103, 108, 142, 247-8, 357, 364
Farmer, Sarah 345
Feast of the Covenant 152
Fellbach 168, 174, 177, 214, 236, 312
Festive Year 249
Finch, Ida 101, 104-5, 109
First Congregational Church 18
Fisher, Edwin 2, 50-59, 60-62, 63-4, 66, 71-3, 75-6, 78-80, 84-5, 87-8, 90, 91-4, 95-6, 112, 118, 120, 128, 129-30, 132, 138-9, 141-4, 147, 150, 152, 156, 160, 162, 172, 173, 176, 180, 185, 189, 192, 198, 200-01, 208, 239, 240, 247, 261, 396, 397
  Tablet from 'Abdu'l-Bahá 54, 61
Fisher, Edwin (junior) 51-2
Fisher, Dr (of Brooklyn, NY) 176, 414
Fisher, Josephine Dickinson 51, 54
Fisher, Luitgard 247
Fisher, Mr (in Berlin) 161
Fisher, Mrs F. 54
Fisher, Olga Wilhelmina 51, 53
Fisher, Mrs Wally 425
Fitzgerald, Colonel 19
Fitzgerald, Nathan 30
Flässel, Mr 246
Fletcher, Clayton 345
Florida 2, 19, 200, 327-30, 332, 334-44, 356-8, 364-5, 367-8
Florida Intergroup Meeting 343, 344
Florida Normal School and Industrial Institute 329, 330, 344, 356
Flowers Culled from the Rose Garden of Acca 109
Flüelin, Switzerland 233, 273

Ford, Reverend 329
Forel, Dr Auguste 290
Forester, Mrs 89
Forest Hill, GA 370
Formative Age 306
Frain, George 370
France, French 4, 14, 32-3, 51, 74, 77, 79, 80, 81, 135, 162, 168-9, 199, 200, 236, 238, 252, 255, 257, 259, 277, 282
   French language 80, 84, 236, 252
   see also Paris
Franco-Prussian War 199
Frank family 193
Frankfurt 6, 125, 297, 312, 353
French, Mrs (Nell) 352
Frauen Club (Women's Club)
   Leipzig 187-8, 242
   Stuttgart 75, 76, 79, 82, 85, 129, 136, 140, 147, 148, 151, 158, 174, 175, 181, 193, 201, 204, 227, 235, 264
Freiburg 295-6, 309
Freudenstadt 70, 75, 282, 312
Frey, Miss 72, 75, 76, 93
Fry, Paula 264
Fugitive Slave Act 37
Fuhrman, Carrie 364
Fulmer, John Patrick 370

Gambler, Miss 276
Gautzsch 246
Gebhardt, Miss 296
Gehde, Johanna Christine 5
Geislingen 312
Geneva 116, 162
Georgia, US 2, 345, 355, 356-7, 363, 366, 367, 368, 370
Gera 125, 246-7, 260, 273, 277, 285, 295, 312
Germany
   German Assembly 6

Bahá'í community *see* Bahá'í community: Germany
   Confederation 6
   Empire 6, 60, 259
   Constitution 60
   German language (and translation into) 66, 78, 79-81, 84-5, 87, 112, 125, 126, 128-31, 132, 133, 139-42, 151, 161, 173, 180, 183, 185, 190, 208, 219-20, 227, 230, 253, 259, 260, 262, 278, 312, 314, 321
   German Orphan Asylum 25
   German Revolution (1918-19) 286, 289
Gestapo 297, 352-3
Getsinger, Edward 58, 207
Getsinger, Lua 17, 58, 62, 99, 109, 142, 182, 293
Gibbons, Louise 54, 56
Gisela, Princess of Bavaria 267
Glassford, Mary Stuart 121-2
Gleichmann, Eva 295
Glitz, Richard 242, 245-6, 254, 277, 290
   Tablet from 'Abdu'l-Bahá 245-6
Glover, Clair 356, 364, 368, 370
Gmünd 236, 264
Golden, Carolyne 370
Golden, Jackson Herbert 370
Golden, Lillian Poole 369-70
Golden, Nell 370
Golden, Robert 370
Golmer, Mr 308
Goodall, Ella (Cooper) 277
Goodall, Helen 58
Göppingen 303, 312, 351
Gotha 215, 244-5, 246, 250, 273, 302
   Tablet from 'Abdu'l-Bahá 244-5, 426
Götz, Emil 268
Grand Rapids, Michigan 325

INDEX

Greatest Holy Leaf *see* Bahíyyih Khánum
Greatest Name 18, 108, 141, 152, 174, 201, 210, 259, 260, 261, 271, 273, 375
  ringstones 18, 108, 201, 260, 271
Green Acre, NH 14, 17, 35, 325, 345
Greenleaf, Mrs 371
Greenville 365, 368, 375, 378
Greeven, Max 353
Gregory, George 40
Gregory, Louis, 2, 40, 136, 158, 159, 202, 301, 327-8, 330, 331-2, 333, 339, 357
Grimm, Anna 426
Grimm family 244
Grossmann, Anna 319, 352, 353
Grossmann, Elsa Marie 352, 354
Grossmann, Hartmut 353
Grossmann, Hermann 2, 294, 314, 317-19, 352, 354
Grünzweig, Julius 60, 71, 72, 287
Guy, Walter Bryant, and Mrs 327, 329-30, 334-7, 340, 342, 344, 345

Haddad, Anton 17
Häfner, Samuel, and Mrs 168, 214, 236, 287
Häfner, Otto 168, 214-15
Haifa 5, 71, 101-9, 142-3, 144, 218, 246, 248, 263, 291, 297, 303-5, 314, 322, 342, 344, 354, 375
  German Consul 250
  Governor 315
Haigis, Mr 89, 160, 168, 175
Hakím, Luṭfulláh 235
Hamburg 6, 250, 285, 294, 297, 312, 314, 317, 319
Hamilton, Mass. 300
Hannen, Carl viii, 9, 34, 68, 137, 139, 283, 299, 319, 325, 326, 348, 364, 371, 373, 380
Hannen, Gladys 9
Hannen, Joseph Anthony 1, 8, 9, 10-11, 18-20, 33, 42, 68, 79, 97, 137, 191, 262, 282, 288, 292-3, 345, 372, 373, 380
  Tablet from 'Abdu'l-Bahá 293
Hannen, Mineola 325, 371, 380
Hannen, Paul 9, 299, 364, 375
Hannen, Pauline
  accepts Bahá'í Faith 11-15, 17-8
  Bahá'í service
    in South Africa 18, 319, 326
    in United States 22, 27-8, 34, 42, 158, 193, 215, 282, 302, 357
  Cabin John 332, 366, 371-3
  early life 7-8
  ill health 279, 326, 332, 348, 349, 356, 364-5, 371-2
  marriage and family 8-9, 20, 22, 137, 283, 292-3, 299, 319, 325, 364, 371-3, 375-380
  pilgrimage 96, 122
  relationship with sisters 1, 271, 293, 299, 338, 343, 372
  correspondence with Alma 43, 64, 68, 97-8, 121, 122, 123, 138, 144, 146, 150, 157, 167, 179, 193, 232, 233, 239, 257, 265, 272, 273, 276, 282, 293, 296, 300, 325, 336, 337, 349, 354, 365, 371, 372, 374
  financial support of Alma 240, 265, 299, 326, 327, 332, 333, 371
  and Shoghi Effendi 348-9, 372-3
  Tablets from 'Abdu'l-Bahá 96, 293
Harrell, Virginia and Jack 359-63, 365-7, 374, 378
Harper, Mrs 306

Harris, Hooper and Gertrude 299, 302
Hauff, Johanna 303-4
Hauptman von Sonntag, Mrs 79, 131
Hawaii 252, 301
Haynes, Susie 333
Hearst, Phoebe 17, 56, 58, 342
Heidelberg 281, 284, 303, 351
Heilbronn 75, 82, 125, 296, 303, 309
Helling, Emma 295, 308
Hellock, Mrs 252
Hensteckel, Mrs 96
Heroic Age 306
Herrigel, Marie 118, 132-3, 137, 145, 152, 156, 160, 167-8, 169, 172-3, 175-6, 192, 202, 222, 264, 308
Herrigel, Wilhelm 80-81, 85, 87, 112, 118, 126, 128, 131-4, 136-8, 139-42, 144, 146-7, 150, 152-3, 155-60, 162, 167-8, 169, 172-3, 175-6, 179-85, 188, 189, 192-3, 198, 201-4, 208, 210-11, 213, 215, 218, 219-24, 231, 236, 238, 261, 264, 277, 284, 285, 287, 296, 305, 308-16, 320, 321, 324
    Tablets and messages from 'Abdu'l-Bahá 118, 132-3, 156, 157, 185, 188, 198, 201
Heydran, Pastor 285
Hidden Words 14, 83, 85, 111, 126, 264
Himmler, Heinrich 352
Hitchcock, Miss 30
Hitler, Adolf 350, 367
Hoagg, Emogene 17, 364
Hoboken, NJ 249
Hochkirch, Mr and Mrs 241-2
Holland (Netherlands) 196, 252, 295, 353m 432
Holley, Horace 327
Holt, Mrs 345

Holy Land 5, 15, 19, 28, 30, 54, 61, 95-7, 103, 111-12, 117, 130, 133, 136, 158, 207, 218, 253, 262, 290. 291, 294, 303-4, 370
Holy Roman Empire 4
Hoke, Lucille 358, 360
Holzhausen, Mrs 426
Hooper, Mrs 338
Horn, Edith 296-7, 314
    Tablet from 'Abdu'l-Bahá 296
Hotel Marquardt, Stuttgart 207-8, 213
Hotel Seminole, Jacksonville 334, 336
House, Colonel 278
Housatonic (cargo ship) 282
Hungary, Hungarian (*also* Austro-Hungary) 4, 77, 126, 219-20, 222, 253, 257, 351
Ḥuqúqu'lláh 88, 157
Hutchinson, Elizabeth 369

Imhoff, Mr and Mrs 89, 130-31
India 104, 111, 126, 225, 253, 351
International Baháʼí Bureau 116
International Conference of Socialist Women 135
International Progressive Thought League, Buffalo 34-5, 43
International Teaching Centre 216
International Women's Conference 135
Iran, Iranians 96, 351 *see also* Persia
Iraq 351
Isaiah (prophet) 21
Islam 83, 183, 203, 275
Italy 51, 77, 185

Jack, Marion 75, 90, 95-6, 111, 112, 122, 164, 294, 352, 354
Jackson, Jas. H., Mr and Mrs 345, 360, 368
Jacksonville, FL 329, 334-9, 341-2, 344, 345

Spiritual Assembly 341
Jaeger family 236, 308
Jaffa 102
Jahn, Mrs 285
Japan 253, 256
Jarvis, Henry 376
Jenkyn, Daniel 276, 432
Jerusalem 151
Jesus Christ 7, 11, 12, 13, 18, 24, 26, 46, 71, 102, 113, 167, 178, 191, 211, 213, 221, 226, 228, 245, 366
Jews, Jewish 211, 213, 220, 225
Jim Crow (laws) 2
Johannesburg 292
Jolly, Alvina 330
Jones family (Spartanburg) 369
Jones, Mrs (Washington DC) 11-14
Junker, Siegried 268, 271

Kaiser (Emperor of Germany) 248, 249, 258, 259, 266, 276, 285, 288 *see also* Wilhelm II
Kaiser, Mrs 42
Kälble, Mrs 285
Karlsruhe 82, 281, 284, 294, 295, 303, 309, 312, 351
Kassel 196
Kenosha, Wis. 207, 325
Kersetten, Switzerland 96
Kershaw, Dr Marie 345, 360, 363-5, 367, 368-9
Keyes, Mr and Mrs 306
Khan, Ali-Kuli 12-13, 17-20, 54-5
Khan, Youness 315
Kheiralla, Ibrahim 17
Khudabakhsh, Habíbu'lláh *see* Moayyad, Habíb
Kiel, Frida 426
Kinney family 99
Kirchner, Mrs 273
Kiser, Mrs 377-8
Kitáb-i-Aqdas 83
Kitáb-i-Íqán 83

Klebs, Margaret 345, 368
Kloss, Dr 335
Kniffin, Dr 50
Knobloch, Amalie 1, 5-9, 22-7, 29, 32, 35, 46, 49, 63, 66-7, 68, 92, 97-100, 121, 261, 373, 380
  Tablets from 'Abdu'l-Bahá 15, 25, 46-7, 66
  Tablet of Visitation for 99-100
Knobloch, Alma
  accepts Bahá'í Faith 1, 13-14
  and 'Abdu'l-Bahá 1, 14, 47-9, 65-7, 80, 99-100, 101, 103-9, 115-16, 129, 142, 145-6, 161, 172, 177-8, 181, 187, 188, 191, 193, 208-9, 217-18, 222, 230, 231, 233, 239, 246, 263, 268, 271, 273, 283, 286, 298, 315-16
    'American girl' 238-9
    letters to 15, 163-7, 169-70, 279
    meetings with 102-09, 163, 198-202, 208-9, 216, 217, 218-19, 222, 230
    Tablets and messages from 15, 28-9, 36, 38, 46, 48, 66, 117-18, 127, 132, 145-6, 155, 170, 178, 180, 183-4, 187, 188, 191, 239-40, 263, 281, 283, 293, 297-8, 301, 315-16, 380
    Tablets of the Divine Plan 1, 67, 68, 280-81, 346, 380
  and Anna Köstlin 87, 137, 152, 157, 168, 182-3, 191, 200-01, 218, 354
  and Annemarie Schweizer 88, 137, 157, 191, 200-01, 354
  Bahá'í service in
    Austria 2, 126-7
    Canada 37-8

Germany 1, 63-6, 69-70, 194, 209, 238, 240, 266, 272, 297-8, 309, 317-224, 350, 354-5
  Berlin 281
  Gera 246, 247, 273, 285
  Gotha 244, 273
  Heidelberg 281, 284
  Karlsruhe 281, 284, 294, 295
  Leipzig 95, 153, 172, 175, 178, 181, 186-8, 195, 241-4, 249, 252-3, 255, 279, 288, 293-4, 296, 310
  Mannheim 2, 284, 289, 296
  Munich 266-7, 281, 283
  Nuremberg 284, 294, 295
  Stuttgart 71-90, 101, 110-25, 128-32, 171, 172-83, 188-9, 190, 201-2, 204-5, 240, 244, 254-60, 262-5, 272, 282, 286-7, 293
  for other places *see* individual entries
United States
  Baltimore 19, 110, 349
  Buffalo 34-7, 42, 48-9, 64-6
  Cabin John 332, 348, 364-5, 371-3, 377-8
  Milwaukee 319, 325-6, 341
  Southern states (Florida, Georgia, Tenne*see*, South Carolina) 2, 200, 327-32, 332-45, 349, 355, 356-70
  Springfield, Mass. 2, 300-01, 302
  Washington DC 2, 27-9, 302, 333, 374, 377
  for other places *see* individual entries
'brain' photograph 94
'Call to Germany, The' 355
citizenship
  German 123-4, 263, 272, 291-2, 293-4, 298
and Edwin Fisher 50, 60, 64, 71, 73, 75-6, 78, 87, 91-4, 120, 129-30, 138, 139, 141-2, 150, 173, 180, 185, 198, 200-01, 239
health 13
family
  early life 5-18
  in Germany 70-71, 97-8, 153, 162, 178-9, 186-7, 189, 195-6, 205, 241, 243, 255, 260, 283
  mother, Amalie Knobloch 9, 63, 67, 97-9, 121, 140
  sisters Fanny and Pauline 1, 64-5, 68, 94, 99, 233, 271, 281, 292-3, 299, 302, 326, 332, 338, 343, 364, 372-4, 379-80
  correspondence with *see* Hannen, Pauline; Knobloch, Fanny
financial constraints 240-41, 249, 263, 266, 281-2, 298, 299-300, 309, 318, 327, 332-3, 338-41, 361, 365
  support from Fanny and Pauline *see* Hannen, Pauline; Knobloch, Fanny
  investments 121, 240, 299, 332, 365
and Hermann Grossmann 2, 294, 317-19, 354
and Jean Stannard 111-16
and Lady Blomfield 172, 174-6, 179-80, 185
and Louis Gregory 159-60, 327-9, 331-2, 333

and Lutheran Concordia Church, Washington 1, 6, 13, 20, 21-6, 29, 68-9
and Margarethe Döring 72-3, 74, 75-6, 78, 125, 128-9, 132, 153, 157, 158-9, 181, 187-8, 190, 207, 217, 236, 259-60, 272-3, 281-2, 283-5, 293-4
and Marion Jack 95-6, 111-12, 164
and Mason Remey 19, 22, 29, 34, 36, 44, 89-90, 98, 136, 159, 278, 295-6, 307, 311, 354-5
and Mírzá Abu'l-Faḍl 18-20, 21-2, 25, 30-31, 33, 110, 115
and Odette d'Astre 32-3
pilgrimage 30-31 96-8, 99, 101-9
race unity 2-3, 9, 27-9, 41, 302, 306-7, 344, 356, 358, 362
and Seven Year Plan, pioneer offer 377
and Shoghi Effendi 2, 105, 290, 306-7, 320, 322, 324, 331, 335, 336-7, 338, 339-41, 346, 348, 349, 357, 362-3, 364, 373, 375, 377
and Virginia Harrell 359-63, 365-7
and Wilhelm Herrigel 81, 133, 136-7, 139, 146-7, 150, 152, 155, 156, 159-60, 172-3, 179, 180, 181, 185, 188, 192, 202, 204, 221, 285, 311, 321
and World War I 162, 248, 254, 257-9, 263-5, 276-8, 283, 289-90
Knobloch, Bruno 7
Knobloch, Fanny
accepts Bahá'í Faith 10-12
Bahá'í service in
South Africa 18, 292-3, 300, 302, 319, 326-7, 332-3
United States 27, 32-3, 334, 372, 377-8
Cabin John 332, 355, 366, 372
early life 5-8
employment 9, 10, 120-21, 282, 299, 352
ill health 232-3, 279, 326, 371, 377, 378, 380
meetings with 'Abdu'l-Bahá 121, 232-3
pilgrimage 96-8, 99, 101-9
relationship with sisters 1, 64-5, 68, 94, 99, 233, 281, 292, 299, 302, 326, 332, 364, 373-4, 379-80
correspondence with Alma 35, 49, 50, 63-4, 68, 72, 73, 76, 79, 92, 93-4, 121, 122, 123, 144, 151, 155, 167, 171, 186, 193, 196, 204, 239, 241, 242, 247, 248, 257, 266-7, 279, 289, 292, 298, 299, 348, 354, 360, 361, 365, 371, 372
financial support of Alma 2, 64-5, 72-3, 87, 88, 120-22, 138, 179, 196, 234, 240-41, 282, 292, 298, 350
and Shoghi Effendi 326-7, 378, 379
Tablets and messages from 'Abdu'l-Bahá 47, 66, 84, 96, 146, 193, 238, 260, 292
Translations 84, 260
visits to
Germany 112, 232, 233, 234, 319
Paris 232-3
Switzerland 233, 273
Knobloch, Gottfried 4-5
Knobloch, Ida 5-6
Knobloch, Johanna (Gehde) 5
Knobloch, Karl August 4-8, 71, 380

Knobloch, Martin (Leipzig) 153, 187, 278
Knobloch, Mina 70, 71, 97-8, 153
Knobloch, Pauline *see* Hannen, Pauline
Knobloch, Paul Martin 6, 8
Knobloch, Wilhelm 5, 70, 71, 97-8, 153, 162
Kohler, Richard, and Mrs Kohler 137, 158, 190, 260, 261, 277, 309
König, Mr 277, 286
Kosky, Rosa 126, 136, 137
Köstlin, Anna 87-8, 137, 152, 155-6, 157, 159-61, 168-71, 175, 177, 182, 186, 190, 191, 193, 198, 213, 215, 218-19, 221, 236, 267, 287, 314-15, 352, 354
  Tablets and messages from 'Abdu'l-Bahá 155, 161, 177, 191
Köstlin, Mr 87
Köstlin, Mrs 137, 152, 157, 183, 193, 236
Kretz, Olive 282, 300, 302, 327, 328, 334, 342
Krieger, Mayor 161, 190, 267
Krieger, Klara (Böttger) 161, 267-8, 278
Krunke, Miss 69-70
Krunke, Olga 69-70
Krüttner, Karl 126-7, 190, 195
  Tablet and message from 'Abdu'l-Bahá 126-7
Kusterer, Mrs 159, 161, 186, 192
Küstner, Mr 314

Ladies Baptist Missionary Society 329
Lakewood 344
Larkins, Wil, Mr and Mrs 361
Langenbrück, Dresden 243
League of Nations 116, 350

Ledroit Park, Washington DC 13
Leipzig viii, 4, 70, 72, 88-9, 95, 96-7, 101, 111, 153, 162, 172, 175-9, 181-3, 186-8, 190-91, 195-6, 209, 241-4, 246, 249-50, 252-5, 260, 263, 277, 279, 282, 286, 288, 293-6, 301, 307, 309, 310, 312, 314-15, 354
  Battle of 187, 249
  Frauen Club 187-8, 242
  English Church 2244
  Gewerbe school 244
  Messages from 'Abdu'l-Bahá 243, 301
  Naw-Rúz celebration, first 243
  petitions to 'Abdu'l-Bahá 242
  Police Department 187, 282
  University 5
  Völkerschlachtdenkmal 187
Leiser, Rabbi Joseph 367
Leopold, Prince of Bavaria 267
Lewis, Mr 333
Lima, Ohio 71, 375
Local Spiritual Assemblies 306, 312
  see also individual towns and cities
Lohse, Doris 352
London, England 80, 81, 95, 121-2, 130, 155-6, 199, 247-8, 253, 282
  'Abdu'l-Bahá's visits 163-9, 171, 173, 175-6, 188, 196
  Bahai Assembly (first) 432
  Unity Meetings 174-5
  University 163
Los Angeles 247
Ludwigsburg 50, 60, 150, 161, 255
Ludwigshafen 281, 284, 296, 303, 309, 312
Lusitania, RMS 278
Lutz, Albert 148, 233, 425
Luzern/Lucerne 96, 233

MacNutt, Howard 30, 31-2, 34, 55
MacNutt, Mary 34

Maier, Mr and Mrs 264
Maihöfer, Johannes 217-18
Malachi (prophet) 71
Mannheim 2, 82, 161, 284, 289, 296, 309
Manshádí, Siyyid Táqi 109
Markgraf family 295, 310
Marney-Connor, Elizabeth 35
Marseilles 175, 236
Marx, Karl 5
Mary Magdalene 37
Mason-Dixon Line 349
Maui, Hawaii 301, 307
Maxwell, Mary 352 *see also* Amatu'l-Bahá Rúḥíyyih Khánum
Maxwell, May 281, 322, 327-8, 331, 352, 374-5
Mecklenburg 317
Menzel, Pastor 21-4, 69
Metzeroth, Fritz 186
Metzeroth, Mrs 186
Mexico 51
Miami, FL 328, 329-31, 334, 343, 344, 345, 360, 378
  Spiritual Assembly 329
Milan, Italy 101, 253
Mills, John Fell 34-5, 42
Mills, John Harrison 34-5, 42
  message from 'Abdu'l-Bahá 47
Mills, Henrietta Fell 34-6, 42-3, 45-6, 47-9
  Tablet and message from 'Abdu'l-Bahá 45-6, 47-8
Mills, Mountfort 151
Milwaukee, Wisconsin
Moayyad, Habíb (Khudabakhsh) 254-5, 261-2, 291
Mohammed, Mohammedans *see* Muhammad, Muslims
Montclair, NJ 188
Montreal, Canada 41
Moore, Daisy 345, 368, 369-70
Moore, Mr 220
Morgan, J.P. 206-7

Mormonism 60, 82
Morstadt, Alfred 125
Morton, Marjorie 19
Most Great Peace 346
Mount Carmel 5, 71, 102, 130, 251
  Bahá'í Terraces 5
  Ben Gurion Avenue 5
Muhammad (Mohammed), Prophet 24
Muḥammad-'Alí, Mírzá 15
Mühlschlegel, Adelbert 350
Munavvar Khánum 112, 123, 142
Munich 2 75, 136, 161, 266-8, 270-71, 281, 283, 309, 312
  petitions to 'Abdu'l-Bahá 268-71
Muníríh Khánum 102, 108, 129
Muslims 86, 148, 225
Mystic Lake, FL 361, 366

Nagel, Bruce 192-3
Naples, Italy 101, 207
Napoleon (Bonaparte) 4, 187, 249
Nashville, TN 339, 345
  Spiritual Assembly 339
National Spiritual Assembly 306
  Germany 88, 215, 218, 277, 308, 311, 313-14, 317-18, 321, 350, 353
  United States and Canada 324, 327, 329, 339, 352, 368
Naumberg 254
Naw-Rúz 85, 148, 158, 182, 204, 243, 271, 300, 329
Nazism, Nazis 88, 159, 218, 350, 352
NSDAP (National Socialist German Workers' Party) 350
Nemmens, Miss 86
Netherlands, 452 *see also* Holland
Newton family 342, 373
New Haven, Connecticut 300
New York City 2, 6, 8, 17, 22, 34, 44, 50, 51, 54-5, 60, 150, 176, 192, 193, 207, 208, 247, 252,

255, 281, 296, 298, 302, 329
Board of Counsel 44
Church of the Ascension 166
Genealogical Hall 302
McAlpin Hotel 281
Spiritual Assembly 151
Stock Exchange 207
New York Herald 278
New Zealand 37
Nice, France 236, 307
Nidwalden, Switzerland 96
Nieuw Amsterdam, steamship 296
Nineteen Day Feast 117, 136, 162, 191-2, 343, 374
North Augusta, SC 368-70
 Spiritual Assembly 368-70
North Carolina 7, 8, 53-4
Nottenrode, v., Baron and Baroness 267
Nourse, Mrs (Elizabeth) 307
Nuremberg 192, 254, 284-5, 294, 295, 297, 312

Ober, Grace 294-5
Ober, Harlan 294-5, 299
Obere Museum Stuttgart 216-17
Oberholz 188
Oberlin College 38
Oetzsch 246
Olgastrasse, Stuttgart 76
Opez, Mrs 426
Orlando, FL 200, 330, 342-4, 345, 373
 Intergroup Meeting 344
Osborne, Ralph 44
Ostseebad Dahme 285

Palm, Anna 73-6, 125
Paris 31, 74, 111, 115, 159, 214, 259, 278
 'Abdu'l-Bahá's visits 163, 168, 173, 198-205, 206, 220, 223, 228, 230, 232-6, 286
 Avenue de Camöens 168

Bahá'í community in 33, 95, 116, 151, 168-9, 194, 199-200, 252, 291
 Tablet from 'Abdu'l-Bahá 291
German Association 201
Trianon Palace Hotel 252
Parker family (Marcella, Myrtle, Mr) 358-9, 363, 365-6
Parsons, Agnes 207, 302
Patzer, Mr 302
Pax, Clara and Mathilde 425
Perron, Mr 312
Persia, Persians 12, 17, 20, 31, 58, 102, 166-8, 192, 199-200, 213, 219, 225, 230, 235, 262, 291, 362
Persian-American Educational Society 20
Persian language 84, 90, 106, 130, 157, 165, 269
Peterson, Carrie 342-3
Pfadelbach 70, 75, 76, 89, 125
Pfankuche, Helina 81
Pfister family 296
Pfisterer, Gertrude 284
Pfisterer, Mrs 284
Pfutzner, Clara 425
Phelps, Mrs, and Grandma Phelps 14
Pine Castle, Orlando 342-3
Pittsburgh 344
Pitzer, Dr 242
Plessner, Hans and Marie 244, 273, 426
Plochingen 219
Pöllinger, Franz 158, 314, 315, 353, 354
Pollock, Susan 215, 244, 256, 273, 302, 426
Pope, Pocahontas 27-9, 33, 392
 Tablet from 'Abdu'l-Bahá 28, 392
Portland, Oregon 278
Port Said, Egypt 15, 54, 109

Powell, Mrs 19
Pretoria, South Africa 325, 327
Prospect Hill Cemetery, Wahington DC 100, 372, 380
Provincial Freeman, The 40
Prussia 4-6, 199, 249

Qur'án, Koran 83, 223

Rabbani, Hussein 339, 340
Race, racial, racism 7, 159
  amity (and Conventions) 302, 306
  difference, an optical illusion 251
  disunity 302
  diversity 302
  identity 41, 64
  interracial, multiracial communities, meetings 302, 327, 344
  prejudice 9, 40, 164, 213
  principles 338
  segregation 306
  unity 2, 302
Racine 325
Randall, Mrs 334-5
Ransom Kehler, Keith 332
Rapps, Dora 284
Rebmann, Miss 287
Red Cross 248, 255, 288, 289
Redson, Dorothy and Harvey 348
Refugee Home Society 41
Regiment of Colored Troops, 104M 40
Reichert, Mr 314
Remey, Charles Mason 18, 19, 22, 29, 34, 36, 44, 58, 88, 89-90, 98, 136, 150, 159, 202, 252-5, 261-2, 266, 278, 294-6, 307, 310, 311, 333, 345, 354-5
  Tablets from 'Abdu'l-Bahá 29, 36-7
  Through Warring Countries 355
Revell, Jessie 355

Rexford, Orcella 334-5
Rhodesia (Zimbabwe) 18, 319, 326
Riḍván Garden, Holy Land 107
Rieger, Otto 79-80, 81, 85, 128, 130
Riehmann, Miss 76, 126
Ripley family: Annie, Bessie (Wigfall), William 19, 200, 342, 345
Roche, Joseph 33
Rock Bluff 362, 366
Rohleder, Pastor 228
Rohr family 243-4, 310
Rohr, Rudolph (Rudi) 295, 310
Rome, Italy 37, 101, 252
Root, Martha 353
Rosenberg, Ethel 175, 306
Rössler, Amalie von 5 *see* Knobloch, Amalie
Rössler, Arthur 97, 195, 277, 425
Rössler, Bruno von 6, 97, 190, 195, 205, 298
Rössler, Clara 186, 195
Rössler, Emma 195
Rössler, Karl Gabriel von 5-6
Rössler, Melanie 255
Roster, Conrad 286
Rostock 317
Rotterdam 255, 298
Rupp, Maria 264, 281
Rúhá Khánum 205
Ruhi Institute 19
Ruoff, Babette 81, 131, 139-42, 155, 261
  Tablets from 'Abdu'l-Bahá 139-40, 142, 155, 181
  Tablet of Visitation for 236-7, 261
Ruoff, Emil 81, 85, 123, 131, 132, 139-42, 152, 155, 175, 181, 208, 261, 287
  Tablets from 'Abdu'l-Bahá 139-40, 142
Russia 77, 253-4, 286, 310
Russian language 294-5

Saint Augustine, FL 327-30, 337, 344, 345
  Spiritual Assembly 344
St Catherines, Ontario 37-8, 41
St Gallen 148, 233
St John's Westminster 165-6
St Paul's Church, Wilmington 8
St Peter's Church, Bautzen 5-6
St Peter's, Rome 101
Sailors' Revolt 285
Salem Chapel, St Catherines 38
Sample, Carlton 370
Sander family 161
San Francisco 9, 223-4
Sarasota, FL 344
Sargent, Sarah Etat 10-12
Sassenburg, Mrs 76
Saxony, 4-6, 72, 123
  King of 249
Scandinavia 324
Schadd, Hans and Elizabeth 39
Schaefer, Miss 75-6, 125
Schaffhausen 193
Scheffler, Carl 36, 50, 60, 72
Scheiling, Miss 125
Scheuerle, Miss von 70, 75, 89, 125
Scheurle, Mrs 76
Schiller, Friedrich 212
Schlenzig 244
Schloss Solitude 212
Schmand, Willy 261, 286
Schneebeli, Mr 141-7, 151-3, 157, 159-61, 181-2
Schoenfeld, Mrs 273
Scholz, Fritz 97, 187, 195-6, 261
Scholz, Jennie 97, 178-9, 187, 195-6, 241, 243, 260, 425
Schröder, Mr 243
Schütz, Miss 308
Schwab, Heinrich 137, 158, 190, 193, 236, 286-7, 309
Schwarz, Alice 162, 210-12, 216, 217-19, 221, 223, 227, 229-30, 233-4, 236, 261, 270, 272, 274, 281, 291, 296, 305, 308, 309, 310, 315, 317, 321, 355
Schwarz, Consul Albert 162, 210-2, 215, 217-19, 222, 224, 227-30, 233-4, 236, 248, 255, 260, 277, 281, 290, 291, 206, 305-6, 308, 311, 315, 321, 324, 355
Schwarz, Eva 426
Schwarz, Olly, Ollie 217 229-30, 255
Schwarz, Rosa 74, 87, 137, 150, 161, 191, 264, 272, 286, 379
Schweizer, Alfred Khurshed 156, 353
Schweizer, Annemarie (Warnke) 81, 87-8, 137, 150, 153, 155, 156, 157-8, 161, 168-9, 170, 175-6, 181, 190, 193, 198, 216, 219, 221, 236, 287, 308, 310, 314, 318, 353-4
  home blessed by 'Abdu'l-Bahá 216, 236
  Tablets from 'Abdu'l-Bahá 155-6, 161
Schweizer, Friedrich 81, 88, 137, 149-50, 153, 155, 156, 158, 160-61, 169-70, 175-7, 181, 183, 190, 191, 196, 216, 236, 277, 3212, 353-4
  home blessed by 'Abdu'l-Bahá 216, 236
  Tablets from 'Abdu'l-Bahá 155-6, 161, 191
Schweizer, Nur 170
Schwerin 317
Sead, South Dakota 342-3
Sego, Esther 345, 356, 363, 367
Sehn, Mr 152
Seker family 344
Serbia 253
Seven Valleys 83, 190, 414
Seven Year Plan (North America) 345-6, 377-8
Shadd, Abraham Doras and Harriet 39-40

INDEX

Shadd, Abram William 40
Shadd, Amelia (Williamson) 37-41
  Tablet and message from 'Abdu'l-Bahá 38-9
Shadd, Emeline (Simpson) 40-41
Shadd, Mary Ann (Cary) 40-41
Sheldon, Grace Carew 35-6
Sheldon, James 35
Sherman, Mr 219
Shoghi Effendi 2, 89, 105, 116, 158, 206, 275-6, 280, 289, 295, 297, 304-8, 312, 315, 318, 320-34, 325, 317, 329, 331, 335, 336, 338-40, 346, 348-53, 357, 361, 364, 375, 380
Simpson, Emeline Shadd 40-41
Södel, Miss 242
Sohrab, Ahmad 18, 19, 30, 48-9, 50, 54-5, 57, 59, 61, 63, 66, 68, 71, 96, 117, 120, 132, 154, 156, 157, 161, 172, 174-5, 196, 198, 205, 206, 208-9, 231-14, 218, 220, 224-6, 243, 251
  Tablets from 'Abdu'l-Bahá 49, 64-6
Sonne der Wahrheit (Sun of Truth) 312-13
Sonntag, Mrs Hauptmann von 79, 131
South Africa 18, 292-3, 300, 301, 302, 319, 326-7, 332-3
South Carolina 2, 364-5, 367-70
  First Spiritual Assembly 368
Spartanburg, SC 365, 368, 370
Spiedel, Sudovika 150
Sprague, Margaret Mills 34-5, 42-4, 46-9
  Messages from 'Abdu'l-Bahá 47-8
Sprague, Sydney 79-81, 86-7, 116, 126, 132-3, 142, 152-3, 159, 162, 247-8
Springfield, Mass. 2, 282, 300-02, 328

Stäbler, Elise 74, 87; 137, 146, 153, 158, 186, 205, 261, 308
Stäbler, Julia 74, 79, 80, 87, 118, 137, 153, 158, 168, 169-70, 174, 186, 191, 192, 205, 216, 236, 261, 268, 310, 354
  Tablet and message from 'Abdu'l-Bahá 118, 191
Stäbler, Mr 192, 310
Stäbler, Sophie 153, 182, 261
Stäbler, Otto 161
Stannard, Jean 111-12, 114-16, 168
Star of the West (*Bahai News*) 130, 151, 250, 255, 312
Staub, Max, and family 244, 277, 279, 286
Staunton, VA 378
Steinmetz, Professor 242
Stevenson, Pastor 306
Still, Mr and Mrs (Grace) 333
Stockholm, Sweden 288
Strasbourg 159, 161, 255, 290
Struven, Edward 68
Struven, Howard 150-51
Sturm, Wolfgang 171
Stuttgart 2, 50, 60-61, 69-70, 71, 78, 125, 135-6, 162, 254-5, 257-8, 289, 291
  'Abdu'l-Bahá's visits to 188, 192-3, 195, 196, 198, 201-3, 206-19, 221-31, 244
  Bahá'í community 72-4, 78-9, 81-2, 85-9, 101, 106, 111-12, 115, 120-21, 126, 128-34, 136, 143, 144-7, 148-53, 155-62, 167-71, 172-85, 186, 188-9, 190-93, 202-3, 204-5, 208, 221, 226, 208, 235-6, 240, 244, 250, 254-6, 259-62, 272, 282-3
  Bahá'í Centre, Friesengasse 216
  Board of Counsel (Assembly) 130-33

473

petitions to 'Abdu'l-Bahá
  89-90, 101, 112, 114, 117,
  128, 150, 201-4
Spiritual Assembly 216, 236,
  313
Tablets and messages from
  'Abdu'l-Bahá 101, 118-19,
  133, 149-50, 155-7, 158,
  161-2, 170-71, 177-8,
  179, 183, 184-5, 192, 209,
  235, 236, 301
unity meetings 74, 80, 95,
  125, 136, 140, 168, 169-
  70, 174-5, 181, 227, 236,
  260-61
Working Committee 85, 87,
  125, 176, 179, 181-2, 192
Bürger Museum 81, 85, 172,
  173, 179, 193, 201, 213,
  222-4, 235
Frauen Club 75, 76, 79, 82, 85,
  129, 136, 140, 147, 148, 151,
  158, 174, 175, 181, 193, 201,
  204, 227, 235, 264
Hotel Marquardt 207-8, 213
Obere Museum 216-17
Railway Station 71, 219, 221,
  230
YMCA 158-9
See also Air Bath, Christian
  Science
Sufism 111
Swabian Alps 264
Swedenborg Society 78, 79, 85, 115
Switzerland 13, 51, 53, 96, 111,
  133, 145, 148, 151, 152, 162,
  176, 179, 211, 233, 236, 253,
  273, 380
Syracuse, NY 44

Tablets of the Divine Plan vii, 1,
  67, 68, 280-81, 329, 340-41,
  346, 380
Ṭáhirih 176

Takoma property 240, 320, 332
Taylor, SC 364
Telle, Marie 425
Temple Emmanuel, San Francisco
  223
Temple, Wilmette (Mashriqu'l-
  Adhkar) 166, 326, 339, 340-41,
  347, 349
  Foundation Hall 326
  Fund 273, 278
Templers 5, 50, 71, 151, 218, 235,
  291
Tennessee 339, 367
Theological Ministries of Europe 125
Theosophical Monthly 253
Theosophical Society
  Leipzig 295
  London 169
  Paris 199
  Vienna 220, 223-4
Theurer, Miss 287
Thirty Years War 5
Thompson, Mrs 338
Thonon-les-Bains 162
Thornburgh-Cropper, Mrs 166,
  174-5
Titanic 207
Thüringen 137, 272
Tokyo 267
Tornstrom, Doris 342
Trainer, Dr 284
Trenton, NJ 50-54, 94, 247
Trenton Evening Times 52
Triple Entente 77
True, Corinne 348
Tübingen 74, 125, 312
Tubman, Harriet 38
Turkey, Turkish Government 31,
  183, 271, 316
Turner, Mrs 27

Übelhack, Alma 284
Übelhack, Freda and family 284
Ulm 312

INDEX

Ulrich, Dr 285
Underground Railroad 38, 39
United Kingdom 196, *see also* England
United Nations 116
United States 1, 2, 6, 8, 17, 19, 34, 35, 40-41, 51-2, 54, 70, 90, 109, 110, 120, 123, 135, 142, 184, 185, 187, 207, 247, 278, 282-3, 288, 293-5, 296, 298, 304, 306, 309, 311, 313, 319, 320, 322, 325-6, 332, 350, 352, 370, 375, 379, 380
 Bahá'í community *see* Bahá'í community: United States and Canada
 Civil War 6, 7, 37, 40
 Congress 37, 362
 Consul 255
 emigration to from Germany 6, 50
 Revolutionary War 39
 South, Southern states 2-3, 37-8, 328-32, 338-45, 349-56, 359, 363-72, 373-5, 377 *see also* individual entries
Universal House of Justice 280, 305, 353, 370
Universal Peace Conference, Bern (1919) 211
Universal Races Congress 163-4
Unveiling the Divine Plan 281

Verdun, Battle of 282, 286
Vernon, Kathryn 336, 337, 344
Vernon, Mrs 336, 337, 338, 344
Verona, VA 377
Versailles, Conference and Treaty 290, 311, 350, 445
Vevey, Switzerland 162
Viavi company 9, 10, 120-22, 282, 299-301, 326-7, 390
Vienna, Austria 81, 219, 220-21, 223, 309, 312, 314-15

 Bahá'í community 309, 312, 314-15
 Spiritual Assembly 315
Vienna Declaration of Trust 315
Villa Wagenburg 216
Vogel, Miss 285
Vollrath, Hugo 253-4, 294
Von der Fange, Mrs 241, 244
Von Steiner, Mrs 151
Von Struten, Miss 76

Wagner, Priska 195
Wagner, Mr 195
Waiblingen 312
Waldschmidt, Dr and Mrs 287, 308
Wallace, Dr and Mrs 336
Warnke, Annemarie *see* Schweizer, Annemarie
Washington DC 6-9, 12, 14, 21, 27-8, 71, 121-2, 262, 292, 299, 319-20, 332, 366, 372, 380
 'Abdu'l-Bahá's visit 342
 Bahá'í community 1-2, 11-15, 17, 27, 33, 34, 61, 70, 99-100, 110, 193, 215, 301-2, 306, 333, 342, 357, 364, 374-5, 377
 Spiritual Assembly 374
Washington Houses of Faith 28
Washington Post 357
Washington Times 17
Waterloo, Battle of 294
Weigle, Fanny and Richard 151, 161
Weimar 212
Weimar Republic 288
Weinberg 125
Wermsdorf 195, 246
West Virginia 39
White, Ruth 313-15
Wieland, Helene 228
Wiesbaden 314
Wigfall, Elizabeth (Bessie, née Ripley) 342, 345

Wilberforce, Archdeacon 165-6
Wiles, Georgie 339, 342, 345
Wilhelm II, Kaiser (Emperor) of
  Germany 215, 248, 249, 258-9,
  260, 276, 285, 288
Wilhelm II, King of Württemberg
  53, 227, 229, 258, 289
Wilhelm, Roy 99, 312
Wilhelmsbad 190
Wilhelmshafen 285
Wilhelm Tell 233
Willacoochee, GA 365
Williams, Roy 302
Williamson, Amelia Cisco Shadd
  37-41
  Tablet and message from 'Abdu'l-
    Bahá 38-9, 41
Williamson, David Thomas 39
Williamson, Dr Jerry and family
  365, 368-9
Wilmette, Ill. 166, 340, 348-9, 364,
  371
Wilmington, North Carolina 7-8
Wilson, President Woodrow 278,
  346, 445
Wilt, Mrs 10-11
Windust, Albert 184, 261, 633
Winnetka, Ill. 348
Wise, Miss 329
Wittendorf 4
women 8-9, 37, 40, 71, 74-5, 94,
  129, 135-8, 176, 187, 217, 227,
  242
Woodcock, Percy 30
World Bahá'í Youth Symposium
  351
World War
  First 2, 77, 183, 199, 220, 229,
    249, 253-65, 268-74, 275-8,
    280-87, 289-91, 295, 309,
    354
    Allies 256, 278, 283, 285
    Landsturm 259
    Lazarettos 263, 268
    Western Front 295
  Second 88, 216, 297, 353, 354,
    375-7
    Eastern Front 353
    see also Gestapo, Nazism
Württemberg 5 *see also* Wilhelm II,
  King of

Yazdi, Ahmad 15, 30-31, 54, 96,
  109, 133
Yazdi, Ḥusayn 102
Yazdi, Muḥammad 102
York, Carrie 27-8
Young, Edward 357-8, 361, 363,
  365-6, 448
Young Turk Revolution 96

Zárqání, Maḥmúd 205, 206
Zayn, Munír 130, 143, 259
Zeitgeist 183, 221
Zimbabwe 18, 319, 326
Zimmer, Mr and Mrs 277, 283, 286
  Tablet from 'Abdu'l-Bahá 283-4
Zion Baptist Church, St Catherines
  38
Zittau 88, 123-4
Zuffenhausen 87-8, 137, 144, 147,
  150, 153, 157-8, 174-5, 177,
  181-2, 193, 216, 236, 250, 258,
  261, 309, 312, 321
Zurich, Switzerland 101, 141, 151

ABOUT THE AUTHOR

Jennifer Wiebers lives with her husband Carsten and their three children in Frankfurt am Main, Germany. She is a Soil Physicist by training and has recently entered the field of Agrobiotechnology. Jennifer has a passion for Bahá'í history, which she has been studying for more than 30 years. For the past ten years she has been meticulously researching the life of Alma Knobloch and has thereby uncovered important details of the early Bahá'í activities in Washington, DC; Buffalo, New York and various other US locations including Florida, Georgia and South Carolina, as well as in St Catherine's, Canada; Germany, Switzerland, Austria and the Czech Republic. In addition, she has studied the historic visit of 'Abdu'l-Bahá to six European countries just before the First World War. Jennifer is strongly involved in the Bahá'í Institute Process which contributes to the betterment of the world and a peaceful future for all mankind.

www.ingramcontent.com/pod-product-compliance
Lightning Source LLC
Chambersburg PA
CBHW060512230426
43665CB00013B/1488